Praise for *Modeling Business Objects with XML Schema*

This is definitely the book I have been waiting for: one that bases the development of XML schemas on a sound methodology. There are no heuristics here. *Modeling Business Objects with XML Schema* is knowledgeable, well-founded, and always practice-oriented. The reader is presented with the entire functionality of XML Schema, and also with manageable solutions for when the barriers of this schema language are reached. Berthold Daum discusses Sumerian cuneiform, Asset Oriented Modeling, canonical XML, object language binding, and schema evolution with equal virtuosity, and in doing so he manages to have jazz trumpeter Miles Davis perform as an XML element. A must-read for every XML developer.

> —Roland Böndgen, Program Manager, The XML Academy,
> Software AG

Modeling Business Objects with XML Schema is an excellent resource for XML Schema authors who model and build enterprise class systems with XML.

> —Tom Marrs, J2EE/XML Architect, Distributed Computing
> Solutions, Inc.

Modeling Business Objects with XML Schema is an informative book that effectively explains its subject by providing a meaningful perspective and enlightening examples.

> —Daniel Krech, Semantic Web Technologist, Eikco, LLC.

D1361876

Modeling Business Objects with XML Schema

Modeling Business Objects with XML Schema

BERTHOLD DAUM

MORGAN KAUFMANN PUBLISHERS

AN IMPRINT OF ELSEVIER SCIENCE

AMSTERDAM   BOSTON   LONDON   NEW YORK
OXFORD   PARIS   SAN DIEGO   SAN FRANCISCO
SINGAPORE   SYDNEY   TOKYO

dpunkt.verlag

Heidelberg, Germany

Copublished by Morgan Kaufmann Publishers and dpunkt.verlag

Morgan Kaufmann Publishers

Senior Editor: Tim Cox
Publishing Services Managers: Edward Wade,
    Simon Crump
Editorial Coordinator: Stacie Pierce
Project Managers: Howard Severson, Kevin Sullivan
Cover Design: Yvo
Cover Image: I. Burgum and P. Boorman/Getty Images
Text Design: Side by Side Studios
Composition: TBH Typecast, Inc.
Illustration: Dartmouth Publishing, Inc.
Copyeditor: Judith Brown
Proofreader: Jennifer McClain
Indexer: Ty Koontz
Interior Printer: The Maple-Vail Book Manufacturing Group
Cover Printer: Phoenix Color

dpunkt.verlag

Senior Editor: René Schönfeldt

Designations used by companies to distinguish their products are often claimed as trademarks or registered trademarks. In all instances in which Morgan Kaufmann Publishers is aware of a claim, the product names appear in initial capital or all capital letters. Readers, however, should contact the appropriate companies for more complete information regarding trademarks and registration.

Morgan Kaufmann Publishers
An Imprint of Elsevier Science
340 Pine Street, Sixth Floor
San Francisco, CA 94104-3205, USA
http://www.mkp.com

Available in Germany, Austria, and Switzerland from
dpunkt.verlag GmbH
Ringstraße 19b
D-69115 Heidelberg, Germany
http://www.dpunkt.de

Printed in the United States of America

07 06 05 04 03   5 4 3 2 1

Library of Congress Control Number: 2003102703

MK ISBN: 1-55860-816-8

dpunkt ISBN: 3-89864-218-6

This book is printed on acid-free paper.

Contents

12 Schema Evolution 445

Foreword

Dave Hollander
CTO, Contivo, Inc.
Co-chair, W3C XML Schema Working Group

"Too complicated! Way too much to learn! Nobody will understand this! Do we really have to implement this?"

XML is simple—why are XML schemas so complex?

In spite of early criticisms, World Wide Web Consortium (W3C) XML schemas have become an important part of our evolving information infrastructure. How important? Internet search engines can find over one quarter of a million documents that discuss XML schemas. Web Services, ebXML, OAGI, and most recent e-commerce specifications use W3C XML schemas. Vendors like BEA, IBM, Microsoft, Oracle, Sun, and a host of others have implemented schemas. In short, understanding XML Schema and its complexities has become essential for architects, developers, and managers who are building information-driven systems.

To understand Schema's complexity, we have to look at its origins. In August of 1998, the group that developed XML gathered at the Metastructures 1998 & XML Developers Conference in Montreal to understand how the community at large was adopting our work. After the conference, 45 attendees gathered to outline how to continue what the XML 1.0 Recommendation had started. Schemas were one of the five work areas identified. Teams formed, chairs were nominated, and the effort began to formally charter working groups under the W3C. In November of 1998, we had our first meeting, gathering face-to-face in Chicago.

XML is simple. It is simple because during its creation, we were able to rely on over 100 years of combined experience in the Standardized Generalized Markup Language (SGML). This shared experience helped us to establish the ten design goals that are listed at the beginning of the XML 1.0 Recommendation. We had a common understanding of these goals; for example, when we declared, "It shall be easy to write programs which process XML documents," we all meant that programmers should be able to write the basic code "over a holiday weekend." XML's simplicity is the direct result of asking ourselves, at nearly every meeting, "Is this necessary for success?" and using our shared experience and goals to answer "No" as much as possible.

XML schemas are complex. The W3C XML Schema Working Group did not have the benefit of a single, shared experience like SGML. The Working Group had to find a way to combine ideas and features from a wide variety of sources: Document Type Definitions (DTDs) from SGML; submissions to the W3C, including DDML, SOX, DCD, and XML-Data; and experience from other technology areas such as object-oriented programming, databases, and UML. The Working Group members, whose experience ranged from database standards, to e-commerce, to the study of ancient manuscripts, all brought needs and requirements with them.

For 30 months, the Working Group met 16 times face-to-face, held teleconferences once or twice a week, and formed dozens of task forces. We produced countless drafts and analyzed comments from thousands of reviewers. It became clear that we could not create a simple specification. This concerned the Working Group, yet we knew that it was important to finish our work and that others would fill in the gaps. In May of 2001 we released our three specifications and continued our work. As I write this, we are preparing the agenda for the 23rd face-to-face meeting.

Today, complaints continue, but at a much lower volume. Developers who are implementing schema-aware tools are filling one of the critical gaps. While these tools make it a lot easier for users of XML schemas, they cannot be expected to do all the work. Writing schemas is more than getting the syntax of XML Schema right. The schemas should be designed in such a way that the documents they describe are easy to author, update, and retrieve. They should be prepared for evolution and take into consideration corporate standards.

In fact, XML and XML schemas are now taking the enterprise world by storm. Understanding how to leverage their abilities is essential to those who already use XML in fields such as the Web, content and knowledge management, and e-business. But it is equally important that experts in other technologies, such as object-oriented or relational technology, build their understanding of XML schemas.

This book guides you through understanding schemas in a systematic way, from the basic concepts—type systems, type derivation, inheritance, and namespace handling—through advanced concepts in schema design. The early chapters describe the problem domain that schemas address. They provide insight into the motivations behind schemas and the problems that they can solve. The middle of the book delivers detailed explanations and examples of how to use the myriad features available in XML Schema and compares these to other similar languages. These chapters illustrate the design issues that the Working Group faced and that schema designers will face. The final chapters put it all together and describe how schemas can be applied to real applications.

Specifications such as the XML Schema Recommendations produced by the W3C Working Group must focus on defining technology and do not have the luxury of explaining motivation, design issues, and applications. This book fills that need admirably.

Acknowledgements

The production of a book is always teamwork, but the merits (or the blame) mostly go to the author whose name happens to be on the cover. So, the following paragraphs not only express my deep-felt gratitude toward all the people that helped to bring this book into the world, but also serve the purpose of self-protection.

In particular, if you are feeling uncomfortable with the book's content, don't blame me; blame the reviewers, Daniel Krech and Dave Hollander. Personally, I think they did a wonderful job and really helped to bring the book into shape. Especially enjoyable were my discussions with Dave about the intricacies of the XML Schema type system and the Unique Particle Attribution. There were also two anonymous reviewers who preferred to remain in the dark—probably for good reasons. So, this is also in honor of the Unknown Reviewer.

The next ones to blame are the people at Morgan Kaufmann Publishers and dpunkt.verlag for giving me the opportunity to publish this work. Maybe they already regret it. Thanks go especially to Tim Cox and Stacie Pierce from Morgan Kaufmann, who patiently helped me through the materialization and publication of the book, and to René Schönfeldt from dpunkt. Production was managed at Morgan Kaufmann by Howard Severson initially, then later in the process by Kevin Sullivan, who took over from an already exhausted Howard.

Copyediting and proofreading were done by Judith Brown and Jennifer McClain, respectively. They are the ones to blame for any problems with grammar and spelling. Authors are never responsible for these sorts of problems. They can adopt a rather liberal attitude to grammar and orthography. The copyeditors and proofreaders have to do all the hard work. I think they deserve a big hand.

If you dislike the page layout, blame goes to the interior designer, Mark Ong at Side by Side Studios. I, in fact, like it a lot. My first reaction to the finished proofs was, "Wow, this really looks nice!" So, a big hand for Mark, and for Bill Turner at TBH Typecast, who did the typesetting. Thanks for that, Bill.

Finally, big thanks—I think from all of us—go to you, the reader. (If you acquired this book by unlawful means, ignore this and don't read on.) By buying this book, you made this production possible. And despite all the electronic gadgets I own, I still like making books.

Berthold Daum
berthold.daum@bdaum.de
February 2003

Introduction

XML Schema is an industry standard. No, it did not become an industry standard by gradual adoption—it was a standard defined under the direct collaboration of various IT industry groups such as middleware manufacturers and database manufacturers. In fact, it was adopted by the contributing industry groups long before the final recommendation was published, a fact that marks the transition of XML from a documentation language to a mainstream data definition language for the whole IT industry.

XML Schema is the result of a political process. Different interests had to be negotiated, and the result is a compromise—a compromise that probably does not make everybody perfectly happy, but a compromise everybody can live with. The outcome of such a political process usually is complex in nature, and XML Schema is no different in that respect. Sure, some early concepts were dropped and the hierarchy of built-in types was streamlined in the final recommendation, but XML Schema is still a "fat" schema definition language by any standard. Just have a look at Figure 5.3 (page 140).

Confused? Just wait until you have a look into the standard itself. It is not easy reading, by any means. The language is highly formal (a delight for mathematicians), and the semantic network of definitions and constraints is very delicate. Getting into it requires time, effort, and patience. The XML Schema Primer [Fallside2001], which has been published as Part Zero of the recommendation, is, in contrast, much more accessible and serves as a first introduction into XML Schema authoring.

In the meantime, most of the critical voices have ceased. The developers who have to implement validating parsers and schema editors are simply too busy to complain, and most users have calmed down now that the first XML Schema–aware schema editors have appeared on the market. Editors such as Altova's XML Spy (*www.altova.com*) and Tibco's TurboXML (*www.tibco.com*) have made working with XML Schema a lot easier. I, for example, have used XML Spy in the process of writing this book to validate the schemata and create the schema diagrams.

None of the existing validators and editors was fully conforming to the XML Schema Recommendation at the time of writing; even the W3C's reference implementation XSV (XML Schema Validator) was incomplete in some points. This shows that the implementation of the standard is quite a project, indeed. By the time this book hits the bookshops, however, existing validators should be quite complete and standard conforming. Some recent validating parsers, such as Apache's Xerces 2.0.0, are already quite impressive.

HOW THIS BOOK IS ORGANIZED

This book does not start with XML Schema right away. I believe that the appearance of XML marks a major shift, a paradigm change in data models. The simple data structures of the past such as relational tables or object-oriented–type hierarchies cannot satisfy the requirements of global computer networks, especially not the requirements of application-to-application communication in electronic business. XML marks a shift toward data structures that are defined by grammars. In fact, XML is nothing but a language for defining grammars. We call such data models "grammar driven."

Part I, "The Model," introduces therefore the mathematical foundations of *grammars* and document schemata. We begin the design of a related set of document schemata by defining a *conceptual model,* a practice that is well established among the database community, but is fairly uncommon among the documentation crowd.

- In Chapter 1, "Foundations," we introduce the basic concepts of document creation, beginning with some really ancient concepts. We then present the mathematical theory of regular sets, regular grammars, and regular types, which can serve as a solid foundation for most document types, in particular for XML documents.
- In Chapter 2, "Conceptual Modeling," we discuss Asset Oriented Modeling (AOM), a modeling method that is based on these theories and that produces models that can be easily transformed into XML schemata. We will also introduce our first example, the conceptual model of a simple bookshop.
- In Chapter 3, "Everybody Likes Jazz," we introduce the second major example, a knowledge base about jazz music and jazz musicians. This model will explain most principles of conceptual modeling and serve as a basis for later XML examples.

Part II, "The Implementation," introduces XML Schema. We do not, however, ignore what is going on beyond XML Schema. Although XML Schema has been adopted widely as the industry standard for schema definition, some critical comments regarding XML Schema have resulted in the creation of a leaner schema language: Relax NG. During the course of this book we will compare the concepts of XML Schema with the concepts of Relax NG. This should allow a clearer understanding of the shortcomings and advantages of both schema languages. We will also have a look at a validation language with a different scope than XML Schema and Relax NG: Schematron. We are then going to implement the conceptual models developed in Part I using XML Schema and Relax NG.

- Chapter 4, "XML Basics," serves as a refresher for your XML knowledge. We discuss XML namespaces, the XML information set, the XML canonical form, and how to write Document Type Definitions (DTDs). We do not repeat the basic XML syntax—you should already know where to put the angle brackets.
- Chapter 5, "XML Schema," discusses the XML Schema recommendation in detail. Starting from a very simple example, we move into the type system of XML Schema, discussing simple and complex types.
- Chapter 6, "Authoring XML Schema," discusses the namespace concept of XML Schema, as well as the possibilities for reuse and schema composition. Finally, we present some usage patterns, such as chameleon components, type substitution, and dangling types.
- In Chapter 7, "Relax NG," we introduce Relax NG as an alternate schema definition language and discuss the pros and cons of Relax NG compared to XML Schema.
- In Chapter 8, "From Conceptual Model to Schema," we translate our conceptual model from Chapter 2 (the bookshop) into XML Schema and Relax NG. This chapter serves as a longer example of implementation techniques with both schema languages.
- Chapter 9, "Validation beyond XML Schema," discusses alternate concepts for defining *constraints* on document types. We analyze which constraints can be defined with the means of XML Schema and for which constraints we have to look elsewhere. We show how to implement constraint validation with imperative programming, XSLT, or Schematron.

In Part III, "The Environment," we discuss issues of schema design in large environments. XML Schema, in particular, was not primarily designed as an improved DTD for the SGML community but rather as a schema language to support the application of XML in new scenarios such as databases and application-to-application messaging. For example, there are close connections between XML Schema and SQL-99, and many concepts that existed already in SQL-99 were adopted, refined, and extended by XML Schema. Yet, object-oriented concepts such as type hierarchies are also found in XML Schema, so it makes sense to investigate how XML schemata can be mapped to object-oriented structures, and vice versa.

- In Chapter 10, "Reality Check: The World Is Object-Oriented," we compare the concepts of XML Schema with object-oriented concepts. We show how XML structures can be bound to object-oriented structures.

- In Chapter 11, "Reality Check: The World Is Relational," we compare the concepts of XML Schema with relational concepts. We show how XML structures can be mapped to relational structures and discuss two commercial implementations.
- In Chapter 12, "Schema Evolution," we discuss schema evolution. We show how new schemata can be derived from existing schemata in a conservative manner, and how we can author schemata that are extensible and evolvable.
- In Chapter 13, "Schemata in Large Environments," we discuss some techniques that allow the application of XML schemata in large environments, such as mediation and decentralized change management. We show how views across multiple schemata can be formulated, for example with XQuery.
- In Chapter 14, "Outlook," we draw some conclusions and argue that XML Schema has transformed XML from a niche technology into a mainstream technology.

WHO SHOULD READ THIS BOOK?

The first group of people who should read this book is, of course, schema designers. System architects, programmers, and document authors will also find useful information here.

Because XML is taking the enterprise world by storm, people educated in other technologies, such as object-oriented technology or relational technology, will come in touch with XML. This can happen at any stage of application development, from conceptual modeling over schema design to implementation. Understanding the basic concepts of XML Schema—type system, type derivation, inheritance, namespace handling—is essential for any of those specialists. This book covers all the necessary steps. For two examples, we first develop a conceptual model and then derive XML schemata from those models.

Database administrators especially will have increasing exposure to XML and XML Schema. For these persons, the book will provide insight into the concepts of XML Schema and how it can be mapped to relational structures.

Application programmers will also find some helpful information. We discuss how the inheritance hierarchies in object-oriented languages correlate with the type hierarchies in XML Schema, and we develop a methodology to generate language bindings from XML schemata.

WHAT ARE THE PREREQUISITES?

Basic knowledge of XML—especially of the XML syntax—is required. If you are new to XML, you will find *The XML Handbook* by Charles Goldfarb and Paul Prescod [Goldfarb2000] a good introduction.

In Chapter 9 especially, you will need some knowledge of XSLT. Michael Kay's *XSLT Programmer's Reference* [Kay2001] is an excellent introduction to XSLT.

Chapter 10 will be easier to read if you already have basic knowledge of object-oriented concepts. There is a wide range of literature about these topics, including Bertrand Meyer's *Object-Oriented Software Construction* [Meyer 1997], and the less voluminous *An Introduction to Object-Oriented Programming* [Budd1997].

Similarly, Chapter 11 will be easier if you already have an understanding of relational concepts. *Database System Concepts,* by Abraham Silberschatz, Henry F. Korth, and S. Sudarshan [Silberschatz2001], for example, is a good and comprehensive introduction into that topic.

Modeling Business Objects with XML Schema

THE MODEL

Foundations

After a browse through the history of documentation and scripture, this chapter discusses some basic concepts that determine the structure of documents. We then turn to schema definition and give a first glimpse of the three schema languages featured in this book: DTD, XML Schema, and Relax NG.

Beginning with Section 1.6, the chapter becomes somewhat mathematical. Readers with an aversion to mathematics may skip the rest of the chapter. Those of you who stick with it will gain a better understanding of how schema languages are constructed and used. First, we discover that schema definition is closely related to the mathematical discipline of formal languages and that each schema definition (or most of it) can be expressed with a grammar.

Regular expressions are a popular method for constraining string expressions. The marriage of regular expressions with grammars results in the definition of regular languages that form a solid basis for the definition of XML schemata. Finally, we extend this calculus to the definition of data types, an important aspect when we consider that XML, programming languages, and database technology increasingly grow together.

1.1 A CORE CONCEPT

The document metaphor seems to be a core concept in business, administration, science, and information technology. The following sections give a brief overview of its historical development, and how this metaphor has been generalized today into a more abstract concept.

1.1.1 Life Is a Document

It seems that in modern societies the document is more important than what the document is about. A person, for example, only exists in the view of institutions and state officials if there are documents that certify the existence of that very person. A person who cannot produce documents certifying her nationality would be regarded as stateless. A person without "papers" does not have an official identity.

The same applies to business: Although a legally binding business contract can be established by the shaking of hands, it is common practice to put such a business contract in writing. Basically every exchange of goods, services, and money is accompanied by documents: purchase orders, bills of material, general ledger, invoices, receipts, and so on. A whole industry sector is dedicated to producing and consuming documents. While blue-collar workers are mainly responsible for the production of industrial goods, the task of white-collar workers is to produce and consume documents.

Documents are also all important in science. They are used to communicate scientific results between scientists, and scientific study—apart from experimental work and field study—consists mainly of studying documents. The reputation of a scientist is measured by how many documents this scientist has published, and how often these documents are referenced in documents produced by other scientists. This is important for designers of documentation systems: The easier a system makes cross-referencing, the more likely it will be adopted by the scientific community.

More and more we find the document metaphor at the core of the infrastructure of large IT systems, not only because the authoring, managing, and retrieval of documents is an important application area, but also because software components are becoming more and more complex. In the early days of programming with assembler or FORTRAN, subroutines were simple constructs that could easily be controlled with simple parameters: plain integers, floating-point numbers, strings, and addresses. Today, reusable software components can be huge and highly complex modules, controlled via similarly complex interfaces. Take, for example, a web service. The protocol of a web service is described with a language called WSDL (Web Service Description Language) [Christensen2001], and the syntax of messages passed to a web service can be described with the language XML Protocol [Williams2001], formerly called SOAP.

The following example shows how a purchase order could be serialized in XML. This document could be sent to a shopping system that would execute the order.

```xml
<?xml version="1.0" encoding="UTF-8"?>
<order orderNo="NILE01709" orderDate="04/23/2002">
  <customer customerNo="BD023432">
    <name>
      <first>John</first>
      <last>Doe</last>
    </name>
    <address>
      <street>747 Sunset Strip</street>
      <town>Miami</town>
      <zip>99999</zip>
      <state>FL</state>
      <country>USA</country>
    </address>
  </customer>
  <orderItem amount="1">
  <CD productNo="9488149012" year="1999">
    <title>suite africaine</title>
      <publisher>harmonia mundi</publisher>
      <contributor kind="performer">Romano</contributor>
      <contributor kind="performer">Sclavis</contributor>
      <contributor kind="performer">Texier</contributor>
      <contributor kind="performer">Le Querrec</contributor>
    </CD>
  </orderItem>
  <orderItem amount="1">
    <book ISBN="0140053972" year="1977">
      <title>On Photography</title>
      <publisher>Penguin</publisher>
      <author>Susan Sontag</author>
      <price>19.95</price>
    </book>
  </orderItem>
</order>
```

Because this message is formulated in a well-established document standard, it can be checked for valid syntax before it is passed to the executing software component, provided the syntax has been described in a document schema. We come to this shortly.

By using document standards and document technology in core areas of the IT infrastructure such as databases and messaging, the IT industry can draw on almost 9,000 years of human experience. Join me for a quick tour through ancient information processing.

1.1.2 Scripture

In common understanding the concept of documents is intrinsically linked with the concept of scripture. However, there are also other forms of documents, which will be discussed in the next section.

The advent of writing systems dates back 9,000 years and seems to coincide with the transition from hunter-gatherer societies to more agrarian societies. The first evidence of writing systems appeared in stones with incisions, which were used as counting tokens, probably to count property such as land, animals, or measures of grain (see Figure 1.1.)

Writing in the form of pictographs (see Figure 1.2) appeared between 4100 and 3800 B.C. in the Sumerian culture, in Mesopotamia (Iraq). These pictographs represented concepts such as hand, sun, woman, head. Stylized pictographs—impressed in clay with a wedge-shaped stylus—became the script known as *cuneiform,* as shown in Figure 1.3.

Similar to the Sumerian script, Chinese script is based on pictographs. However, it is not known whether Chinese script was influenced by Sumerian script or vice versa. The first recorded Chinese pictographs date back to 2500 B.C., and a full writing system was developed by the nineteenth century B.C. (In the pro-

Figure 1.1 Incised counting tokens from the Neolithic Age.

Figure 1.2 Sumerian pictographs representing the concepts great and man, meaning king.

Figure 1.3 Assyrian cuneiform. This cuneiform appeared in two roles—either as an ideogram representing the Assyrian word *irsitu* (earth), or as an acrophon representing the syllable *ki.*

cess, the Chinese also invented paper.) These pictographs underwent a gradual stylization into the well-known "square characters." Since pictographs can only express "real-world" concepts, combinations of pictographs were introduced to express abstract ideas. To a certain extent, characters for phonetic sounds were also introduced. Chinese script was adopted by other Asian countries, and in the fourth century B.C. the Japanese developed their script from Korean and Chinese.

Near the end of the fourth millennium B.C., the Egyptian culture introduced the concept of sound. Pictographs–*hieroglyphs*—represented syllables. Hieroglyphs (see Figure 1.4), however, only represented consonants, not vowels. They were used to represent the first sound in the word depicted by the pictograph, a concept called *acrophony*. The same concept is found in Phoenician script, which influenced Aramaic, Hebrew, and Greek script. It was up to the Greeks (about 800 B.C.) to represent vowels with letters and basically to invent our modern alphabet. The Greek alphabet led to Latin (see Figure 1.5) and Cyrillic, while Aramaic led to Arabic and most of the scripts used in India.

Figure 1.4 Egyptian hieroglyph representing the sound of *F.*

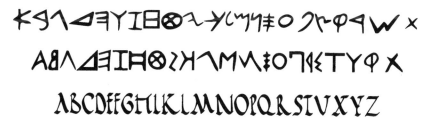

Figure 1.5 Phoenician, early Greek, and Roman alphabets (fonts courtesy of Jack Kilmon).

1.1.3 Other Forms of Documents

Long before scripture drawings and painting were used in documents, there were cave paintings dating to 25,000 B.C. Whether these paintings were used as documents or were purely decorative we don't know. But it seems probable that such paintings had a documentation purpose, maybe for teaching. Hunter-gatherer societies also had a requirement for records. We know, for example, that the X-ray drawings by Australian Aborigines—made on tree bark or in the sand—served to distribute the result of a hunt among relatives.

However, hunter-gatherers and nomadic societies had a problem with tangible documents: They would have to carry them around. So, these societies used a different form of documentation: information encoded into songs and tales that could be transmitted orally. While these nontangible formats have not always been regarded as documents, our digital age widens our understanding of what is a document. Digital documents are nontangible, too—not bound to a particular material manifestation. We recognize document formats that include media other than writing or drawing, such as images, voice, sound, or video clips. They may not necessarily be persistent and may exist only during a limited, possibly short, time span, such as messages between middleware components, SMS messages, or traffic jam notifications to a car's navigation system. In this sense we can define a *document* as an artifact with the purpose of conveying information. And in this book, we deal predominantly with documents based on script.

1.2 LINEAR CONCEPTS

Before we look into document schemata in detail, let's first investigate which principles guide the organization of document instances. This will help to explain the purpose of certain schema language constructs, such as the `choice` or `sequence` operators in XML Schema.

1.2.1 Sequence

It is in the very nature of script that text is ordered in a sequential fashion. Unlike images or drawings, which leave the initiative to the eye of the reader, script leads the reader along a narrative. This has been the case from the beginning of writing, when pictographs were set one after each other (see Figure 1.6). The direction of writing varies from culture to culture: Western scripts (even Klingon) run from left to right, Hebrew and Arabic run from right to left, and Chinese script (and scripts derived from Chinese) run from top to bottom.

The sequential organization of documents results from the fact that script is the manifestation of speech. Speech happens in time, which establishes a natural order between the spoken words. Sequential organization of text is essential to support the text's narrative.

However, there are also cases where sequence establishes an order of a higher kind. Consider, for example, an encyclopedia or dictionary. The sequence of topics in an encyclopedia does not support a narrative because there is no narrative that runs across topics. Here, a sequence of topics is established to make navigation easy. Because the topics are ordered alphabetically we know that we can find the topic *saxophone* between the topics *saw* and *say*.

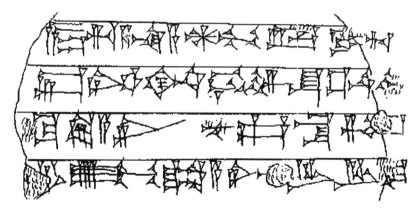

Figure 1.6 Four proverbs in Sumerian cuneiform. The sequential pattern of each proverb is clearly visible.

The following piece of code shows an XML description of a jazz album listing the tracks in sequential order. The position of the track nodes within the album node defines an order relationship between the track nodes.

```
<album>
   <title>The Koeln Concert</title>
   <track><title>Part I</title></track>
   <track><title>Part IIa</title></track>
   <track><title>Part IIb</title></track>
</album>
```

1.2.2 Hierarchy

The concept of hierarchy, too, is older than the art of writing. Poems and songs, for example, are structured into stanzas and verses, so there is a relationship between the part and the whole. This structuring of information is necessary for various reasons. There are physical reasons: A singer may run out of breath when a verse is too long, a story may be too long to be told during an evening, or an output buffer may be too small to hold the whole message. Early business applications, for example, had to restrict the physical length of messages to 80 bytes, a format inherited from punched card technology. There are also reasons caused by perception: The human short-term memory can only hold a limited amount of information. Structuring information into groups of smaller units makes it easier for the listener or reader to process that information.

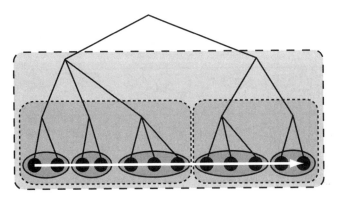

Figure 1.7 Sequence and hierarchy.

Any structure of a linear text sequence can be easily transformed into a hierarchy. Text elements are structured into groups, these form larger groups, and this process can be repeated until only a single group exists. As shown in Figure 1.7, such hierarchical group structures do have a 1:1 mapping to tree structures. Tree structures are the dominant structuring principle for text documents, and as we have already seen in Section 1.1.1, XML supports this concept by allowing us to decorate each tree node with a tag.

The following listing of the marked-up description of Carla Bley's *Escalator over the Hill* exhibits a clear hierarchical structure: title and track elements are child nodes of album. The track elements, in turn, consist of child elements title and duration.

```
<album>
  <title>Escalator over the hill</title>
  <track>
    <title>Hotel Overture</title>
    <duration>PTM13S12</duration>
  </track>
  <track>
    <title>This is here...</title>
    <duration>PTM6</duration>
  </track>
  <track>
    <title>Like animals</title>
    <duration>PTM1S20</duration>
  </track>
</album>
```

1.3 NONLINEAR CONCEPTS

Sequential order is certainly the dominating principle for the arrangement of text elements within a document. However, there are many cases where it is not possible to establish a clear sequential order. This means that different readers might read the text elements in a different sequence (and different authors would place text elements differently in the document layout). Additional navigational concepts are required to help the reader move around within the document.

1.3.1 Bags

Take for example the Sumerian cuneiform from Figure 1.6. While the narrative of the proverb defines the sequential order of each proverb, the order in which the proverbs are arranged on the document is not obvious. In fact, the order in which these proverbs are arranged probably did not matter at all. Or, the author might have placed the proverb that was most important to him at the top. But that is a subjective decision.

We find the same situation in our modern newspapers. Articles in a newspaper are not arranged in a strict logical order. The most important news is placed on the front page (although for many readers it is debatable what is most important), while the rest of the articles are grouped along themes into several sections: politics, business, regional, cultural, sports. Within these sections the arrangement of articles on a page is more a matter of aesthetics and perception than logic: The page must look well balanced, and in Western cultures the articles considered important are positioned at the top, while more obscure topics vanish in the corners at the bottom.

In software systems we sometimes have to use a prescribed sequence of elements, especially if these elements are not identified within a message. A Java message call, for example, requires the parameters to be in the same order as in the definition of the method. Other systems that identify parameters by names may allow varying sequences of parameters. For example, in XML-RPC, parameters are represented without parameter names—parameters are identified by position only. SOAP, which evolved from XML-RPC, identifies parameters by their names, so sequence does not matter.

We call collections of items for which a clear logical order cannot be established, or is not required, a *bag*. The following two XML representations for a jazz performance are equally valid: It does not matter if we give the location first or if we give the time first.

```
<performedAt>
  <location>Dixie Park</location>
  <time>1910-03-27T17:15:00</time>
</performedAt>
```

```
<performedAt>
  <time>1910-03-27T17:15:00</time>
  <location>Dixie Park</location>
</performedAt>
```

1.3.2 Annotations

Some texts have more footnotes than regular text. The purpose of a footnote is to introduce a new aspect or an additional explanation or example without disrupting the main narrative.[1] But footnotes are only one possible form of annotation; there are many others such as margin notes, sidebars, or help texts.

Margin notes act as entry points into a text. Readers can quickly scan the margins for a topic of interest and, if found, continue to read about this topic in the text. Margin notes support nonlinear reading: Readers are not forced to read through the text until they get to the point of interest, but can easily skip text areas.

Sidebars are used to place background information or elements of entertainment into separate text units without disrupting the main narrative. Take for example the description of a route in a travel guide. Readers would expect the main narrative to help them organize the trip along that route. Background information embedded in the text, such as a fairy tale from that region or an article about the regional flora and fauna, would disturb readers in their effort to organize the trip. So, it is better to place this information in a visually separated sidebar.

Help texts assist readers in performing a certain task. Usually, these texts are kept out of sight. Readers who already know how to perform the given task do not have to scan through the sometimes-extensive help texts. Readers who need assistance can navigate to these help texts in order to get the necessary instructions. A typical application for help texts is computer software, but printed documents also come with help texts. Take for example the tax form. The instructions on how to fill out the form are usually printed on a separate sheet or on the back of the main document. To establish a relation between the single elements of the main document and specific help texts, cross-referencing techniques are used. For example, the elements on the main document are numbered and so are the help instructions, so that they can be easily located.

---

1. Too many footnotes indicate a bad writing style and document the author's inability to get a clear understanding of the inner logic of his material.

1.3.3 Cross-References

Annotations introduce a variation into the concept of sequence, but they never question the main narrative. After reading a footnote or a sidebar, the reader continues with the main text. Cross-references are different in that respect. A cross-reference points to a remote text element from which the reader may or may not return. Texts that are extensively cross-referenced establish—besides the main narrative given by the text sequence—a multitude of alternate narratives given by the different paths that follow sequences of cross-references.

The concept of cross-references has led to the development of the hypertext metaphor. This goes back to 1945 when Vannevar Bush postulated the idea of associative indexing in the article "As We May Think" [Bush1945]. Ted Nelson coined the term *hypertext* in an article published in *Literary Machines:*

> By "hypertext" (we) mean non-sequential writing—text that branches and allows choice to the reader, best read at an interactive screen. [Nelson1982]

While cross-references within a document can add to the consistency of a document because they can relate the different parts of a document to each other, cross-references between different documents can become disturbing to the reader. "Lost in hyperspace" is a common buzz phrase that describes the loss of orientation when readers follow hyperlinks from document to document.

Unlike the previously discussed nonlinear concepts (bags and annotations), cross-references cannot be modeled as a tree. For bags and annotations this is still possible by allowing tree nodes to contain unordered sets of child nodes. Cross-references, in contrast, completely ignore the concept of hierarchy. To describe cross-references formally, other concepts must be understood, such as node-and-arc models or primary/foreign keys. Cross-referencing allows for arbitrarily complex document structures. And so, it is possible, for example, to serialize the content of a relational database into a single document where the relations between the database tables are kept as cross-references.

The following piece of XML shows a cross-reference from a child element sample to a child element track: The node sample specifies in attribute trackRef a reference to the trackNo attributes of track nodes.

```
<album>
  <title>The Koeln Concert</title>
  <track trackNo="t1"><title>Part I</title></track>
  <track trackNo="t2"><title>Part IIa</title></track>>
  <track trackNo="t3"><title>Part IIb</title></track>
  <sample trackRef="t2">
    http://www.nile.com/cds/mp3/koelnConcert/part2.mp3
  </sample>
</album>
```

1.4 DOCUMENT-CENTRIC VS. DATA-CENTRIC CONTENT

This brings us to two juxtaposed document concepts, which are discussed in the SGML and XML communities under the names document-centric content model and data-centric content model. (I am not perfectly happy with this wording: "Document-centric document" sounds a bit like "humane human.") The previous section already gave an example of a data-centric document: A relational database, for example, can be seen as a data-centric document. But there are simpler examples for data-centric documents: the phone book, company directories, index cards, and punched cards.

Now, what differentiates a document-centric document from a data-centric document? Apart from presentation issues, the main difference is that document-centric content follows a narrative, but data-centric content does not. This implies that the sequence of document elements in a data-centric document is not determined by a narrative but by logical criteria: The entries in a phone book, for example, are ordered lexically by name. In a relational database table the table entries are not ordered at all; they can be retrieved in any order as requested by the user.

Of course, these two document forms are not mutually exclusive. Document-centric documents may contain data-centric parts, and vice versa. For example, a product description that follows a narrative may contain a (data-centric) table that lists the product features, and a data-centric document such as a product catalog may contain descriptive elements (mini-narratives) within each product entry.

Historically, data-centric documents are as old as document-centric documents, probably older. Script was invented to record information, not to write novels. The earliest documents we know (the incision stones shown in Figure 1.1) seem to be data-centric. But perhaps these stones were placed in sequence to tell a story. Who knows?

1.5 DOCUMENT SCHEMATA

Document schemata define *document types* by defining constraints on the document structure and document content. We say that a document instance that complies with a given document schema belongs to the document type defined by this document schema. We call two document schema definitions *equivalent* when both define the same document type; that is, when the set of valid documents described by each schema is identical.

While constraints on the document content affect the semantics of a document, constraints on the document structure can be regarded as syntactical constraints. In Section 1.6 we will see that structural constraints can be well described with the help of formal grammars. A document instance can thus be regarded as a sentence of some formal language. Since the theory of formal languages is a well-studied and generally well understood discipline, we can gain substantially from this approach. But before we start to explore the fundamentals of grammars, let's first look at three document schemata that actually define the same document type.

1.5.1 A First Schema

The following three listings serve as a first look at the three schema languages used in this book: DTD, XML Schema, and Relax NG. All three listings define the same document type. The purchase order shown in Section 1.1.1 is a valid instance of this document type. Of course, there exist many other schema languages, such as DSD, SOX, TREX, and XDR, but DTD, XML Schema, and Relax NG are currently the most relevant schema languages.

■ XML DTD was introduced with the XML 1.0 specification [Bray2000].
■ XML Schema became a W3C recommendation by May 2, 2001 [Fallside-2001], [Thompson2001], [Biron2001].
■ Relax NG was published by the Organization for the Advancement of Structured Information Standards (OASIS) on December 3, 2001 [Clark2001], [Murata2001].

These first examples introduce the three schema languages and give a first impression of the code. You need not understand these schemata in every detail yet, as the three schema languages will be covered in Chapters 4, 5, 6, and 7.

During the course of this book, schemata will be presented in all three schema languages. Note that these schema languages are not mutually exclusive. It is possible—and sometimes necessary—to define both a DTD and a schema in another schema language such as XML Schema or Relax NG. DTDs don't provide a rich type system and have no namespace support. XML Schema, on the other hand, does not provide means to specify document composition, and with Relax NG, it is not possible to define default and fixed values for elements and attributes. So, sometimes it is necessary to combine.

DTD

We'll start with the DTD version of the purchase order document.

```
<?xml version="1.0" encoding="UTF-8"?>
<!ELEMENT order (customer, orderItem+)>
<!ATTLIST order
  orderNo CDATA #REQUIRED
  orderDate CDATA #IMPLIED
>
```

```
<!ELEMENT customer (name, address)>
<!ATTLIST customer
  customerNo CDATA #REQUIRED
>
<!ELEMENT orderItem (CD | book)>
<!ATTLIST orderItem
  amount CDATA #REQUIRED
>
<!ELEMENT name (first, middle?, last)>
<!ELEMENT address (street, town, zip, state, country?)+>
<!ELEMENT CD (title, publisher, contributor*,price)>
<!ATTLIST CD
  productNo CDATA #REQUIRED
  year CDATA #IMPLIED
>
<!ELEMENT book (title, publisher, author*, price)>
<!ATTLIST book
  ISBN CDATA #REQUIRED
  year CDATA #IMPLIED
>
<!ELEMENT first (#PCDATA)>
<!ELEMENT middle (#PCDATA)>
<!ELEMENT last (#PCDATA)>
<!ELEMENT street (#PCDATA)>
<!ELEMENT town (#PCDATA)>
<!ELEMENT zip (#PCDATA)>
<!ELEMENT state (#PCDATA)>
<!ELEMENT country (#PCDATA)>
<!ELEMENT title (#PCDATA)>
<!ELEMENT contributor (#PCDATA)>
<!ELEMENT price (#PCDATA)>
<!ATTLIST contributor
  kind CDATA #REQUIRED
>
<!ELEMENT publisher (#PCDATA)>
<!ELEMENT author (#PCDATA)>
```

Readers fluent in XML will have no trouble interpreting this schema. The element order is made up of the elements customer and orderItem. Element customer is required exactly once, while orderItem can have one or several occurrences, indicated by the + modifier. In addition, the element order must have the attribute orderNo and may have the attribute orderDate. Similarly, the other elements are described in the same way, until the whole document tree is covered. The leaf elements of this tree—the elements first, middle, last, etc.—contain character data, indicated by #PCDATA. Interesting, too, is the definition of the element orderItem that consists of a choice of the elements CD and book. We will discuss choices in more detail in the next section. DTDs are covered in Section 4.4.

XML Schema

The next listing shows the same schema formulated with XML Schema. In fact, the DTD in the previous listing was generated from the schema shown here with the help of a commercial tool (XML Spy).

```
<?xml version="1.0" encoding="UTF-8"?>

<xs:schema xmlns:xs="http://www.w3.org/2001/XMLSchema"
elementFormDefault="qualified" attributeFormDefault="unqualified">

  <xs:element name="order">

    <xs:complexType>

      <xs:sequence>

        <xs:element name="customer">

          <xs:complexType>

            <xs:sequence>

              <xs:element name="name">

                <xs:complexType>

                  <xs:sequence>

                    <xs:element name="first" type="xs:string"/>

                    <xs:element name="middle" type="xs:string"
                                                  minOccurs="0"/>

                    <xs:element name="last" type="xs:string"/>

                  </xs:sequence>

                </xs:complexType>

              </xs:element>

              <xs:element name="address" maxOccurs="unbounded">

                <xs:complexType>

                  <xs:sequence>
```

```
                         <xs:element name="street" type="xs:string"/>
                         <xs:element name="town" type="xs:string"/>
                         <xs:element name="zip" type="xs:string"/>
                         <xs:element name="state" type="xs:string"/>
                         <xs:element name="country" type="xs:string"
                                                   minOccurs="0"/>
                  </xs:sequence>
                </xs:complexType>
              </xs:element>
          </xs:sequence>
          <xs:attribute name="customerNo" use="required"/>
        </xs:complexType>
    </xs:element>
    <xs:element name="orderItem" maxOccurs="unbounded">
      <xs:complexType>
        <xs:choice>
          <xs:element name="CD">
            <xs:complexType>
              <xs:sequence>
                <xs:element ref="title"/>
                <xs:element ref="publisher"/>
                <xs:element name="contributor" minOccurs="0"
                                     maxOccurs="unbounded">
                  <xs:complexType>
                    <xs:simpleContent>
                      <xs:extension base="xs:string">
                        <xs:attribute name="kind" use="required"/>
                      </xs:extension>
                    </xs:simpleContent>
                  </xs:complexType>
                </xs:element>
                <xs:element name="price" type="xs:decimal"/>
              </xs:sequence>
              <xs:attribute name="productNo" use="required"/>
              <xs:attribute name="year" use="optional"/>
            </xs:complexType>
```

```
            </xs:element>
            <xs:element name="book">
              <xs:complexType>
                <xs:sequence>
                  <xs:element ref="title"/>
                  <xs:element ref="publisher"/>
                  <xs:element name="author" type="xs:string"
                        minOccurs="0" maxOccurs="unbounded"/>
                  <xs:element name="price" type="xs:decimal"/>
                </xs:sequence>
                <xs:attribute name="ISBN" use="required"/>
                <xs:attribute name="year" use="optional"/>
              </xs:complexType>
            </xs:element>
          </xs:choice>
          <xs:attribute name="amount" use="required"/>
        </xs:complexType>
      </xs:element>
    </xs:sequence>
    <xs:attribute name="orderNo" use="required"/>
    <xs:attribute name="orderDate"/>
  </xs:complexType>
</xs:element>
<xs:element name="title" type="xs:string"/>
<xs:element name="publisher" type="xs:string"/>
</xs:schema>
```

This looks quite different. One reason is that XML Schema uses the XML syntax itself. XML Schema is a bit more verbose than a DTD: Cardinality constraints, for example, are spelled out as minOccurs and maxOccurs instead of using the cryptic, albeit convenient, DTD notations ?,*, and +. The same is true for the choice clause, which replaces the "|" compositor, and the sequence clause, which replaces the "," compositor.

The other main difference is that the structure of a schema formulated with XML Schema exhibits the same hierarchy as the later document instances: Elements that are nested into other elements are nested into those elements in the schema definition, too. This allows for defining elements with a local scope. In DTDs, in contrast, all element definitions have a global scope.

In this listing we have defined three elements with a global scope: the root element order, and the elements title and publisher that are reused in different places. Within the hierarchy, these elements are referred to by the clauses ref="title" and ref="publisher".

Of course, in XML Schema we could define title and publisher locally, too. This would allow us, for example, to use publisher elements with a different layout for CDs and books. In contrast, such a schema could not be represented as a DTD because all elements are declared globally. In a DTD we would have to rename the publisher element as book-publisher and as CD-publisher to cater to differing element structures. This is not always desirable, so this example demonstrates a clear advantage of XML Schema over DTDs. Chapters 5 and 6 will discuss XML Schema in its full glory.

Relax NG

Finally, here is the same document type defined in Relax NG:

```
<?xml version="1.0"?>

<grammar ns="" xmlns="http://relaxng.org/ns/structure/1.0"
datatypeLibrary="http://www.w3.org/2001/XMLSchema-datatypes">
  <start>
    <element name="order">
      <optional>
        <attribute name="orderDate"/>
      </optional>
      <attribute name="orderNo"/>
      <element name="customer">
        <attribute name="customerNo"/>
        <element name="name">
          <element name="first">
            <data type="string"/>
          </element>
          <optional>
            <element name="middle">
              <data type="string"/>
            </element>
          </optional>
          <element name="last">
            <data type="string"/>
          </element>
```

```
      </element>
      <oneOrMore>
        <element name="address">
          <element name="street">
            <data type="string"/>
          </element>
          <element name="town">
            <data type="string"/>
          </element>
          <element name="zip">
            <data type="string"/>
          </element>
          <element name="state">
            <data type="string"/>
          </element>
          <optional>
            <element name="country">
              <data type="string"/>
            </element>
          </optional>
        </element>
      </oneOrMore>
    </element>
    <oneOrMore>
      <element name="orderItem">
        <attribute name="amount"/>
        <choice>
          <element name="CD">
            <attribute name="productNo"/>
            <optional>
              <attribute name="year"/>
            </optional>
            <ref name="titlePattern"/>
            <ref name="publisherPattern"/>
            <zeroOrMore>
```

```
                    <element name="contributor">
                      <data type="string"/>
                      <optional>
                        <attribute name="kind"/>
                      </optional>
                    </element>
                  </zeroOrMore>
                  <ref name="pricePattern"/>
                </element>
                <element name="book">
                  <attribute name="ISBN"/>
                  <optional>
                    <attribute name="year"/>
                  </optional>
                  <ref name="titlePattern"/>
                  <ref name="publisherPattern"/>
                  <zeroOrMore>
                    <element name="author">
                      <data type="string"/>
                    </element>
                  </zeroOrMore>
                  <ref name="pricePattern"/>
                </element>
              </choice>
            </element>
          </oneOrMore>
        </element>
    </start>
    <define name="publisherPattern">
      <element name="publisher">
        <data type="string"/>
      </element>
    </define>
    <define name="titlePattern">
      <element name="title">
```

```
        <data type="string"/>
      </element>
    </define>
    <define name="pricePattern">
      <element name="price">
        <data type="decimal"/>
      </element>
    </define>
</grammar>
```

Relax NG also uses an XML syntax to describe schemata. The first difference is that a schema is not called a schema but a grammar, giving a clear hint that schemata can be described with grammars. Section 1.6 will introduce grammars—so be prepared. What is different, too, is that cardinality constraints are not expressed with minOccurs and maxOccurs but by enveloping an expression in an optional, oneOrMore, or zeroOrMore clause.

However, these are minor differences. A more important difference is that Relax NG does not recognize global element definitions as DTDs and XML Schema do. Instead it introduces the concept of *patterns,* which are declared by a define clause. These constructs and the ability to combine various patterns and grammars are the strong points of Relax NG. They make it possible to develop complex schemata from simple building blocks. Another nice twist is the uniform syntax for attribute and element definition. Relax NG is discussed in detail in Chapter 7.

1.5.2 Choice

The concept of sequence is the dominant organizing concept within documents. Constraining the sequence of elements is the most frequent operation that we encounter when defining a schema for a given document type. For example, the customer section within a document must consist of the customer's name and address, given in this sequence. The customer's name is made up of the elements first, middle, last, which must always appear in the document in this sequence. As we have seen in the schemata above, each schema language has the means to specify a prescribed sequence.

However, if we only had to deal with sequence, we would not need a schema. It would be sufficient simply to provide an example document. A schema is only required if there is an element of choice in how we can author a document. In fact, our example already contains an element of choice: A single orderItem element may contain either a CD element or a book element, as shown in Section 1.1.1. This choice is specified explicitly, using a "|" in the DTD, or the choice clause in XML Schema and Relax NG.

But choices are not limited to these explicitly specified alternatives. Choices can come in other disguises, too:

- Optional elements are another form of choice. For example, the customer's name may be given with or without a middle name. Formally, we can describe an option as an alternative between a content element and an empty element.
- Repeating elements contain an element of choice, as it is up to the document author when to stop the repetition. Repeating elements can be formally described as a combination of recursion (see next section) and choice.

1.5.3 Recursion

Recursion is a universal and powerful concept, especially in the formulation of grammars. *Recursion* means to perform an operation, and then to perform the same operation on the results of the previous operation, and so on. We can easily see that recursion is one of the main ingredients of life. For example, the growth of a single biological cell into a complex organism can be seen as a recursive process. A cell doubles its genetic information and then splits into two cells. The same process is again performed by these two cells, resulting in four cells. Then the four cells repeat this process, and so on. At some point this process stops, however, and that is where the concept of choice plays a role in recursion. Recursion without choice results in cancer.

Now, where does recursion play a role in document schemata? We have already mentioned repeating elements. A list of elements can be defined by the following recursive process:

1. Add a single list entry to the document.
2. Add an empty element to the document (in this case the list ends), or add a list to the document.

But recursion can create more complex structures than simple repetitions. A typical example is a list for machine parts where each part entry contains entries for subparts, which in turn contain entries for sub-subparts, and so on:

1. Create a part entry.
2. Within the part entry create entries for subparts.
3. Treat each subpart entry as a part entry.

This is different from ordinary repetition: With recursion we can specify hierarchical structures of arbitrary depth. Without recursion we could only specify structures of limited depth.

The following listings give a short example of a recursive part structure in the three schema languages. Similar structures are found in genealogies, in taxonomies, in arithmetic expression, or in the folder structure of your computer's file system. First, in the DTD the part element definition refers to itself in the list of child elements:

```
<?xml version="1.0" encoding="UTF-8"?>
<!ELEMENT partlist (part+)>
<!ELEMENT part (description, part*)>
<!ATTLIST part
  partNo CDATA #REQUIRED
>
<!ELEMENT description (#PCDATA)>
```

In XML Schema the part element definition refers to itself in the sequence of child elements:

```
<?xml version="1.0" encoding="UTF-8"?>
<xs:schema xmlns:xs="http://www.w3.org/2001/XMLSchema"
elementFormDefault="qualified" attributeFormDefault="unqualified">
  <xs:element name="partlist">
    <xs:complexType>
      <xs:sequence>
        <xs:element ref="part" maxOccurs="unbounded"/>
      </xs:sequence>
    </xs:complexType>
  </xs:element>
  <xs:element name="part">
    <xs:complexType>
      <xs:sequence>
        <xs:element name="description" type="xs:string"/>
        <xs:element ref="part" minOccurs="0" maxOccurs="unbounded"/>
      </xs:sequence>
      <xs:attribute name="partNo" use="required"/>
    </xs:complexType>
  </xs:element>
</xs:schema>
```

Finally, in Relax NG the part list is constructed by referring to the partPattern recursively:

```
<?xml version="1.0"?>
<grammar ns="" xmlns="http://relaxng.org/ns/structure/1.0"
datatypeLibrary="http://www.w3.org/2001/XMLSchema-datatypes">
  <start>
```

```
      <element name="partlist">
        <oneOrMore>
          <ref name="partPattern"/>
        </oneOrMore>
      </element>
    </start>
    <define name="partPattern">
      <element name="part">
        <attribute name="partNo"/>
        <element name="description">
          <datatype="string"/>
        </element>
        <zeroOrMore>
          <ref name="partPattern"/>
        </zeroOrMore>
      </element>
    </define>
  </grammar>
```

The following sections will demonstrate that the three basic concepts

- sequence
- choice
- recursion

are sufficient to describe document structures of a complexity that suits almost any purpose.

1.6 GRAMMARS

This introduction to formal grammars will provide a sound mathematical basis for XML schemata, because any schema can be regarded as a grammar that defines a particular language. The whole concept of XML is to provide a "language factory," and the many existing XML-based markup languages demonstrate clearly that this factory produces some output.

Grammatical analysis goes back to the fourth century B.C. when Panini in India defined a grammar for Sanskrit. Plato also studied the grammar of the Greek language in his dialogue *Cratylus*. The study of formal grammars, however, in which we are interested here, began as late as the mid-1950s when Noam Chomsky [Chomsky1956] published his work on structural linguistics.

1.6.1 Formal Grammars

The theory of formal grammars is closely related to other theories of computation, such as the theory of recursive functions (Gödel), the theories of Turing on computation, and Kleene's theory of regular sets and regular expressions (see Section 1.6.3).

Mathematicians define a formal grammar G as a *production system* consisting of the following:

- A finite alphabet Σ. The concept of an alphabet used here is a very general one. An alphabet can, for example, consist of all Unicode characters; but it may also consist of all keywords of a programming language, all pictographs of the Sumerian script, the sounds of a bird song (bird songs do have a grammar![2]), or the element and attribute names defined for an XML document type.
- A finite set of non-terminal symbols N. As the name says, these symbols will not appear in the final document instance but are used only in the production process.
- A start symbol S taken out of the set of non-terminal symbols N.
- A finite set of generative rules R. Each rule transforms an expression of non-terminal symbols and alphabet symbols (terminal symbols) into another expression of non-terminal symbols and alphabet symbols.

Such a system is called a production system because it can be used to produce language sentences (or document instances) from the language (or document type) defined with grammar G. The production starts with the start symbol S. By applying the rules first to S, and then recursively to the outcome of the previous transformation, it is possible to generate a valid "sentence" of the formal language defined by the grammar. The production stops when the expression contains no more non-terminal symbols. All valid "sentences" of a given language can be generated in this way. The process of generation is completely mechanistic and can be easily transferred to a computer. Let's look at an example. The following little grammar generates currency amounts.

The alphabet is

```
{0,1,2,3,4,5,6,7,8,9, $, . }
```

The set of non-terminal symbols is

```
{ CURR, NUMBER, DIGIT }
```

---

2. This is not really surprising. Any message emitted from a finite state automaton—through which a brain can be seen—complies to a grammar.

The start symbol is

CURR

The rules are

(1) CURR -> $ NUMBER . DIGIT DIGIT

(2) NUMBER -> DIGIT

(3) NUMBER -> DIGIT NUMBER

(4) DIGIT -> 0

(5) DIGIT -> 1

   . . .

(13) DIGIT -> 9

Now we can generate a bit:

CURR	Start symbol
$ NUMBER . DIGIT DIGIT	after rule (1)
$ DIGIT NUMBER . DIGIT DIGIT	after rule (3)
$ DIGIT DIGIT NUMBER . DIGIT DIGIT	after rule (3)
$ DIGIT DIGIT DIGIT . DIGIT DIGIT	after rule (2)
$ 9 3 4 . 50	after rules (13), (7), (8), (9), (4)

Conversely, the grammar can be used to construct a parser that decides for a given input stream if that input stream is a valid sentence of the language defined by the grammar G. This is basically what XML parsers do. Actually, there are two parsers: The first checks if the input document complies with the XML syntax as defined in the XML 1.0 specification. A document that passes that test is called *well formed*. The second parser is constructed from the schema definition. A document that passes this test, too, is called *valid*.

Unfortunately, the general parsing problem is undecidable. Constructing a parser from a grammar can result in a parser that never stops (except, perhaps, with a stack overflow exception). Thus, for several decades, researchers have aimed to constrain grammars in such a way that it is always possible to decide if an input stream belongs to the language defined by the grammar—in other words, that the parser always stops with a positive or negative result.

1.6.2 Backus-Naur-Form (BNF)

The class of decidable grammars is actually very clearly defined. It consists of all so-called context-free grammars, meaning that the left-hand side of the grammar rules must only contain a single non-terminal symbol. A grammar that cannot be expressed in such a way is not decidable.

One particular notation of context-free grammars is the Backus-Naur-Form (BNF). John Backus and Peter Naur introduced this class of grammars with their formal notation to describe the syntax of the ALGOL 60 programming language. Today, BNF remains the most frequently used grammar notation to define programming languages and other formal languages.

The BNF notation is quite simple. It introduces only a few metasymbols:

Symbol	Meaning
::=	is defined as
|	alternative, or
< >	angle brackets surround non-terminal symbols

Terminal symbols are the symbols from the grammar's alphabet and are written without the angle brackets.

A BNF rule has the following form:

```
non-terminal ::= sequence_of_alternatives consisting of strings of
                 terminals or non-terminals separated by |
```

Our little example from above would look like this in BNF:

```
<CURR> ::= $ <NUMBER> . <DIGIT> <DIGIT>
<NUMBER> ::= <DIGIT> | <DIGIT <NUMBER>
<DIGIT> ::= 0 | 1 | 2 | 3 | 4 | 5 | 6 | 7 | 8 | 9
```

Although BNF was designed to describe the syntax of ALGOL 60, it is interesting to know that it did not succeed in defining the language completely. The definition of ALGOL 60 required additional constraints. Only programs that satisfy these additional constraints are valid ALGOL 60 programs. One of these constraints requires that program variables that are referenced in a statement must be declared in the declaration part of the program. It can be proven that this constraint *cannot* be defined with the formalism of BNF.

What has this to do with documents? Well, syntactically the declaration and usage of variables in ALGOL 60 is equivalent to cross-referencing within a document (the ID-IDREF construct in SGML and XML). Each cross-reference in a document must point to the cross-reference's definition within the document. Dangling cross-references (cross-references that point to nowhere) are not allowed. This cross-reference constraint cannot be captured with the means of BNF.

The question is, should such a constraint be captured in a grammar? This would be possible by adopting a grammar model that is more general than BNF, but experience tells us that such grammars result in parsers that are difficult to build and are slow in execution. It is better to keep the parser simple, and to test the additional constraints separately.

The problem with BNF for document processing is that even BNF is too general in many cases. BNF languages require parsers that may have to look far ahead in the input stream to decide which branch to take. This makes the parser slow and resource hungry. Let's look into alternative grammar models in order to see if we can find something more efficient.

1.6.3 Regular Sets and Regular Expressions

A well-known calculus to describe sets of string expressions is the calculus of regular expressions. For Perl and Python programmers, regular expressions are daily exercise, and as Java 1.4 introduces a library for regular expressions, Java programmers should soon know them by heart as well.

Regular expressions are algebraic expressions that describe patterns. String patterns are the most popular, but patterns of other items can also be described. We will revisit regular expressions (patterns) in this role in Section 5.2.7 and in the appendix, where we discuss the lexical representation of XML data types in XML Schema. Here, we are more interested in how regular expressions can be utilized to describe the structure of documents or document parts; that is, how regular expressions can be used to describe how document parts must be arranged to form a valid document.

Regular expressions (and also the term itself) were invented by the mathematician Stephen Cole Kleene [Kleene1956] in the mid-1950s as a notation to describe "regular sets" of symbol strings. The basics of regular set algebra are quite simple. We assume a finite alphabet Σ. Again, this alphabet can contain any kind of symbols, but for the purpose of this explanation, we assume that it only contains ASCII letters.

We can define the following constants:

Symbol	Definition
{}	The empty set
ε	The empty string
a	Literal character with a contained in Σ

And we can define the following three operations:

Notation	Definition	Example
RS	Concatenation. RS denoting the set { ab | a in R and b in S }	{"ab", "c"}{"x", "yz"} = {"abx", "abyz", "cx", "cyz"}
R | S	The set union	{"ab", "c"} | {"x", "yz"} = {"ab", "c"", "x", "yz"}

| R* | The "Kleene" star, also call *powerset*. R* denotes the smallest superset of R that contains ε and is closed under string concatenation. This is the set of all strings that can be constructed by concatenating zero or more strings in R. Obviously, R* consists only of the empty string (if R contained only the empty string) or is infinite. | {"ab", "c"}* = {ε, "ab", "c", "abab", "abc", "cab", "cc", "ababab", "ababc", "abcab", "abcc", "cabab", "cabc", "ccab", "ccc", . . . }. Obviously, Σ* denotes the set of all strings that can be constructed from alphabet Σ. |

An expression combined from the above constants and operators is called a regular expression and describes a regular set. Each regular set can be obtained from a given alphabet with a finite number of concatenations, unions, and "Kleene" star operations.

Look familiar? Well, a DTD model group definition looks very much the same, and something like

```
(CD | book)*
```

is in fact a regular expression.

The 11 axioms and two rules in Table 1.1 (page 32) define the complete algebra for regular expressions. Such algebra can come in handy when we want to refactor schema definitions and other regular expressions. All theorems about regular expressions can be derived from these axioms with the help of the two rules.

The rich set of regular expression operators, as we know them from languages such as Perl, can all be derived from the three basic operators, concatenation, set union, and powerset. The extreme simplicity of regular expressions allows the construction of very simple and fast parsers. However, regular expressions are far less powerful than BNF grammars.

In the context of document processing, regular expressions are interesting because they can easily describe the nodes of a tree-structured document. They can cover all the basic structures of sequence, choice, and repetition. However, regular expressions cannot describe the depth structure of a whole document. This is because regular expressions do not cover recursion. So it is impossible to describe, for example, a parts list of arbitrary depth with a regular expression. What we therefore have to do is to combine recursion with regular expressions. One way to achieve this is to introduce *regular grammars*.

1.6.4 Trees, Hedges, and Forests

The Hedge-Regular Grammar (HRG) [Murata1995] is such a combination. HRGs (sometimes also called Forest-Regular Grammars or simply Hedge-Grammars) have obtained much attention recently because they are well suited to describe

Table 1.1 All theorems about regular expressions can be derived from these 11 axioms and 2 rules.

Axiom/Rule	Description
Axiom 1: $(R\|S)\|T = R\|(S\|T)$	Set union is associative.
Axiom 2: $(RS)T = R(ST)$	Concatenation is associative.
Axiom 3: $R\|S = R\|S$	Set union is commutative.
Axiom 4: $R(S\|T) = RS\|RT$	Concatenation is left distributive to the set union.
Axiom 5: $(R\|S)T = RT\|ST$	Concatenation is right distributive to the set union.
Axiom 6: $R\|R = R$	Set union is idempotent.
Axiom 7: $R\varepsilon = R$	The empty string is neutral to the string concatenation.
Axiom 8: $\{\}R = \{\}$	The empty set is the null element for string concatenation.
Axiom 9: $\{\}R\| = R$	The empty set is neutral to the set union.
Axiom 10: $R* = RR*\|\varepsilon$	The empty string reconstructs the powerset that was concatenated with its own operand.
Axiom 11: $R* = (R\|\varepsilon)*$	The empty string added to the operand of a powerset does not influence the powerset.
Rule of Substitution	Let R, S, T, R', and S' be regular expressions with: $R=S$ Let α be a symbol that occurs in both R and S. If R' is obtained by the substitution of α in R with T, and S' is obtained by the substitution of α in S by T, then $R'=S'$
Rule of Solution of Equations	Let R, S, and T be regular expressions with: $R = SR\|T$ If S does not include ε then $R=S*T$

XML documents. Parsers obtained from HRGs are simple and fast, and HRGs have additional benefits, which will be discussed below. In particular, the definition of RELAX and Relax NG (see Chapter 7) is directly based on HRGs.

Now what exactly is an HRG? An HRG consists of

- A finite alphabet Σ.
- A finite set N of non-terminal symbols.
- A starting set S. This starting set is a regular set of non-terminal symbols out of N. If X consists of a single non-terminal symbol out of N, we speak of a Tree-Regular Grammar.

■ A finite set R of production rules. Each of these rules has the form

```
A ::= x(r)
```

where A is a non-terminal symbol out of N, x is a terminal symbol out of Σ, and r is a regular expression of non-terminal symbols out of N. In particular, r can be empty.

Let's look at an example. We want to define a grammar for documents containing a part list, similar to the one in Section 1.5.3. Each part list contains an unlimited number of parts. Each part description consists of a part number, a description, and a list of subparts. We can define a grammar for such documents in the following way:

The alphabet Σ consists of the terminal symbols

```
{part-list(), part(), part-no(), description(), a, b, c,..., z, 0, 1,..., 9}
```

The set N of non-terminal symbols consists of

```
{LIST-OF-MATERIALS, PART, PART-NO, DESCRIPTION, LETTER, DIGIT}
```

The starting set X consists of a single non-terminal symbol

```
{LIST-OF-MATERIALS}
```

The set R of production rules consists of

```
LIST-OF-MATERIALS ::= part-list(PART*)
PART ::= part(PART-NO DESCRIPTION PART*)
PART-NO ::= part-no(DIGIT*)
DESCRIPTION ::= description(LETTER*)
LETTER ::= (a|b|...|z)
DIGIT ::= (0|1|...|9)
```

We have defined here a tree-regular grammar because the start set consists only of a single non-terminal symbol. Basically, documents that consist of a single root node can be described with a tree-regular grammar. Document nodes such as XML elements, however, are not trees but hedges (ordered lists of trees). This is the case for the document node part(). If we wanted to describe the content of this node with a grammar, we could use the same grammar except that we would define the start set as {PART-NO DESCRIPTION PART*}.

The grammar above also contains a recursion: A part() node can contain other part() nodes. This possibility makes the HRG more expressive than plain regular expressions. However, HRGs are not as powerful as BNF grammars; they can only describe treelike or forestlike structures. But they are more powerful than DTDs.

In particular, HRGs allow us to describe context-sensitive content models. Take for example the following production rules:

```
CATALOGUE ::= catalogue(LIST-OF-MATERIALS PRICELIST)
```

```
LIST-OF-MATERIALS ::= part-list(PART*)

PART ::= part(PART-NO DESCRIPTION PART*)

PRICELIST ::= pricelist(PART-WITH-PRICE*)

PART-WITH-PRICE ::= part(PART-NO DESCRIPTION PRICE)

PRICE ::= price(DIGIT*)

...
```

Here, we describe a `catalogue` document containing two lists. Both lists contain elements tagged with `part()`, but the first list contains the classical explosion `part-list`, while the second contains a flat part list where each part element has an additional `price` element.

Such a content model cannot be defined with DTDs because DTDs do not differentiate between non-terminal and terminal symbols.

In contrast, both XML Schema and Relax NG provide a mechanism for representing non-terminal symbols. In Relax NG a pattern definition (see Section 7.2.2) is equivalent to the usage of a non-terminal in a grammar. In XML Schema, groups and attribute groups serve the same purpose (see Sections 6.2.2 and 6.2.3).

One nice feature about HRGs is that HRG languages can be combined using Boolean set operators (union, intersection, negation) and still stay HRG languages. This allows for a highly modular design of document schemata and the automatic generation of complex document schemata from simple building blocks.

1.7 REGULAR TYPES

We have seen how regular grammars can be used to define document types. We have seen, too, that DTDs use regular expressions to define the type of document nodes. XML Schema also provides an explicit constructor (`complexType`) for type definition. Therefore, it seems sensible to provide a unified formalism for both document type definition and element type definition. We achieve that by introducing a new *substitution* operation into regular expressions. This operation replaces the powerset operator and makes regular expressions equivalent to regular grammars.

An exciting aspect of these regular types is that they can be applied to general data types, allowing much finer control over content than traditional data type declarations.[3] Functional programming languages such as ML or Haskell can exploit the possibilities of regular types. Examples are the *fxp* parser for ML, the *HaXml* libraries for Haskell, and the development of XDuce [Hosoya2000a], a functional language based on ML with built-in support for XML data types.

---

3. A datatype should be understood not as a particular physical representation of data values, but as a set of constraints describing a set of values.

These languages handle XML document nodes in a type-safe way—the compiler is able to check on the type-safety of operations applied to document nodes. But also in imperative languages such as Java, C++, or C#, the typing of document nodes plays a crucial role when we bind a document schema to an object-oriented class hierarchy, as discussed in Chapter 10.

We will use regular types in the context of conceptual modeling as discussed in Chapter 2.

1.7.1 Types as Regular Expressions

The classic data types, as we know them from early programming languages and database systems, are fairly basic: String, Integer, Float, Boolean, Binary, Date, Time make a typical working set of data types. A whole generation of programmers has happily lived with this set of data types.

Later, abstract data types were introduced, an idea that was picked up and made more sophisticated by object-oriented programming. Abstract data types did widen the concept of data types, as they also subsumed complex data types. A new data type can be constructed by forming a pattern out of existing data types, in particular the above-mentioned primitive data types.

While this approach allows the construction of rather complex data types and similarly complex type hierarchies (for a comparison between object-oriented type models and document-oriented type models, see Chapter 10), it does not allow the finer control over the content of primitive data types. In classical type systems, a text document is a string is a string is a string. The internal structure of the string is of no concern to the type system.[4]

This situation is totally unacceptable when it comes to the exchange of documents and text-based messages. Help comes in the form of regular expressions. As regular expressions allow us to restrict textual documents to certain patterns, they allow us to effectively sub-type strings and thus introduce whole hierarchies of document types. The following sections discuss the basics of such a type theory. The discussion is based on [Hosoya2000], but is extended with the introduction of the substitution operation.

1.7.2 Basic Composition

To define a full set of regular expressions, we need three basic notations:

- *Variable.* A variable stands for an arbitrary expression. We denote a variable with an uppercase character, such as X.

---

4. Even in classical programming this is not always satisfactory. Take for example a Java program that wants to send an SQL command to a relational database via JDBC. The SQL command is just a string constant (or variable) and cannot be syntax checked by the Java compiler. The result is that bugs that could be detected at compile time are detected later, during the execution of the program.

■ *Tagged expression.* This is denoted by t[X]. In XML a tagged expression would be represented by a tagged element, the element content representing the expression in the brackets. An empty element is denoted by t[].

■ *Empty sequence.* We denote this with (). In XML an empty sequence would be represented by nothing.

To combine these elements we only need three simple operators: concatenation, union, and substitution. The principles of concatenation are as follows:

■ X,Y denotes a concatenation of the expressions X and Y.

■ Concatenation is an associative operation: (X,Y),Z is equivalent to X,(Y,Z). See also Axiom 2 in Table 1.1.

■ Concatenation is not a commutative operation: X,Y is not necessarily equivalent to Y,X.

The union operator follows these principles:

■ X|Y denotes that a pattern can consist of either X or Y.

■ This is an associative operation: (X|Y)|Z is equivalent to X|(Y|Z) (Axiom 1).

■ It is also a commutative operation: X|Y is equivalent to Y|X (Axiom 3).

■ Both concatenation and tagging are distributive in respect to the union: X,(Y|Z) is equivalent to (X,Y)|(X,Z) (Axioms 4 and 5), and t[X|Y] is equivalent to t[X]|t[Y].

To use substitution, an expression can be enclosed by curly brackets and decorated with a label:

1{X}

A *later* reference to that label is substituted with the content between the curly brackets. The syntax for the referencing label consists only of the label name:

1

For example:

1{X,Y},Z,1

is equivalent to

X,Y,Z,X,Y

In particular, substitution can be used to express recursive structures. For example:

1{t[1,1]|()}

denotes a binary tree structure. Note that the union with the empty sequence is essential here because it allows for stopping the recursion process. Without this possibility of choice, the expression would match only infinite structures.

The operations described in the following paragraphs are all derived from the previous three operators.

- *Option.* X? denotes X or the empty sequence. X? can be derived from the union operator:

X? == X|().

- *Powerset.* X* denotes the set of recurring concatenation of X. This includes the empty sequence. X* can be derived from the previous operators in the following way:

X* == 1{(X,1)?

- *Interleaving.* X&Y denotes that X is concatenated with Y, or that Y is concatenated with X. X&Y can be derived from the previous operators by

X&Y == X,Y | Y,X.

- *Non-empty powerset.* X+ denotes recurrence of X, which happens at least once. X+ can be derived from the previous operators by

X+ == X,X*.

As we have seen, recursive types can be expressed with three basic constructs: concatenation, union, and substitution. All other operators can be derived from these.

1.7.3 Basic Type Algebra

The distributive properties of concatenation and tagging in respect to the union allow us to factor out certain expression parts when we construct a union from two different types:

t[X,Y,Z]| t[X,Y]

First, we factor out the tag:

t[(X,Y,Z)|(X,Y)]

Then we can factor out the first concatenation operand:

t[X,((Y,Z)|(Y))]

We then expand the clause (Y) with the empty sequence:

`t[X,((Y,Z)|(Y,()))]`

and factor out the next concatenation operand:

`t[X,Y,(Z|())]`

Finally, we abbreviate the union expression:

`t[X,Y,Z?]`

In Section 1.7.6 we will see that this technique is essential when converting nondeterministic expressions into deterministic ones.

1.7.4 Subtypes

When we define data types on the basis of regular expressions, we can establish a hierarchy of types. Type hierarchies play a role in XML Schema when it comes to deriving element types from existing complex element types by restriction or extension. We say that a type X is a subtype Y (X <= Y), if any valid instance of X is also a valid instance of Y. The subtype relationship forms a partial order for regular expression types: We may have two types for which no subtype relationship exists. However, it is always possible to construct a supertype that encloses both types as subtypes.

It is possible to deduct the subtype relationship from the regular expressions that define both types. We can start with simple expressions:

`X <= X | Y`

because the right side is a union of X with some other expression type. From this it follows that

`X <= X?`

as X? is defined by X|().
It is also true that

`X,X,...,X <= X*`

as X* contains concatenations of X with itself in any length. Furthermore, concatenation, union, and tagging are conservative regarding the subtype relation: If X <= Y then also

`X,Z <= Y,Z`

and

```
X | Z <= Y | Z
```

and

```
t[X] <= t[Y]
```

This is also true within a recursion: If X <= Y then also

```
1{t[X,1]} <= 1{t[Y,1]}
```

and

```
1{t[X | 1]} <= 1{t[Y | 1]}
```

1.7.5 Generic Types

Finally, the generic tagged expression ~[X] is a supertype to any t[X]:

```
t[X] <= ~[X]
```

Using a generic tagged expression and recursion we can define a completely generic type:

```
1{(~[1]|String|Integer|Float|Boolean|Binary|Date|Time)*}
```

This type subsumes all tagged structures and all of the specified primitive types.

1.7.6 Deterministic Types

A deterministic type is a type that can be described with a deterministic regular expression. An advantage to deterministic types is that their instances are easier and faster to parse.

A regular expression is deterministic if at each choice point of the parsing process it is possible to decide which branch to take without having to look ahead.

Take for example the regular expression

```
((a,b)|(a,c))
```

This expression is not deterministic because each branch begins with a. At this point, it is impossible to decide which branch to take without looking one step ahead: The branches are only differentiated by b and c.

The XML 1.0 specification, for example, requires that a content model definition made with a DTD be deterministic. This is to maintain compatibility with SGML: SGML processors may flag a nondeterministic content model as *ambiguous*. XML Schema also requires a deterministic content model (*Unique Particle Attribution*). In Relax NG this requirement has been dropped.

In many cases it is possible to transform a nondeterministic expression into a deterministic expression. In the example above, we can factor out the a and get

`a,(b|c)`

Now it is possible to decide at the choice expression which branch to take because each branch begins with a different expression (b and c).

Similarly, `(a,b)|(c&a)` is not deterministic because the expression (c&a) allows valid instances of (a,c). Here we would need to resolve the expression first into

`(a,b)|((a,c)|(c,a))`

Then, by using the fact that the union operator is associative, we can transform it into

`((a,b)|(a,c))|(c,a)`

and finally into

`(a,(b|c))|(c,a)`

Conceptual Modeling

To some this chapter might come as a surprise: Conceptual modeling is a topic that is not frequently discussed in the context of XML. But XML has become a mainstream enterprise technology with applications far beyond the classical document applications of SGML. In enterprises, XML plays a role as an integration format for diverse data formats, typically for inter-application messaging. Relational databases are equipped with XML layers, and native XML-database and XML-enabled middleware has appeared on the market. In these application fields, solid engineering practices dominate and conceptual modeling is an issue indeed.

In this chapter we investigate how traditional conceptual modeling methods such as Entity Relationship Diagrams might be applied to the complex XML data structures. We then introduce a new conceptual modeling method, Asset Oriented Modeling (AOM), that is particularly suited for the grammar-based data structures of XML.

2.1 MOTIVATION

Conceptual modeling techniques are well known in enterprise software construction. Up to 80% of effort goes into the design phase of an implementation, only 20% into the implementation. Prior to the implementation of an application, a requirements analysis is performed, which results in an informal description of the business domain. Based on the requirements analysis, the conceptual model captures the business domain with more formal (and mostly visual) means.

A sound conceptual model documents that the participating analysts and engineers have understood the problem. It defines a common reference point for discussion between the different groups involved in the development of an application or an application system. The conceptual model thus forms the basis for the technical architecture. In particular, this is true when projects use different implementation paradigms side by side. For example, if we want to store data in a relational database, but communicate with client applications and peers in XML format, and in addition need an object-oriented Java access layer, things are becoming less than simple. Keeping, for example, the inheritance hierarchies in such an environment in sync can prove more difficult than managing a bag of bees.

A conceptual model can be of great benefit here (see Figure 2.1). It defines the reference point from which all particular implementations are derived. Therefore, the conceptual model itself should be independent from a given technical infrastructure—it should not matter if SQL or XML is used to store the

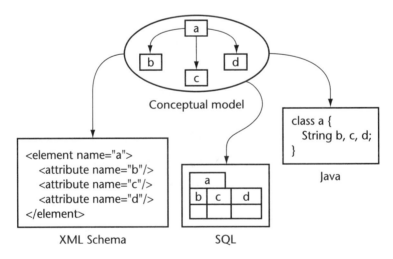

Figure 2.1 The conceptual model as a central point of information. Implementations that are derived from the model are always synchronized.

data. Changes to the information structure are applied to the conceptual model first, and are then carried through to the various implementations.

That a model should be implementation neutral does not mean that the selection of the correct modeling method does not depend on the technology used for the implementation. In the development of IT we have witnessed how the different paradigms in information representation have also spawned related conceptual modeling methods. When relational databases were introduced, Entity Relationship Diagrams became the conceptual method of choice. When object-oriented languages became popular, UML (an object-oriented modeling method) evolved. Now, with XML becoming a mainstream technology, we should expect to see modeling methods that are particularly close to grammars and the information model of XML. In fact, we will present such a modeling method in the following chapters.

Choosing a modeling method that follows the current trend in information technology has several advantages:

- The model is better understood by programmers; implementation is easier and faster.
- Older modeling methods may not be suited to capturing the structure of the new application domains that evolve with the new technologies.
- A modeling method that closely matches the implementation method is better suited to support roundtrip engineering.

2.2 PRINCIPLES OF CONCEPTUAL MODELING

What is the purpose of a conceptual model? A conceptual model is created—as the name suggests—at an early stage during the project development cycle, usually after requirements analysis, when most of the details are still unclear. This differentiates a conceptual model from an implementation model. An implementation model serves as a blueprint for a concrete implementation; the conceptual model, in contrast, provides the audience with a bird's-eye view and does not drown them in detail.

The purpose of a conceptual model is *communication*—communication between the various parties involved in development. It may be faster to implement an application without creating a conceptual model first. However, developers may have a nasty surprise when clients tell them that the delivered application was not what they bargained for. A conceptual model adds extra safety to the development process. It helps to detect errors and misconceptions in an early phase of development. CASE tools (computer-aided software engineering) can help to generate code parts directly from a conceptual model, so some of the extra effort is rewarded when implementing the application.

The language used to describe the model must therefore be easy to understand by all parties involved, not only by those who are going to implement the system. This excludes implementation languages as modeling languages. I therefore do not advocate the use of markup languages, such as XML and SGML and their schema definition languages, as modeling languages. A model formulated in XML Schema or Relax NG would, for example, be well understood by schema authors, but all other parties, such as business architects, systems analysts, and database specialists, would be left out.

Now, what makes a good conceptual model? The following guiding principles are based on Esko Marjomaa's research [Marjomaa2002]:

- *Conceptualization.* Only conceptual aspects of the modeled domain (Universe of Discourse) should be taken into account when constructing the conceptual schema.
- *Completeness.* The conceptual schema should describe all the relevant aspects of the modeled domain.
- *Formalization.* It should be possible to formalize conceptual schemata in order to allow unambiguous implementation.
- *Intelligibleness.* Conceptual schemata should be easy to interpret and understand.
- *Correspondence.* There should be a one-to-one correspondence between the entities of the model and the entities of the modeled domain.
- *Invariance.* Conceptual schemata should be constructed on the basis of such entities that are invariant during certain time periods within the modeled domain.
- *Decomposition.* In order to construct a good conceptual schema it is important first to construct relevant subschemata and then to search for connections between them.

The principles of formalization and intelligibleness are somewhat opposite to each other. A highly formalized model may not be understood by everyone. Sometimes an informal description can be more useful.

2.3 ENTITY RELATIONSHIP DIAGRAMS

The first conceptual modeling method, Entity Relationship Modeling, was invented by Peter Chen in the 1970s [Chen1976]. ERM is so simple that everybody can understand it: For ERM the world consists of *entities*. Entities may have *attributes*, and we can have *relationships* between entities. Entities of the same type form an *entity set*, and relationships of the same type form a *relationship set*. All this is defined in a rather informal way.

As an example of the Entity Relationship method, we reverse engineer the document schemata given in Chapter 1 and present the conceptual model in the original notation of 1976. Figure 2.2 shows the results. The rectangles represent entity sets. Entity attributes are represented by ellipsoids. Double-outlined rectangles represent weak entities (entities that are subordinate to other entities). The triangle represents a generalization (product is a generalization of

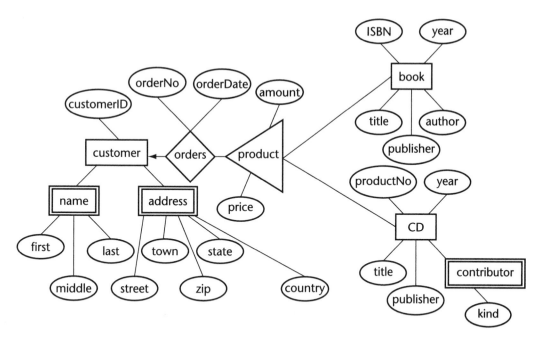

Figure 2.2 Preserving the heritage: the purchase order example as an Entity Relationship Diagram.

book and CD). Relationships are represented by rhombs. An arrow restricts the cardinality to 1; otherwise the cardinality is not restricted. In our example, one customer can order several products, and each product is attributed with an amount.

This example, however, has a few problems. First, a book can only have one author, as author is represented as an entity attribute. This restriction does not apply to contributor, as contributor is represented as an entity. However, contributor looks a bit incomplete. It has, for example, no attribute for a name.

Also, in terms of a conceptual model, authors, contributors, and publishers should be modeled as entities in their own right. Authors, contributors, and publishers are, after all, real-world entities and not mere attributes of books and CDs. However, this semantic information is not contained in the document schemata. Here, we see the limits of reverse engineering.

Figure 2.3 shows the conceptual model that we would prefer; still, this model also has shortcomings. ERM was developed when relational databases came into use, and although it is a fairly generic modeling method, it reflects some of the limitations of relational technology. First, attributes must be atomic; that is, they cannot exhibit a deeper structure. That is why name is modeled as an entity—the only way to equip it with the structure of first, middle, last. But in the real world a name is not so much a first-order entity as a property of an entity. Second, we have no way of showing that some attributes, such as middle,

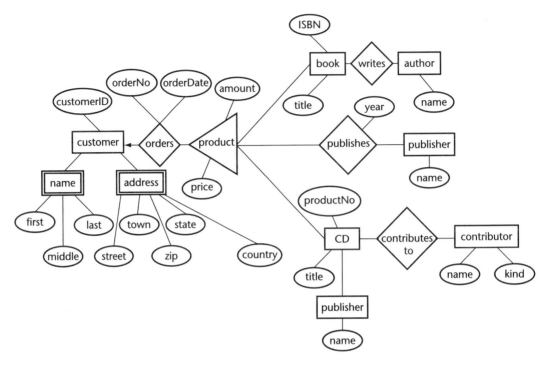

Figure 2.3 Improved version of our order example.

year, or orderDate, are optional. In relational technology there are no optional fields in a record; absent values are represented as null values.

In the years after the invention of ERM, many dialects appeared using different notations. Among them was Information Engineering, developed by Clive Finkelstein [Finkelstein1998], and made popular through his collaboration with James Martin [Martin1993].

When the world turned object-oriented, various object-oriented dialects of ERM appeared, such as Semantic Object Modeling (SOM), developed by David Kroenke [Kroenke1995], and Nijssen's Information Analysis Methodology (NIAM), which finally became the Object Role Modeling (ORM) method [Halpin1999] used in Microsoft's Visio product. This development culminated in the definition of the Unified Modeling Language (UML) by the Object Management Group [Booch1997]. UML, however, has abandoned the idea of a generic conceptual modeling method and offers instead a variety of specialized modeling methods such as class diagram, business case diagram, state diagram, activity diagram, connectivity diagram, and deployment diagram. This puts UML more into the league of object-oriented implementation modeling languages.

2.4 REALITY OF CONCEPTUAL MODELING

Conceptual modeling did not remain the pen-and-paper method originally devised by Peter Chen. Modeling tools were introduced that allow for designing models interactively on the computer screen. Most of the modeling also allows for deriving some code from the model definition. This, however, poses a problem. Today, development cycles are not linear. You don't start with a conceptual model, implement it, and that's it. Instead, after implementing a first version, you go through various tests, gather experiences from the users, and design a new version. Development, today, happens incrementally and iteratively. During these iterations, the conceptual model, the implementation model, and the code must be kept in sync.

One technique to achieve synchronization is called *roundtrip engineering*. This means that changes made to the code are automatically reflected back into the model. The model always stays informed about the current state of the application code and vice versa. When changes are made to the model, it is possible to automatically carry these changes forward to the code.

Roundtrip engineering requires a high degree of integration between code management and model management and the consistent use of the same modeling tools throughout the project. In small and medium projects this should not be difficult to ensure. In large projects, however, it becomes almost impossible. Hundreds of developers may be working on the same project, probably located all over the world, and probably working with different tools. Under these circumstances it is almost impossible to synchronize all changes made to the code and automatically reflect them back into the model.

So, conceptual modeling can become a drag factor when code changes must be reflected back into the model. This is especially true when the philosophy of the enterprise data model is used. This philosophy postulates that the whole enterprise must be seen as one consistent information model. When this huge model is centrally administered and every change must be approved by the central administration, the result is a cumbersome bureaucracy that can slow down the development process considerably. The same is true for large document schemata that are centrally administered. Section 13.2 will discuss some issues surrounding centralized and decentralized change management for schemata.

Ad hoc business collaborations as we find them in electronic business and virtual enterprises have the opposite requirements. Here, the partners do not want to integrate their various information models into a single consistent model. What they require are information systems that collaborate in a loosely coupled fashion, usually with the help of mediating middleware between the participating software systems. The same is true for company mergers. Here, too, the systems have simply to collaborate, but with the prospect of long-term integration. Conceptual modeling must tackle this area as well.

2.5 INTRODUCING ASSET ORIENTED MODELING

Asset Oriented Modeling (AOM) is a new conceptual modeling method that was designed especially for XML and open environments. AOM is used throughout the book to represent information structures visually. There are two reasons why we should use a new modeling method:

- The classic enterprise information model is giving way to an open network information model. The new scenario exposes problems in the existing classical modeling methods: They are not flexible enough for network structures and are too slow for Internet speed.
- With XML we have a powerful technology to describe complex information structures based on a document model. Again, problems with classical modeling methods are revealed: They are not expressive enough for the highly complex document structures, and they are often too complex to be easily adopted by schema designers.

AOM was born out of these requirements. It is a lean modeling method with only a few concepts to grasp. What differentiates this method from other modeling methods are the following points:

- A unified approach to entities and relationships allows us to describe information structures that are beyond the scope of traditional modeling methods—for example, relationships between relationships and inheritance between relationships.
- Regular expressions, regular grammars, and regular types (see Sections 1.6 and 1.7) play a central role in AOM. In particular, this allows XML-like structures to be defined in a very compact way.
- Namespaces allow merging of models and model parts.

The following sections introduce the basic concepts of AOM and demonstrate its application with some step-by-step examples. Chapter 3 will discuss a larger model that will then be transformed into XML Schema in Relax NG in Chapter 8. You can also find detailed information about AOM on its web site, *www.aomodeling.org*.

2.5.1 AOM Basics

The main components in AOM for describing the structure of an information model are *assets* and *arcs*. Unlike the various flavors of Entity Relationship Modeling, AOM does not distinguish between entities and relationships (or between classes and associations as UML does). Assets are not the same as entities, and arcs are not the same as relationships. AOM uses assets and arcs more in the way the Resource Description Framework (RDF) uses nodes and arcs. The classical entities and relationships are both represented in AOM as assets. Or, to be precise, AOM treats everything—even entities—as relationships. Let's see how this works.

Take for example a classical entity type, Customer. Let's say this entity type is related to entity type Person by an is_a relationship, and with entity type Account by a has relationship. So the classical model would have three entity types: Customer, Person, and Account, and two relationship types: is_a and has.

However, we could interpret this situation quite differently. We could see Customer as a binary relationship that relates an account to a person. If we also want to include the fact that a customer resides at a given address, then Customer becomes a ternary relationship between Person, Account, and Address. In fact, a relationship might relate any number of items to each other. Generally, we allow *n*-ary relationships.

Do we also have 1-ary (unary) relationships? Of course we have. Take for example a bicycle. A bicycle can be seen as a binary relationship because it relates the front wheel and the back wheel to each other. What about a monocycle? Obviously, a monocycle represents a unary relationship. That might sound like one hand clapping, but mathematically it is perfectly correct.

Let's put this all together and look at a first example. What was said for the monocycle applies in the model in Figure 2.4 to OrderItem. OrderItem is a unary relationship referring to CD. The binary relationship orders relates the two

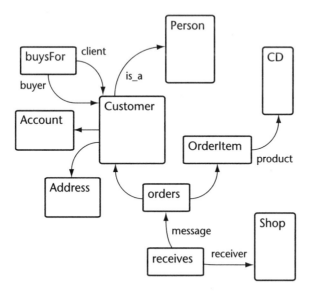

Figure 2.4 Simple model for a music shop. Note that arcs do not represent a relationship but simply connect an asset with other assets that play a role in the context of the first asset. Arcs can be decorated with role names.

relationships `Customer` and `OrderItem` to each other. Finally, the binary relationship `receives` relates the relationships `orders` and `Shop` to each other.

Modeling this example in a classical modeling method would give us some trouble because in classic theory it is not clear if `orders` is a relationship or an entity. If we decided for a relationship `orders`, we would have trouble with relationship `receives`, as this relationship would now relate an entity (`Shop`) with another relationship (`orders`)—a concept that is not supported in classical modeling methods.

In classical ERM, if we decided for an entity, we would first have to *reify* the act of ordering into an entity `Order`. (To reify means to make into a thing.) Then we would have to invent additional relationships to relate `Order` to `Customer` and `CD`. The model gets bigger. Unfortunately, these scenarios where we would have to treat relationships as entities are not uncommon. In modern business scenarios, any business relationship manifests itself sooner or later as a business document and, alas, becomes an entity.

So far, we have not discussed how to represent the end nodes of our graph: `Person`, `CD`, `Account`, `Address`, and `Shop`. Shouldn't we represent these assets differently—as entities? I think not. These assets are always potential relationships. For example, if we add an asset `Department` to `Shop`, then `Shop` becomes a unary relationship. As long as `Department` is not added, `Shop` is, well, a 0-ary relationship. If this sounds a bit uncommon, consider that the concept of zero was uncommon itself until the number zero was invented only some time ago in Arabia. The advantage is that with this concept, a given model is easier to extend. When we want to add `Department` to `Shop`, we just connect it with an arc, but we do not have to convert `Shop` from an entity into a relationship.

AOM's concept of using relationships over relationships is based on Bernhard Thalheim's Higher Order Entity Relationship Modeling (HERM) [Thalheim-2000], although Thalheim still differentiates between entities and relationships. In this respect AOM is closer to the relational approach, where both entities and relationships are represented as tables. It was E. F. Codd, the father of relational algebra, who stated that there is no reason to distinguish between entity type and relationship type [Codd1991]). Consequently, relational database schemata translate nicely into AOM.

The following sections will introduce AOM's language elements in a more formal way.

2.5.2 Assets

Now, let's take a closer look at the definition of assets (Figure 2.5):

- *Label.* The asset label is optional and defines one or several *display names* for asset instances. If omitted, the display name of instances is identical to the asset name. Labels are not necessarily unique.

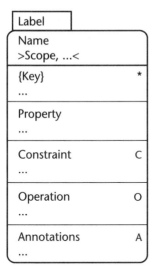

Figure 2.5 Asset definition schema.

A solid label without display names denotes an abstract asset, that is, an asset that cannot have instances.

- *Name.* The asset name *identifies* an asset within a scope.
- *Scope.* The scope defines one or several *contexts* for assets. All asset definitions are only valid within the specified scope(s). A typical example for using scopes is versioning. If no scope is specified, the model scope applies.
- *Key.* One or several optional *primary keys* identify asset instances uniquely. Composite keys must be decorated with a name. For single property keys, the name defaults to the name of the property.
- *Property. Properties* contain the "data" of asset instances (see next section). Optionally, a property can be constrained by a data type definition.
- *Constraints.* These can be used to define additional *restrictions* for properties. Constraints can be defined for single properties, across properties, or across assets.
- *Operations.* Asset operations define abstract *access methods* to asset instances. The semantics depend on the implementation.
- *Annotations.* These are an *extension* mechanism, similar to tagged values in UML. AOM allows XML syntax for annotations.

At this point we need a proper definition of a key: In the most general sense a key can be expressed as a function over some asset properties $k = f(n1, n2, . . .)$, which uniquely identifies the asset. However, for many implementation systems this definition is too general. AOM therefore only supports keys defined by the following specification:

A key is constituted by an unordered set of properties that uniquely identifies an asset. A *primary key* is constituted by the minimal set of such properties.

The distinction between asset name and display label is an important one. It gives AOM the same descriptive power as a regular grammar. The asset name takes the function of a non-terminal symbol, while the display names act as terminal symbols.

2.5.3 Arcs and Clusters

Arcs and clusters are the "glue" between assets. While arcs introduce an element of hierarchy into the model, clusters represent choice.

Arcs

Assets are connected by directed arcs. An arc that points from asset A to asset B, as shown in Figure 2.6, indicates that asset B plays a role in asset A. Arcs do not represent relationships in the sense of Entity Relationship Diagrams. Relationships are represented in AOM as assets. Let's take a closer look at the elements in Figure 2.6:

- *Role*. Arcs can be decorated with a *role name*. If no role name is defined, the implicit role name is the name of the target asset.
- *[n..m]*. In addition, an arc can be decorated with a *cardinality constraint* (see Table 2.1).
- *>range*. The range attribute is an additional constraint for arcs, restricting the possible set of target instances to a specific container (for details see Section 2.5.8).
- *(key)*. In the rare cases where a target asset specifies more than one primary key, the key can be specified by its name.

When the cardinality constraints like the ones defined in Table 2.1 are used to decorate the edges of a graph (such as the arcs in a conceptual model), this can result in constraints that can never be satisfied. For example, in Figure 2.7, each instance of asset type C requires the existence of at least two instances of asset type A and at most one instance of asset type B. This contradicts the

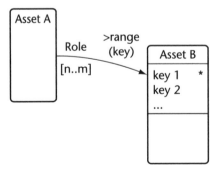

Figure 2.6 Arc connecting assets.

Table 2.1 Cardinality constraints for arcs.

Notation	Description
[n..m]	0 <= n <= m
	An unlimited upper bound is denoted with an asterisk *.
*	[∅..*]
+	[1..*]
?	[0..1]
no decoration	[1..1]

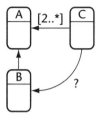

Figure 2.7 Contradictory cardinality constraints.

implicit constraint between B and A, which dictates a 1:1 relation between both.

Therefore, we should always make sure that the intersection of all constraint cardinalities used within a complex structure is not empty. This is always the case when we only use the last four constraint types (*, +, ?, no decoration): Their intersection always contains [1..1].

Clusters

Arcs can be clustered. A cluster describes a situation where an arc leads from one asset to a set of *alternative* assets. As shown in Figure 2.8 (page 54), a cluster is denoted with a small circle at the origin point, containing the choice operator |. Clusters can also be used in classification relationships. Figure 2.9 (page 54) shows how a cluster can be applied to is_a arcs. What this says is that a customer is either a person or a company.

2.5.4 Properties

In AOM, properties can be atomic or complex. Again this is different from classical modeling methods where properties (or attributes) can only be atomic. Properties in AOM can have

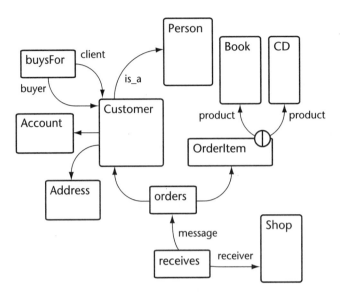

Figure 2.8 The example from Figure 2.4 extended with a cluster. A customer now orders either a CD or a book.

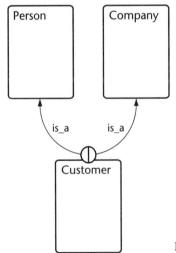

Figure 2.9 A clustered is_a relationship.

- An undefined type. In this case, only the name of the property is specified.
- An explicitly defined type (see next section).
- A local type definition.

Local types are defined via a regular expression (see Section 1.7) using the following syntax:

Syntax	Description	Example
prop(...)	Complex property, consisting of property name and a particle containing subproperties.	See following rows.
(...)	A property particle. The parentheses contain nested expressions combining the following operators.	
(sub,...,sub)	Sequence (ordered list)	author(name(first,last), birthDate)
		Property author consists of subproperty name, followed by subproperty birthDate. Subproperty name consists of subproperty first followed by subproperty last.
(sub&...&sub)	Bag (unordered list)	part(id,(maker&grade))
		Property part consists of subproperties id, maker, and grade, with id always in the first position and maker and grade following in any order.
(sub|...|sub)	Choice (alternative)	speaker((bass,middle,treble) | (low,high))
		A speaker system is either a three-way bass-middle-treble system or a two-way low-high system.

Both properties and particles can be suffixed with one of the following modifiers:

Syntax	Description	Example
(no modifier)	mandatory *[1..1]*	last
		A last name is always required.
?	optional *[0..1]*	middle?
		Not everybody has a middle name, so this property is optional.

+	repeated *[1..n]*	phoneNo+
		At least one phone number is required.
*	optional and repeated *[0..n]*	sponsor(name,url)*
		An arbitrary number of sponsors is allowed.
[n..m]	minimum of *n* occurrences and a maximum of *m* occurrences with $0 <= n <= m$	phoneNo[1..4]
		The number of phone numbers is restricted to a maximum of 4.

Recursive structures can be defined by using the substitution operation as introduced in Section 1.7. We use the following syntax to define recursive properties:

Syntax	Description	Example
label{}	**Label declaration.**	sect{title,para*}
	Establishes a reference point for the expression within the curly brackets. Unlike a tag, a label does not appear in instances. It is a pure metanotation.	represents the property sequence
		title,para*
		and allows this sequence to be referenced by label sect.
label	**Label reference.**	block(sect{title,para*}, anno,sect,sect)
	Refers to an earlier defined reference point. The current label occurrence is substituted with the expression designated by the earlier label declaration.	is equivalent to
		block(title,para*,anno,title, para*,title,para*)
		In particular, labeling allows the definition of recursive structures.
		recur{part(recur*)}
		is a typical treelike part list:
		part(part(part(...)*)*)*
		Note that the use of a modifier such as * or ? is essential here. It ensures that the definition can

have finite instances. In contrast, the expression

`recur{part(recur+)}`

would have only infinite productions.

Figure 2.10 shows how this syntax can be used within an asset definition. The definition of properties is straightforward:

- `customerID` is a property with a (yet) undefined type. This property is also used as a primary key, as denoted in the slot under the asset name.
- `name` contains subproperties `first`, `middle`, and `last`. Subproperty `first` may occur several times, and subproperty `middle` is optional.
- `title` is optional but may occur several times.
- `phone` must occur at least once and at most four times.
- `shippingAddress` and `billingAddress` are identically structured, but `billingAddress` is optional.

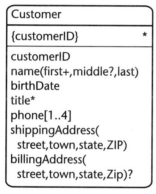

Figure 2.10 Definition of a Customer asset.

2.5.5 Types

Simple types can be assigned to a property in order to constrain the values of that property to atomic values of the type's value domain. The notation is simple:

`type propertyname`

AOM does not introduce its own type system but allows the use of existing type systems, for example, Java types, SQL types, and XML Schema built-in types. The default type system for properties is defined in the global model definition; however, it is also possible to mix types from several type systems into one model. Types not belonging to the default type system are prefixed with a type system identifier, for example, `sql_TIME`, or `xs_string`.

AOM allows extending, restricting, or combining simple types by specifying type expressions.

Syntax	Description	Example
`type`	Single type	`float` Property contains a floating-point value.
`(type1|type2)`	Type union	`(float|int)` Property contains a floating-point or integer value.
`(type1,type2)`	Type sequence	`(NMTOKEN,int)` Property contains a name token followed by an integer value, such as "USD 5".

`{value1,value2,...0}`	Type restriction by enumeration. The listed values are the only values possible for the property.	`int{1,2,3}`
		
		 Property contains one of the listed integers.
		
		 `{I,II,III}`
		
		 Property contains one of the listed values of undefined type.

`type(param=value)`	Type parameter. Depends on the type system used (for example, restricting facets in XML Schema— see Section 5.2.7).	`decimal(fractionDigits=2)` Property contains decimal values with two fractional digits.

The following type modifiers can be used:

Syntax	Description	Example
`?`	Optional type (used in sequences)	`(NMTOKEN?,int)` Property contains an integer that can optionally be prefixed with a name token.
`+`	List extension of type with at least one occurrence	`(NMTOKEN,int+)` Property contains a name token that is followed by at least one integer.

*	Optional list extension of type	`(NMTOKEN,int*)`
		Property contains a name token that may be followed by integers.
[n..m]	List extension of type with at least *n* occurrences and at most *m* occurrences with 0 <= *n* <= *m*.	`(NMTOKEN,int[2:4])`
		Property contains a name token followed by 2–4 integers.

Complex properties are defined via a local definition, as shown earlier. Alternatively, a complex property may be defined via a complex type definition, which is nothing but the name of an asset that defines the structure of the property. Any asset can be used as a type.

With AOM, we can combine several complex types with the union operator:

Syntax	Description	Example
`type`	Complex type	`person`
		Property contains a structure as defined in asset `person`.
`(type1|type2)`	Type union	`(person|company)`
		Property contains either a structure as defined in asset `person` or a structure as defined in asset `company`.

In the example shown in Figure 2.11, all properties have been decorated with type definitions. The atomic types are borrowed from XML Schema, assuming

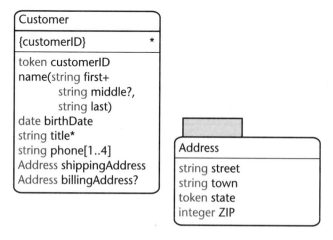

Figure 2.11 Completely typed `customer` asset.

XML Schema was defined as the default type system on the model level. The only complex type is Address, which is used for both shippingAddress and billingAddress. This type is defined as an abstract asset (note the grayed-out asset label), so it cannot have instances of its own.

2.5.6 Inheritance

In AOM, the is_a relationship defines an inheritance relationship (see Figure 2.12). Features of the target asset, such as properties, keys, constraints, operations, annotations, in- and outgoing arcs, are inherited by the origin asset. The origin asset may override inherited features.

Multiple inheritance is possible, provided the definitions made in assets A1 and A2 are compatible. Definitions inherited by asset B from both A1 and A2 are constructed by intersection: If two definitions are incompatible, their intersection is empty. Figure 2.13 shows how to construct an asset CDforSale from assets CD and Product by multiple inheritance. What this says is that CDforSale is *both* a CD and a product.

Clustered inheritance works like a generalization. The inherited definitions are combined by the choice operator. In Figure 2.14, a customer is *either* a person *or* a company.

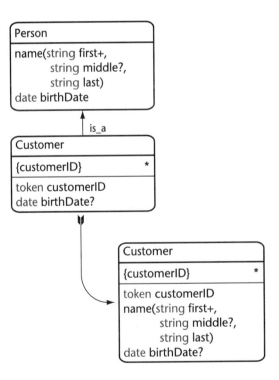

Figure 2.12 Asset Customer inherits properties from asset Person but overrides the definition of property birthDate by making it optional.

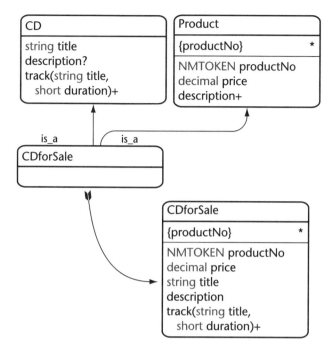

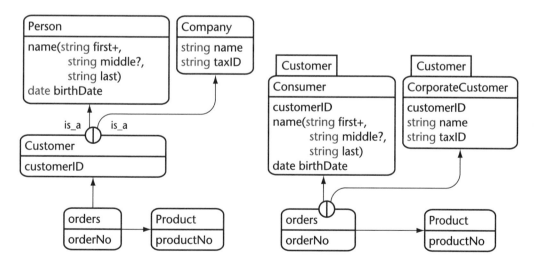

Figure 2.13 Multiple inheritance. The asset CDforSale inherits properties from both CD and Product. As the definitions of property description clash, the intersection of both definitions is constructed. The intersection of cardinality constraint [0..1] (?) with cardinality constraint [1..*] (+) results in [1..].

Figure 2.14 Clustered inheritance. The diagram on the right shows how clustered inheritance can be resolved. We get two different asset types Consumer and CorporateCustomer, but united under the same display label Customer. Consequently, instances would all be named Customer.

2.5.7 Constraints

Again, AOM does not introduce its own constraint language but allows the use of existing constraint languages. One example is OCL, which is mostly used in UML scenarios. This book uses an XPath-like constraint language, which will allow us, for example, to transform conceptual constraints easily into Schematron expressions (discussed in Chapter 9) or to use XPath-enabled DOM implementations for constraint checking.

Constraints can be defined in order to introduce additional restrictions for properties. In AOM constraints can be defined

- for single properties or subproperties
- between subproperties of a single property
- between properties of a single asset
- and across different assets

For example, say we want to require that a middle name not be specified if there is more than one first name specified. This would read as

```
not(name/first[2]) or not(name/middle)
```

To relate a constraint expression to a specific property or subproperty, a constraint can be equipped with a *context expression* that is separated from the constraint expression with a double colon. For example, we can transform the above constraint to

```
name:: not(first[2]) or not(middle)
```

by factoring out name.

A constraint that needs to access property values in other assets can do so by exploiting the access structure provided by the arcs between assets. Let's assume that we want to add a constraint to asset A that needs to access values in asset B. If there is an arc leading from asset A to asset B, we can access properties in asset B from asset A by

```
B/propname
```

If a role name is specified for the arc, we can use

```
rolename/propname
```

instead. Figure 2.15 shows a constraint between the two assets orders and Customer.

2.5.8 Level 2 Structures

The language elements outlined above are sufficient to define the basic structure of an information system. Assets can represent both the entities and re-

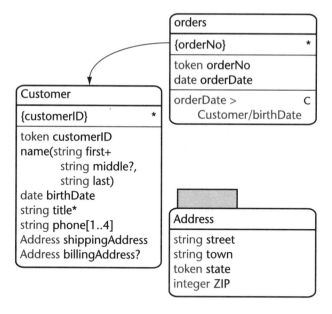

Figure 2.15 Defining a constraint between two assets. The property orderDate in instances of asset orders must always contain values that are larger than those in property birthDate in the corresponding instances of asset Customer.

lationships of a conceptual model. The ability to specify structured property avoids the need to introduce artificial entities and keeps the model compact.

However, large systems require large models, and viewers can get lost in the cobweb of interrelated assets. AOM therefore introduces a notation for additional structures defined on top of an existing model. These are generically called Level 2 Structures (L2S).

L2S serve three interrelated purposes:

- L2S improve the perceptibility of the model by arranging assets that are closely connected into groups, and by demarcating these groups.
- L2S usually represent real-world objects. Within a business scenario, typical Level 2 Structures represent *business objects* and *business documents*.

    Business objects are assets or groups of assets that play a role in a business process.
    Business documents are assets or groups of assets that are exchanged as messages between business objects within the context of a business process.

- L2S provide a hint regarding modularization for later implementations of the model. In XML Schema, for example, an L2S would typically be implemented as a separate schema file. In Java, an L2S would typically be implemented as a separate package.

Each L2S can group together several assets (and/or other L2S, as L2S can be nested). They are demarcated by a labeled box. Multiple labels (aliases) are possible. Figure 2.16 shows how to group the assets in a simple shop model. Customers can order books or CDs. When they do so, they may order several items in varying amounts. Items consist either of books or CDs. The shop receives those orders.

Customers, books, CDs, and shops are first-order business objects because they play a role in the business process. Not so clear is where to put the assets orders, OrderItem, and receives. Since each act of ordering will result in a purchase order (a business document) that will list multiple order items, we place the assets orders and OrderItem into the same L2S. Receiving an order is a function of the Shop business object, so the asset receives goes into one L2S with asset Shop.

Within each L2S, one designated asset acts as the *identifying asset* (each marked with a bold outline). In our example the following assets are used as identifying assets: Customer, CD, Book, orders, Shop.

The following constraints apply to identifying assets:

■ Identifying assets should have a *key*. A key allows identifying instances of L2S uniquely. This makes sense: Especially in an open environment, each business object and each business document should have a globally unique identifier that can be used as a key. Each web page has one!

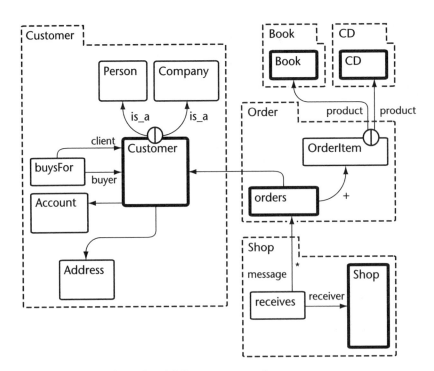

Figure 2.16 Applying Level 2 Structures, step 1.

- Starting from the identifying asset of an L2S, we must be able to reach any asset belonging to that L2S by following the arcs in the indicated direction. This constraint will allow us to interpret each L2S as an aggregation and will later allow us to easily implement Level 2 Structures as hierarchical structures, such as XML document types.

The example in Figure 2.16 presents a problem: We would like to use asset Shop as the identifying asset of L2S Shop, but the arc coming from asset receives has the wrong direction. This is a common problem when grouping into L2S.

To comply with this constraint we must reverse the direction of the offending arc. This reversal represents a change of interpretation: An asset that was originally superior to the identifying asset now becomes a subaltern of the identifying asset.

Arc reversal renders any cardinality constraint of that arc invalid. Therefore, the reversed arcs are decorated with "*" to indicate that no cardinality constraint exists for this arc.

In addition, the reversal of an arc renders its role name invalid. It may require the specification of a new role name.

Let's see what this operation does to our Shop example (Figure 2.17). We have reversed the arc leading from asset receives to asset Shop. We can interpret this

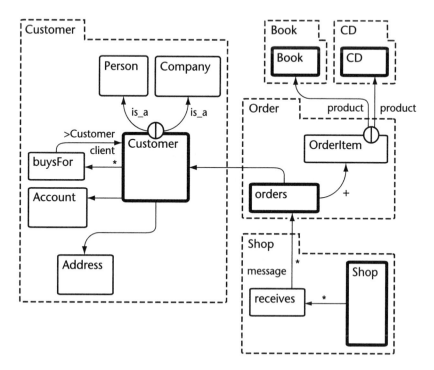

Figure 2.17 Applying Level 2 Structures, step 2.

as an acquisition of asset receives by asset Shop. To comply with the rules, we have also dropped the role name and the cardinality constraints (by adding an asterisk).

The same operation was applied to the arc with the role name buyer leading from Customer to buysFor. We had the same problem there: buysFor could not be reached from identifying item Customer. We have reversed this arc, removed any cardinality constraints, and dropped the role name.

But what have we done to the arc with the role name client? This arc points back to asset Customer. Arcs that are local to an L2S are also local to any instance of the business object represented by the L2S. For example, the arc leading from Customer to Account would lead in an instance A from Customer A to Account A and not to an arbitrary account. This is the desired behavior for most arcs connecting assets within an L2S, and consequently the range of these arcs is by default restricted to one *instance*.

Not so for arc client. For this arc it would not make sense to point back to the same customer instance. Instead we want this arc to point at other Customer instances. We therefore must loosen the *range* constraint of this arc, and we do this by decorating the arc with the name of the L2S, which in our case is Customer, too. By doing so, we indicate that this arc may point to all instances of the L2S Customer.

2.5.9 Models and Namespaces

In AOM each model can consist of

- Assets
- Arcs connecting assets
- Level 2 Structures (L2S) that group items together
- Global definitions

Figure 2.18 shows the graphical representation of the global definitions that can be made in AOM and a concrete example.

- *Name.* The name of the model.
- *Namespaces.* The *default namespace* and additional namespaces with their *prefixes* (see below). Namespaces are identified by a globally unique URI. The definition of a default namespace is mandatory.

  The syntax for namespace prefixes is prefix=namespace.
- *Scopes.* A user-defined *context* for the model. Multiple scopes are allowed. A typical application for using scopes is versioning. If no scope is supplied, the model is valid in a global scope.
- *Type systems.* The type systems used for simple types, such as Java, XML Schema, SQL. Type systems should be specified with a globally unique URI.

  First, a *default type system* is defined, followed by additional type systems with their *prefix*.

Name	
Namespaces	
Scopes	
Type systems	
Constraint languages	
Operation vocabulary	
Annotations	

(a)

Name	CDOrderModel
Namespaces	http://www.jazzshop.com/orders jaz=http://www.jazz.org
Scopes	Vers1 Vers2 Vers2.1
Type systems	http://www.w3.org/2001/XMLSchema

(b)

Figure 2.18 The global model settings describe the use of namespaces, type systems, constraint languages, and other information.

- *Constraint language.* The language used for specifying constraints, such as OCL or XPath. Constraint languages should be specified via a globally unique URI.

  First, a *default constraint language* is defined, followed by additional constraint languages with their *prefix*.
- *Operation vocabulary.* The vocabulary namespaces for defining abstract operations. These vocabularies are user defined. First, a *default operation vocabulary* is defined, followed by additional operation vocabularies with their *prefix*.
- *Annotations.* An extension mechanism, similar to tagged values in UML. However, AOM allows XML syntax.

The example in Figure 2.18(b) defines a default namespace, an additional namespace with prefix *jaz*, three scopes, and a default type system.

The purpose of namespaces in AOM is to globally identify assets in a unique way. The default namespace that must be defined with each model applies to all assets, unless these items use an explicit namespace prefix (separated from the name with a colon). The combination of name and namespace identifies an item unambiguously within a given scope. This feature allows for merging models. The ability to merge two or more models becomes important in large scenarios, where applications are developed by multiple groups, or when formerly distinct applications grow together. Using different namespaces for different models prevents clashes between equally named assets or L2S. On the other hand, it is also possible to force assets from different models to merge, by assigning them to a common namespace and giving them the same name.

When two models are merged, the result is basically a union of both models. However, the following rules apply when definitions clash:

- Equally named assets belonging to the same namespace and the same scope are merged.
- Level 2 Structures are merged when their identifying assets are merged. In this case their labels are combined by a union.

When two assets are merged, their properties are combined per union. Equally named properties are combined in a single particle with the help of a choice operator.

Similar rules apply to asset labels, keys, constraints, operations, and annotations. Detailed merging rules are documented on the AOM web site (*www.aomodeling.org*).

Figure 2.19 shows our completed bookshop model. Section 13.1 shows how to combine two models using the model developed in this chapter and the model developed in Chapter 3.

2.5.10 Summary

AOM is a new modeling method that is particularly (but not exclusively) targeted at XML environments. Its main features can be summarized as follows:

- *AOM is expressive.* By representing relationships in their reified form as assets, AOM allows us to define, describe, and visualize higher-order relationships — that is, relationships between relationships. AOM Level 2 Structures can be used to model large-scale objects by aggregating several lower-level assets. These structures are closely related to objects of the real world and allow an intuitive and natural model of the business domain. They are also easy to implement in the form of XML documents.
- *AOM is compact.* Due to the fact that AOM allows the definition of properties with complex structures, AOM models are usually very compact. The regular

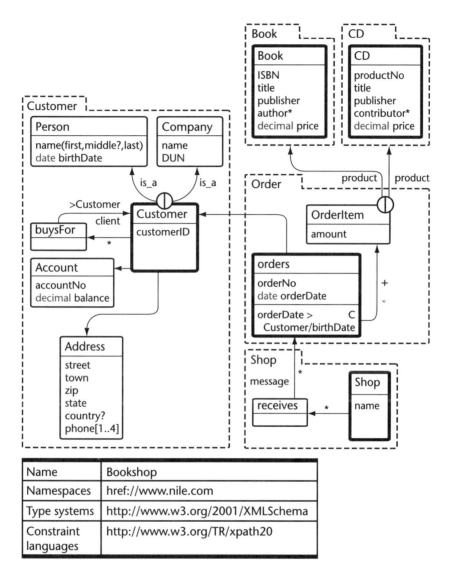

Figure 2.19 The completed bookshop model. Note the namespace definitions for model, type system, and constraint language.

expression syntax for properties allows the definition of structures of arbitrary complexity.

■ *AOM is modular.* By attaching globally unique namespace identifiers to models and/or assets, AOM is able to merge models both horizontally and vertically. This allows the distributed development of models and the integration of foreign models.

- *AOM is simple.* The metamodel (Figure 2.20) of AOM is very simple, which makes AOM easy to learn and to use.

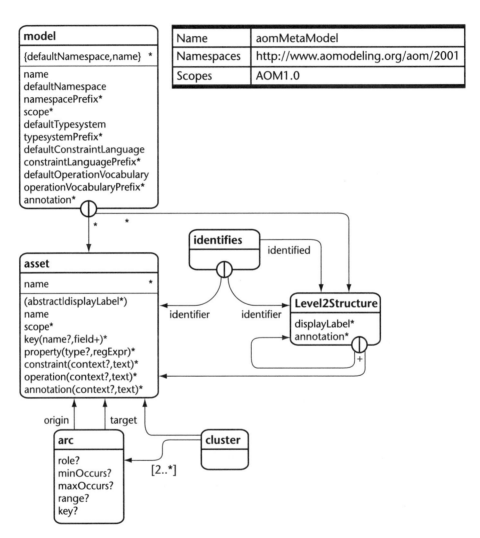

Figure 2.20 AOM metamodel. The recursive arc at the Level2Structure asset indicates that L2S can be nested. In this, the nested L2S may act as an identifying item of the containing L2S.

Everybody Likes Jazz

In this chapter we will model a small knowledge base. This will provide us with the information structures from which we can draw examples for the following chapters. I have chosen an example about jazz music and jazz musicians, first, because I think this example is pretty cool, and second, because it allows us to apply our modeling techniques to an area that is not so well understood as the classical purchase order example.

As you probably know, the relationships among jazz musicians are manifold and complex. New bands and projects are set up all the time, and there are many forms of collaboration. In this respect, jazz music very much resembles electronic business, where business relations are much more short-lived than in the old economy. This chapter develops this example in detail, starting with an informal verbal description and then formalizing this description into a conceptual model.

3.1 INFORMAL DESCRIPTION

A popular method for modeling an information domain is to start with an informal, verbal description of the scenario. The scenario should be described in short, simple sentences.

```
A jazz musician is a person.

A person has a name and a birth date.

The birth date may not be known.

A jazz musician collaborates with other jazz musicians.

During a certain period of time a jazz musician belongs to a style.

A style is dominant during a certain period of time.

Instrumentalists, jazz singers, jazz composers are jazz musicians.

An instrumentalist plays one or several instruments.

A jam session is a form of collaboration.

A jam session is performed at a location and at a particular time.

A project is a form of collaboration (during a certain period of time).

A band is a form of collaboration (during a certain period of time).

A collaboration can result in one or several albums.

An album has a publisher, a product number, and a title.

An album has one or several tracks.

A track has a duration and a title.

An album may have one or several samples.

A sample provides an MP3 URL for a track.

A jazz musician may produce a solo album.

Albums and jazz musicians are reviewed in magazines by critics.

A critic is a person.
```

The actual relationships are, as a matter of fact, much more complicated. For example, we could include a full taxonomy for musical instruments and styles. But for the purpose of this example, this description might do.

To prepare the construction of the conceptual model, we perform a simple grammatical analysis. In each sentence we identify the nouns (jazz musician, person, name, birth date, band, collaboration, location, album, etc.) and verbs (is, has, collaborate, plays, etc.). This will help us to identify relevant information items.

3.2 THE CONCEPTUAL MODEL, FIRST DRAFT

We are now going to transform this informal description into a more formal conceptual model. In traditional conceptual modeling (such as ERM or Object Role Modeling), nouns would end up as entities (or attributes) and verbs would end up as relationships. But we will use AOM instead, so both nouns and verbs will become assets. This simplification will spare us the classical design dilemma: Do I choose an entity or relationship to model an item that could be both? In our example, this is collaboration-collaborate. In one sentence it behaves like an entity; in another sentence it acts as a relationship. In AOM this dilemma does not exist, and the only choice is which name to choose for the asset. In such cases we usually decide for the noun form, which is collaboration.

When modeling verbs as assets, there are two notable exceptions:

■ The verb *has* indicates either that an asset has a property, as in

A person has a name and a birth date.

or that an asset aggregates other assets, as in

An album has one or several tracks.

In this case we represent the verb *has* with a simple arc leading from asset type album to asset type track. As explained in Section 2.5.1, it is the asset type album that could be regarded as a relationship between tracks.

■ The expression *is a* indicates a classification:

A jazz musician is a person.

The noun on the right-hand side (person) is usually the more general term than the noun on the left-hand side (jazz musician). Again, we represent the verb *is* with a simple arc leading from jazz musician to person. We indicate the special role of this connection by decorating the arc with is_a.

3.3 ASSET OR PROPERTY?

There is still a design decision to make. Especially for aggregations, we have to decide if we want to model the aggregated items as assets or as properties of the aggregating item. This distinction is not always easy. However, there are a few guidelines:

■ Anything that plays a certain role in the context of our business is definitely an asset. So, the decision about what becomes an asset and what a property may depend on the business process. For example, in the context of our jazz knowledge base, it may be sufficient to model instrument as a property. But if we plan to implement a supply chain for a music shop, instrument would definitely be an asset, and an important one.

- In many cases the distinction between a property and an asset can be made using a simple rule: A property can belong to an asset, but an asset cannot belong to a property. For example, a duration cannot have a track.
- An item that is only connected to a single asset is always a candidate for becoming a property. In contrast, an item that has other connections, too, must be modeled as an asset. Take for example:

An album has one or several tracks of a given duration.

track could be modeled as a property of project if we did not have the following:

An album may have one or several samples.

and

A sample provides an MP3 URL for a track.

There is a cross-reference between sample and track that could not be modeled if sample and track were properties. sample puts track in relation to an MP3 URL. So we must model both track and sample as separate assets, but we can model the MP3 URL as a property of sample.

- Because AOM allows complex properties, we will find that complex information items that must be modeled in classical modeling methods as separate entities may be modeled as structured properties in AOM. This will result in a compact model.

3.3.1 The Jazz Model

Let's discuss the model, shown in Figure 3.1, from left to right. First, a **style** has a name. This is not mentioned in the informal description. Informal descriptions usually make assumptions about the background knowledge of the reader, for example, the knowledge that most things and concepts do have a name. So, we have introduced a name, and we have declared it as a key, assuming that the name of a style is unique.

We have introduced two subproperties for the period, defining the start and the end of the period. Again, this stems from background knowledge. Periods do have a start and an end. At this point we do not determine how precise the start and end date should be. Here, for describing the period when a certain jazz style was dominant, it would be sufficient to specify both dates by year only. Alternatively, we could specify a period by giving a start date and the length of the interval. Notice that we have also introduced a description property. Although not required by the informal description, it may be useful to describe the style in a few words.

The asset **belongsTo** establishes a relationship between a style and a jazz musician. This is a many-to-many relationship because one jazz musician may belong to several styles during his or her life, and of course many jazz musicians belong to one style. This relationship is attributed again with a period, which

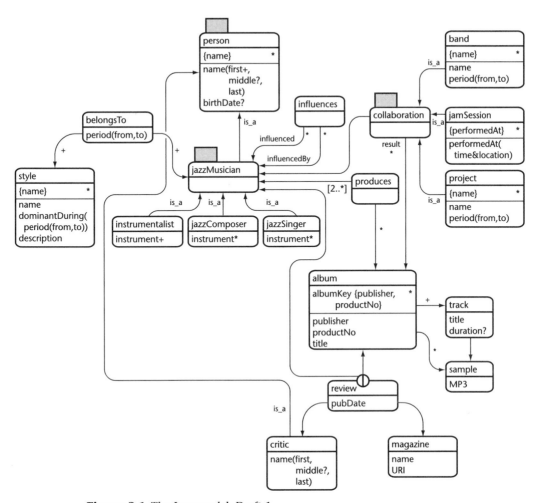

Figure 3.1 The Jazz model, Draft 1.

may differ from the period defined in the style. This attribute defines a period during which a given jazz musician belongs to a given style.

The asset **jazzMusician** does not have its own properties but inherits everything from the asset person. jazzMusician itself is marked as an abstract asset, indicated by the solid label box. So there will be no jazzMusician instances. Instances will be instrumentalists, jazzComposers, or jazzSingers.

The assets **instrumentalist**, **jazzComposer**, and **jazzSinger** have a property instrument. In case of an instrumentalist, this property is constrained by the cardinality [1..*] (+) because an instrumentalist has to play at least one instrument. The others are free to play as many instruments as they like, or not to play any instrument at all.

The definition of **person** is straightforward. At this stage we have declared the name property as a key, which will cause us some trouble later. We have made property birthDate optional because of The birth date may not be known.

The asset **influences** relates jazz musicians to other jazz musicians. Again, this is a many-to-many relationship, as one musician can influence many others but also can be influenced by several others. For this asset, the definition of role names is mandatory to differentiate both arrows leading to jazzMusician.

The asset **produces** describes the relationship between jazz musicians and solo albums. A jazzMusician may produce several solo albums, so this is a one-to-many relationship.

The asset **collaboration** acts as a classification for the various concrete collaborations such as jamSession, project, and band. Because it does not have its own instances, it is marked as abstract. Collaboration relates at least two jazz musicians (otherwise it wouldn't be a collaboration) to an unlimited set of albums.

The modeling of **album** is straightforward. To identify an album uniquely, we have chosen both properties publisher and productNo to form a composite key. Because composite keys must be named, we have given it the name albumKey.

We have chosen to model the verb *reviewed* as a noun and to attribute it with a publishing date of the review. The result is asset **review**. This asset relates a critic, a magazine, and an album or jazz musician to each other—a ternary relationship. The choice between album and jazz musician is modeled via a *cluster*.

The asset **critic** inherits everything from asset person but overrides the property name because it needs only one occurrence of first. The modeling of asset **magazine** is straightforward. The assets **band** and **project** are very similar. Both have a name and a period during which they exist. We assume that the name is unique, so we use it as a key.

The asset **jamSession** is different. A jam session is performed at a certain time and at a certain place. We have modeled this with property performedAt. Because we are not interested in a particular sequence of location and time, we have used the operator & here. We have declared performedAt as a key, which should be sufficiently unique.

3.4 NORMALIZATION

After we have obtained a first draft of our model, we should normalize it. Unlike relational technology, XML and object-oriented formats allow a physical data format that follows the structures of the actual business data very closely. There is no need to break complex information items into a multitude of "flat" tables. We will find that an XML document can represent a conceptual asset almost unmodified. This does not mean that no normalization is required. We must still make sure that our information model does not have redundancies, and that we end up with an implementation that not only consistently matches the real-world relationships between information items but is also easy to maintain. We make sure that

- Asset types are *primitive*; that is, their properties do not contain information structures that could be modeled as independent asset types. For example, the asset type `album` must not embed data from `jazzMusician`.
- Asset types are *minimal*; that is, they do not contain redundant properties, meaning none of their properties can be derived from other properties. For example, the asset type `person` must not contain a property `age`, as this can be derived from `birthDate`.
- Asset types must be *complete*; that is, other assets that may be present in the real-world scenario can always be derived from the asset types defined in the model. Our model is not complete. A jazz album typically lists the participating musicians and which instruments each musician played on this album. This requires that we introduce a sentence like

  `A jazz musician plays one or several instruments on an album.`

  into our informal description and model it appropriately (see Section 3.5).
- Asset types must *not be redundant*; that is, none of the defined asset types in the model can be derived from other asset types in the model. In our example, we have a redundant asset. A band is a kind of project—the main difference is that it exists over a longer period of time and probably produces more albums. On an informal level, there is a semantic difference between both, but structurally they are the same.

  We fix this by deleting the asset `band`. In order to allow instances of `band`, however, we decorate asset `project` with two display labels: `band` and `project`. The consequence is that in the schema, both are treated equally but instances can have either name.
- All asset types must have a *unique meaning*.
- Assets should have a *key*. Keys must be minimal; that is, they must consist of the smallest set of properties that can uniquely identify an instance. In our example, not every asset has a key. (For example, `belongsTo`, `influences`, `review`, `critic`, and `magazine` don't have a key.) We should introduce suitable keys for these assets. `jazzMusician`, `instrumentalist`, `jazzSinger`, and `jazzComposer` do not need their own key, because they inherit one from `person`. If an asset type does not have suitable properties that can act as keys, we can easily equip them with some kind of a unique property (for example, by generating a UUID for each instance).

  In particular, keys are required when an asset has outgoing arcs and we plan to implement the model in a relational environment. Here, in our XML environment, it is very likely that we will implement the triangle `album`, `track`, `sample` with relational techniques (such graphs cannot be reduced to tree structures). Therefore we equip asset `track` with a new property `trackNo` that we declare as a key.

3.5 PARTITIONED NORMAL FORM

While the steps mentioned before result in a pretty robust model, there is one more thing we can do. Assets ultimately result in XML elements or documents, and can thus be subject to transformations (for example, via an XSLT stylesheet). To make the keys robust against such transformations, we should make sure that each asset is in *Partitioned Normal Form* (PNF).

> An asset type or property is in Partitioned Normal Form (PNF) if the atomic properties of an asset constitute a key of the asset and all non-atomic properties and subproperties are in Partitioned Normal Form themselves.

Or, in other words:

> All complex structures in the model (assets and complex properties) must have atomic child nodes that can act as a key.

What is the PNF good for? If we plan to store assets in relational databases, PNF is essential. Relational technology requires us to fragment all complex structures into flat relational tables. Keys that span complex structures would be lost during such a transformation to First Normal Form (1NF) (see Section 11.5). But also in an XML environment, keys constituted from atomic fields are a good idea. For cross-references, XML Schema allows multifield keys (see Section 5.3.17), but each field must be atomic. DTDs and Relax NG, however, are even more limited: They allow only a single atomic field as a key for cross-references.

In our example, the following assets are not in PNF:

- person, because the key name(first,middle?,last) is a composite. A solution would be to introduce a personal ID. Here, we opt to introduce an atomic ID composed from last name, middle name, and first name, such as MingusCharles.
- jamSession, because the key performedAt(time&location) is a composite. Here, we opt for a different solution. We resolve the property performedAt into two independent properties: time and location. These two properties are atomic and can thus constitute a multifield primary key that conforms to PNF. An implementation of this key with DTDs or Relax NG would, however, cause troubles because these schema languages do not support multifield keys.

  Because AOM requires us to name a composite key, we decorate this key with the name jsKey.

Figure 3.2 shows our conceptual Jazz model after we have applied the changes suggested by normalization. We have made the following changes:

- Removed the redundancy between assets band and project by deleting asset band and decorating asset project with the two display labels band and project.
- Introduced a new property ID into asset person and declared it as the primary key.

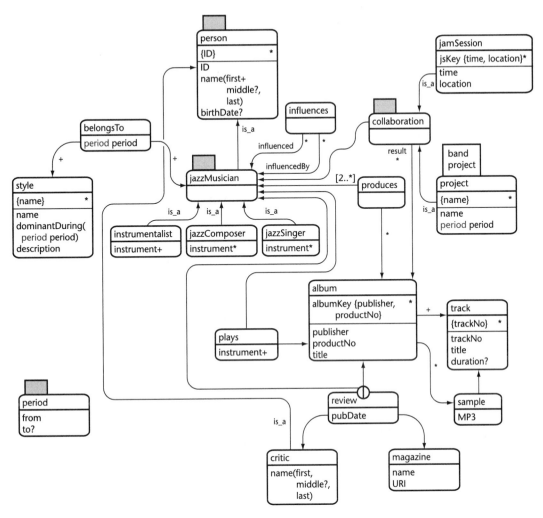

Figure 3.2 The Jazz model, Draft 2.

- Resolved property `performedAt` in asset `jamSession` into `time` and `location`. We declared the combination of these two properties as a primary key and named it `jsKey`.
- Introduced a new asset `plays` that relates albums and jazz musicians. It is attributed with an `instrument` property. At least one instrument must be specified. (For a jazz singer, that would be "vocals.")
- Factored out the definition of complex property `period` into an abstract asset `period`. We use this asset as a *type* definition. We have also improved this definition by making the subproperty `to` optional. This allows us to model periods that have not ended yet.

3.6 RESOLVING is_a RELATIONSHIPS

In the next step we "flatten" the model by resolving some of the is_a relationships. We do this to prepare the model for implementation with different technologies. While object-oriented technologies are well suited to capture deep hierarchies of superclasses and subclasses (although this may sometimes result in less than well maintainable implementations), the implementation of such data structures with relational technology or with XML would be rather awkward. XML Schema does support inheritance relationships between data types (although only single inheritance), but it does not support inheritance between document nodes.

For the purpose of manual conversion of the Jazz model into XML schemata (see Chapter 8), it is a good idea to resolve the is_a relationships wherever this is possible. When using a modeling tool such as KLEEN [KLEEN2002], this step should not be necessary because the modeling tool should be able to resolve inheritance relations before generating code.

We have the following options:

- Explicitly copy the features of the parent into the child asset types, then remove the parent asset. For example, we could copy the arcs and properties of asset type collaboration into the asset types jamSession and project. This would also allow us to sharpen the cardinality constraints for jamSession: A jam session produces at most one album.

    For asset jazzMusician, this operation would be far from simple, despite the fact that there are no properties to inherit. We would also need to copy the incoming and outgoing arcs. For the incoming arcs (from influence, collaboration, produces, plays, belongsTo), we would need to introduce *clusters* at the origin point of each arc.
- Fold the child assets into the parent asset. This is possible when the children don't differ very much from each other. The result is a very compact model.

    Take for example instrumentalist, jazzSinger, and jazzComposer. These assets only differ in the cardinality of instrument. If we can tolerate losing that differentiation (we could later remedy this loss by introducing an explicit constraint), we move instrument into the parent asset jazzMusician, then remove the children. The cardinality of instrument is set to "*" (obtained by union of the individual cardinalities).

What remains is to introduce a feature that indicates the type of the child instance. Here we have two options:

- Create a property that specifies the instance type. For example, we can indicate instrumentalist, jazzSinger, and jazzComposer by an extra property named kind. We can declare the property as an enumeration type with the values instrumentalist, jazzSinger, and jazzComposer. Note that with this approach, the asset instances are no longer named `instrumentalist`, `jazzSinger`, and `jazzComposer`, but `jazzMusician`.

To remedy the cardinality problem, we can introduce a constraint saying that `kind` must either be different from "instrumentalist" or there must be at least one `instrument` child.

```
kind != instrumentalist or count(instrument) > 0
```

■ Indicate the child type by display labels in the parent type. For example, we could add three display labels `instrumentalist`, `jazzSinger`, and `jazzComposer` to `jazzMusician`. Instances of `jazzMusician` would then be `instrumentalist`, `jazzSinger`, or `jazzComposer` instances.

To remedy the cardinality problem, we can introduce a constraint:

```
not(self::instrumentalist) or count(instrument) > 0
```

For asset `jazzMusician`, the second option (using multiple display labels) would be the most elegant option. But for tutorial purposes the additional property `kind` is created.

After applying these operations, our model would look like Figure 3.3 (page 82), which reflects the following changes:

■ We have combined the assets `instrumentalist`, `jazzComposer`, and `jazzSinger` into a generic asset `jazzMusician`. In this asset we have introduced a new property, `kind`. The (yet undefined) type of this new property is restricted by the enumeration `instrumentalist`, `jazzComposer`, `jazzSinger`. To capture the restriction for instrumentalists, we have defined an explicit constraint.

■ We have resolved the abstract asset `collaboration` into the concrete assets `jamSession` and `project`. These assets only inherited arcs from `collaboration`; there were no properties to inherit.

■ We did not resolve abstract asset `person` into the concrete assets `jazzMusician` and `critic`. This would introduce too many redundant definitions into the model. We also want to keep at least one abstract asset, to see how we can deal with it later, during implementation.

3.7 INTRODUCING LEVEL 2 STRUCTURES

In our model we use Level 2 Structures (L2S) to model business objects. Business objects are assets that play a prominent role in our scenario. Identifying a business object requires that we have an idea not only about the structure of the information, but also about the purpose of that information.

In our example, all `jazzMusician` asset types, `style`, all `collaboration` asset types, `album`, and `review` could be L2S. Jazz musicians are clearly the most important topic in our knowledge base, but similarly important are style and the various collaborations. `album` could play a role if we plan to connect our knowledge base with an online shop for CDs. The asset `magazine` does not play a prominent role in our scenario; therefore, we include it in the L2S `review`.

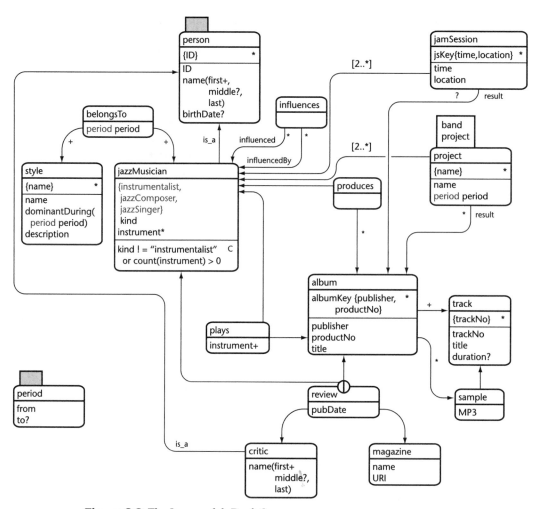

Figure 3.3 The Jazz model, Draft 3.

After determining all the dominant assets in our model, we group the remaining assets around these selected assets, demarcate these groups with a Level 2 box, and arrive at the diagram shown in Figure 3.4.

Remember the constraint that must be enforced when constructing L2S from assets:

> Starting from the identifying asset of an L2S, we must be able to reach any asset belonging to that L2S by following the arcs in the indicated direction.

This constraint will allow us to interpret each L2S as an aggregation and later make it easy to implement the L2S in the form of hierarchical data models such as XML documents.

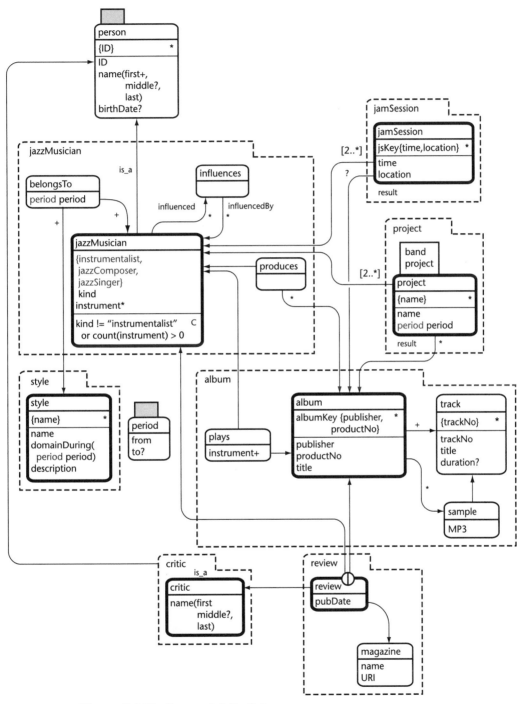

Figure 3.4 The Jazz model, Draft 4.

When we check this constraint for our model, we encounter three problems:

- From the assets belongsTo and influences, both arrows lead to asset jazzMusician. This is bad, because when starting at jazzMusician, we cannot reach belongsTo and influences.
- Asset produces cannot be reached from jazzMusician.
- Asset plays cannot be reached from album.

To solve these problems, we simply reverse one of the arcs for each of the assets belongsTo and influences. This results in a slightly different interpretation. We are now saying:

A jazzMusician has a "belonging" to a style.

and

A jazzMusician has influences from other jazz musicians.

In the case of influences, the decision as to which of the two arrows to reverse depends on which jazz musician should be assigned influence assets: the one who is influenced, or the one who influences others. It is better to take the first option: Jazz musicians might tell you who influenced them, but they are not likely to tell you who they influenced.

We also reverse the arcs leading from album to plays and from jazzMusician to produces. We decorate each reversed arc with an asterisk to remove any cardinality constraint and remove its role name.

We also take the opportunity to fix a problem with keys. The asset review definitely needs a key, because it is an identifying asset of L2S review. The identifying asset of an L2S should indeed always have a key, because otherwise, instances of such an L2S could become inaccessible when stored in a database. We therefore have introduced a property ID for asset review, which could be a generated identifier such as a UUID or a URL for a web page. Figure 3.5 shows the results.

There is still one problem with asset influence: Jazz musicians hardly influence themselves, but this is exactly what we have specified. Remember that arcs that are local to an L2S are also local to instances of the L2S. To allow a jazz musician to be influenced by other jazz musicians, we must loosen the range constraint of the arc influencedBy. We do this by decorating this arc with >jazzMusician (the display name of the L2S).

Structurally, our conceptual model is now complete. We finish the definition of the model by rendering a few more details, such as global model settings (default namespace, default type system, and default constraint language), and by decorating atomic properties with data types from XML Schema (see Section 5.2). There is one exception: Later, we want the property description to contain complex XHTML content, but at the moment we do not want to specify this further. We therefore extract this property as an empty asset for later detailing. Figure 3.6 (page 86) shows the results.

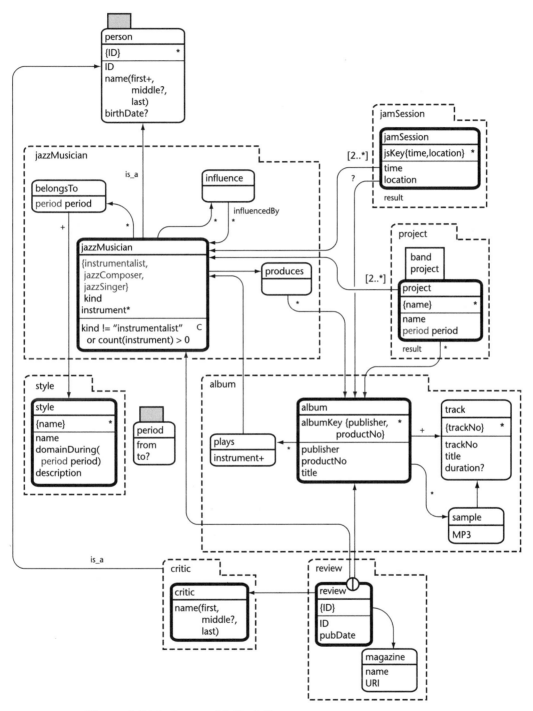

Figure 3.5 The Jazz model, Draft 5.

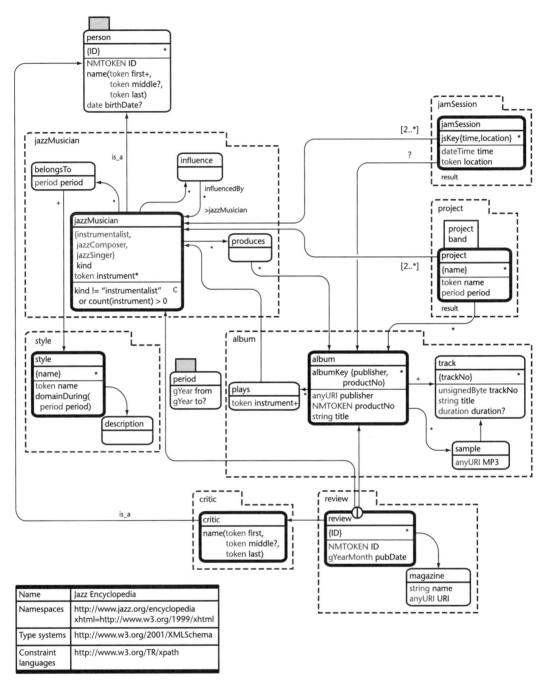

Figure 3.6 The Jazz model, final draft.

THE IMPLEMENTATION

XML Basics

In this part of the book we will implement the conceptual models that we have developed in Part I as XML schemata in three ways—in the form of DTDs, in XML Schema, and in Relax NG. But before we do so, an overview of the concepts and facilities of all three schema languages is presented.

This chapter deals with the DTD as it is defined in the XML 1.0 specification [Bray2000]. But before we go into the DTD details, we will look at some advanced XML topics, such as XML namespaces, the XML information model, and canonical XML. A good understanding of namespaces and the XML Information Set is essential for appreciating the various features in XML Schema definition languages.

This discussion assumes that you are already familiar with the XML syntax. If not, there are many excellent books that provide an introduction to XML.

4.1 NAMESPACES

XML namespaces are defined in [Bray1999]. Namespaces are important for schema composition. Using namespaces helps to avoid name conflicts. Take for example a document that includes parts described by different document standards, such as XHTML, SVG, SMIL, SOAP, and your own schema definitions. Without namespaces it would be almost impossible to avoid name clashes. For this reason I recommend that you always define a target namespace with a schema, and I discourage the use of DTDs for schema definition.

Namespaces must be declared in an XML document instance with the help of the xmlns attribute or an attribute with the prefix xmlns:. The first defines the default namespace; the second defines namespaces that are associated with a namespace prefix. For example:

```
xmlns ="http://www.w3.org/2001/XMLSchema"
```

defines the XML Schema namespace as the default namespace. In contrast,

```
xmlns:xs="http://www.w3.org/2001/XMLSchema"
```

associates the XML Schema namespace with the prefix xs:.

The scope of such a namespace definition is the element where it is defined plus all child elements (unless a child element overrides it with another namespace declaration). So, if we declare namespaces in the root element of a document, their scope is usually the whole document.

We say that the name of an element is *qualified* if the element is within the scope of a default namespace declaration, or if its name is specified with a namespace prefix. Attributes are qualified if they are specified with a namespace prefix. (Default namespaces do not apply to attributes.) For example:

```
<customer xmlns="http://www.nile.com/customers"
          xmlns:a="http://www.nile.com/addresses"
          customerNo="BD023432">
  <name>
    <first>John</first>
    <last>Doe</last>
  </name>
  <a:address>
    <a:street>747 Sunset Strip</a:street>
    <a:town>Miami</a:town>
    <a:zip>99999</a:zip>
    <a:state>FL</a:state>
```

```
    <a:country>USA</a:country>
  <a:address>
</customer>
```

In this example all elements are qualified. The ones without a prefix belong to namespace `http://www.nile.com/customers`, and the ones with prefix `a:` belong to namespace `http://www.nile.com/addresses`. The attribute `customerNo` is not qualified.

Care must be taken if documents are composed from multiple entities (see Section 4.4.6). If namespace declarations were contained in an unexpanded entity (see Section 4.2.6), they would not be visible and the whole document would not be processed correctly.

4.2 THE XML INFORMATION MODEL

The principal information model of XML is defined in a W3C recommendation called the "XML Information Set" [Cowan2001]. The XML Information Set is independent of the actual representation of a document; the document may exist in the serialized form of an XML text file, in the form of a DOM tree, in the form of Java objects, and others. So, for the discussion of the XML information model, the concrete XML syntax is irrelevant.

In its current state this recommendation describes the abstract data model of the XML 1.0 recommendation [Bray2000], including XML namespaces [Bray1999], but does not cover new features introduced with XML Schema. In particular, it does not support type definitions for elements. For attributes, only those types that can be defined with a DTD are featured. Also, there is no support for the advanced integrity constraints that can be defined with XML Schema such as the `key`, `keyref`, and `unique` clauses (see Section 5.3.17).

4.2.1 Overview

Table 4.1 (page 92) lists all the information items that constitute the XML Information Set, with examples in serialized XML form. The XML Information Set has a tree structure, with the nodes of the tree made up of the information items in Table 4.1. Figure 4.1 (page 94)shows the structure of the XML Information Set using the AOM modeling language defined in Chapter 2.

Note that the information set of a document instance defined under a DTD changes when a DTD-aware parser processes the document. Default and fixed values declared in the DTD may change the value of attributes in the document instance. Attributes declared in the DTD may be added to the attribute set of a document element in the document instance. Notations and unparsed entities declared in the DTD are added to the document node of the document instance. If this additional information is contained in an external DTD subset and the parser chooses to use this information (nonvalidating parsers are free to

Table 4.1 Information items of the XML Information Set.

Information Item	Description
Attribute	Attributes can be specified with elements. Example: `<order orderDate="2002-05-03">...</order>`
Character	Characters that appear in the content of an element, as a character reference, or in a CDATA section are first-order information objects in the XML information model. Example: `<last>Brubeck</last>`
Comment	A comment block within a document. Example: `<!--Schema created by KLEEN XSD generator version 0.01-->`

Document	The whole document entity.
	Example:
	`<?xml version="1.0" encoding="UTF-8"?>`
	`  <order>`
	`  ...`
	`  </order>`

Document type declaration	A declaration that defines the type of a document. A document type declaration can define an internal subset and a reference to an external subset (DTD).
	Example:
	`<!DOCTYPE book SYSTEM`
	`        "http://www.book.org/book">`

Element	Either the root element of a document or a child element of another element.
	Example:
	`<name>`
	`  <last>Brubeck</last>`
	`</name>`

Namespace	A definition that establishes a separate space for element names in order to avoid name conflicts.
	Example:
	`<xs:schema`
	`  xmlns:xs="http://www.w3.org/2001/XMLSchema">`

Notation	The notation declaration serves as an extension mechanism. It allows you to associate an internal name with an external or public identification. Example: `<!NOTATION jpeg SYSTEM "viewer.exe">`

(continued)

Table 4.1 *Continued*

Information Item	Description

Processing instruction	An instruction that advises XML processors about actions to take.
	
	`<?xml:stylesheet type="text/xsl"`
	`                    href="xml-shockwave.xsl"?>`

Unexpanded entity	An entity reference that for some reason could not be expanded. Example:
	
	`<!ENTITY smallprint SYSTEM`
	`    "http://www.shady.org/legal404.xml">`

Unparsed entity	Unparsed entities are non-XML entities, such as images, audio files, binaries, etc. Example:
	
	`<!ENTITY picture SYSTEM`
	`    "http://www.jazz.org/ellington.jpg" NDATA jpeg>`

make use of an external DTD or not), the information set of the document instances changes.

Similarly, a schema defined with XML Schema may change the information set of a document instance: Default and fixed values declared in the DTD may change the value of attributes *and elements* in the document instance. Attributes declared in the DTD may be added to the attribute set of a document element in the document instance.

The following sections discuss each of these information items in detail.

4.2.2 Document Node

An XML document is defined as a document node in its own right. This node has the following properties:

- *Children.* A document node can own exactly one element node—the root element, also called *document element*. Besides this element, a document node can contain other child nodes: processing instructions, comments, and a document type declaration. Processing instructions and comments defined in the Document Type Definition (DTD) are not included in the information set of the document node. (Processing instructions defined in the Document Type Definition are child nodes of the document type declaration node, discussed in Section 4.2.9.)
- *Document element.* The root element of the document. This element contains all other document elements as children, grandchildren, and further descendants.

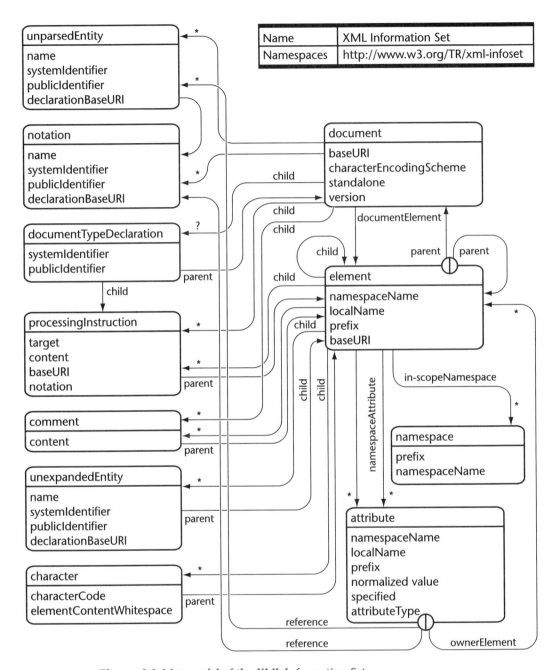

Figure 4.1 Metamodel of the XML Information Set.

- *Notations.* An unordered set of notation information items, one for each notation declared in the DTD (see Section 4.2.11).
- *Unparsed entities.* An unordered set of unparsed entity information items (see Section 4.2.10), one for each unparsed entity declared in the DTD.
- *Base URI.* The base URI of the document entity. Base URIs can be specified explicitly with the `xml:base` attribute as defined in the "XML Base" recommendation [Marsh2001].
- *Character encoding scheme.* The code system used for this document. By default, XML uses the UTF-8 code system for character encoding. However, it is possible to declare other code systems such as UTF-16 for a document. In an XML file this is done with an encoding declaration in the document prolog:

```
<?xml version="1.0" encoding="UTF-16" standalone="yes"?>
```

- *Standalone.* An indication of the standalone status of the document. The value "true" indicates that a document does not rely on external markup definitions such as default values or entity declarations.
- *Version.* The XML version of the document, currently 1.0.

4.2.3 Elements

Element nodes may have one or several child nodes. They can be other elements, attributes, processing instructions, comments, character data, unparsed and unexpanded entities, and in-scope namespaces. Elements can repeat within a context, except the document element, which must occur exactly once.

An element has the following properties:

- *Namespace name.* The name of the namespace of the respective element type. The chosen namespace name should be globally unique.
- *Local name.* The local part of the element type name (excluding namespace prefix).
- *Prefix.* The namespace prefix in the element type name. This prefix serves as a shorthand notation for the element's namespace.
- *Children.* An *ordered* list of child nodes. This can be other elements, processing instructions, unexpanded entities, characters, and comments.
- *Attributes.* An *unordered* set of attribute information items, one for each attribute (either specified in the document instance or defaulted from the DTD).
- *Namespace attributes.* An *unordered* set of attribute information items, one for each namespace declaration (specified or defaulted from the DTD). Namespace attributes are declared by using the prefix `xmlns:`. For example,

```
<xs:schema
  xmlns:xs="http://www.w3.org/2001/XMLSchema">
```

defines a namespace attribute for the XML Schema namespace. This attribute is owned by the `<xs:schema>` element.

In addition, a declaration of the form `xmlns=""`, which undeclares the default namespace, counts as a namespace attribute.

■ *In-scope namespaces.* An *unordered* set of namespace information items, one for each of the namespaces in effect for this element. These are not only namespaces that have been declared with this element but also namespaces that have been declared with parent elements, or the default namespace. In addition, XML's own namespace, `http://www.w3.org/XML/1998/namespace`, with the prefix `xml`, belongs to the in-scope namespaces.

■ *Base URI.* The base URI of the element. Base URIs can be specified explicitly with the `xml:base` attribute, as defined in the "XML Base" recommendation [Marsh2001].

■ *Parent.* A reference to the parent node, either the document node or an element node.

4.2.4 Attributes

The attribute nodes of an element always form an unordered list—that is, it is not possible to make statements about the order in which the attributes of an element occur. Attributes are always leaf nodes; they do not have child nodes. Each attribute has a *local name* and can have a *namespace identifier*. The local name (also, the combination of local name and namespace identifier) is not required to be unique within a document: Attributes with the same name may appear in different contexts in a document (under different owner elements). Attributes must not repeat within a context.

Attributes have the following properties:

■ *Namespace name.* The name of the namespace of the respective attribute type.

■ *Local name.* The local part of the attribute type name (excluding namespace prefix).

■ *Prefix.* The namespace prefix in the attribute type name.

■ *Normalized value.* The normalized attribute value, consisting of a normalized character string. A character string is normalized by reducing whitespace within the string to a single whitespace character and by removing any whitespace from the beginning and end of the string.

■ *Specified indicator.* Indicates whether this attribute was actually specified in the start tag of its element, or if it was defaulted from the DTD.

■ *Attribute type.* An indication of the type declared for this attribute in the DTD. Legitimate values are ID, IDREF, IDREFS, ENTITY, ENTITIES, NMTOKEN, NMTOKENS, NOTATION, CDATA, and ENUMERATION (see Section 4.4.3).

■ *References.* An attribute may refer to another document item depending on its type:
  Attributes of type IDREF and IDREFS refer to elements.
  Attributes of type ENTITY, ENTITIES refer to unparsed entities.
  Attributes of type NOTATION refer to notation items.

■ *Owner element.* A reference to the element that owns the attribute.

4.2.5 Processing Instructions

Processing instructions are evaluated by XML processors. For example, a processing instruction can cause a web browser to invoke an XSLT processor to convert the document into HTML:

```
<?xml:Stylesheet href="convert.xsl" type="text/xsl"?>
```

A processing instruction information item has the following properties:

- *Target.* A string representing the *target part* of the processing instruction. In the example above, this is `xml:Stylesheet`.
- *Content.* A string representing the *content* of the processing instruction. In the example, `href="convert.xsl" type="text/xsl"`.
- *Base URI.* The base URI of the processing instruction. Base URIs can be specified explicitly with the `xml:base` attribute, as defined in the "XML Base" recommendation [Marsh2001].
- *Notation.* The notation information item named by the target (see Section 4.2.11).
- *Parent.* A reference to the element that contains the processing instruction.

4.2.6 Unexpanded Entity Reference

Normally, the information set describes an XML document with all parsed entities expanded. However, there may be cases when a processor chooses not to expand an entity, for example, when the entity definition is not accessible. In this case, the entity is represented by an unexpanded entity information item with the following properties:

- *Name.* The name of the entity referenced.
- *System identifier.* The system identifier of the entity.
- *Public identifier.* The public identifier of the entity, consisting of a normalized character string. A character string is normalized by reducing whitespace within the string to a single whitespace character and by removing any whitespace from the beginning and end of the string.
- *Declaration base URI.* The base URI relative to which the system identifier should be resolved (that is, the base URI of the resource within which the entity declaration occurs). Base URIs can be specified explicitly with the `xml:base` attribute, as defined in the "XML Base" recommendation [Marsh2001].
- *Parent.* A reference to the element that contains the unexpanded entity reference.

4.2.7 Character

There is a character information item for each data character that appears in the document, whether literally, as a character reference, or within a CDATA section. A character information item has the following properties:

- *Character code.* The ISO 10646 (Universal Multiple-Octet Coded Character Set (UCS)) character code. The character code ranges from 0 to #x10FFFF, though not every value in this range is a legal XML character code:

  `#x9 | #xA | #xD | [#x20-#xD7FF] |`
  `[#xE000-#xFFFD] | [#x10000-#x10FFFF]`

  This is the complete range of Unicode characters except xFFFE and xFFFF.

- *Element content whitespace.* A Boolean indicating whether the character is whitespace appearing within element content.
- *Parent.* A reference to the element that contains the character.

The XML Information Set specification does not specify how these character information items are aggregated in text nodes. This has resulted in various incompatible text node implementations. For example, XPath combines all characters within a node in a text child node, while DOM allows several text fragment child nodes. (DOM Level 3 remedies this situation by introducing an additional attribute, wholeText.)

4.2.8 Comment

A comment information item has the following properties:

- *Content.* A string representing the content of the comment.
- *Parent.* A reference to the element that contains the comment.

4.2.9 Document Type Declaration

If the XML document has a document type declaration, then the information set contains a single document type declaration information item, which has the following properties:

- *System identifier.* The system identifier of the external DTD subset.
- *Public identifier.* The public identifier of the external DTD subset, consisting of a normalized character string. A character string is normalized by reducing whitespace within the string to a single whitespace character and by removing any whitespace from the beginning and end of the string.
- *Children.* An *ordered* list of processing instruction information items representing processing instructions appearing in the DTD.
- *Parent.* A reference to the document node that contains the document type declaration.

4.2.10 Unparsed Entity

There is an unparsed entity information item for each unparsed general entity declared in the DTD. Unparsed entities are non-XML entities, such as images, audio files, and binaries. An unparsed entity information item has the following properties:

- *Name.* The name of the entity.
- *System identifier.* The system identifier of the external subset.
- *Public identifier.* The public identifier of the external subset, consisting of a normalized character string. A character string is normalized by reducing whitespace within the string to a single whitespace character and by removing any whitespace from the beginning and end of the string.
- *Declaration base URI.* The base URI relative to which the system identifier should be resolved (that is, the base URI of the resource within which the entity declaration occurs). Base URIs can be specified explicitly with the `xml:base` attribute, as defined in the "XML Base" recommendation [Marsh2001].
- *Notation.* The notation information item named by the notation name (see next section).

4.2.11 Notation

There is a notation information item for each notation declared in the DTD. Notations are used to identify the format of unparsed entities, the format of attributes declared with type NOTATION, and the processor for a processing instruction. A notation information item has the following properties:

- *Name.* The internal name of the entity.
- *System identifier.* The system identifier of the referenced entity.
- *Public identifier.* The public identifier of the referenced entity, consisting of a normalized character string. A character string is normalized by reducing whitespace within the string to a single whitespace character and by removing any whitespace from the beginning and end of the string.
- *Declaration base URI.* The base URI relative to which the system identifier should be resolved (that is, the base URI of the resource within which the entity declaration occurs). Base URIs can be specified explicitly with the `xml:base` attribute, as defined in the "XML Base" recommendation [Marsh2001].

4.2.12 Namespace

Each element in the document has a namespace information item for each namespace that is in scope for that element (see Section 4.2.3). A namespace information item has the following properties:

- *Prefix.* The prefix whose binding this item describes. Syntactically, in a namespace declaration this is the part of the attribute name following the `xmlns:` prefix.
- *Namespace name.* The URI of the namespace to which the prefix is bound.

4.2.13 An Example

For the following (very small) XML document, let's discuss the XML Information Set.

```
<j:album xmlns:j="http://www.jazz.org/encyclopedia"
        productNo="1064">
  <j:publisher>http://www.ecmrecords.com</j:publisher>
</j:album>
```

Document Node

The document node has only one *child node*: the element j:album. This is also the *document element*. There are no *notations* or *unparsed entities*. There is no explicit base URI specification, so the *base URI* defaults to the actual location of the document that we assume at http://www.jazz.org/albums/. There is also no explicit XML prolog, so the default values apply for the XML *version*, the *encoding scheme*, and the *standalone attribute*: "1.0," "UTF-8," and "yes."

Elements

Element j:album has several *child nodes*: the *namespace attribute* xmlns:j, the *attribute* productNo, the *child* element j:publisher, and several whitespace characters. j:album has the *namespace name* of "http://www.jazz.org/encyclopedia," the *local name* is "album," the *prefix* is "j." There is a single *in-scope namespace* "http://www.jazz.org/encyclopedia." There is no explicit base URI specification, so the *base URI* is inherited from the *parent node* that is the document node.

Element j:publisher has 25 *child nodes*: the characters of "http://www.ecmrecords.com." j:publisher has the *namespace name* of "http://www.jazz.org/encyclopedia," the *local name* is "publisher," the *prefix* is "j." There is a single *in-scope namespace* "http://www.jazz.org/encyclopedia." There is no explicit base URI specification, so the *base URI* is inherited from the *parent node,* which is the element j:album.

Attributes

The attribute productNo has the *namespace name* "http://www.jazz.org/encyclopedia," which it has inherited from its *owner element* j:album. The *local name* is "productNo," but there is no *namespace prefix*. The normalized *value* is "1064," the *specified indicator* is "true," the *attribute type* has no value. The attribute does not *refer* to other document items.

Characters

There are 25 non-whitespace character nodes and several whitespace characters (line feeds, carriage returns, and blanks) contained in the document. Each character is *coded* under ISO 10646. The whitespace characters all belong to *parent* element j:album, while the non-whitespace characters belong to parent element j:publisher. For the whitespace characters, the *whitespace indicator* is set to true.

Namespaces
There is one namespace defined in this document—"j" is the *prefix*, and "http://www.jazz.org/encyclopedia" is the *namespace name*.

4.3 XML CANONICAL FORM

The XML Information Set as discussed above represents XML documents in an abstract form. The lexical form of an XML document allows many variations for the same content. For example, attributes may appear in arbitrary order, redundant namespace declarations are possible, character content may be expressed with or without CDATA, and so on. This makes it difficult for humans and machines to determine whether two given XML documents are equivalent—not identical by the letter but equivalent by content. And this is not the only problem. Cryptographic methods used by message digests and digital signatures rely on the textual representation of a document. With different text representations, equivalent documents would, for example, have different digital signatures. The proposed W3C recommendation "XML-Signature Syntax and Processing" [Eastlake2002] therefore relies on the existing methods for producing canonical XML.

The W3C recommendation "Canonical XML" [Boyer2001] defines a canonical form for XML documents, a syntactical form that allows simple character string comparison of two XML documents. However, this recommendation does not cover the new features introduced with XML Schema, such as the canonical form for the various new data types. Therefore, XML Schema itself defines a canonical form for the lexical representation of all built-in data types defined in XML Schema.

4.3.1 Canonical Text

Acceptable forms of text in XML documents meet the following requirements:

- Canonical XML documents are always encoded in UTF-8.
- All line breaks are normalized to #xA.
- Character entity references are resolved—that is, they are replaced by the referenced entities. Here, the character entity euro is replaced with its definition in the ENTITY clause:

Noncanonical	Canonical
`<...!ENTITY euro #x20AC>`	`<price>&#x20AC; 50.00</price>`
`<price>&euro; 50.00</price>`	

- Canonical text does not contain the characters &, <, >, nor the carriage return character (#xD). These characters are replaced by &, <, >, and .

- CDATA sections are replaced with their character content. Here, the CDATA wrapping around the `if` instruction is removed. By doing so, the unparsed character data becomes parsed character data, so we have to replace < with <.

Noncanonical	Canonical

`<![CDATA[`
 	
`if (pubYear < 100)`
`    pubYear+=1900;`
 	
`]]>`
	`if (pubYear &lt; 100)`
	`    pubYear+=1900;`

4.3.2 Canonical Whitespace

Acceptable forms for whitespace in canonical XML documents meet the following requirements:

- Whitespace outside of the document element and within start and end tags is normalized. (A character string is normalized by reducing whitespace within the string to a single whitespace character and by removing any whitespace from the beginning and end of the string.)
- Attribute values are normalized; that is, whitespace within the attribute value string is reduced to a single whitespace character, and whitespace at the beginning and end of the string is removed.
- All whitespace in character content is retained (excluding characters removed during line feed normalization—see above). Here, all whitespace within tags, and within the value of attribute `ref`, is normalized:

Noncanonical	Canonical

`<album   >`
 	
`    <title>So    long</title>`
`    <reviews    ref="r1    r2">`
`</    album>`
	`<album>`
	
	`    <title>So    long</title>`
	`    <reviews ref="r1 r2">`
	`</album>`

4.3.3 Resolved References

The resolution of parsed entity references involves the following steps:

- Parsed entity references are replaced by the referenced entities.
- Default attributes and fixed attributes are added to each element if not already present. Here, we have resolved entity `legalDoc` with the content of the file `http://www.book.org/modules/legal` to which it refers. We have also included the default value of attribute `review` in the document content.

Noncanonical	Canonical
`<!ENTITY legalDoc SYSTEM`	`<review version="1.0">`
	Buy this book!
`"http://www.book.org/modules/legal">`	`<legal>This article does not express the opinion of its author.</legal>`
`...`	
`<!ATTLIST review`	`</review>`
`     version CDATA "1.0">`	
`...`	
`<review>`	
`Buy this book!`	
`&legaldoc;`	
`</review>`	

4.3.4 Removal of Redundant Nodes

In canonical XML, the XML declaration and Document Type Definition (DTD) are removed. The XML declaration is no longer necessary since the canonical document is always a standalone document in UTF-8 code. The DTD is no longer necessary, as all default and fixed values and all referenced entities have been resolved.

Redundant namespace nodes are also removed. An element's namespace node is redundant when the nearest parent element has a namespace node in the node-set with the same local name and value. Here, we have removed the namespace declaration in element `title` because the parent element `book` already declared the same namespace. We have also removed the XML declaration and the `DOCTYPE` declaration.

Noncanonical	Canonical
`<?xml version="1.0"?>`	`<book xmlns="http://www.book.org>`
`<!DOCTYPE book SYSTEM`	`<title>`
`     "http://www.book.org/book">`	`The light of the day`
`<book xmlns=`	`</title>`
`     "http://www.book.org">`	`</book>`
`  <title xmlns=`	
`     "http://www.book.org">`	
`   The light of the day`	
`  </title>`	
`</book>`	

4.3.5 Canonical Elements

The child nodes of an element (elements, attributes, processing instructions, comments, character data, unparsed and unexpanded entities, and in-scope namespaces) are ordered in the following sequence:

1. The element itself.
2. Namespaces: Namespaces are ordered in lexical sequence.
3. Attributes: The attribute nodes are sorted lexicographically, with the namespace URI as the primary sort criterion and the local name as the secondary sort criterion.
4. Child elements in the given sequence.

Empty elements are expanded to start-end tag pairs. Here, we have brought namespace declarations and attributes into the correct order. We have also expanded the empty element `<isPayed/>` to a start tag and end tag.

Noncanonical	Canonical
`<instrument name="saxophone"`	`<instrument`
`        maker="Selmer"`	`xmlns="http://www.jazz.org"`
`        id="71r8"`	`id="71r8" maker="Selmer"`
`    xmlns="http://www.jazz.org">`	`name="saxophone">`
`<isPaid/>`	`<isPaid></isPaid>`
`</instrument>`	`<\instrument>`

4.3.6 Canonical Attributes

The canonical form of an attribute consists of

- a space character
- the attribute's qualified name
- an equality sign
- a double quote
- the value as a canonical string with normalized whitespace (see Section 4.3.2)
- a double quote

Here, we have normalized the whitespace in the attribute value, removed whitespace between element name and attribute and between equality sign and quote, and replaced the single quotes with double quotes:

Noncanonical	Canonical
`<instrument`	`<instrument name="tenor saxophone"/>`
`    name= 'tenor    saxophone '/>`	

4.3.7 Canonical Processing Instructions

Processing instruction (PI) nodes consist of

- the opening PI symbol (<?)
- the PI target name of the node
- a leading space and the string value if the string value is not empty
- the closing PI symbol (?>)
- for PIs outside the document element, a separating #xA character between processing instruction and document element

Here, we have removed unnecessary whitespace:

Noncanonical	Canonical
| ```
<?xml:stylesheet
  type="text/xsl"
  href="xml-shockwave.xsl"    ?>
``` | ```
<?xml:stylesheet
  type="text/xsl"
  href="xml-shockwave.xsl"?>
``` |

4.3.8 Canonical Comments

For canonical XML without comments, all comments are removed. For canonical XML with comments, comments are normalized in the following way:

- the opening comment symbol (<!--)
- the string value of the node
- the closing comment symbol (-->)
- for comments outside the document element, a separating #xA character between comment and document element

4.4   THE DOCUMENT TYPE DEFINITION (DTD)

In this section we move from the instance to the schema. As stated in Section 1.5, a schema defines a document type (or a class of documents) by imposing a set of constraints on the document instances. For example, we can postulate that documents of type book must start with an introduction, followed by a table of contents, followed by one or several chapters, followed by an index. This schema would clearly reject any document with the table of contents somewhere between the chapters.

Traditionally, document types are defined in XML with the help of a Document Type Definition (DTD). The DTD has its legacy in SGML. Because of its deficiencies (see Section 4.4.8), it has sparked a variety of alternate schema languages for XML, among them schema languages such as XDR, RELAX, Trex, or SOX. This has culminated in the definition of the W3C's XML Schema, the now official way to define XML schemata.

However, DTDs are still popular. DTDs are much simpler than XML Schema. Schemata defined with a DTD are more compact than those defined with XML Schema. Tool support for XML Schema is still patchy but, fortunately, is quickly improving. Last but not least, there is a large pool of XML and SGML experts who are well versed in DTDs, while a similar skill pool for XML Schema has still to develop. Therefore, the rest of the chapter discusses how to define a document schema with a DTD.

4.4.1 Document

The first thing to know about a Document Type Definition is that a document instance does not necessarily need one. A document instance without a Document Type Definition is only constrained by the XML syntax—it must only be well formed, provided that no other schema definition exists for this document instance (through XML Schema, XDR, Relax NG, etc.). This well-formedness is sufficient for parsers and similar XML processors to process any XML document even if no DTD exists, or if the DTD cannot be accessed.

Note, however, that processing a document without the DTD can yield different results from processing with the DTD. A DTD can contain definitions that are relevant for the document content, such as default and fixed values and entity declarations. Only when a document is declared as *standalone* (see Section 4.2.2) is it semantically safe to process it without its DTD. When a DTD is specified and can be accessed, XML can validate the content of the document instance against the Document Type Definition. Since not all XML processors are able to do so, we differentiate between validating and nonvalidating XML processors.

The next important thing to know about a Document Type Definition is that it comes in parts. A DTD can consist of an internal and an external subset. The external subset exists as a separate physical entity, such as a file, and is referenced by a document instance via a DOCTYPE declaration with a SYSTEM identifier:

```
<!DOCTYPE book SYSTEM "http://www.book.org/book">
```

or via a DOCTYPE declaration with a PUBLIC identifier:

```
<!DOCTYPE HTML PUBLIC "-//W3C//DTD XHTML 1.1//EN"
```

The SYSTEM identifier points via a URI to the physical entity containing the external DTD subset. The PUBLIC identifier identifies a publicly known document type such as a W3C standard. Such DTD subsets are usually built into the XML client, for example, into an XHTML browser. The document instance, however, may specify an additional URI after the public identifier to help the client to locate the DTD subset.

The internal subset of a DTD is specified within the document instance. In this case, too, a DOCTYPE declaration is used, but without the SYSTEM identifier. Instead, DTD components are specified locally.

```
<!DOCTYPE book [
  ...
]>
```

Of course, it does not make much sense to define a document type for a single document instance. But the internal subset makes much more sense when it is combined with an external subset. It allows us to extend the definition of the external subset for individual document instances. For example, if we have a book that also has a glossary, we might append the definition for the glossary within the internal DTD subset of this document. The most common reason for internal subsets is to define, redefine, or extend entities—both character entities and the entities that define the structure of documents.

When we define both an external and internal DTD subset, we can combine both DOCTYPE declarations into one:

```
<!DOCTYPE book SYSTEM "http://www.book.org/book" [
  ...
]>
```

4.4.2 Elements

Now, let's look at the components of a Document Type Definition. In a DTD, all XML elements are defined on a global level. This means that it is not possible to define identically named elements of different types in different contexts. For example, if we have a document

```
<CD>
  <title>Sahara</title>
  <track>
    <title>Ebony Queen</title>
    <duration>8:58</duration>
  </track>
 <track>
    <title>Rebirth</title>
    <duration>5:19</duration>
  </track>
</CD>
```

all title elements must have the same type definition. It would not be possible to have different element type definitions for CD/title and CD/track/title. This is fine in the above example, but a serious restriction in other cases.

The definition of elements in a DTD is very close to the definition of regular sets. In fact, we could see a DTD as a Hedge-Regular Grammar (HRG) (see Section 1.6.4). The ELEMENT and ATTLIST components of a DTD could be seen as production rules of such a grammar.

The following example could be a complete DTD for the document type book mentioned above:

```
<!ELEMENT book (title+,authors)>
<!ELEMENT title ANY>
<!ELEMENT authors (author+)>
<!ELEMENT author (firstName,middleName?,lastName)>
<!ATTLIST author
          author-id ID #REQUIRED
          role (contributor|editor) "contributor">
<!ELEMENT firstName (#PCDATA)>
<!ELEMENT middleName (#PCDATA)>
<!ELEMENT lastName (#PCDATA)>
```

The difference between a DTD and the definition of a regular grammar is that all non-terminal symbols are identical with the tag names in the document instances. This identity is the reason for the fact that DTDs do not allow us to define identically named elements of differing types in different contexts (which XML Schema and Relax NG allow). It is also responsible for the fact that DTDs are *not equivalent* with Hedge-Regular Grammars; they only define a subset of HRG languages.

But back to the basics. The DTD statement

```
<!ELEMENT book (title+,authors)>
```

can be seen as a grammar's production rule because it describes the production of a <book>...</book> element. The <book> tags enclose the rest of the production consisting of (title+,authors). The production of the non-terminal symbols title and authors is defined in the following rules. Recursive definitions are possible, as in

```
<!ELEMENT section (title,(abstract?,section+)|body)>
```

The production stops when a terminal symbol is reached. The following terminal symbols are possible:

ANY   Wildcard: The element can contain mixed content, including character data and child elements.

EMPTY   Denotes an empty element.

#PCDATA   The element contains parsed character data. (Parsed character data must not contain characters such as < or &.)

Model Groups

If the right side of a production rule contains non-terminal symbols, then this is either a single non-terminal symbol or a model group. Basically, a model group is a regular expression (see Section 1.6.3) consisting of non-terminal and/or terminal symbols.

The following operators (also called connectors) can be used to combine these symbols:

`(child)`	Single symbol, no operator required
`(child1,child2,...,childn)`	Sequence, elements separated by comma
`(child1|child2|...|childn)`	Choice, elements separated by the vertical bar
`(child1,(child2|(child3,child4)),child5)`	Parentheses are used to denote complex structures

In addition, non-terminal symbols and expressions in parentheses can be postfixed with a modifier that denotes the cardinality of the symbol or expression:

Symbol	Cardinality Constraint
No modifier	One occurrence, item is mandatory [1..1]
?	One occurrence, item is optional [0..1]
+	Multiple occurrences, item is mandatory [1..n]
*	Multiple occurrences, item is optional [0..n]

In the example given earlier we defined

```
<!ELEMENT authors (author+)>
```

because the element `<authors>` can contain multiple `<author>` elements, but must contain at least one of them. We defined

```
<!ELEMENT author (firstName, middleName?, lastName)>
```

because the element `<author>` must contain the elements `<firstName>` and `<last-Name>`, but may or may not contain the element `<middleName>`.

4.4.3 Attributes

Each non-terminal symbol (each tag name) may have a supplementary ATTLIST production rule for the definition of attributes. ATTLIST rules list all attributes of an element:

```
<!ATTLIST author
          author-id ID #REQUIRED
          role (contributor|editor) "contributor">
```

Here, ATTLIST defines the attributes for element `author`. These are `author-id` and `role`. Each single attribute definition consists of an attribute name, an attribute type, and a default value specification.

ATTLIST rules are always terminal because XML attributes cannot have a complex structure. The attribute types can be selected from a few built-in primitive types:

CDATA	Character data.
NMTOKEN	Nametoken. Valid nametokens consist of letters, digits, and the characters ., -, _, or : from the XML character set (see Section 4.2.7).
NMTOKENS	NMTOKEN list (separated by whitespace).
(writer|editor|artist)	Enumeration. Each token must be a valid nametoken.
NOTATION (n1|n2|...)	Enumeration of notation symbols (see Section 4.4.5).
ID	Element identifier. This must be a valid name. Element identifiers must be unique in the context of a document. (Names start with a letter or with _ and can contain letters, digits, ., -, or _. Names must not start with the string "xml" or variations thereof, such as XML, xML, XmL, etc.)
IDREF	Reference to an element ID.
IDREFS	IDREF list (separated by whitespace).
ENTITY	Reference to an unparsed entity. The referenced ENTITY must have been declared with an ENTITY instruction.
ENTITIES	ENTITY list (separated by whitespace).

The following default value specifications can be used for attribute definitions:

#IMPLIED	Attribute is neither required nor does it have a default value.
#REQUIRED	Attribute must be specified in document instance.
"yes"	Default value. An attribute with the specified default value is inserted into the document instance when the instance does not specify the attribute.

`#FIXED "v1"`   Fixed content. If the instance specifies the attribute, it must have this value. If not, the attribute with this value is inserted into the instance.

In our example,

```
<!ATTLIST author
        author-id ID #REQUIRED
        role (contributor|editor) "contributor">
```

defines that an `author` element must always specify an attribute `author-id` of type `ID`. If the attribute `role` is specified, it must have either the value "contributor" or "editor". If this attribute is not specified, the default value `role="contributor"` is inserted into the document. For example,

```
<author author-id="AmblerEric">...</author>
```

results in

```
<author author-id="AmblerEric" role="contributor">...</author>
```

4.4.4 Cross-References

The `ID` and `IDREF` attribute types can be used to establish cross-references between elements. This allows us to establish networklike document structures that cannot be captured in tree structures. In particular, it is possible to define documents that mimic relational tables by using the `ID` and `IDREF` constructs. Attributes of type `ID` act as primary keys, while attributes of type `IDREF` act as foreign keys. Most XML DOM implementations allow for locating elements by `ID`, too.

4.4.5 Extension Mechanisms

The `NOTATION` attribute type acts as a type extension mechanism for elements. A `NOTATION` type attribute refers to one or several `NOTATION` declarations. For example:

```
<!NOTATION arabianYear
        SYSTEM "http://www.book.org/datatypes/arabianYear">
<!NOTATION romanYear
        SYSTEM "http://www.book.org/datatypes/romanYear">
<!ATTLIST book
        pubDate NOTATION (arabianYear|romanYear) "romanYear">
```

By referring to several NOTATION declarations, a NOTATION attribute can implement a *type union*. Each NOTATION declaration declares a specific data type. A custom XML processor can check this data type, possibly by using a helper application.

In practical applications, the NOTATION construct is rarely used, especially as there are now better ways to define data types for XML attributes and elements with XML Schema.

4.4.6 Document Composition

A DTD can declare user-defined entities. These entities can be used within the document text and are replaced in the document by the entity definition when the document is processed and when the entity definition is accessible. Locally defined entities are used to abbreviate frequently used terms and phrases or to introduce a symbolic notation for commonly needed constants. For example:

```
<!ENTITY legal "All rights preserved">
<!ENTITY piAlmost "3.141593">
```

Externally defined entities are used to modularize schemata. For example,

```
<!ENTITY legalDoc SYSTEM "http://www.book.org/modules/legal">
```

includes the contents of file http://www.book.org/modules/legal in the document content.

Using external entities can modularize both the definition of schemata and document instances. This can be helpful when documents are very large and complex. External entities can contain references to other entities, so it's possible to construct large entity trees. SGML authors, especially, have developed a high art of modularization with entities.

However, when external entities are used too extensively for modularization, the maintenance of schemata becomes difficult. In addition, the use of external entities in some application areas is not recommended. For example, if XML is used as a message format, external entities should be avoided; standalone documents are preferred. Also, XML database systems will usually resolve all external entities before they store a document. When the document is retrieved again, it looks different: The external entities are now included.

Both entity types discussed above are parsed entities (they contain XML content that can be parsed). In addition, XML recognizes unparsed entities—entities that contain non-XML data such as images, audio files, and video clips. An unparsed image entity, for example, can be referenced with

```
<!ENTITY cover
         SYSTEM "http://www.book.org/images/dimitrios.gif" NDATA GIF>
```

4.4.7 Schema Composition and Reuse Mechanisms

Parameter entities are only used within a DTD; they do not appear within the content of XML instances. A parameter entity is an abbreviation for a string that is used frequently within a DTD, thus allowing these strings to be factored out.

A parameter entity can be declared through

```
<!ENTITY % entity-name "string-value">
```

All occurrences of %entity-name within the DTD will be substituted with string-value. Because the string value may contain other references to parameter entities, the concept of parameter entities is quite powerful.

A parameter entity may not only relate to a simple string value but also to a public identifier or to a system identifier. This makes it possible to compose a DTD from several parts. Typically, a complex DTD consists only of a small root unit containing a set of parameter entity declarations referring to the various components that constitute the DTD. Our book DTD could look like this:

```
<!ENTITY % common SYSTEM "common.ent">
<!ENTITY % author SYSTEM "author.ent">
%common;
%author;
```

The file common.ent could, for example, contain the definitions

```
<!ELEMENT book (title+,authors)>
<!ELEMENT title ANY>
<!ELEMENT authors (author+)>
```

while the file author.ent would contain the definitions

```
<!ELEMENT author (firstName,middleName?,lastName)>
<!ATTLIST author
        author-id ID #REQUIRED
        role (contributor|editor) "contributor">
<!ELEMENT firstName (#PCDATA)>
<!ELEMENT middleName (#PCDATA)>
<!ELEMENT lastName (#PCDATA)>
```

However, this technique quickly reaches its limits. Document schemata made up of dozens of separate entity files are difficult to manage; because there is no namespace concept, name clashes are all too common.

One important application of parameter entities is to implement a schema extension mechanism. Take for example our book schema. A book instance may only consist of one or several title elements and one authors element. We are not allowed to add some detail information to specific instances, such as comments, a table of contents, or reviews.

If we want to allow arbitrary extensions to a document schema on the instance level, we can utilize parameter entities. First we define the external DTD subset in the following way:

```
<!ENTITY % details "">
<!ELEMENT book (title+,authors %details;)>
...
```

Here, we define an empty parameter entity named details and append it to the definition of element book. So, this definition is equivalent to

```
<!ELEMENT book (title+,authors)>
```

But if we override the definition of entity details within the internal DTD subset, things look completely different:

```
DOCTYPE book SYSTEM "http://www.book.org/book" [
<!ENTITY % details ",publishersReview" >
<!ELEMENT publishersReview ANY>
]>
```

Now the rule

```
<!ELEMENT book (title+,authors %details;)>
```

is resolved to

```
<!ELEMENT book (title+,authors,publishersReview)>
```

and we can add a publishersReview element as a child element to the book element.

4.4.8 DTD Deficiencies

In the past, DTDs were the standard way to define a schema for an XML document type. This has changed with the release of the XML Schema Recommendation by the W3C. Compared to XML Schema, DTDs have several deficiencies:

- The syntax of a DTD is different from XML syntax. This inhibits the use of the vast array of XML tools for editing, validating, parsing, and transforming DTDs.

- DTDs do not support namespaces. Although DTDs allow the use of `prefix:name` combinations for element and attribute names, they interpret these combinations as simple names. This can lead to confusion.
- DTDs only recognize a small range of built-in data types that can only be applied to attributes. For example, we cannot define elements and attributes that must be numeric or integers. Thus, the content of elements and the value of attributes are always regarded as character data. This can have unpleasant effects when a processor wants to compare two elements containing numeric values. Because the processor does not know that the element content is numeric, 6 is regarded as greater than 139594; -1 is regarded as smaller than -5; the floating-point number 3.7e-10 is regarded as larger than 2.0e+16; and so on. Languages such as XPath, therefore, have explicit means of interpreting the content of an element or attribute as numeric.
- There is no standard way to create user-defined data types. Type definitions with the NOTATION mechanism require custom extensions to XML processors and are rarely portable.
- DTDs do not provide a special mechanism for specifying sequences of elements with no specified order. For a given model group (e1,e2,e3) the elements e1...e3 must appear in the document instance in the exact sequence as defined in the DTD. To simulate such an unordered sequence (a bag), all possible permutations must be given as alternatives: ((e1,e2,e3) | (e1,e3,e2) | (e2,e1,e3) | ...). In contrast, SGML allows for specifying such sequences with (e1&e2&e3). We will see that XML Schema provides means for specifying bags, too.
- The definition of general cardinality constraints such as [2:4] is not supported. Again we must enumerate all possible combinations: ((e,e),(e,e,e), (e,e,e,e)). When there is no upper bound, such as [4:*], we need to write this as (e,e,e,e+).
- In DTDs all elements are defined on the global level. This makes it impossible to define context-sensitive elements—elements with the same name but different structures in different contexts.
- DTDs do not allow the definition of multifield cross-reference keys, nor is it possible to use element values as keys (only attributes can be defined as type ID). Keys cannot be scoped, either; they are always defined on the global level. This can require document authors to construct rather complex key values to simulate multifield keys or scoped keys.

  Section 3.5 showed how to construct a composite key value. In a document where we want to index `jazzMusician` elements by name, for example, we have to construct a composite key value from the constituents of the name element, such as `MingusCharles`. If in the same document we also want to index jazz musicians by instrument, we must prefix the key values with a scope prefix in order to distinguish musician keys from instrument keys, for example, `musician#MonkThelonious` and `instrument#piano`.

XML Schema

The XML Schema Working Draft was first published in May 1999, and the final recommendation was released in May 2001. It consists of three parts. Part Zero is a very readable (but non-normative) XML Schema primer, written by David C. Fallside (*http://www.w3.org/TR/xmlschema-0*). Part One specifies XML Schema structures (*http://www.w3.org/TR/xmlschema-1*), and Part Two specifies XML Schema data types (*http://www.w3.org/TR/xmlschema-2*). These parts are harder to read, sometimes resembling certain legal texts.

During their work, the XML Schema Working Group could include experiences with several other already existing schema languages, such as XSchema, DDML, XML-Data, XDR, and SOX. Now, with the XML Schema recommendation released, most XML communities are moving toward XML Schema.

This chapter gives a complete introduction to the type system of XML Schema. We begin with simple XML Schema data types—the most important advantage of XML Schema over DTDs apart from the support for namespaces. XML Schema data types have also been adopted by other schema languages such as Relax NG (see Chapter 7). The rest of the standard will be covered in Chapter 6.

117

5.1 AN APPETIZER

Although XML Schema is a complex standard, moving from a DTD to XML Schema is quite simple: Just feed your schema editor a DTD, and export it in XML Schema format. Things become more complicated when you move into advanced concepts: user-defined data types, for example, or modularized schemata with multiple namespaces. But these are things that you can't do at all with DTDs.

Becoming an XML Schema expert requires some effort to master the language and exploit its full potential. Moving from DTD authoring to XML Schema authoring is like moving from a Model T Ford to a Porsche: If you can't control it, you will easily drive it through the next fence. On the other hand, you don't have to go uphill in reverse gear (for lack of a fuel pump in the Model T).

Just as an appetizer let's look at a very small DTD:

```
<!ELEMENT person (name, birthDate)>
<!ELEMENT name (#PCDATA)>
<!ELEMENT birthDate (#PCDATA)>
```

And here is the equivalent schema for a simple person element containing a name and birth date written in XML Schema:

```
<?xml version="1.0" encoding="UTF-8"?>
<xs:schema xmlns:xs="http://www.w3.org/2001/XMLSchema">
  <xs:element name="person">
    <xs:complexType>
      <xs:sequence>
        <xs:element name="name" type="xs:string"/>
        <xs:element name="birthDate" type="xs:string"/>
      </xs:sequence>
    </xs:complexType>
  </xs:element>
</xs:schema>
```

Well, that doesn't look too difficult. Here, we define a document type with a root element named person. This root element has two child elements named name and birthDate. When we look at the schema diagram in Figure 5.1, the concept is even easier to grasp.

We see that XML Schema works quite differently from DTDs: Elements can be defined within the element definition of another element. One advantage is that the code (and also the diagram) displays the later tree structure of the doc-

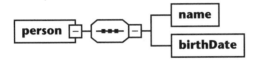

Figure 5.1 The person element contains name and birthDate in a sequence.

ument instances quite well. Global element definitions as in a DTD are possible, too, but we will deal with this later.

We also see that an element containing other elements is defined as a complex type element. Type declarations, type="xs:string", replace the (#PCDATA) declarations from the DTD. This brings us to one of the most outstanding features of XML Schema and—apart from its support for namespaces—its most important improvement over DTDs: its support for data types. We will therefore start with an extensive discussion of simple data types in XML Schema. Later sections discuss how data structures (that is, complex data types) can be defined and how namespaces are handled. Finally, we will have a look at XML Schema's reuse mechanisms that allow the modularization of schemata and the construction of type libraries. We will see that XML Schema offers concepts like inheritance, generic types, and polymorphism that are similar to concepts found in object-oriented programming, yet at the same time are quite different.

In contrast to DTDs, XML Schema uses XML syntax for schema definition. The concepts throughout this chapter are explained using the following notation to document the features of a syntactical construct in XML Schema:

Name	Attributes	Contains
simpleType	final?	annotation?
	id?	(restriction | list | union)
	name?	

The Name column specifies the element name of the construct (the tag name). The Attributes column contains the attributes that this element may have. (The question mark denotes an optional attribute.) The Contains column defines the possible child elements.

The definition for simpleType given above would allow, for example, the following schema clause:

```
<xs:simpleType name="price">
 <xs:restriction base="xs:decimal">
  <xs:fractionDigits value="2"/>
  <xs:minInclusive value="0.00"/>
 </xs:restriction>
</xs:simpleType>
```

5.2 SIMPLE DATA TYPES

Simple data types in XML Schema are constructed by means of a few basic concepts: value space, lexical space, fundamental facets, constraining facets, and type extensions. The following sections discuss these basic concepts and then present the data types that are built into XML Schema.

5.2.1 Value Space

The type system of XML Schema makes a clear distinction between *value space* and *lexical space*. While the value space consists of an abstract collection of valid values for a data type, the lexical space contains the lexical representation of these values—that is, the tokens as they appear in the XML document. Take for example an integer. The value of integer 5 is always the same; the lexical representation, however, can differ: 5, 005, five, V, *****, and so on.

5.2.2 Lexical Representations and Canonical Representation

The XML Schema recommendation defines which lexical representations are valid for a given data type. In some cases, there is only one possible representation, but in many cases, various kinds of lexical representations are allowed. Take for example data type `boolean`: XML Schema allows the representation "true" and "false" but also the representation "1" (for "true") and "0" (for "false").

In such cases where XML Schema allows several lexical representations, one representation is designated as the *canonical* representation. For data type `boolean` this is the representation "true" or "false." Canonical representations are important when we want to compare two document instances for equality: It is first necessary to convert both documents into the canonical form, before they can be compared by character string comparison. Section 4.3 already discussed the W3C recommendation "Canonical XML" [Boyer2001]. Because XML data types are not covered by this recommendation, the XML Schema specification explicitly defines the canonical formats of its own data types.

5.2.3 Fundamental Facets

XML Schema defines basic data types in a very systematic way. The properties of data types are classified in so-called *facets*. Each facet describes a specific aspect of a data type, such as equality, cardinality, and length. Again, these facets are classified into two categories:

- *Fundamental facets* define the basic value space properties of data types. They are used to declare the *primitive* data types that are built into the standard. They are *not* used to declare derived data types (built-in or user defined).

■ *Constraining facets* are used, as the name says, to constrain the value space or lexical space of a data type. They are used to derive new data types from existing data types by restriction. This is discussed in detail in Section 5.2.7.

XML Schema defines the following fundamental facets:

Facet	Description
equal	Defines equality between values of a data type. For example, two items are equal if their values (not necessarily their string representations in the lexical space) are equal. Every value space in XML Schema supports the notion of equality, so this facet has the value "true" for every data type.
ordered	Defines order relations between values of a data type. The order relation can be *total* or *partial*. For example, numeric values are totally ordered, date values are partially ordered, and string values are not ordered at all. This may seem odd, but the ordering of strings depends on the localization context, and for date values it is impossible to determine an order relation between a date that specifies a time zone and one that comes without one.
bounded	Defines whether the values of a data type are restricted by an upper and/or lower bound. For example, float values are bounded (due to their IEEE 754-1985 representation), while decimal values are not bounded.
cardinality	Defines whether the value space of a data type is finite or countable infinite. (Uncountable infinite data types do not exist in the recommendation.) For example, enumerations are finite, and integer numbers are countable infinite. Float values are also finite due to their IEEE 754-1985 representation, although in mathematics real numbers are uncountable infinite.
numeric	Defines whether a data type is numeric or not.

5.2.4 Built-in Primitive Data Types

Using fundamental facets, XML Schema defines a set of built-in primitive data types. Table 5.1 lists these data types with their respective lexical representations. Canonical representations are printed in **bold**, and the other representations are followed by the reason why they are not canonical. The table also lists which constraining facets may be applied to each data type in order to derive other data types from it (see Section 5.2.7).

Table 5.1 Built-in primitive datatypes in XML Schema. Canonical representations are printed in bold typeface. Built-in datatypes belong to the XML Schema namespace, which is represented here with prefix "xs:".

Data Type	Description	Lexical Representation	Possible Constraining Facets
xs:string ordered=no bounded=no cardinality=infinite numeric=no	Character string of unlimited length. XML Schema does not define an ordering relation for strings!	Some string	length minLength maxLength pattern enumeration whiteSpace
xs:boolean ordered=no bounded=no cardinality=finite numeric=no	Boolean value.	**true, false** 1, 0	pattern whiteSpace
xs:decimal ordered=total bounded=no cardinality=infinite numeric=yes	Decimal number. A minimum precision of 18 digits must be supported by conforming processors.	**–1.23** **126.54** **0.0** +100000.00 (+ sign) 210 (no decimal point)	totalDigits fractionDigits pattern whiteSpace enumeration maxInclusive maxExclusive minInclusive minExclusive
xs:float ordered=total bounded=yes cardinality=finite numeric=yes	A single-precision 32-bit floating-point type according to IEEE 754-1985.	**127.433E12** **–12.78E-2, 12** **INF, -INF, 0, –0** **NaN** –1E4 (no decimal point) +22.0 (+ sign) 1.20e+04 (lowercase *e*)	pattern enumeration whiteSpace maxInclusive maxExclusive minInclusive minExclusive

(continued on next page)

Data Type	Description	Lexical Representation	Possible Constraining Facets
xs:double ordered=total bounded=yes cardinality=finite numeric=yes	A double-precision 64-bit floating-point type according to IEEE 754-1985.	127.433E12 –12.78E-2, 12 INF, –INF, 0, –0 NaN –1E4 (no decimal point) +22.0 (+ sign) 1.20e+04 (lowercase *e*)	pattern enumeration whiteSpace maxInclusive maxExclusive minInclusive minExclusive
xs:duration ordered=partial bounded=no cardinality=infinite numeric=no	Specifies a period of time. The value space is a six-dimensional space where the coordinates designate the Gregorian year, month, day, hour, minute, and second.	The lexical representation follows the format PnYnMnDTnHnMnS. An optional fractional part for seconds is allowed. Negative durations are allowed, too. Examples: **PT5H3M33.3S** **P1Y3M** **–PT5H** **PT40H**	pattern enumeration whiteSpace maxInclusive maxExclusive minInclusive minExclusive
xs:time ordered=partial bounded=no cardinality=infinite numeric=no	A specific time of day as defined in § 5.3 of ISO 8601.	The lexical representation follows the format hh:mm:ssZ. An optional fractional part for seconds is allowed. Z denotes an optional time zone: Z for UTC time, or a signed time difference in format hh:mm. Examples: **05:20:23.2** **20:00:00Z** **13:20:00–05:00** (explicit time zone used)	pattern enumeration whiteSpace maxInclusive maxExclusive minInclusive minExclusive

(continued on next page)

Table 5.1 *(continued)*

Data Type	Description	Lexical Representation	Possible Constraining Facets
xs:date ordered=partial bounded=no cardinality=infinite numeric=no	A Gregorian calendar date according to § 5.2.1 of ISO 8601.	The lexical representation follows the format CCYY-MM-DDZ. Z denotes an optional time zone. To accommodate values outside the range 1–9999, additional digits and a negative sign can be added to the left. (The year 0000 is prohibited.) Examples: **1999-05-31** **2000-01-01Z** 2001–07–17+05:00 (explicit time zone used)	pattern enumeration whiteSpace maxInclusive maxExclusive minInclusive minExclusive
xs:dateTime ordered=partial bounded=no cardinality=infinite numeric=no	A specific instant of time (a combination of date and time) as defined in § 5.4 of ISO 8601.	The lexical representation follows the format CCYY-MM-DDThh:mm:ssZ with T acting as a separating character between date and time. Z denotes an optional time zone. Examples: **2001-12-01T05:20:23.2** 1999-05-31T13:20:00-05:00 (explicit time zone used)	pattern enumeration whiteSpace maxInclusive maxExclusive minInclusive minExclusive
xs:gYearMonth ordered=partial bounded=no cardinality=infinite numeric=no	Represents a specific Gregorian month in a specific Gregorian year.	The lexical representation follows the format CCYY-MMZ. Z denotes an optional time zone. Example: **2001-12**	pattern enumeration whiteSpace maxInclusive maxExclusive minInclusive minExclusive

(continued on next page)

Data Type	Description	Lexical Representation	Possible Constraining Facets
xs:gYear ordered=partial bounded=no cardinality=infinite numeric=no	Represents a Gregorian year.	The lexical representation follows the format CCYYZ. Z denotes an optional time zone. Example: **2001**	pattern enumeration whiteSpace maxInclusive maxExclusive minInclusive minExclusive
xs:gMonthDay ordered=partial bounded=no cardinality=infinite numeric=no	Specifies a recurring Gregorian date.	The lexical representation follows the format --MM-DDZ. Z denotes an optional time zone. Example: **--04-01**	pattern enumeration whiteSpace maxInclusive maxExclusive minInclusive minExclusive
xs:gMonth ordered=partial bounded=no cardinality=infinite numeric=no	Denotes a Gregorian month that recurs every year.	The lexical representation follows the format --MM--Z. Z denotes an optional time zone. Example: **--05--**	pattern enumeration whiteSpace maxInclusive maxExclusive minInclusive minExclusive
xs:gDay ordered=partial bounded=no cardinality=infinite numeric=no	Denotes a Gregorian day that recurs every month.	The lexical representation follows the format ---DDZ. Z denotes an optional time zone. Example: **---01**	pattern enumeration whiteSpace maxInclusive maxExclusive minInclusive minExclusive

(continued on next page)

Table 5.1 *(continued)*

Data Type	Description	Lexical Representation	Possible Constraining Facets
xs:hexBinary ordered=no bounded=no cardinality=infinite numeric=no	Arbitrary hex-encoded binary data.	**FFFF3** **0100** 9a7f (lowercase letters)	length minLength maxLength pattern enumeration whiteSpace
xs:base64Binary ordered=no bounded=no cardinality=infinite numeric=no	Base64-encoded arbitrary binary data. The entire binary stream is encoded using the Base64 Content-Transfer-Encoding defined in Section 6.8 of RFC 2045.	**aGVsbG8gd29ybGQh**	length minLength maxLength pattern enumeration whiteSpace
xs:anyURI ordered=no bounded=no cardinality=infinite numeric=no	A Uniform Resource Identifier (URI) reference.	**http://www. xmlarchitecture.org**	length minLength maxLength pattern enumeration whiteSpace
xs:QName ordered=no bounded=no cardinality=infinite numeric=no	XML qualified names consisting of namespace name and local part.	**xsl:for-each** **xs:attribute**	length minLength maxLength pattern enumeration whiteSpace
xs:NOTATION ordered=no bounded=no cardinality=infinite numeric=no	Represents the NOTATION attribute type from XML attributes.	This data type is *abstract;* the user must derive his or her own data type from it.	length minLength maxLength pattern enumeration whiteSpace

5.2.5 Constructed Types

XML Schema derives additional built-in data types from these primitive data types. This is done with a `simpleType` declaration.

Name	Attributes	Contains
simpleType	final?	annotation
	id?	(restriction | list | union)
	name?	

XML Schema uses three methods for constructing built-in data types.[1] These methods can also be employed by schema authors to construct their own data types.

- *Restriction.* The value space or the lexical space of the original data type is restricted by constraining facets. For example, the data type `integer` is derived from the primitive data type `decimal` by constraining the facet `fractionDigits` to 0. For details see Section 5.2.7.
- *Extension by list.* This allows a sequence of values of the same simple data type. For example, the data type `NMTOKENS` is constructed from data type `NMTOKEN` by concatenating a list of `NMTOKEN` values. For details see the next section.
- *Extension by union.* The value space of the new data type is a union of the value spaces of multiple existing simple data types. This extension method is not used to construct built-in data types but can be used to define user-defined data types. For details see Section 5.2.10.

The application of these methods by XML Schema to the built-in data types results in a rather large hierarchy of built-in derived data types, which are listed in Section 5.2.8. In terms of the theory of regular types, restrictions create subtypes (see Section 1.7.4), while extensions create supertypes.

When defining user-defined types, users have the ability to inhibit further type construction. This is done with the `final` attribute, which can take one of the following values: `#all`, `list`, `union`, `restriction`. This allows inhibiting further construction by any method (`#all`) or by a specific method.

5.2.6 Extending Data Types by List

Most data types can be extended to a list of this base data type. Within an XML element or attribute instance, the values of a list are separated by whitespace. Therefore, this extension method can only be applied to data types that do not

---

1. The XML Schema Recommendation Part Two uses the term "derived" instead of "constructed" in this context. Since this terminology clashes with the semantics defined for "derived" in Part One of the recommendation, we use the term "constructed."

allow whitespace in the lexical representation. In particular, it is not possible to nest lists.

In contrast to the type system of Relax NG (see Chapter 7), XML Schema does not allow the construction of lists with members of different data types.

Name	Attributes	Contains
list	id	annotation?
	itemType	simpleType?

The following example shows how we can define a vector consisting of an arbitrary number of double-precision floating-point numbers:

```
<xs:simpleType name="tVector">
  <xs:list itemType="xs:double"/>
</xs:simpleType>
```

A possible instance of such a type could look like the following:

```
127.433E12  0  -12.78E-2
```

Extension by list defines a *supertype* of the base data type. The value space of the base data type is just a subset of the value space of the list data type (list length = 1).

5.2.7 Restricted Data Types

In contrast, constructing a data type by applying constraints results in a *subtype* of the base data type, because the value space of the new data type is restricted; that is, it is a subset of the value space of the base data type.

Name	Attributes	Contains
restriction	base	annotation?
	id?	simpleType?
		(minExclusive | minInclusive | maxExclusive | maxInclusive | totalDigits | fractionDigits | length | minLength | maxLength | enumeration | whiteSpace | pattern)*

XML Schema classifies the constraints that can restrict a data type into constraining facets. Each facet controls a different aspect of a data type, for example, the total number of digits or the number of fractional digits for a decimal data type. As shown earlier in Table 5.1, each primitive data type defines which constraining facet may be applied to it.

The following constraining facets are available in XML Schema:

Facet	Description

`length`	Defines the length for an atomic data type value (number of characters for strings, number of octets for binary, etc.).
	
	```<xs:simpleType name="tUsZip">```
	  ```<xs:restriction base="xs:string">```
	   ```<xs:length value="5"/>```
	  ```</xs:restriction>```
	```</xs:simpleType>```
	
	Defines the number of elements for a list type.
	
	```<xs:simpleType name="tVector">```
	  ```<xs:list itemType="xs:double"/>```
	```</xs:simpleType>```
	```<xs:simpleType name="tVector3D">```
	  ```<xs:restriction base="tVector">```
	    ```<xs:length value="3"/>```
	  ```</xs:restriction>```
	```</xs:simpleType>```

`minLength`	Defines the minimum length for atomic types or the minimum number of elements for list types.
`maxLength`	Defines the maximum length for atomic types or the maximum number of elements for list types.

`pattern`	Constrains the values of a data type by constraining the lexical space of a data type to match a specified character pattern. Patterns are defined via regular expressions. The syntax for the specification of patterns uses almost the same tokens and escape symbols as other languages that support patterns. (See the appendix for a complete listing of the pattern language.)
	
	Example:
	
	```<xs:simpleType name="tRegNo">```
	  ```<xs:restriction base="xs:string">```
	   ```<xs:pattern```
	     ```value="((\p{Lu}|\d){4}-){4}(\p{Lu}|\d){4}"/>```
	  ```</xs:restriction>```
	```</xs:simpleType>```

	Constrains the string to five substrings separated by "-". Each substring consists of four uppercase letters or decimal digits. Example:
	`E343-8873-KYZO-733A-4844`
`enumeration`	Constrains the value space of a data type to a specified enumeration of values.

Example:

```
<xs:simpleType name="tColorName">
  <xs:restriction base="xs:string">
    <xs:enumeration value="red"/>
    <xs:enumeration value="green"/>
    <xs:enumeration value="blue"/>
  </xs:restriction>
</xs:simpleType>
```

`whiteSpace`	This is not really a constraining facet, but it defines a policy of how whitespace in input values is handled: *preserve* (keep all whitespace characters), *replace* (replace each whitespace character with the blank character), *collapse* (reduce all sequences of whitespace characters to a single blank character).
`maxInclusive/` `maxExclusive`	Upper bound for the value space of a data type. `maxInclusive` includes the specified value, `maxExclusive` excludes the specified value.
`minInclusive/` `minExclusive`	Lower bound for the value space of a data type. `minInclusive` includes the specified value, `minExclusive` excludes the specified value.

Example:

```
<xs:simpleType name="tGrade">
  <xs:restriction base="xs:integer">
    <xs:minInclusive value="1"/>
    <xs:maxExclusive value="6"/>
  </xs:restriction>
</xs:simpleType>
```

Specifies an integer data type with the possible values 1, 2, 3, 4, 5.

`totalDigits`	Maximum total number of decimal digits in values of data types derived from data type `decimal`.

fractionDigits   Maximum number of decimal digits in the fractional part of values of data types derived from decimal.

Example:

```
<xs:simpleType name="tAccount">
  <xs:restriction base="xs:decimal">
    <xs:totalDigits value="15"/>
    <xs:fractionDigits value="2"/>
  </xs:restriction>
</xs:simpleType>
```

Defines a decimal data type with at most 15 decimal digits and two fractional digits.

5.2.8 Built-in Constructed Data Types

By applying the constraining facets explained above and by applying list extensions, XML Schema defines a hierarchy of built-in constructed data types (see Table 5.2 and Figure 5.2). Built-in data types belong to the XML Schema namespace, represented here with prefix "xs:".

Table 5.2 Built-in constructed data types in XML Schema. Built-in data types belong to the XML Schema namespace, represented here with the prefix "xs:".

Data Type	Derived By

xs:normalizedString
 	
A string with normalized whitespace; that is, the string must not contain the carriage return (#xD), line feed (#xA), or tab (#x9) characters.
	`<xs:restriction base="xs:string">`
	`  <xs:whiteSpace value="replace"/>`
	`</xs:restriction>`
	Examples:
	`"A normalized     string"`
	`"Not a`
	`     normalized string"`

xs:token
 	
A string that does not contain the line feed (#xA) or tab (#x9) character, does not have leading or trailing spaces (#x20), and does not have internal sequences of two or more spaces.
	`<xs:restriction`
	`        base="xs:normalizedString">`
	`  <xs:whiteSpace value="collapse"/>`
	`</xs:restriction>`
	Examples:
	`"A valid token"`
	`"Not a    valid token "`

(continued on next page)

Table 5.2 *(continued)*

Data Type	Derived By

`xs:language`
 	
Language identifiers as defined by ISO 639 and ISO 3166.
	`<xs:restriction base="xs:token">`
	  `<xs:pattern value=`
	`"([a-zA-Z]{2}|[iI]-[a-zA-Z]+|[xX]-[a-zA-`
	`Z]{1,8})(-[a-zA-Z]{1,8})*"/>`
	`</xs:restriction>`
	Examples:
	`"en-GB"`
	`"en-US"`
	`"fr-CA"`

`xs:NMTOKEN`
 	
Represents the corresponding attribute type from XML 1.0 (DTD). (See Section 4.4.3.)
	`<xs:restriction base="xs:token">`
	  `<xs:pattern value="\c+"/>`
	`</xs:restriction>`
	Examples:
	`"nametoken"`
	`"not a nametoken"`

`xs:NMTOKENS`
 	
Represents the corresponding attribute type from XML 1.0 (DTD). (See Section 4.4.3.)
	`<xs:restriction>`
	  `<xs:simpleType>`
	    `<xs:list itemType="xs:NMTOKEN"/>`
	  `</xs:simpleType>`
	  `<xs:minLength value="1"/>`
	`</xs:restriction>`
	Examples:
	`"nametoken1 nametoken2 nametoken3"`

`xs:Name`
 	
Represents the corresponding attribute type from XML 1.0 (DTD).
	`<xs:restriction base="xs:token">`
	  `<xs:pattern value="\i\c*"/>`
	`</xs:restriction>`
	Examples:
	`"goodName"`
	`"5badName"`

(continued on next page)

Data Type	Derived By

`xs:NCName`
 	
Represents the corresponding attribute type from XML 1.0 (DTD).
	```<xs:restriction base="xs:Name">```
	  ```<xs:pattern value="[\i-[:]][\c-[:]]*" />```
	```</xs:restriction>```
	Examples:
	`"goodNCName"`
	`"ex:badNCName"`

`xs:ID` Represents the corresponding attribute type from XML 1.0 (DTD). (See Section 4.4.3.)	```<xs:restriction base="xs:NCName"/>```
`xs:IDREF` Represents the corresponding attribute type from XML 1.0 (DTD). (See Section 4.4.3.)	```<xs:restriction base="xs:NCName"/>```

`xs:IDREFS`
 	
Represents the corresponding attribute type from XML 1.0 (DTD). (See Section 4.4.3.)
	```xs:restriction>```
	  ```<xs:simpleType>```
	    ```<xs:list itemType="xs:IDREF"/>```
	  ```</xs:simpleType>```
	  ```<xs:minLength value="1"/>```
	```</xs:restriction>```

`xs:ENTITY` Represents the corresponding attribute type from XML 1.0 (DTD). (See Section 4.4.3.)	```<xs:restriction base="xs:NCName"/>```

`xs:ENTITIES`
 	
Represents the corresponding attribute type from XML 1.0 (DTD). (See Section 4.4.3.)
	```<xs:restriction>```
	  ```<xs:simpleType>```
	    ```<xs:list itemType="xs:ENTITY"/>```
	  ```</xs:simpleType>```
	  ```<xs:minLength value="1"/>```
	```</xs:restriction>```

(continued on next page)

Table 5.2 *(continued)*

Data Type	Derived By

`xs:integer`
 	
The standard mathematical integer data type of arbitrary length.
	`<xs:restriction base="xs:decimal">`
	  `<xs:fractionDigits`
	      `value="0" fixed="true" />`
	`</xs:restriction>`
	Examples:
	`"1234567"`
	`"123.40"` (not an integer)

`xs:nonPositiveInteger`
 	
Integer less than or equal to zero.
	`<xs:restriction base="xs:integer">`
	  `<xs:maxInclusive value="0"/>`
	`</xs:restriction>`

`xs:negativeInteger`
 	
Integer less than zero.
	`<xs:restriction`
	        `base="xs:nonPositiveInteger">`
	  `<xs:maxInclusive value="-1"/>`
	`</xs:restriction>`

`xs:long`
 	
Integer in the range of –9223372036854775808 to 9223372036854775807.
	`<xs:restriction base="xs:integer">`
	  `<xs:minInclusive`
	      `value="-9223372036854775808"/>`
	  `<xs:maxInclusive`
	      `value="9223372036854775807"/>`
	`</xs:restriction>`

`xs:int`
 	
Integer in the range of –2147483648 to 2147483647.
	`<xs:restriction base="xs:long">`
	  `<xs:minInclusive`
	      `value="-2147483648"/>`
	  `<xs:maxInclusive`
	      `value="2147483647"/>`
	`</xs:restriction>`

`xs:short`
 	
Integer in the range of –32768 to 32767.
	`<xs:restriction base="xs:int">`
	  `<xs:minInclusive value="-32768"/>`
	  `<xs:maxInclusive value="32767"/>`
	`</xs:restriction>`

(continued on next page)

Data Type	Derived By

xs:byte
 	
Integer in the range of –128 to 127.
	```<xs:restriction base="xs:short">```
	``` <xs:minInclusive value="-128"/>```
	``` <xs:maxInclusive value="127"/>```
	```</xs:restriction>```

xs:nonNegativeInteger
 	
Integer greater than or equal to zero.
	```<xs:resriction base="xs:integer">```
	``` <xs:minInclusive value="0"/>```
	```</xs:restriction>```

xs:unsignedLong
 	
Integer in the range of 0 to 18446744073709551615.
	```<xs:restriction```
	```base="xs:nonNegativeInteger">```
	``` <xs:maxInclusive```
	``` value="18446744073709551615"/>```
	```</xs:restriction>```

xs:unsignedInt
 	
Integer in the range of 0 to 4294967295.
	```<xs:restriction base="xs:unsignedLong">```
	``` <xs:maxInclusive```
	``` value="4294967295"/>```
	```</xs:restriction>```

xs:unsignedShort
 	
Integer in the range of 0 to 65535.
	```<xs:restriction base="xs:unsignedInt">```
	``` <xs:maxInclusive value="65535"/>```
	```</xs:restriction>```

xs:unsignedByte
 	
Integer in the range of 0 to 255.
	```<xs:restriction base="xs:unsignedShort">```
	``` <xs:maxInclusive value="255"/>```
	```</xs:restriction>```

xs:positiveInteger
 	
Integer greater than zero.
	```<xs:restriction```
	```base="xs:nonNegativeInteger">```
	``` <xs:minInclusive value="1"/>```
	```</xs:restriction>```

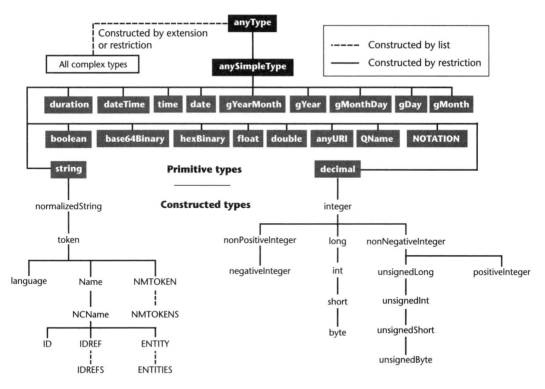

Figure 5.2 Built-in data types in XML Schema. Primitive data types are printed in reverse. Dashed lines indicate construction by list; solid lines indicate derivation by restriction.

5.2.9 The Hierarchy of Built-in Primitive and Constructed Data Types

The built-in primitive data types listed in Section 5.2.4 and the built-in constructed data types listed in Section 5.2.8 establish a hierarchy of data types as shown in Figure 5.2. Constructed data types are obtained from primitive data types and other constructed data types by restriction and list extension. Please note that these operations do not establish a hierarchy in terms of subtype and supertype. While type restriction always results in a subtype of the base type, list extension always results in a supertype of the base type. This is the reason why we use the term *constructed data type* in contrast to *derived data type* as used in the XML Schema Recommendation, Part Two. The formal definition of *derived* in Part One of the recommendation does not allow for type extension by list or union.

5.2.10 Union Types

With the union operation, it is possible to combine disparate data types in a single data type. The new data type is a supertype to all the contributing member data types: Its value space is the union of the value spaces of all contributing member data types. The member data types can be either referenced by name in the memberTypes attribute or defined locally using simpleType declarations within the union element.

Name	Attributes	Contains
union	id	annotation?
	memberTypes	simpleType*

In the following schema fragment, a string data type tISBN is defined. The pattern facet restricts valid strings to the typical ISBN patterns, such as 0-646-27288-8. (For an explanation of the pattern syntax, see the appendix.) A second data type, tProductNo, is defined next, representing custom product numbers. These product numbers start with "9-" followed by two groups of three to five decimal characters, followed by a single decimal character, for example, 9-234-9393-0.

We can then use these two type definitions to construct a union type tISBNorProductNo allowing both patterns. We could use this combined data type for a catalog containing books and other products.

```
<xs:simpleType name="tISBN">
  <xs:restriction base="xs:string">
    <xs:pattern value="(\d)-(\d){3}-(\d){5}-(\d)"/>
  </xs:restriction>
</xs:simpleType>


<xs:simpleType name="tProductNo">
  <xs:restriction base="xs:string">
    <xs:pattern value="9-((\d){3,5}-){2}(\d)"/>
  </xs:restriction>
</xs:simpleType>


<xs:simpleType name="tISBNorProductNo">
  <xs:union memberTypes="tISBN tProductNo"/>
</xs:simpleType>
```

In this example the patterns of the two member types tISBN and tProductNo are chosen in such a way that their lexical value domains overlap. In such cases the sequence of the member types given in the union clause matters: An XML Schema–aware processor would first try to match an instance string to the tISBN pattern, and if that failed, to the tProductNo pattern. However, individual instances may enforce the usage of a specific member type via the xsi:type attribute (see Section 6.2.4).

5.2.11 User-Defined Data Types

As mentioned in Section 5.2.5, it is possible for users to construct their own data types from built-in data types. Let's look at an example. We want to declare a schema for asset jazzMusician defined in Figure 3.5. We choose to represent the property kind as an attribute. Since only three values are allowed, we want to declare the attribute accordingly, restricting its value range to instrumentalist, jazzSinger, and jazzComposer. We can achieve this with the following definition:

```
<xs:attribute name = "kind">
  <xs:simpleType>
    <xs:restriction base = "xs:NMTOKEN">
      <xs:enumeration value = "instrumentalist"/>
      <xs:enumeration value = "jazzSinger"/>
      <xs:enumeration value = "jazzComposer"/>
    </xs:restriction>
  </xs:simpleType>
</xs:attribute>
```

What we do is declare a simple data type on the fly. This new anonymous data type is only used for the attribute with the name "kind" and is derived from the built-in data type xs:NMTOKEN by restriction. We then use three occurrences of the xs:enumeration facet to define the three possible values.

Similarly, we could define an element duration (for the duration property of asset track):

```
<xs:element name = "duration">
  <xs:simpleType>
    <xs:restriction base = "xs:duration">
      <xs:maxInclusive value = "PT77M"/>
```

```
    </xs:restriction>
   </xs:simpleType>
  </xs:element>
```

Here, we use a restricted form of the built-in data type `xs:duration` in that we only allow durations smaller or equal to 77 minutes.

5.3   STRUCTURE IN XML SCHEMA

As you can see in Figure 5.3 (page 140), the definition of a document structure with XML Schema is a rather complex undertaking. Understanding the interrelated concepts of XML Schema takes a while of reading forward and backward. Be patient. The best method is to learn the most basic constructs first and worry about advanced features such as global definitions and reuse mechanisms later:

1. The *root element* of a document is defined on the schema level via an *element* definition.
2. This root element has a *complex type*.
3. Complex type declarations combine other (global and local) elements that again may have a complex type, or otherwise have a simple type.
4. This combination is achieved via *model groups* consisting of *sequences*, *choices,* or *bags.*
5. *Particles* can further constrain model groups by introducing cardinality constraints.

5.3.1 Hierarchy

XML documents have a clear hierarchical structure. There is a root element that has child elements that in turn can have other child elements, and so on. Additionally, each element may be decorated with attributes.

On the schema level, two types of elements can be defined:

- The first element definition specifies the root element for all document instances.
- Subsequent element declarations on the schema level are used to specify global elements. They may or may not appear in instance documents, and will certainly not appear in root position. Instead, this set of element definitions acts as a kind of local library for element definitions.

Readers will find this concept similar to the definition of a document structure with DTDs, where all element definitions happen on the global level. Typically, we define elements that occur in several places as global elements to avoid

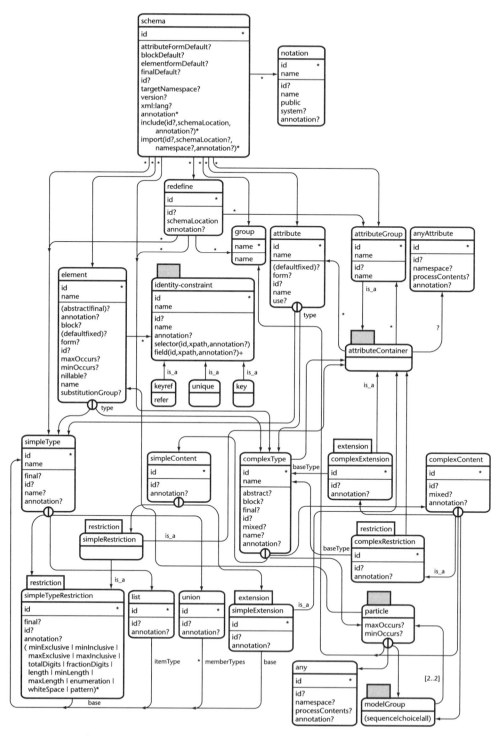

Figure 5.3 The XML Schema metamodel. The relationships between the different syntactical elements of a schema definition are complex, indeed.

redundant local definitions. Also, global element definitions can be used to specify recursive element structures. Section 5.3.12 discusses global elements in more detail.

5.3.2 Elements and Complex Types

Elements are defined in XML Schema with the `element` clause:

Name	Attributes	Contains
element	(abstract | final)?	annotation?
	block?	(simpleType | complexType)?
	(default | fixed)?	(unique | key | keyref)*
	form?	
	id?	
	maxOccurs?	
	minOccurs?	
	(name | ref)	
	nillable?	
	substitutionGroup?	
	type?	

All these attributes and child elements of the element clause will be discussed in the following sections. Let's begin with the most basic ones. The required attribute `name` defines the name of the element (the tag):

```
<xs:element name="location"/>
```

Optionally, each element definition can include a type specification. This can be a simple type, as discussed in Section 5.2. The `type` attribute can refer to a built-in type or to a user-defined type. In the following example we refer to the built-in type `normalizedString`. (The prefix `xs:` was defined as a prefix for the XML Schema namespace—see Section 6.1.)

```
<xs:element name="location" type="xs:normalizedString"/>
```

Where there is a simple type there must also be a complex type. Indeed, the `complexType` declaration in XML Schema is used to aggregate several XML elements and attributes into a single data type. Consequently, each node in an XML document has a data type—whether explicitly defined or not. Leaf nodes—elements without child elements and attributes, and attributes—adhere to a simple data type, while all other nodes are of a complex type.

Name	Attributes	Contains
complexType	abstract?	annotation?
	block?	simpleContent
	final?	complexContent
	id?	(group | all | choice | sequence)?
	mixed?	(attribute | attributeGroup)*
	name?	anyAttribute?

Complex types are always user-defined types with one notable exception: The built-in type xs:anyType is a generic complex type, to which all other complex types are subtypes. Complex types can be defined at a global level, or locally as implicit data types. Here is an example for such a local type definition:

```
<xs:element name = "period">
  <xs:complexType>
    <xs:sequence>
      <xs:element name="from" type="xs:date"/>
      <xs:element name="to" type="xs:date"/>
    </xs:sequence>
  </xs:complexType>
</xs:element>
```

Here is the equivalent DTD (ignoring type declarations):

```
<!ELEMENT period (from, to)>
<!ELEMENT from (#PCDATA)>
<!ELEMENT to (#PCDATA)>
```

In this example, the complex type consists of a *particle*—a complex structure containing child elements. (The next section will discuss particles in detail.) There are several content models for complex types:

- *Particles* define child element structures.
- *Simple content* relates to a simple data type that can be extended by local definitions.
- *Complex content* relates to an earlier defined complex data type or to the built-in data type xs:anyType. This complex type can then be restricted by local definitions.

All of these content models can contain attribute definitions. Section 5.3.11 discusses the definition of attributes.

Even in the case when an element contains only a single child element, it must be defined via a complex type with a particle (see next section). Since particles are defined via connectors (sequence, choice, all), we have to define a rather meaningless connector—in this example xs:sequence. Semantically it does not matter which one you choose, but for reasons of style, select xs:sequence.

```
<xs:element name="influence">
  <xs:complexType>
    <xs:sequence>
      <xs:element name="influencedBy" type="xs:NMTOKEN"/>
    </xs:sequence>
  </xs:complexType>
</xs:element>
```

5.3.3 Particles and Model Groups

In the example above we defined a particle consisting of a sequence of elements. XML Schema defines a particle as one of the following:

- an element declaration (see Section 5.3.2)
- a wildcard (see Section 5.3.15)
- a model group

In addition, particles can have a cardinality constraint (see Section 5.3.4) specified with minOccurs and maxOccurs.

Model Groups

Model groups are similar to DTD model groups, but the syntax is completely different and there is a new connector. Model groups can be constructed using three kinds of *connectors*:

- sequence
- all
- choice

The xs:sequence connector has the following child nodes:

Name	Attributes	Contains
sequence	id?	annotation?
	maxOccurs?	(element | group | choice | sequence | any)*
	minOccurs?	

This connector has the same semantics as the , connector in an XML DTD or the , operator in a regular expression (see Section 1.7). It specifies an ordered sequence of elements—that is, it requires that instance documents adhering to this schema always use elements in the prescribed sequence. Given the schema fragment

```
<xs:element name = "period">
  <xs:complexType>
    <xs:sequence>
      <xs:element name="from" type="xs:date"/>
      <xs:element name="to" type="xs:date"/>
    </xs:sequence>
  </xs:complexType>
</xs:element>
```

the following instance fragment is valid

```
<period>
  <from>1917-05-23</from>
  <to>1918-11-05</to>
</period>
```

but not

```
<period>
  <to>1918-11-05</to>
  <from>1917-05-23</from>
</period>
```

The xs:all connector has the following child nodes:

Name	Attributes	Contains
all	id?	annotation?
	maxOccurs?	element*
	minOccurs?	

This connector has no equivalent in the XML DTD, but it has the same semantics as the & connector in an SGML DTD or the & operator in a regular expression (see Section 1.7). It does not require a particular order of elements in the document instance—it specifies a *bag* of elements. Given the schema fragment

```
<xs:element name = "performedAt">
  <xs:complexType>
    <xs:all>
      <xs:element name = "location"
                  type = "xs:normalizedString"/>
      <xs:element name = "time" type = "xs:dateTime"/>
    </xs:all>
  </xs:complexType>
</xs:element>
```

both of the following instance fragments are correct:

```
<performedAt>
  <location>Dixie Park</location>
  <time>1910-03-27T17:15:00</time>
</performedAt>
```

```
<performedAt>
  <time>1910-03-27T17:15:00</time>
  <location>Dixie Park</location>
</performedAt>
```

But this is not correct:

```
<performedAt>
  <time>1910-03-27T17:15:00</time>
</performedAt>
```

As you can see, XML Schema makes it easy to specify unordered sequences. With the DTD we had to resort to specifying alternatives of all possible permutations of the child elements, a quite laborious process.

> **Note:** When nesting particles, there is one restriction with the xs:all connector. The xs:all connector cannot directly contain other connectors (but it may contain other complex elements constructed with other connectors). It also may not be a child element of other connectors. This is to avoid nondeterministic expressions and keep parsers simple (see also Sections 5.3.4 and 5.3.18).

The following example is invalid for two reasons: (1) The all connector is the child of an xs:sequence connector, and (2) the all connector contains an xs:choice connector.

```
<xs:complexType>
  <xs:sequence>
    <xs:all>
      <xs:choice>
        ...
      </xs:choice>
    </xs:all>
  </xs:sequence>
</xs:complexType>
```

The `xs:choice` connector has the following child nodes:

Name	Attributes	Contains
sequence	id	annotation?
	maxOccurs	(element | group | choice | sequence | any)*
	minOccurs	

This connector has the same semantics as the | connector in an XML DTD or the | operator in a regular expression (see Section 1.7). It specifies alternatives of elements—that is, it requires that the instance documents use only one element out of the defined list. Given the schema fragment

```
<xs:element name = "message">
  <xs:complexType>
    <xs:choice>
      <xs:element name="from" type="xs:string"/>
      <xs:element name="to" type="xs:string"/>
    </xs:choice>
  </xs:complexType>
</xs:element>
```

the following instance fragments are possible:

```
<message>
  <from>John</from>
</message>

<message>
  <to>John</to>
</message>
```

But this is not possible:

```
<message>
  <from>John</from>
  <to>John</to>
</message>
```

Here is the equivalent DTD:

```
<!ELEMENT message (from | to)>
<!ELEMENT from (#PCDATA)>
<!ELEMENT to (#PCDATA)>
```

The xs:sequence and xs:choice connectors can be nested to create complex element structures. For example:

```
<xs:element name = "collaborationContext">
  <xs:complexType>
    <xs:choice>
      <xs:sequence>
        <xs:element name="from" type="xs:date"/>
        <xs:element name="to" type="xs:date"/>
      </xs:sequence>
      <xs:sequence>
        <xs:element name="location"
                    type="xs:normalizedString"/>
        <xs:element name="time" type="xs:dateTime"/>
      </xs:sequence>
      <xs:sequence>
        <xs:element name="time" type="xs:dateTime"/>
        <xs:element name="location"
                    type="xs:normalizedString"/>
      </xs:sequence>
    </xs:choice>
  </xs:complexType>
</xs:element>
```

Here is the equivalent DTD fragment (ignoring type declarations):

```
<!ELEMENT collaborationContext
          ((from, to) | (location, time) | (time, location))>
<!ELEMENT from (#PCDATA)>
<!ELEMENT to (#PCDATA)>
<!ELEMENT location (#PCDATA)>
<!ELEMENT time (#PCDATA)>
<!ELEMENT time (#PCDATA)>
<!ELEMENT location (#PCDATA)>
```

Here, we have defined an alternative that consists either of a sequence of from and to elements, or of a bag of location and time elements. Note that we have resolved the bag into two xs:sequence connectors, as it is not allowed to define an xs:all connector inside an xs:choice connector.

The following instance fragments would be possible:

```
<collaborationContext>
  <period>
    <from>1917-05-23</from>
    <to>1918-11-05</to>
  </period>
</collaborationContext>


<collaborationContext>
  <performedAt>
    <location>Dixie Park</location>
    <time>1910-03-27T17:15:00</time>
  </performedAt>
</collaborationContext>


<collaborationContext>
  <performedAt>
    <time>1910-03-27T17:15:00</time>
    <location>Dixie Park</location>
  </performedAt>
</collaborationContext>
```

Note: For a discussion of nondeterministic choice groups, see Section 5.3.18.

5.3.4 Cardinality Constraints

Cardinality constraints can be applied to particles. A particle is either an element, a wildcard (see Section 5.3.15), or a model group:

- minOccurs defines the minimum of occurrences of the particular element or particle.
- maxOccurs defines the maximum of occurrences of the particular element or particle.

Obviously, the following constraints apply for the values of minOccurs and maxOccurs:

```
0 <= minOccurs
0 <= maxOccurs
minOccurs <= maxOccurs
```

A special "unbounded" value for maxOccurs allows an unlimited number of occurrences. For both minOccurs and maxOccurs the default value is 1; so, if neither is specified, an element or particle has to appear once and only once. Compared to the cardinality operators available in DTDs (+, ?, *), the combination of minOccurs and maxOccurs offers advanced functionality (see Table 5.3).

Note: A maxOccurs value greater than 1 is not allowed for elements that contain an xs:all connector, or for elements contained in an xs:all connector. This is to avoid nondeterministic expressions (see also Section 5.3.3).

Table 5.3 Cardinality constraints in XML Schema and DTD.

XML Schema		DTD	
minOccurs	**maxOccurs**	**Cardinality Operator**	**Description**
1	1	None	Single element required
1	Unbounded	+	Multiple elements, at least one required
0	1	?	Optional single element
0	Unbounded	*	Multiple elements, optional
n	m	No equivalent	At least n elements, at most m elements
n	Unbounded	No equivalent	At least n elements
0	0	No equivalent	No element

For example, this album has exactly one title and one or several tracks:

```
<xs:element name = "album">
  <xs:complexType>
    <xs:sequence>
      <xs:element name="title" type="xs:string"/>
      <xs:element name="track" type="xs:string" maxOccurs="unbounded"/>
    </xs:sequence>
  </xs:complexType>
</xs:element>
```

Here is the equivalent DTD fragment:

```
<!ELEMENT album (title, track+)>
<!ELEMENT title (#PCDATA)>
<!ELEMENT track (#PCDATA)>
```

5.3.5 Default Values and Fixed Values

DTDs allow us to define default values and fixed values for attributes. In contrast to DTDs, XML Schema allows us to define default values and fixed values for elements, too. This is done via the attributes default and fixed. For example:

```
<xs:element name="kind"
            type="xs:NMTOKEN"
            default="instrumentalist"/>
<xs:element name="version"
            type="xs:decimal"
            fixed="1.0"/>
```

Note that these schema declarations modify—just like the DTD default and fixed values—the content of the instance document. The content seen by a schema-aware application is different from the content seen by a non-schema-aware application parser.

5.3.6 Mixed Content

By default, an element of complex type must only contain attributes and child elements, but no other content, such as text. To allow mixed content—content consisting of child elements and text—we specify the attribute mixed="true" in a complexType declaration. This method of declaring mixed content for an element is superior to the mixed content declaration in a DTD: We can control not only the number and types of child elements but also their sequence, with the help of an xs:sequence connector. If we do not want to control the sequence, we just use an xs:all connector instead. In fact, we may use an arbitrary complex particle consisting of several nested connectors in connection with the mixed declaration.

The following example instance document shows a typical mixed content element description:

```
<description>The album <albumTitle>Truth is Marching In</albumTitle>
from the <performer>Albert Ayler Quintet</performer> consists of
<noOfTracks>2</noOfTracks> tracks: <trackNo>1</trackNo> -
<trackTitle>Truth is marching In</trackTitle>, <trackNo>2</trackNo> -
<trackTitle>Our Prayer</trackTitle>.</description>
```

We can define such an element type with the following specification:

```
<xs:element name="description">
  <xs:complexType mixed="true">
    <xs:sequence>
      <xs:element name="albumTitle" type="xs:string"/>
      <xs:element name="performer" type="xs:string"/>
      <xs:element name="noOfTracks" type="xs:positiveInteger"/>
      <xs:sequence maxOccurs="unbounded">
       <xs:element name="trackNo" type="xs:positiveInteger"/>
        <xs:element name="trackTitle" type="xs:string"/>
      </xs:sequence>
    </xs:sequence>
  </xs:complexType>
</xs:element>
```

Here is the equivalent DTD fragment (ignoring type declarations):

```
<!ELEMENT description (#PCDATA | albumTitle | performer | noOfTracks |
                      (trackNo, trackTitle)+)*>
<!ELEMENT albumTitle (#PCDATA)>
<!ELEMENT performer (#PCDATA)>
<!ELEMENT noOfTracks (#PCDATA)>
<!ELEMENT trackNo (#PCDATA)>
<!ELEMENT trackTitle (#PCDATA)>
```

In this example, we have defined a header consisting of album title, performer, and number of tracks, followed by a repeating group consisting of track number and track title. All the defined elements must appear in the prescribed order, but because we have specified `mixed="true"`, arbitrary text may be interspersed between the elements. Without this declaration the document instance fragment would have to look like this:

```
<description>
  <albumTitle>Truth is Marching In</albumTitle>
  <performer>Albert Ayler Quintet</performer>
  <noOfTracks>2</noOfTracks>
  <trackNo>1</trackNo>
  <trackTitle>Truth is marching In</trackTitle>
  <trackNo>2</trackNo>
  <trackTitle>Our Prayer</trackTitle>
</description>
```

5.3.7 Simple Content

Simple content definitions refer to existing simple data types, as discussed in Section 5.2 (built-in or user defined), via an extension or restriction clause. They are usually used to define leaf elements that may contain attributes (see Section 5.3.11).

Name	Attributes	Contains
simpleContent	id?	annotation?
		(restriction | extension)

Name	Attributes	Contains
extension	base	annotation?
	id?	(attribute | attributeGroup)*
		anyAttribute?

Name	Attributes	Contains
restriction	base	annotation?
	id?	simpleType?
		(minExclusive | minInclusive | maxExclusive | maxInclusive | totalDigits | fractionDigits | length | minLength | maxLength | enumeration | whiteSpace | pattern)*
		(attribute | attributeGroup)*
		anyAttribute?

Here is an example of a simple content definition:

```
<xs:complexType name="weight">
 <xs:simpleContent>
  <xs:extension base="xs:nonNegativeInteger">
   <xs:attribute name="unit" type="xs:NMTOKEN"/>
  </xs:extension>
 </xs:simpleContent>
</xs:complexType>
```

5.3.8 Complex Content

Complex content definitions refer to existing complex data types (user defined or the only built-in complex data type, xs:anyType) via an extension or restriction clause. They are usually used to exploit existing complex type definitions (see also Section 6.2) and to define empty elements (see Section 5.3.10). A type extension can be used to add extra particles and/or attributes to a base type.

Name	Attributes	Contains
complexContent	id?	annotation?
	mixed?	(restriction | extension)

Name	Attributes	Contains
extension	base	annotation?
	id?	(group | all | choice | sequence)?
		(attribute | attributeGroup)*
		anyAttribute?

Name	Attributes	Contains
restriction	base	annotation?
	id?	(group | all | choice | sequence)?
		(attribute | attributeGroup)*
		anyAttribute?

Note: The new definition describes a superset of instances compared to the base type only if the particles and attributes that are added (or all elements contained in those particles) are optional. In this case, the instances of the base type are represented by the new type definition, too. This means that not every extended type is a supertype of the base type.

Given the following type definition,

```
<xs:complexType name="tPeriod">
  <xs:sequence>
    <xs:element name="from" type="xs:date"/>
    <xs:element name="to" type="xs:date"/>
  </xs:sequence>
</xs:complexType>
```

we add an optional mode element to the complex type definition named tPeriod:

```
<xs:complexType name="tPeriodWithMode">
 <xs:complexContent>
  <xs:extension base="tPeriod">
   <xs:sequence>
    <xs:element name="mode" type="xs:normalizedString" minOccurs="0"/>
   </xs:sequence>
  </xs:extension>
 </xs:complexContent>
</xs:complexType>
```

The result would be equivalent to the following type definition:

```
<xs:complexType name="tPeriodWithMode">
  <xs:sequence>
    <xs:element name="from" type="xs:date"/>
    <xs:element name="to" type="xs:date"/>
    <xs:element name="mode" type="xs:normalizedString" minOccurs="0"/>
  </xs:sequence>
</xs:complexType>
```

Because the new element is optional (minOccurs="0"), the definition covers all instances of the original type tPeriod, too. If the new element were not defined as optional, the extension would not be a supertype, because the new instance set would not cover the instances of the original type definition.

Note that additional elements are always added at the end of a child element sequence. XML Schema does not provide a way to specify a particular position where a new element should be inserted.

In contrast, the restriction clause can be used to add constraints to a component. Given the original type definition,

```
<xs:complexType name="tPersonName">
 <xs:sequence>
  <xs:element name="first" type="xs:string" maxOccurs="unbounded"/>
  <xs:element name="middle" type="xs:string" minOccurs="0"/>
  <xs:element name="last" type="xs:string"/>
 </xs:sequence>
</xs:complexType>
```

the following definition describes a subset of the original instance set (only those names with a single first name and no middle name):

```
<xs:complexType name="tPersonNameWithOnlyOneFirstName">
 <xs:complexContent>
  <xs:restriction base="tPersonName">
   <xs:sequence>
    <xs:element name="first" maxOccurs="1"/>
    <xs:element name="last"/>
   </xs:sequence>
  </xs:restriction>
 </xs:complexContent>
</xs:complexType>
```

Here, the definition of maxOccurs="1" is essential because we wish to override the maxOccurs="unbounded" value.

Actually, the original type definition of

```
<xs:complexType name="tPersonName">
 <xs:sequence>
  <xs:element name="first" type="xs:string" maxOccurs="unbounded"/>
  <xs:element name="middle" type="xs:string" minOccurs="0"/>
  <xs:element name="last" type="xs:string"/>
 </xs:sequence>
</xs:complexType>
```

is only an abbreviated form of

```
<xs:complexType name="tPersonName">
 <xs:complexContent>
  <xs:restriction base="xs:anyType">
```

```
    <xs:sequence>
     <xs:element name="first" type="xs:string" maxOccurs="unbounded"/>
     <xs:element name="middle" type="xs:string" minOccurs="0"/>
     <xs:element name="last" type="xs:string"/>
    </xs:sequence>
   </xs:restriction>
  </xs:complexContent>
</xs:complexType>
```

Any complex type in XML Schema is a restriction of the only built-in complex type in XML Schema: xs:anyType.

5.3.9 Type Hierarchies

Extension and restriction applied on complex elements result in type *definition* hierarchies. This should not be misunderstood as a type hierarchy in terms of subtypes and supertypes. Although deriving a complex type A from another complex type B by restriction always results in a true type hierarchy (A being a subtype of B), this cannot be said for type extension. A type obtained by extension is a supertype of the original type only if the added features (elements and attributes) are optional (minOccurs="0"). This is a must if we want to keep the extended schema compatible with existing document instances. Table 5.4 shows under which conditions a type derivation results in a subtype/supertype relation.

On the other hand, many supertypes cannot be derived by type extension. For example, it is not possible to insert an optional child element into a sequence of elements at any position other than the end of the sequence. It is also not possible to add alternatives to elements (that is, replace an element with a choice group).

5.3.10 Empty Elements

Unlike the DTD, XML Schema does not have an explicit notation for empty elements. Instead, the complex content clause can be used for that purpose:

```
<xs:element name="track">
 <xs:complexType>
  <xs:complexContent>
   <xs:restriction base="xs:anyType">
    <xs:attribute name="title" type="xs:string"/>
```

Table 5.4 Constraints for complex type restriction.

Constraint	Supertype	Subtype	Remarks
Default value	No default value	Default value defined	Defining a default value for a child element or attribute excludes those instances that do not contain this element or attribute.
Fixed value	No fixed value	Fixed value defined	Defining a fixed value for a child element or attribute excludes those instances where this element or attribute does contain a different value.
Type	No type declaration	Type defined	No type declaration is equivalent to ur-type in XML Schema. Any type in XML Schema is a subtype of the ur-type.
	Type A defined	Type B defined, and B is subtype of A	
Cardinality [minOccurs, maxOccurs]	[n1,m1]	[n2,m2] with n1 <= n2 and m2 < m1 or n1 < n2 and m2 <= m1	The narrower range [n2,m2] excludes instances that violate that range but are well within the [n1,m1] range.

```
    <xs:attribute name="duration" type="xs:duration"/>
   </xs:restriction>
  </xs:complexContent>
 </xs:complexType>
</xs:element>
```

We use the built-in complex type xs:anyType as a base type. We restrict this generic base type to the two attributes title and duration. These definitions result in valid instance fragments such as

```
<track title="Off Minor" duration="PT3M08S"/>
```

As we saw in Section 5.3.8, we can abbreviate this restriction to xs:anyType with the following, preferred construct:

```
<xs:element name="track">
  <xs:complexType>
    <xs:attribute name="title" type="xs:string"/>
    <xs:attribute name="duration" type="xs:duration"/>
  </xs:complexType>
</xs:element>
```

Here is the equivalent DTD (ignoring type declarations):

```
<!ELEMENT track EMPTY>
<!ATTLIST track
        title CDATA #IMPLIED
        duration CDATA #IMPLIED >
```

The same element without attributes

```
<track/>
```

would have the following definition:

```
<xs:element name="track">
 <xs:complexType>
  <xs:complexContent>
   <xs:restriction base="xs:anyType">
   </xs:restriction>
  </xs:complexContent>
 </xs:complexType>
</xs:element>
```

This can be abbreviated to

```
<xs:element name="track">
 <xs:complexType/>
</xs:element>
```

Here is the equivalent DTD:

```
<!ELEMENT track EMPTY>
```

5.3.11 Attributes

Attributes can be added to all content models: particles, simple content, and complex content. Attributes are defined with the xs:attribute clause.

Name	Attributes	Contains
attribute	(default | fixed)?	annotation?
	form?	simpleType?
	id?	
	(name | ref)	
	type?	
	use?	

This clause always contains the definition of the attribute name. Optionally, it can define a type (simple types only) and can contain a use clause and a default or fixed value definition. The use clause can have the values required, optional, and prohibited.

```
<xs:element name="track">
  <xs:complexType>
    <xs:simpleContent>
      <xs:extension base="xs:normalizedString">
        <xs:attribute name="duration"
                      type="xs:duration"
                      use="required"/>
      </xs:extension>
    </xs:simpleContent>
  </xs:complexType>
</xs:element>
```

Here is the equivalent DTD fragment (ignoring type declarations):

```
<!ELEMENT track (#PCDATA)>
<!ATTLIST track
      duration CDATA #REQUIRED >
```

In this example, we have defined duration as an attribute of track. The type was set to the built-in type xs:duration and the use clause to required, meaning that this attribute must be specified in instance documents. A valid instance of this element would be

```
<track duration="PT3M08S">Off Minor</track>
```

If a type has multiple attributes, the sequence of their definition does not matter, as the attribute nodes of an element form an unordered set (see Section 4.2.4).

Unlike elements, attributes cannot be placed into model groups. The consequence is that we do not have the ability to define elements with mutually exclusive attributes. For example, we might want to define an element person that either has an attribute age or an attribute birthDate. The only option is to define a choice group with two local person elements: one with the attribute age, the other with the attribute birthDate—or even better, to implement both birthDate and age as elements! In Chapter 7 we will see how Relax NG deals with this problem.

5.3.12 Global and Local Types

Both simple types and complex types can be defined on a global level, that is, on the schema level. Such types must be named. This makes it possible to refer to these type definitions when they are used locally. For example,

```
<xs:simpleType name="material">
  <xs:restriction base="xs:string">
    <xs:enumeration value="brass"/>
    <xs:enumeration value="wood"/>
  </xs:restriction>
</xs:simpleType>
```

or

```
<xs:complexType name="tPeriod">
  <xs:sequence>
    <xs:element name="from" type="xs:date"/>
    <xs:element name="to" type="xs:date"/>
  </xs:sequence>
</xs:complexType>
```

Typically, we define global types when these type definitions are used in several places. We can refer to such type definitions in element definitions and in extension and restriction clauses:

```
<xs:element name="period" type="tPeriod"/>
```

or

```
<xs:extension base="tPeriod">
...
</xs:extension>
```

or

```
<xs:restriction base="tPeriod">
...
</xs:restriction>
```

Global types can be defined as abstract using the clause `abstract="true"`. Such types cannot be used for type designation in element definitions, but can only be used to derive other types via extension or restriction. This can be done either within the schema or in the document instance with an `xsi:type` declaration (see Section 6.2.4).

On the other hand, it is possible to declare a global type as final using the attribute `final`. This attribute may specify `"restriction"`, `"extension"`, or `"#all"` as a value. If `"restriction"` is specified, it is not possible to derive other types by restriction. Similarly, `"extension"` means it is not possible to derive other types by extension, and `"#all"`, to derive other types by any method.

5.3.13 Global Elements and Attributes

Similar to types, elements and attributes may also be defined on a global level. Global elements and attributes are defined on the schema level following the definition of the document root element. Again, the definition of global elements and attributes makes sense when we want to refer to this definition from several places.

In the following schema we define a global element `title` after the definition of root element `jazzMusician`:

```
<?xml version="1.0" encoding="UTF-8"?>
<xs:schema ...>
  <xs:element name = "jazzMusician">

  ...

  </xs:element>
<!--Global element definition begin here -->
  <xs:element name = "title" type = "xs:string"/>
</xs:schema>
```

When we want to reuse this definition we simply use an element reference like this:

```
<xs:element ref="title">
```

Global definition is the only way to define an element in a DTD. This has drawbacks: It is impossible to define elements with the same name but of different types in different contexts.

5.3.14 Recursive Structures

Global definition of elements is one way in XML Schema to define recursive element structures. For example,

```
<xs:element name = "part">
  <xs:complexType>
    <xs:sequence>
      <xs:element name="productNo" type="xs:token"/>
      <xs:element ref="part" minOccurs="0" maxOccurs="unbounded"/>
    </xs:sequence>
  </xs:complexType>
</xs:element>
```

defines a recursive tree of part elements. Because the child element definition refers to the containing element, the containing element must be defined as a global element.

Here is the equivalent DTD fragment (ignoring type declarations):

```
<!ELEMENT part (productNo, part*)>
<!ELEMENT productNo (#PCDATA)>
```

This technique has a disadvantage: It is not possible to define context-specific recursive element structures. For example, if we want two different part trees—one allowing mixed content, the other not allowing mixed content—and we want to use them in the same document, we have a problem. However, it is relatively easy to define context-specific recursions by using the group construct, discussed in detail in Section 6.2.2. Groups are defined on a global level and can refer to themselves and thus establish recursive structures. Nothing stops us from defining several recursive groups with different layouts and referencing them from context-specific but equally named elements:

```
<xs:group name="gDetailedListPart">
 <xs:sequence>
  <xs:element ref="productNo"/>
  <xs:element name="part" maxOccurs="unbounded" minOccurs="0">
   <xs:complexType>
    <xs:sequence>
```

```
        <xs:group ref="gDetailedListPart"/>
      </xs:sequence>
    </xs:complexType>
  </xs:element>
  <xs:element name="details" type="xs:string"/>
 </xs:sequence>
</xs:group>

<xs:group name="gShortListPart">
 <xs:sequence>
  <xs:element ref="productNo"/>
  <xs:element name="part" maxOccurs="unbounded" minOccurs="0">
   <xs:complexType>
    <xs:sequence>
      <xs:group ref="gShortListPart"/>
    </xs:sequence>
   </xs:complexType>
  </xs:element>
 </xs:sequence>
</xs:group>

<xs:element name="productNo" type="xs:string"/>
```

Here, we have defined two recursive groups gDetailedListPart and gShort-
ListPart. Note that element productNo is defined as a global element because it
has an identical definition in both groups. We can now set up a root element
containing two different lists in different contexts, but both lists are constructed from elements with tag part (see Figure 5.4).

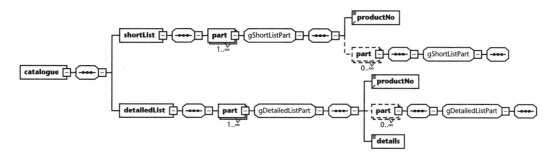

Figure 5.4 Two context-specific recursive lists constructed via groups.

```
<xs:element name="catalogue">
  <xs:complexType>
    <xs:sequence>
      <xs:element name="shortList">
        <xs:complexType>
          <xs:sequence>
            <xs:element name="part" maxOccurs="unbounded">
              <xs:complexType>
                <xs:group ref="gShortListPart"/>
              </xs:complexType>
            </xs:element>
          </xs:sequence>
        </xs:complexType>
      </xs:element>
      <xs:element name="detailedList">
        <xs:complexType>
          <xs:sequence>
            <xs:element name="part" maxOccurs="unbounded">
              \xs:complexType>
                <xs:group ref="gDetailedListPart"/>
              </xs:complexType>
            </xs:element>
          </xs:sequence>
        </xs:complexType>
      </xs:element>
    </xs:sequence>
  </xs:complexType>
</xs:element>
```

Used in this way, groups work similarly to non-terminal symbols in grammars—their names do not appear in instance documents. Consequently, by using group constructs, we should be able to express any schema that can be described by a regular grammar. This is not possible with DTDs!

Here is a valid instance document. (For an explanation of the namespace attributes in the xs:schema clause, see Section 6.1.)

```
<catalogue xmlns:xsi="http://www.w3.org/2001/XMLSchema-instance"
           xsi:noNamespaceSchemaLocation="catalogue.xsd">
```

```
<shortList>
  <part>
    <productNo>234</productNo>
    <part>
      <productNo>345</productNo>
    </part>
  </part>
  <part>
    <productNo>5467</productNo>
  </part>
</shortList>
<detailedList>
  <part>
    <productNo>234</productNo>
    <details>speaker</details>
  </part>
  <part>
    <productNo>345</productNo>
    <part>
      <productNo>5467</productNo>
      <details>valve</details>
    </part>
    <details>amplifier</details>
  </part>
</detailedList>
</catalogue>
```

XML Schema wouldn't be XML Schema if it did not offer at least two solutions to a problem. Another way to define recursive structures in XML Schema is via global complex types. We want to create two part lists—one containing part elements with mixed content, the other containing part elements without mixed content. To do so we define two different types tPart and tPartMixed that introduce part elements of different types locally. These part elements refer recursively to the previously defined type declarations.

Here is the definition of a recursive part structure without mixed content:

```
<xs:complexType name="tPart">
  <xs:sequence>
```

```
    <xs:element name="name" type="xs:string"/>
    <xs:element name="price" type="xs:decimal"/>
    <xs:element name="part" type="tPart"
               minOccurs="0" maxOccurs="unbounded"/>
  </xs:sequence>
</xs:complexType>
```

The definition for the recursive part structure with mixed content looks quite similar:

```
<xs:complexType name="tPartMixed" mixed="true">
  <xs:sequence>
    <xs:element name="name" type="xs:token"/>
    <xs:element name="price" type="xs:decimal"/>
    <xs:element name="part" type="tPartMixed"
               minOccurs="0" maxOccurs="unbounded"/>
  </xs:sequence>
</xs:complexType>
```

We can then use both type definitions to define local part elements that are recursive but have a different type (see Figure 5.5):

```
<xs:element name="root">
  <xs:complexType>
    <xs:sequence>
      <xs:element name="partsWithoutText">
        <xs:complexType>
          <xs:sequence>
            <xs:element name="part"
                       type="tPart" maxOccurs="unbounded"/>
          </xs:sequence>
        </xs:complexType>
      </xs:element>
      <xs:element name="partsWithText">
        <xs:complexType>
          <xs:sequence>
            <xs:element name="part"
                       type="tPartMixed" maxOccurs="unbounded"/>
```

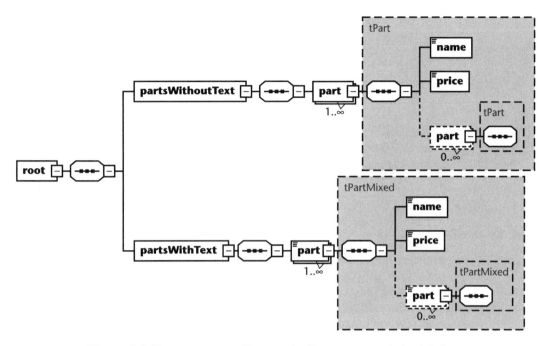

Figure 5.5 Two context-specific recursive lists constructed via global types.

```
        </xs:sequence>
       </xs:complexType>
      </xs:element>
     </xs:sequence>
    </xs:complexType>
  </xs:element>
```

Now we can define a document instance that can contain both types of part elements nested in unlimited depth:

```
<root>
  <partsWithoutText>
    <part>
      <name>mouthpiece</name>
      <price>130</price>
      <part>
        <name>reed</name>
        <price>2</price>
      </part>
    </part>
```

```
    <part>
      <name>body</name>
      <price>1500</price>
    </part>
  </partsWithoutText>
  <partsWithText>
    <part>The part<name>mouthpiece</name>costs<price>130</price>
    and contains: <part>The part<name>reed</name>costs<price>2</price>
    </part></part>
    <part>The part<name>body</name>costs<price>1500</price></part>
  </partsWithText>
</root>
```

5.3.15 Wildcards

A wildcard (an element or attribute of no further specified content) can be declared with the XML Schema elements <xs:any/> or <xs:anyAttribute/>.

Name	Attributes	Contains
any	id?	annotation?
	maxOccurs?	
	minOccurs?	
	processContents?	

Name	Attributes	Contains
anyAttribute	id?	annotation?
	namespace?	
	processContents?	

Using wildcards allows for the inclusion of elements and attributes from foreign schemata and namespaces (see Section 6.1.3). In this way, sections of XHTML, SVG, RDF, or other content could be included in a document. For example:

```
<xs:element name="description">
  <xs:complexType>
    <xs:sequence>
      <xs:any processContents="skip"/>
    </xs:sequence>
  </xs:complexType>
</xs:element>
```

The attributes `namespace` and `processContents` will be explained in Section 6.1.3.

5.3.16 Nullability

DTDs only support the concept of optional elements: An element is either present or absent. Besides allowing optional elements (with `minOccurs="0"`), XML Schema introduces a new concept. Instance elements can be set to "nil" by specifying the attribute `xsi:nil="true"`. (Here, `xsi:` denotes the namespace prefix for XML Schema Instances `http://www.w3.org/2001/XMLSchema-instance`.) In the schema, the attribute

```
<xs:element ... nillable="true"/>
```

declares whether an element is nillable, or not (the default value is "false"). Nilled elements must not have any content, but they are allowed to have attributes!

With the following schema fragment,

```
<xs:element name="bodyPart" nillable="true">
  <xs:complexType>
    <xs:sequence>
      <xs:element name="productNo" type="xs:token"/>
    </xs:sequence>
    <xs:attribute name="color" type="tColorName"/>
  </xs:complexType>
</xs:element>
```

we allow things like colored null values:

```
<bodyPart xsi:nil="true" color="red"/>
<bodyPart color="green">
  <productNo>x93932</productNo>
</bodyPart>
<bodyPart xsi:nil="true" color="blue"/>
```

Exciting!

Note that a nilled element is a new concept: It is neither an absent element (defined via `minOccurs="0"`) nor an empty element (see Section 5.3.10).

In my opinion, the concept of nilled elements is of limited value. It was introduced to improve the compatibility of XML with certain relational database products. However, mapping, for, example, a nullable SQL field to a nillable XML element may work for a specific application, but it is not a general solution. Traditionally, in many applications nullable database fields are already mapped to optional XML elements. So relational null values already have a defined representation in XML (an optional element or attribute). To represent the new nillable elements in object-oriented or relational data models would therefore require a new representation in these applications.

However, the concept makes sense if we wish to express different flavors of nothingness. A value may be absent for different reasons: It could be absent because it represents real nothingness (such as a person without a middle name), because the document author did not know the value (middle name exists, but is unknown), or it could be absent for some technical reasons (server breakdown, for example). These reasons could be coded into the attributes of a nilled element so that appropriate action can be taken.

5.3.17 Uniqueness, Keys, Reference

Similar to the DTDs, XML Schema provides built-in data types ID and IDREF for modeling cross-references between document elements. However, the main purpose of these data types is to provide backward compatibility with existing XML documents.

XML Schema introduces a more flexible concept for keys, key references, and uniqueness with the key, keyref, and unique clauses. These are not hampered by the inherent restrictions of the DTD key concept:

- DTDs do not allow keys to have a specific data type, as keys must be specified with the ID and IDREF data types.
- Elements cannot be declared as keys. Only attributes can be declared as keys with data type ID.
- The data type ID can only define keys that are global for the whole document instance, and therefore must be unique within the scope of the whole document instance.
- ID and IDREF cannot handle composite keys. This may be required when we want to represent relational structures in an XML document. XML Schema allows composite keys. However, it must be noted that using composite keys creates a problem for schema validators: In general, for schemata containing composite keys and key references, it is not possible to determine whether the schema has valid instances [Fan2001].

Unique
The unique clause allows us to define nodes or node combinations that must be unique within a specified scope. This scope is determined by the location where the unique clause is defined.

Name	Attributes	Contains
unique	id?	annotation?
	name	selector
		field+

Name	Attributes	Contains
selector	id?	annotation?
	xpath	

Name	Attributes	Contains
field	id?	annotation?
	xpath	

The name attribute identifies the unique constraint. It can be referenced in a keyref clause (discussed shortly).

The selector element defines in its xpath attribute the document element to which the unique constraint applies. This is done with an XPath expression relative to the location where the unique clause was defined.

Similarly, the field elements (there can be several) define in their xpath attributes which combination of fields constitutes a unique value. Nodes within such a combination may have various data types, such as string, decimal, float, and so on. Here, the XPath expression is relative to the element specified in the selector clause.

The XPath syntax is described fully in [Clark1999]. However, for our purposes, it is sufficient to know that document node hierarchies are expressed by the node names separated by slashes, that attribute names are prefixed with the @ character, that . denotes the current node, and that the choice operator | separates alternative paths.

Let's assume we have a document with a root element album. This root element contains child element track, which in turn contains title elements. We want to make sure that each track has a different title. We must therefore declare the title element as unique. We do so by placing a unique clause into the definition of element track:

```
<xs:element name="album" ...>
  <xs:complexType>
    <xs:sequence>
      <xs:element name="track">
        <xs:complexType>
          <xs:sequence>
```

```
                    <xs:element name="title" type="xs:string"/>
                  </xs:sequence>
                  <xs:attribute name="trackNo" type="xs:short" use="required"/>
                  <xs:attribute name="duration" type="xs:duration"/>
                </xs:complexType>
              </xs:element>
              <xs:element name="sample">
                <xs:complexType>
                  <xs:attribute name="trackRef" type="xs:short"/>
                  <xs:attribute name="mp3" type="xs:anyURI"/>
                </xs:complexType>
              </xs:element>
            </xs:sequence>
          </xs:complexType>

          ...
          <xs:unique name="uniqueTitle">
            <xs:selector xpath="track"/>
            <xs:field xpath="title"/>
          </xs:unique>
        </xs:element>
```

Here we declare the element title as unique within the context of album. That is achieved by placing the xs:unique clause into the scope of element album and by selecting the track element in the xs:selector element of the xs:unique clause. The xpath specification in the field element locates the attribute title relative to the context specified in the xs:selector element.

Key

The key clause allows us to define nodes or node combinations as a primary key within a specified scope. Keys must be unique, too, but they must also be present within the scope where the key clause is defined. Therefore, it does not make sense to define an element that has been declared as a key as optional (minOccurs="0"), nor to define it as nillable.

Name	Attributes	Contains
key	id?	annotation?
	name	selector
		field+

The `name` attribute identifies the `key` constraint. It can be referenced in a `keyref` clause (see next section). The syntax of the `selector` and `key` clauses is the same as for the `unique` specification.

Let's assume we want to refer to `track` elements by their `trackNo` attribute. We place the `key` clause into the scope of the root element `album`:

```
<xs:element name="album" ...>
  ...
  <xs:key name="primaryKeyTrackNo">
    <xs:selector xpath="track"/>
    <xs:field xpath="@trackNo">
  </xs:key>
</xs:element>
```

Keyref

The `keyref` clause allows us to define nodes or node combinations as a foreign key within a specified scope.

Name	Attributes	Contains
keyref	id?	annotation?
	name?	selector
	refer	field+

Again, the syntax of the `selector` and `key` clauses is the same as for the `unique` specification. The `name` attribute is optional and has no defined function.

The attribute `refer` identifies the corresponding `key` or `unique` definition. Yes, you can refer to a `unique` clause! Contrary to a `key` clause, however, the `unique` clause does not guarantee that the reference can be resolved (it allows dangling references).

The type of the `keyref` node (or the combination of types) must match the type (or combination of types) of the corresponding `key` or `unique` definition.

If a document instance contains those nodes that make up a foreign key, it must also contain the document nodes to which the foreign key relates. Otherwise the document would not be valid.

Let's assume our `album` contains a second list, `sample`, where each item refers to an item in the `track` list via its attribute `trackRef`. We could establish a cross-reference between these two lists in the following way:

```
<xs:element name="album" ...>
  ...
  <xs:key name="primaryKeyTrackNo">
    <xs:selector xpath="track"/>
```

```
      <xs:field xpath="@trackNo"/>
    </xs:key>
    <xs:keyref name="foreignKeyISBN" refer="primaryKeyTrackNo">
      <xs:selector xpath="sample"/>
      <xs:field xpath="@trackRef"/>
    </xs:keyref>
  </xs:element>
```

Finally, let's look at a more advanced example. We'll assume our sample element is constructed from a choice group consisting of elements goodSample, badSample, and uglySample. Each of these elements has an attribute trackRef.

How do we construct a foreign key for a choice group? We make use of the XPath choice connector and specify alternate paths in the selector clause. In the following listing we define the complete schema for our album documents. The root element album has two child elements: sample (defined as a global element) and track. The root element also contains a definition for a primary key pkTrack with the selector track and the key field @trackNo. The foreign key is defined with fkSample with the selector sample/goodSample | sample/badSample | sample/uglySample and the key field trackRef.

```
<?xml version="1.0" encoding="UTF-8"?>
<xs:schema xmlns:xs="http://www.w3.org/2001/XMLSchema"
           elementFormDefault="qualified"
           attributeFormDefault="unqualified">
  <xs:element name="album">
   <xs:complexType>
    <xs:sequence>
     <xs:element name="track">
      <xs:complexType>
       <xs:sequence>
        <xs:element name="title" type="xs:string"/>
       </xs:sequence>
       <xs:attribute name="trackNo" type="xs:short" use="required"/>
       <xs:attribute name="duration" type="xs:duration"/>
      </xs:complexType>
     </xs:element>
     <xs:element ref="sample"/>
    </xs:sequence>
   </xs:complexType>
```

```
    <xs:key name="pkTrack">
     <xs:selector xpath="track"/>
     <xs:field xpath="@trackNo"/>
    </xs:key>
    <xs:unique name="uniqueTitle">
      <xs:selector xpath="track"/>
      <xs:field xpath="title"/>
    </xs:unique>
    <xs:keyref name="fkSample" refer="pkTrack">
     <xs:selector
       xpath="sample/goodSample | sample/badSample | sample/uglySample"/>
     <xs:field xpath="@trackRef"/>
    </xs:keyref>
 </xs:element>
  <xs:element name="sample">
   <xs:complexType>
    <xs:choice>
     <xs:element name="goodSample">
      <xs:complexType>
       <xs:attribute name="trackRef" type="xs:short"/>
       <xs:attribute name="mp3" type="xs:anyURI"/>
      </xs:complexType>
     </xs:element>
     <xs:element name="badSample">
      <xs:complexType>
       <xs:attribute name="trackRef" type="xs:short"/>
       <xs:attribute name="mp3" type="xs:anyURI"/>
      </xs:complexType>
     </xs:element>
     <xs:element name="uglySample">
      <xs:complexType>
       <xs:attribute name="trackRef" type="xs:short"/>
       <xs:attribute name="mp3" type="xs:anyURI"/>
      </xs:complexType>
     </xs:element>
    </xs:choice>
```

```
  </xs:complexType>
 </xs:element>
</xs:schema>
```

The following code shows a valid document instance of the schema defined above:

```
<?xml version="1.0" encoding="UTF-8"?>
<album>
 <sample>
  <goodSample trackref="1" mp3="http://www.jazz.org/sampleA.mp3"/>
 </sample>
 <sample>
  <badSample trackref="2"/>
 </sample>
 <track trackNo="1" duration="PTM10S47">
  <title>happy for you</title>
 </track>
 <track trackNo="2" duration="PTM3S13">
  <title>bad feelings</title>
 </track>
</album>
```

> **Note:** This schema could not be expressed as a DTD. The ID/IDREF construct used in DTDs to establish cross-references requires ID and IDREF attributes to have NMTOKEN values. NMTOKEN values, however, must start with a letter. This does not fit with our integer track numbers. In addition, DTDs do not have a `unique` construct.

5.3.18 Deterministic Types

Appendix E of the second edition of the XML 1.0 Recommendation notes that content models *should* be deterministic (unambiguous). This requirement exists for the purpose of compatibility with SGML. SGML parsers may flag a nondeterministic schema as ambiguous. XML Schema also requires content models such as `choice` groups and `all` groups to be deterministic (*Unique Particle Attribution*).

A content model is deterministic if all particles defined in the model can be reduced to a deterministic regular expression (see Section 1.7.6). A regular expression is deterministic if at each choice point it is possible to decide which branch to take without having to look ahead. Let's look at an example:

```
<xs:complexType name="tName">
  <!-- This schema fragment violates the Unique Particle Attribution
constraint! -->
  <xs:choice>
    <xs:sequence>
      <xs:element name="first"/>
      <xs:element name="last"/>
    </xs:sequence>
    <xs:sequence>
      <xs:element name="first"/>
      <xs:element name="middle"/>
      <xs:element name="last"/>
    </xs:sequence>
  </xs:choice>
</xs:complexType>
```

This type definition is not deterministic because both choice branches begin with the same elements. However, the same type can be easily expressed in a deterministic (and more compact) way:

```
<xs:complexType name="tName">
  <xs:sequence>
    <xs:element name="first"/>
    <xs:element name="middle" minOccurs="0"/>
    <xs:element name="last"/>
  </xs:sequence>
</xs:complexType>
```

The Unique Particle Attribution is subject to an ongoing debate. The question is: What is more desirable, efficient parsers or easier schema authoring? Arguably, if somebody should suffer, it should be the machine and not the human. But nondeterminism can cause the parser to suffer very much, indeed, as a look-ahead may stretch across several megabytes. And then it is the end user who suffers because of unacceptable response times.

It is not always possible to make a definition deterministic. The following schema was written to describe a small orchestra consisting of either seven saxophone players or three guitarists. It violates the *Element Declarations Consistent* constraint:

```
<?xml version="1.0" encoding="UTF-8"?>
<xs:schema xmlns:xs="http://www.w3.org/2001/XMLSchema"
           elementFormDefault="qualified"
           attributeFormDefault="unqualified">
  <!-- This schema violates the Element Declarations Consistent
constraint! -->
  <xs:element name="orchestra">
    <xs:complexType>
      <xs:choice>
        <xs:element name="musician" minOccurs="7" maxOccurs="7">
          <xs:complexType>
            <xs:sequence>
              <xs:element name="saxophone"/>
            </xs:sequence>
          </xs:complexType>
        </xs:element>
        <xs:element name="musician" minOccurs="3" maxOccurs="3">
          <xs:complexType>
            <xs:sequence>
              <xs:element name="guitar"/>
            </xs:sequence>
          </xs:complexType>
        </xs:element>
      </xs:choice>
    </xs:complexType>
  </xs:element>
</xs:schema>
```

This structure is nondeterministic because both branches begin with a `musician` tag. There is no way we could refactor this structure into an equivalent nondeterministic structure. In XML Schema, the above schema is illegal: Using an element (`musician`) with different type declarations within the same `choice` clause is not allowed. In such cases we are required to change the document structure, for example, to rename the `musician` elements as `saxophonist` and `guitarist`, or to use a different namespace for each `musician` element.

Authoring XML Schema

Now that you have been introduced to the type system of XML Schema in Chapter 5, we continue our *tour de force* in this chapter. The first section discusses the overall structure of schemata written with XML Schema and how namespaces are handled. The next two sections cover reuse mechanisms and schema composition. (Schema composition is a must if we want to define multi-namespace schemata.) The final section, "Usage Patterns," discusses some best practices for authoring XML schemata with XML Schema.

6.1. NAMESPACES

XML Schema provides full support for XML namespaces (see Section 4.1), so much so that the whole concept of schemata is based on the concept of target namespaces. In addition, schemata can ask their instances to qualify elements and attributes with namespace declarations, and wildcards can be used to include content from foreign namespaces.

6.1.1 Target Namespace

The main mechanism for namespace support with XML Schema is the `target-Namespace` declaration. Each schema file that contains a `targetNamespace` declaration serves as a description of that particular namespace. A schema file may describe only a single namespace, but there can be several schema files for the same target namespace. For example:

```
<xs:schema xmlns:xs="http://www.w3.org/2001/XMLSchema"
           targetNamespace="http://www.jazz.org">
```

As shown in Figure 6.1, the namespace serves as the connecting element between document instances and schemata. For each namespace declared in a document instance, an XML processor will try to find a corresponding schema definition. The document instance may help the XML processor in this process by specifying a schema location. But this is not required, and the XML processor is free to choose a different schema definition, for example, a built-in schema definition (see Section 6.3.2).

It is also possible to define schemata without a target namespace. These schemata can be used to describe unqualified elements (discussed next), or they can be assigned to a namespace when they are used—for example, when they are imported into another schema.

6.1.2 Qualified and Unqualified Names

A schema may ask that the local elements and attributes of its target namespace be specified in qualified or in unqualified form in document instances (see Section 4.1). A document instance has two ways to qualify element and attribute names:

- It can equip elements and attributes with a namespace prefix.
- It can define a default namespace.

A schema can ask for qualified names for each element or attribute individually, using the `form="qualified"` attribute within element and attribute definitions. It can also specify `elementFormDefault="qualified"` or `attributeFormDefault="qualified"` as attributes of the `<schema>` clause. This will ask for qualification of all elements or attributes unless they are specified with `form="unqualified"`.

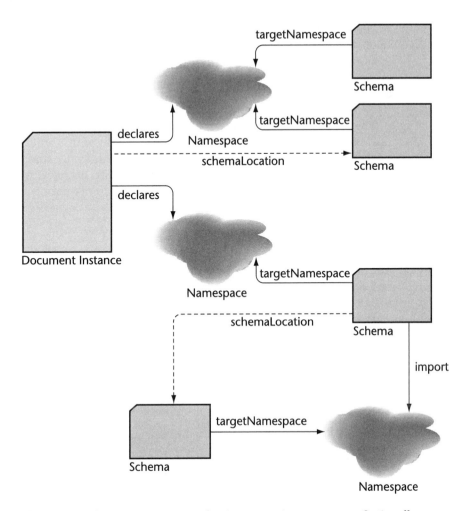

Figure 6.1 Schemata are connected to instances via namespaces. Optionally, an instance may specify a schema location. The same logic applies when a schema imports types from other schemata, as shown in the lower section of this diagram.

Note that these declarations apply only to local elements and attributes, not to global elements (see Section 5.3.13). Global elements must always appear in qualified form in document instances, either qualified by prefix or by using a default namespace. The reason for this is that a processor must be able to locate the schema definition that belongs to an element's namespace. Since local elements always have a global ancestor element, the processor is always able to determine the namespace, because the global ancestor element is always qualified.

However, this can lead to disturbing situations. The combination of `element-FormDefault="unqualified"` and not providing a default namespace in a document instance can make the authoring of document instances difficult. Document authors need to know which elements are defined locally and which elements are defined globally—global elements must be specified with a namespace prefix, while local elements must not be specified with a namespace prefix.

The consequence is: Always use `elementFormDefault="qualified"`. Either decorate both local and global elements consistently with namespace prefixes, or define a default namespace for the document instance and do not prefix local and global elements. Since attributes inherit their in-scope namespaces from their owner elements, it is fine to specify `attributeFormDefault="unqualified"`.

6.1.3 Wildcards

The wildcards `<xs:any/>` and `<xs:anyAttribute/>` are used to declare elements and attributes that can contain content from other namespaces (see Section 5.3.15). This namespace is defined with the attribute `namespace`.

Wildcards can be processed by an XML processor in three ways:

- `processContents="skip"` indicates that there are no constraints regarding the content of the element or attribute. It is sufficient that the content is well formed. An XML processor will not check the content for validity.
- `processContents="lax"` requires that the element or attribute is valid when it is declared. If the processor cannot obtain the corresponding schema definition, the content is not checked.
- `processContents="strict"` requires that the element or attribute is declared in the specified namespace or in the document instance via an `xsi:type` declaration (see Section 6.2.4), and that it is valid. This instruction requires the XML processor to obtain the corresponding schema definition and to perform the necessary checks. This is the default value.

The attribute `namespace` can be used to specify a list of namespace identifiers. This list can contain

- Explicit namespace URIs.
- The string `"##targetNamespace"`. This specifies the target namespace of the current schema.
- The string `"##local"`. This specifies the namespace of the respective document instance.

As an alternative to a list, the following string values can be specified:

- `"##any"`. Any namespace. This is also the default value of the `namespace` attribute. This value is often used together with `processContents="skip"`.
- `"##other"`. Any namespace other than the target namespace.

The following example defines an element `description` that must contain valid XHTML content:

```
<xs:element name="description">
  <xs:complexType>
    <xs:sequence>
      <xs:any namespace="http://www.w3.org/1999/xhtml"
          processContents="strict"/>
    </xs:sequence>
  </xs:complexType>
</xs:element>
```

6.1.4 Schema Default Namespace

Because a schema defined with XML Schema is an XML document, too, it is possible to define a default namespace for the schema itself. This default namespace applies to all elements and attributes used in the schema definition that are not decorated with a namespace prefix. This includes the XML Schema declarations such as `<element>`, `<attribute>`, `<simpleType>`, or `<complexType>`.

Basically, we have three options for assigning a default namespace:

- *Use the target namespace as the default namespace.* In this case we do not have to prefix the items that we define in the schema and that belong to the target namespace. Instead, we prefix all XML Schema declarations with an appropriate prefix such as `xs:`. This is the preferred method for using the default namespace because it makes schema composition easy: Unqualified definitions (those that do not belong to a namespace) from external schema parts that we include (see Section 6.3.3) are automatically added to the default namespace (which is the target namespace). This is the desired behavior. For example:

```
<?xml version="1.0" encoding="UTF-8"?>
<xs:schema xmlns:xs="http://www.w3.org/2001/XMLSchema"
           targetNamespace="http://www.jazz.org"
           xmlns="http://www.jazz.org"
           elementFormDefault="qualified"
           attributeFormDefault="unqualified">
  <xs:element name="jazzMusician" type="tJazzMusician"/>
  ...
</xs:schema>
```

- *Use the XML Schema namespace as the default namespace.* In this case we do not have to prefix the XML Schema declarations, but we have to prefix the elements, types, and attributes that we define in the schema. This method is less flexible than the previous method: Unqualified definitions from included schemata would be added to the XML Schema namespace, which is not desired. For example:

```
<schema xmlns="http://www.w3.org/2001/XMLSchema"
        targetNamespace="http://www.jazz.org"
        xmlns:jazz="http://www.jazz.org"
        elementFormDefault="qualified"
        attributeFormDefault="unqualified">

  <element name="jazz:jazzMusician" type="jazz:tJazzMusician"/>

  ...

</schema>
```

■ *Use no default namespace at all.* In this case we have to prefix XML Schema declarations, and the elements, types, and attributes that we define in the schema. Again, this method causes trouble when unqualified definitions are included from external schemata. These definitions would not belong to any namespace, which results in an error when the schema is used. For example:

```
    <?xml version="1.0" encoding="UTF-8"?>

<xs:schema xmlns:xs="http://www.w3.org/2001/XMLSchema"
        targetNamespace="http://www.jazz.org"
        xmlns:jazz="http://www.jazz.org"
        elementFormDefault="qualified"
        attributeFormDefault="unqualified">

  <xs:element name="jazz:jazzMusician" type="jazz:tJazzMusician"/>

  ...

</xs:schema>
```

Clearly, the first option (using the target namespace as the default namespace) is the way to go.

6.2 REUSE MECHANISMS

XML Schema provides various mechanisms for elements reusing existing declarations, in particular global elements and types and various group constructs.

6.2.1 Global Elements and Global Types

Sections 5.3.12 and 5.3.13 discussed the definition of global elements and global types. The question for the schema author is: When should I use global elements, and when is it better to define a global type?

The answer is easy: Types are much more flexible constructs than elements. In almost all cases, it is better to define a global type instead of a global element. Global types can be used for element declaration, but it is also possible to derive other types from them via restriction and extension. In addition, we can build separate type libraries and import them with the import statement (see Section 6.3.5). In contrast, a global element can only be referred to, and that's it (almost).

There are two exceptions where a global element is more appropriate:

- Defining recursive structures is only possible by reference, and reference requires global elements (see Section 5.3.14). Using global elements is not the only way to define recursive structures, but it is the simplest.
- Elements that are subject to substitution (see Section 6.2.5) must be defined as global elements.

Of course, nothing stops us from using global elements and global types in combination. A global element can always refer to a global type definition. This solution provides the most flexibility. We can easily redefine types and use type libraries, while allowing other schemas that are importing our schema to apply substitution mechanisms to the globally defined elements.

6.2.2 Groups

A group definition can furnish a model group with a name. Groups can only be defined globally on the schema level. In Section 5.3.14 we used groups to define context-specific recursive structures. Groups are the most flexible construct for defining complex document structures.

Name	Attributes	Contains
group	(name | ref)	annotation?
		(all | choice | sequence)?

For example, we define a group:

```
<xs:group name="gName">
  <xs:sequence>
    <xs:element name="first"/>
    <xs:element name="last"/>
  </xs:sequence>
</xs:group>
```

This group can now be referenced by name instead of explicitly specifying a model group:

```
<xs:element name="name">
  <xs:complexType>
    <xs:group ref="gName"/>
  </xs:complexType>
</xs:element>
```

6.2.3 Attribute Groups

Similar to groups, attribute groups can combine several attribute definitions into a single named group. Attribute groups can only be defined globally on the schema level.

Name	Attributes	Contains
attributeGroup	id?	annotation?
	(name | ref)	(attribute | attributeGroup)*
		anyAttribute?

For example, we define the attribute group:

```
<xs:attributeGroup name="aName">
    <xs:attribute name="first" type="xs:string"/>
    <xs:attribute name="last" type="xs:string"/>
</xs:attributeGroup>
```

The whole group can then be referenced by specifying the group name instead of specifying each individual attribute.

```
<xs:element name="person">
  <xs:complexType>
    ...
    <xs:attributeGroup ref="aName"/>
  </xs:complexType>
</xs:element>
```

6.2.4 Instance Type Overriding

XML Schema allows document instances to override the type of elements (but not of attributes) locally with another type definition. This can be done with the `xsi:type` attribute. "xsi:" is the prefix for the namespace `http://www.w3.org/2001/XMLSchema-instance` and must be declared in the document instance. This namespace contains all XML Schema declarations that may appear in document instances.

The new type can be a built-in type or a type defined globally in the schema, but must be a type that is derived[1] from the original type of the element. In the following example from Section 5.2.10, we use an xsi:type definition in the document instance to select a specific member element from a union type:

```
<?xml version="1.0" encoding="UTF-8"?>
<xs:schema xmlns:xs="http://www.w3.org/2001/XMLSchema"
           elementFormDefault="qualified"
           xmlns="href://www.nile.com"
           targetNamespace="href://www.nile.com"
           attributeFormDefault="unqualified">
  <xs:simpleType name="tISBN">
    <xs:restriction base="xs:string">
      <xs:pattern value="(\d)-(\d){3}-(\d){5}-(\d)"/>
    </xs:restriction>
  </xs:simpleType>
  <xs:simpleType name="tProductNo">
    <xs:restriction base="xs:string">
      <xs:pattern value="9-((\d){3,5}-){2}(\d)"/>
    </xs:restriction>
  </xs:simpleType>
  <xs:simpleType name="tISBNorProductNo">
    <xs:union memberTypes="tISBN tProductNo"/>
  </xs:simpleType>
  <xs:element name="product">
    <xs:complexType>
      <xs:sequence>
        <xs:element name="productNo"
                    type="tISBNorProductNo"/>
      </xs:sequence>
    </xs:complexType>
```

---

1. In the case of simple types, XML Schema uses the narrower definition of *derived* as defined in Part One of the XML Schema Recommendation. Derivation by list extension or union is not allowed for instance type overriding. However, the member types of a union or a list are valid derivations of the corresponding union or list type.

```
  </xs:element>
</xs:schema>
```

In a particular document instance, we can ensure that the `tProductNo` type definition is used by an XML processor by overriding the type definition of its `productNo` element via `xsi:type="tProductNo"`:

```
<?xml version="1.0" encoding="UTF-8"?>
<product xmlns="href://www.nile.com">
  <productNo xmlns:xsi="http://www.w3.org/2001/XMLSchema-instance"
      xsi:type="tProductNo">0-646-27288-8</productNo>
</product>
```

This is possible because `tProductNo` is a member type of `tISBNorProductNo`, and consequently is regarded as derived from `tISBNorProductNo`. Without this overriding, the content of this `productNo` instance would be interpreted as of type `tISBN` because `tISBN` is specified first in the `union` clause, and "0-646-27288-8" satisfies the `tISBN` pattern.

Of course, the discrimination between `tISBN` and `tProductNo` does not make much sense if we only want to validate a document. But for other XML processors, different types might imply different semantics; in such cases, type overriding would enforce different behavior.

Overriding schema type definitions in a document instance is, of course, also possible for complex types, provided the complex type definition was not decorated with a `block` attribute. The `block` attribute can take the values `#all`, `restriction`, `extension`, or combinations of `restriction` and `extension`. It is therefore possible to inhibit selectively the restriction or the extension of a complex type in document instances, or to inhibit both. (The `block` attribute is not allowed for simple type definitions. However, we can inhibit the overriding of simple types by using the `block` attribute in the definition of elements.)

Typical use cases for instance type overriding are

- The type defined in the schema is *abstract*. The instance *must* specify a concrete derived type.
- The document schema is fairly generic and does not define the type of elements but leaves this task to document instances. One application that heavily uses this technique is SOAP.
- We want to convey meta-information to the application as in the example given above.

6.2.5 Substitution Groups

Substitution groups are a kind of alias mechanism for elements. An element is called substitutable if it specifies a so-called *head element* via the `substitution-Group` attribute. The element referring to the head element must be of a type that can be derived[2] (via extension or restriction) from the type of the head element, and both the head element and the referring element must be defined globally.

Since head elements and referring elements can belong to different namespaces, substitution groups are a great way to cross namespace borders. For example, when we include or import definitions (see Sections 6.3.3 and 6.3.5) from another schema file, there are always cases when we might not want to use the defined element names but would like to rename. This can be done with substitution groups, as long as the elements were defined globally. Substitution groups allow *mediating* between different namespaces and different schema parts.

Let's assume we have a schema file with target namespace http://www.jazz.org/generic and that this file contains the definition for an element instrument:

```
<xs:element name="instrument" type="xs:string" abstract="true"/>
```

This element is not intended to appear in instance documents, as we have defined it as abstract. We now want to define another schema with target namespace http://www.myMusicShop.com/instruments in which we import the above definition. However, we do not want to keep the name instrument but would prefer to use specific instruments like saxophone and trombone. We can achieve this with a substitution group:

```
<xs:element xmlns:j="http://www.jazz.org/generic"
            name="saxophone" substitutionGroup="j:instrument"/>
<xs:element xmlns:j="http://www.jazz.org/generic"
            name="trombone" type="xs:normalizedString"
            substitutionGroup="j:instrument"/>
```

For the element trombone, we have restricted the type to xs:normalizedString. This is possible, since instrument was defined with xs:string, and xs:normalizedString is a restriction of xs:string. However, if instrument was defined with type xs:token, then the definition of trombone would be invalid because xs:normalizedString is not derived from xs:token (see Section 5.2.9).

It is possible to protect an element against the definition of substitution groups by defining it as final. The final attribute can take the values #all, restriction, and extension, or a combination of restriction and extension. It is therefore possible to protect an element against specific substitution methods.

---

2. In the case of simple types, XML Schema uses a narrower definition of *derived* as defined in Part One of the XML Schema Recommendation. Derivation by list extension or union is not allowed for substitution groups. However, the member types of a union or list are valid derivations of the corresponding union or list type.

Similarly, it is possible to protect an element against the application of sub-stitution groups in document instances by decorating it with a `block` attribute. This attribute can take the value `#all`, the values `restriction`, `extension`, `substitution`, or combinations thereof.

For an application of substitution groups in a larger example, please see Section 6.4.2.

6.3 SCHEMA COMPOSITION

A schema does not necessarily consist of a single file but may consist of several components, may refer to type libraries, and so forth. This section discusses the various possibilities, such as `include`, `import`, and `redefine`, for composing schemata within the same namespace and across namespaces.

Theoretically, these mechanisms allow for construction of very deep inclusion and redefinition hierarchies. (COBOL copy code experts will be delighted.) However, it is good practice to keep these hierarchies as flat as possible. This improves readability and avoids cyclic inclusions and contradicting redefinitions.

6.3.1 The Schema Clause

The `schema` clause is the root element of any schema file.

Name	Attributes	Contains
schema	attributeFormDefault?	(include | import | redefine | annotation)*
	blockDefault?	((simpleType | complexType | group | attributeGroup |
	elementFormDefault?	element | attribute | notation), annotation*)*
	finalDefault?	
	id?	
	targetNamespace?	
	version?	
	xml:lang?	

The `schema` clause defines the default values for the form attributes in attribute definitions, form attributes in element definitions, block attributes, and final attributes. As child elements, it contains definitions that must be made on the schema level such as global types, global elements and attributes, groups and attribute groups, and notation declarations. The `schema` clause may also be decorated with one or several annotations.

6.3.2 Locating Schemata

XML instances may specify the schemata that can be used for validation of the instance via the `xsi:schemaLocation` attribute. Because this declaration is located in the document instance, it must be qualified with the namespace for XML Schema instances that must be declared in the document instance, too.

```
xmlns:xsi="http://www.w3.org/2001/XMLSchema-instance"
xsi:schemaLocation="http://www.jazz.org/encyclopedia
                    http://www.jazz.org/encyclopedia.xsd"
```

The `schemaLocation` attribute contains one or several pairs of URIs. The first URI in each pair identifies the namespace, while the second URI in each pair specifies the location of the corresponding schema. Note that the latter is only a hint from the document author to the XML processor about where to find the schema. It is up to the processor to use this schema reference or not. For example, an SVG processor or a SMIL processor may discard this reference and use its built-in schema definition for the SVG or SMIL namespace. The location of schemata that do not have a namespace can be specified with the attribute `noNamespaceSchemaLocation`.

6.3.3 Include

The mechanisms for inclusion, redefinition, and import allow us to establish and use type libraries. Type libraries are useful because they help to standardize type definitions within a corporation or across corporations.

A schema definition can *include* any number of external schema files. However, there is a condition: An included external schema file must have the same target namespace definition as the including file, or no target namespace definition at all. In the latter case, the definitions in the included schema are adapted to the target namespace of the including schema.

The `include`, redefine (Section 6.3.4), and `import` (Section 6.3.5) clauses must always be located at the beginning of a `schema` clause.

Name	Attributes	Contains
include	id?	annotation?
	schemaLocation	

For example:

```
<xs:include schemaLocation = "http://www.jazzstore.com/cd.xsd"/>
```

This clause has basically the same effect as pasting the content of `http://www.jazzstore.com/cd.xsd` into the current schema file.

6.3.4 Redefine

The redefine clause works similarly to the include clause. A redefined external schema file must have the same target namespace definition as the including file, or no target namespace definition at all. What is different from the include clause is that redefine allows modification of the included definitions. For example, simple types can be restricted, and complex types can be extended or restricted.

The include, import, and redefine clauses must always be located at the beginning of a schema clause.

Name	Attributes	Contains
redefine	id?	(annotation | simpleType | complexType | group | attributeGroup)*
	schemaLocation	

Given the following schema in file tName.xsd,

```
<?xml version="1.0" encoding="UTF-8"?>
<xs:schema xmlns:xs="http://www.w3.org/2001/XMLSchema"
           elementFormDefault="qualified"
           attributeFormDefault="unqualified">
  <xs:complexType name="tName">
    <xs:sequence>
      <xs:element name="first" maxOccurs="unbounded"/>
      <xs:element name="middle" minOccurs="0"/>
      <xs:element name="last"/>
    </xs:sequence>
  </xs:complexType>
</xs:schema>
```

we can now include this type definition in another schema and at the same time redefine it:

```
<xs:redefine schemaLocation="tName.xsd">
  <xs:complexType name="tName">
    <xs:complexContent>
      <xs:restriction base="tName">
        <xs:sequence>
          <xs:element name="first" maxOccurs="1"/>
```

```
          <xs:element name="last"/>
        </xs:sequence>
      </xs:restriction>
    </xs:complexContent>
  </xs:complexType>
</xs:redefine>
```

Note that the name of the redefined complex type and the name of the base type are identical (tName)! This is required by the redefinition mechanism. It is possible to redefine all or only some of the included types.

It is also possible to redefine groups and attribute groups. Given the following schema in file gName.xsd,

```
<?xml version="1.0" encoding="UTF-8"?>
<xs:schema xmlns:xs="http://www.w3.org/2001/XMLSchema"
           elementFormDefault="qualified"
           attributeFormDefault="unqualified">
  <xs:group name="gName">
    <xs:sequence>
      <xs:element name="first"/>
      <xs:element name="last"/>
    </xs:sequence>
  </xs:group>
  ...
</xs:schema>
```

we can now extend this group via a redefinition:

```
<xs:redefine schemaLocation="gName.xsd">
  <xs:group name="gName">
    <xs:sequence>
      <xs:group ref="gName"/>
      <xs:element name="middle" minOccurs="0"/>
    </xs:sequence>
  </xs:group>
</xs:redefine>
```

Again, the redefined group has the same name as the group to which it refers.

6.3.5 Import

In contrast to `include`, the `import` clause can combine several schemata from different target namespaces. This is important since a single schema definition only supports a single target namespace. Multi-namespace schemata or instances must therefore be composed from several schema files.

The `include`, `import`, and `redefine` clauses must always be located at the beginning of a `schema` clause.

Name	Attributes	Contains
import	id	annotation?
	namespace	
	schemaLocation	

A multi-namespace schema defines the namespaces used with their prefixes via a standard namespace declaration in the `schema` element. Directly after the `schema` element, the necessary `import` statements are specified to import the foreign namespaces.

Optionally, the `import` statement may specify the schema location in order to help the XML processor to locate the schema file that defines that namespace. However, for the XML processor, this is only one possible source of information. Document instances may specify schema locations for the various namespaces, too, and the processor is free to use built-in namespace definitions for particular namespaces (see Section 6.3.2).

The following schema imports the XHTML namespace and assigns the prefix `html:` to it. We can then, for example, refer to the XHTML `blockquote` element definition.

```
<?xml version="1.0" encoding="UTF-8"?>
<xs:schema xmlns:xs="http://www.w3.org/2001/XMLSchema"
        xmlns:html="http://www.w3.org/1999/xhtml"
        targetNamespace="http://www.jazz.org"
        xmlns="http://www.jazz.org"
        elementFormDefault="qualified"
        attributeFormDefault="unqualified">
  <xs:import namespace="http://www.w3.org/1999/xhtml"/>
  <xs:element name="description">
    <xs:complexType>
      <xs:sequence>

        ...

        <xs:element ref="html:blockquote">
```

```
      <xs:sequence>
    <xs:complexType>
   </xs:element>
</xs:schema>
```

Note: The `namespace` attribute in the `import` clause is optional, too. An import without a `namespace` attribute imports definitions without namespace qualification. Consequently, it allows unqualified references (references without a namespace prefix or a default namespace) to external definitions.

6.3.6 Notation

The `notation` element supports the simple abstract type `NOTATION` and provides the functionality known from the XML 1.0 NOTATION declarations (see Section 4.2.11). Its purpose is to provide compatibility for the translation of DTDs into XML Schema.

Name	Attributes	Contains
notation	id?	appinfo?
	name	
	public?	
	system?	

The following example includes a jpeg image in a document and defines application viewer.exe as its processor.

```
<xs:notation name="jpeg" public="image/jpeg" system="viewer.exe"/>
```

6.3.7 Annotations

Any element of an XML Schema definition can contain one or several annotations. Annotations can contain both `appinfo` elements and `documentation` elements as child elements. `appinfo` elements contain user-defined information for machine consumption, while `documentation` elements contain information for human readers.

Name	Attributes	Contains
annotation		(appinfo | documentation)*

Here is an example of using `appinfo` to describe physical properties of a schema element to a native XML database (Software AG's Tamino, see also Section 11.11.1):

```xml
<?xml version="1.0" encoding="UTF-8"?>
<xs:schema xmlns:xs="http://www.w3.org/2001/XMLSchema"
    xmlns:x="http://www.w3.org/1999/xhtml"
    xmlns:tsd=
      "http://namespaces.softwareag.com/tamino/TaminoSchemaDefinition"
    targetNamespace="http://www.nile.com"
    xmlns="http://www.nile.com"
    elementFormDefault="qualified"
    attributeFormDefault="unqualified">
  <xs:element name = "productNo" type = "xs:NMTOKEN">
    <xs:annotation>
      <xs:appinfo>
        <tsd:elementInfo>
          <tsd:physical>
            <tsd:native>
              <tsd:index>
                <tsd:standard/>
              </tsd:index>
            </tsd:native>
          </tsd:physical>
        </tsd:elementInfo>
      </xs:appinfo>
      <xs:documentation>
        Element <x:i>productNo</x:i> is to be stored as a native XML
        element. It is used as a standard index to allow efficient
        access to album documents by <x:i>productNo</x:i>.
      </xs:documentation>
    </xs:annotation>
  </xs:element>
</xs:schema>
```

Note that XHTML is used to mark up the documentation text. This should be adopted as a best practice. (Similarly, HTML is consistently used to mark up documentation in Java source code and JavaDocs.)

6.4 USAGE PATTERNS

The following sections discuss some advanced techniques that exploit the modularity and reuse mechanism of XML Schema. These patterns also qualify as best practices recommendations.

6.4.1 Chameleon Components and Type Libraries

Reusing XML Schema components requires some consideration. It requires that we design the single components with their possible reuse purposes in mind. One aspect of this is how we treat namespaces.

When furnishing a generic schema component such as a type library with a fixed target namespace, we have already restricted the possible reuse scenarios. We have removed one point of variation (one degree of freedom)—the component has lost some flexibility. It now contains type definitions that belong to a dedicated namespace; we cannot use it in other scenarios where other namespaces are in effect.

So, it is a good idea not to equip generic components with a target namespace. Such components are called *chameleon* components. They can easily be inserted into other schema files that do have a target namespace, and of course, we want them to blend into that target namespace. This is in fact the case: XML adds included components that do not have a target namespace to the target namespace of the including schema.

Let's look at an example. We define a small type library named customer.xsd (see Figure 6.2) with just a single type tCustomer:

```
<?xml version="1.0" encoding="UTF-8"?>

<xs:schema xmlns:xs="http://www.w3.org/2001/XMLSchema"
           elementFormDefault="qualified"
           attributeFormDefault="unqualified">

  <xs:complexType name="tCustomer">

    <xs:sequence>

      <xs:element name="customerID" type="xs:string"/>

        <xs:element name="name">

          <xs:complexType>
```

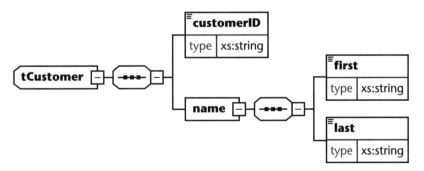

Figure 6.2 The chameleon component customer.xsd.

```
            <xs:sequence>
              <xs:element name="first" type="xs:string"/>
              <xs:element name="last" type="xs:string"/>
            </xs:sequence>
          </xs:complexType>
        </xs:element>
      </xs:sequence>
    </xs:complexType>
</xs:schema>
```

We can use this type definition in a schema such as the following invoice schema (see Figure 6.3):

```
<?xml version="1.0" encoding="UTF-8"?>
<xs:schema targetNamespace="http://www.nile.com/billing"
         xmlns:xs="http://www.w3.org/2001/XMLSchema"
         xmlns="http://www.nile.com/billing"
         elementFormDefault="qualified"
         attributeFormDefault="unqualified">
  <xs:include schemaLocation="customer.xsd"/>
    <xs:element name="invoice">
      <xs:complexType>
        <xs:sequence>
          <xs:element name="customer" type="tCustomer"/>
          <xs:element name="item">
            <xs:complexType>
              <xs:sequence>
                <xs:element name="Amount" type="xs:positiveInteger"/>
                <xs:element name="productNo" type="xs:string"/>
                <xs:element name="price" type="xs:decimal"/>
              </xs:sequence>
            </xs:complexType>
          </xs:element>
        </xs:sequence>
      </xs:complexType>
    </xs:element>
</xs:schema>
```

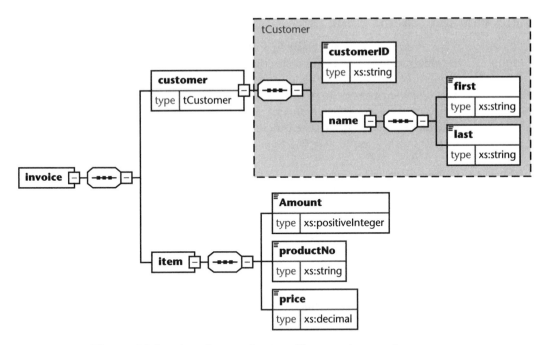

Figure 6.3 Invoice schema using type library `customer.xsd`.

What is important here is how we define the default schema namespace. As you can see, the default schema namespace is the same as the target namespace, while the XML Schema namespace is linked with the prefix `xs:`. Consequently, we have to decorate each XML Schema term, such as `sequence` or `complexType`, with the prefix `xs:`, while—and this is important—the elements of `invoice` do not need a qualifying prefix. If we had chosen to define the default schema namespace differently, we would need to qualify all elements of `invoice` with a prefix because they belong to the target namespace. This would also apply to the elements included from the type library `customer.xsd`. This, of course, is not possible, as `customer.xsd` is defined without a namespace.

So, the golden rule for schema design is

target namespace = default schema namespace

With this policy and with chameleon components, we can easily create type libraries that can be included in schemata of different target namespaces.

Note that we can also apply this technique on the document instance level. We can include chameleon components into document instances using the `noNamespaceSchemaLocation` declaration, as discussed in Section 6.3.2. The component will be added to the default namespace of the document.

6.4.2 Defining Schema Families

A common problem, especially in electronic businesses, is adapting schemata to national, regional, or cultural standards and customs. For example, the address element of an invoice looks different in Europe and in the United States. We would rather not have to provide an extra document schema for each local context. One way to achieve this is to define an abstract master schema. This schema defines the basic structure of the document but leaves the details to the various localized schema extensions.

Using Substitution Groups

An elegant way to define such a master schema and later extend it is to make use of substitution groups (see Section 6.2.5). Remember, a substitution group allows us to use the members of a substitution group in lieu of the head element to which each member of the substitution group refers.

The strategy we use is to define the master schema in such a way that any document node where we need variability can act as the head element for a substitution group. We define such head elements as global elements (a requirement for substitution groups), and we define them as *abstract* elements. This ensures that we cannot create document instances before we have actually substituted all head elements with a concrete implementation.

Here is an example for an invoice master schema (see also Figure 6.4):

```xml
<?xml version="1.0" encoding="UTF-8"?>
<xs:schema xmlns:xs="http://www.w3.org/2001/XMLSchema"
           elementFormDefault="qualified"
           attributeFormDefault="unqualified">
  <xs:element name="invoice">
    <xs:complexType>
      <xs:sequence>
        <xs:element ref="abstractAddress"/>
        <xs:element name="item" maxOccurs="unbounded">
          <xs:complexType>
            <xs:sequence>
              <xs:element name="amount" type="xs:positiveInteger"/>
              <xs:element name="productNo" type="xs:string"/>
              <xs:element name="price" type="xs:decimal"/>
            </xs:sequence>
          </xs:complexType>
        </xs:element>
      </xs:sequence>
    </xs:complexType>
  </xs:element>
```

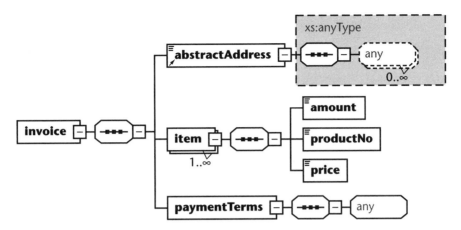

Figure 6.4 Master schema for country-independent invoices.

```
<xs:element name="paymentTerms">
  <xs:complexType>
    <xs:sequence>
      <xs:any processContents="skip"/>
    </xs:sequence>
  </xs:complexType>
</xs:element>
    </xs:sequence>
  </xs:complexType>
</xs:element>
<xs:element name="abstractAddress" type="xs:anyType" abstract="true"/>
</xs:schema>
```

Here, we have included the element abstractAddress as a point of variability. This element is defined as a global element and is referred to in the definition of the root element invoice. We have declared element abstractAddress as abstract.

We have also declared the type as xs:anyType. This is the only built-in complex type in XML Schema, and it is a type from which all other complex types can be derived. Remember that the member of the substitution group that will later replace element abstractAddress must have a type that can be derived from the type of abstractAddress. xs:anyType gives us the most flexibility. The only limitation is that we cannot replace abstractAddress with an element of a simple type.

Of course, we could define head element `abstractAddress` with a specific complex type, if we wish to restrict the possible replacements for this element. However, as we cannot foresee the future, we may at some time be faced with an address format that cannot be derived from the type of `abstractAddress`. For this reason we have chosen `xs:anyType`, which allows us any address format, even if it is an address on Mars.

Now, let's see how we can instantiate this abstract master schema with a concrete address definition (see Figure 6.5).

```xml
<?xml version="1.0" encoding="UTF-8"?>
<xs:schema xmlns:xs="http://www.w3.org/2001/XMLSchema"
           elementFormDefault="qualified"
           attributeFormDefault="unqualified">
  <xs:include schemaLocation="invoiceMaster.xsd"/>
  <xs:element name="UKAddress" substitutionGroup="abstractAddress">
    <xs:complexType>
      <xs:sequence>
        <xs:element name="name" type="xs:string"/>
        <xs:element name="street" type="xs:string"/>
        <xs:element name="city" type="xs:string"/>
        <xs:element name="country" type="xs:string"/>
```

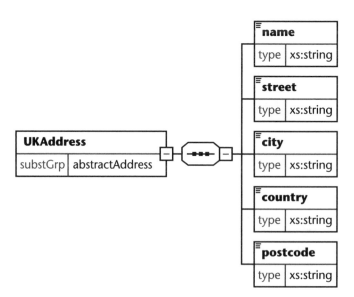

Figure 6.5 Concrete address element definition.

```
        <xs:element name="postcode" type="xs:string"/>
      </xs:sequence>
    </xs:complexType>
  </xs:element>
</xs:schema>
```

Here, we have defined a complete localized invoice schema for the United Kingdom. First, we have included our master schema. Then we have defined a global element UKAddress and have declared it as a member of the substitution group abstractAddress. Because abstractAddress was defined with type xs:any-Type, we can now furnish UKAddress with any complex type definition of our choice.

Based on this schema definition we can now create a document instance:

```
<?xml version="1.0" encoding="UTF-8"?>

<invoice xmlns:xsi="http://www.w3.org/2001/XMLSchema-instance"
         xsi:noNamespaceSchemaLocation="UKInvoice.xsd">

  <UKAddress>
    <name>Mary O'Donerthy</name>
    <street>107 Oxford Street</street>
    <city>Cambridge</city>
    <country>United Kingdom</country>
    <postcode>CB1 1JR</postcode>
  </UKAddress>
  <item>
    <amount>2</amount>
    <productNo>4711-3</productNo>
    <price>9.95</price>
  </item>
  <item>
    <amount>1</amount>
    <productNo>1278-4</productNo>
    <price>5.00</price>
  </item>
  <paymentTerms><b>Pay soon!</b></paymentTerms>

</invoice>
```

This instance is a valid instance of schema `UKInvoice.xsd`. Note that we must use element `UKAddress` instead of element `abstractAddress` because `abstractAddress` was defined as abstract. In the same way, we could define invoice schemata for the United States, Germany, France, Italy, and so on, all based on `invoiceMaster.xsd`.

Substitution groups are a good way to achieve variability in a single namespace, but they also have drawbacks:

- All variable elements and their substitutions must be defined as global elements, so it is not possible to define context-specific (local) elements here.
- Things get out of hand when there are several *context drivers*. For example, the address of an invoice may depend on the location, the layout of the items in the invoice may depend on the industry sector, and the layout of the payment terms may depend on the target audience (corporate, consumer). As these context drivers may appear in various combinations, the number of possible concrete schemata can become quite large.

Using Type Substitution

Another technique to allow variability in schemata is to use abstract types. When a particular schema instance is written, concrete types substitute for these abstract types. The schema supplies these concrete types in the form of a type library, so that instance authors may select the types they need from that library. The library can be defined in the same schema, or it can be defined in a separate file that is then included in the schema file.

The following example illustrates this technique. Again, we have implemented an invoice schema (see Figures 6.6 and 6.7). This time all elements (except the root element) are defined as local elements, but they refer to abstract types that are defined globally.

```
<?xml version="1.0" encoding="UTF-8"?>
<xs:schema xmlns:xs="http://www.w3.org/2001/XMLSchema"
           elementFormDefault="qualified"
           attributeFormDefault="unqualified">

  <xs:element name="invoice">
    <xs:complexType>
      <xs:sequence>
        <xs:element name="address" type="tAddress"/>
        <xs:element name="item" type="tItem" maxOccurs="unbounded"/>
        <xs:element name="paymentTerms" type="tPaymentTerms"/>
      </xs:sequence>
    </xs:complexType>
  </xs:element>
```

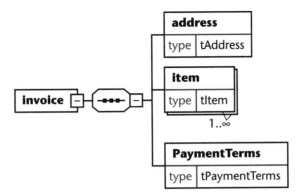

Figure 6.6 A master schema for invoice using abstract types.

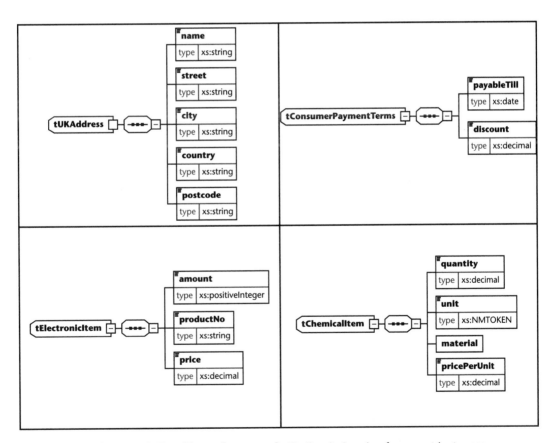

Figure 6.7 Type library for type substitution in invoice document instances.

```
<xs:complexType name="tAddress" abstract="true">
  <xs:complexContent>
    <xs:restriction base="xs:anyType"/>
  </xs:complexContent>
</xs:complexType>


<xs:complexType name="tItem" abstract="true">
  <xs:complexContent>
    <xs:restriction base="xs:anyType"/>
  </xs:complexContent>
</xs:complexType>


<xs:complexType name="tPaymentTerms" abstract="true">
  <xs:complexContent>
    <xs:restriction base="xs:anyType"/>
  </xs:complexContent>
</xs:complexType>


<!-- type library for address types --->
  <xs:complexType name="tUKAddress">
    <xs:complexContent>
      <xs:restriction base="tAddress">
        <xs:sequence>
          <xs:element name="name" type="xs:string"/>
          <xs:element name="street" type="xs:string"/>
          <xs:element name="city" type="xs:string"/>
          <xs:element name="country" type="xs:string"/>
          <xs:element name="postcode" type="xs:string"/>
        </xs:sequence>
      </xs:restriction>
    </xs:complexContent>
  </xs:complexType>


<!-- type library for item types -->
  <xs:complexType name="tElectronicItem">
```

```xml
      <xs:complexContent>
        <xs:restriction base="tItem">
          <xs:sequence>
            <xs:element name="amount" type="xs:positiveInteger"/>
            <xs:element name="productNo" type="xs:string"/>
            <xs:element name="price" type="xs:decimal"/>
          </xs:sequence>
        </xs:restriction>
      </xs:complexContent>
    </xs:complexType>

    <xs:complexType name="tChemicalItem">
      <xs:complexContent>
        <xs:restriction base="tItem">
          <xs:sequence>
            <xs:element name="quantity" type="xs:decimal"/>
            <xs:element name="unit" type="xs:NMTOKEN"/>
            <xs:element name="material"/>
            <xs:element name="pricePerUnit" type="xs:decimal"/>
          </xs:sequence>
        </xs:restriction>
      </xs:complexContent>
    </xs:complexType>

<!-- type library for payment term types -->
  <xs:complexType name="tConsumerPaymentTerms">
    <xs:complexContent>
      <xs:restriction base="tPaymentTerms">
        <xs:sequence>
          <xs:element name="payableTill" type="xs:date"/>
          <xs:element name="discount" type="xs:decimal"/>
        </xs:sequence>
      </xs:restriction>
    </xs:complexContent>
  </xs:complexType>
</xs:schema>
```

Also in this case, the concrete types that substitute for the abstract types must have been derived from the corresponding abstract types. We see that, for example, tConsumerPaymentTerms was defined with a base type tPaymentTerms. It can, therefore, substitute for tPaymentTerms in any occurrence that specifies tPaymentTerms.

We have also defined the abstract types with the most general complex type (xs:anyType). This allows us maximum flexibility for the types in the respective type libraries.

Applying this technique requires a bit more work on the part of document authors. The document author has to specify which type is used with which element:

```xml
<?xml version="1.0" encoding="UTF-8"?>
<invoice xmlns:xsi="http://www.w3.org/2001/XMLSchema-instance"
         xsi:noNamespaceSchemaLocation="invoiceMaster2.xsd">
  <address xsi:type="tUKAddress">
    <name>Mary O'Donerthy</name>
    <street>107 Oxford Street</street>
    <city>Cambridge</city>
    <country>United Kingdom</country>
    <postcode>CB1 1JR</postcode>
  </address>
  <item xsi:type="tElectronicItem">
    <amount>2</amount>
    <productNo>4711-3</productNo>
    <price>9.95</price>
  </item>
  <item xsi:type="tChemicalItem">
    <quantity>12.5</quantity>
    <unit>liter</unit>
    <material>double destillated water</material>
    <pricePerUnit>0.52</pricePerUnit>
  </item>
  <paymentTerms xsi:type="tConsumerPaymentTerms">
    <payableTill>2002-05-20</payableTill>
    <discount>0</discount>
  </paymentTerms>
</invoice>
```

The concrete types for address, item, and paymentTerms elements are determined within the document instance. This allows a wide variety of document flavors without the need to create a huge number of schemata. Context-specific (local) elements are also possible.

Once again, this approach has a few drawbacks:

- It requires more effort from document authors.
- It cannot be used to extend a schema from the "outside." The master schema must define or include a library containing all valid types.
- It may allow the document author too much freedom. For example, a certain industry sector may only want items of a specific type used in an invoice, but document authors are free to mix item types at their discretion. For instance, in this example we mixed electronic items and chemical items in one invoice.

Using Dangling Type Definitions

Our final technique is based on multiple namespaces. We use the fact that the definition of a schema location in the import directive is optional, and that a document instance may specify schema locations for namespaces used in the document. Note that the declaration of a schema location is only a hint to the XML processor about where a schema for that namespace may be found (see Section 6.3.5).

In the master schema we simply avoid declaring types that we want to keep variable. Instead, we import the namespaces that contain these type definitions but don't tell the processor where to find these namespaces.

```
<?xml version="1.0" encoding="UTF-8"?>
<xs:schema targetNamespace="http://www.nile.com/billing"
           xmlns:xs="http://www.w3.org/2001/XMLSchema"
           xmlns:ba="http://www.nile.com/billing/types/address"
           xmlns:bi="http://www.nile.com/billing/types/item"
           xmlns:bp="http://www.nile.com/billing/types/terms"
           xmlns="http://www.nile.com/billing"
           elementFormDefault="qualified"
           attributeFormDefault="unqualified">
  <xs:import namespace="http://www.nile.com/billing/types/address"/>
  <xs:import namespace="http://www.nile.com/billing/types/item"/>
  <xs:import
      namespace="http://www.nile.com/billing/types/terms"/>
  <xs:element name="invoice">
    <xs:complexType>
      <xs:sequence>
        <xs:element name="address" type="ba:tAddress"/>
```

```
        <xs:element name="item" type="bi:tItem" maxOccurs="unbounded"/>
        <xs:element name="paymentTerms" type="bp:tPaymentTerms"/>
      </xs:sequence>
    </xs:complexType>
  </xs:element>
</xs:schema>
```

This approach is called "dangling types" because the types for the elements address, item, and paymentTerms are not declared in the schema (see Figure 6.8). Instead, we have put these types into namespaces of their own, which we import via corresponding import statements. Because these import statements do not have a schemaLocation attribute, it is still unclear where the type declaration resides.

Three schema files containing the necessary type declarations are presented next.

UKAddress.xsd

```
<?xml version="1.0" encoding="UTF-8"?>
<xs:schema
        targetNamespace="http://www.nile.com/billing/types/address"
        xmlns:xs="http://www.w3.org/2001/XMLSchema"
        xmlns="http://www.nile.com/billing/types/address"
        elementFormDefault="qualified"
        attributeFormDefault="unqualified">
  <xs:complexType name="tAddress">
    <xs:sequence>
      <xs:element name="name" type="xs:string"/>
```

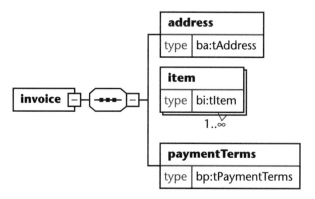

Figure 6.8 The master invoice schema with dangling types.

```
        <xs:element name="street" type="xs:string"/>
        <xs:element name="city" type="xs:string"/>
        <xs:element name="country" type="xs:string"/>
        <xs:element name="postcode" type="xs:string"/>
      </xs:sequence>
    </xs:complexType>
</xs:schema>
```

ElectronicItem.xsd

```
<?xml version="1.0" encoding="UTF-8"?>
<xs:schema targetNamespace="http://www.nile.com/billing/types/item"
           xmlns:xs="http://www.w3.org/2001/XMLSchema"
           xmlns="http://www.nile.com/billing/types/item"
           elementFormDefault="qualified"
           attributeFormDefault="unqualified">

  <xs:complexType name="tItem">
    <xs:sequence>
      <xs:element name="amount" type="xs:positiveInteger"/>
      <xs:element name="productNo" type="xs:string"/>
      <xs:element name="price" type="xs:decimal"/>
    </xs:sequence>
  </xs:complexType>
</xs:schema>
```

ConsumerPaymentTerms.xsd

```
<?xml version="1.0" encoding="UTF-8"?>
<xs:schema
    targetNamespace="http://www.nile.com/billing/types/terms"
    xmlns:xs="http://www.w3.org/2001/XMLSchema"
    xmlns="http://www.nile.com/billing/types/terms"
    elementFormDefault="qualified"
    attributeFormDefault="unqualified">

  <xs:complexType name="tPaymentTerms">
    <xs:sequence>
      <xs:element name="payableTill" type="xs:date"/>
      <xs:element name="discount" type="xs:decimal"/>
    </xs:sequence>
```

```
    </xs:complexType>
</xs:schema>
```

We can now create a document instance. Within the document instance we connect the namespaces with the files that define the respective types. Other document instances may assign other document declaration files to the corresponding type namespaces, and so, can customize the schema.

```
<?xml version="1.0" encoding="UTF-8"?>
<invoice
  xmlns="http://www.nile.com/billing"
  xmlns:ba="http://www.nile.com/billing/types/address"
  xmlns:bi="http://www.nile.com/billing/types/item"
  xmlns:bp="http://www.nile.com/billing/types/terms"
  xmlns:xsi="http://www.w3.org/2001/XMLSchema-instance"
  xsi:schemaLocation=
   "http://www.nile.com/billing
    http://www.nile.com/billing/invoiceMaster3.xsd
    http://www.nile.com/billing/types/address
    http://www.nile.com/billing/types/address/UKAddress.xsd
    http://www.nile.com/billing/types/item
    http://www.nile.com/billing/types/item/ElectronicItem.xsd
    http://www.nile.com/billing/types/terms
    http://www.nile.com/billing/types/terms/ConsumerPaymentTerms.xsd"
>
  <address>
    <ba:name>Mary O'Donerthy</ba:name>
    <ba:street>107 Oxford Street</ba:street>
    <ba:city>Cambridge</ba:city>
    <ba:country>United Kingdom</ba:country>
    <ba:postcode>CB1 1JR</ba:postcode>
  </address>
  <item>
    <bi:amount>2</bi:amount>
    <bi:productNo>4711-3</bi:productNo>
    <bi:price>9.95</bi:price>
  </item>
  <item>
    <bi:amount>1</bi:amount>
    <bi:productNo>1713-2</bi:productNo>
```

```
    <bi:price>5.00</bi:price>
  </item>
  <paymentTerms>
    <bp:payableTill>2002-05-20</bp:payableTill>
    <bp:discount>0</bp:discount>
  </paymentTerms>
</invoice>
```

This technique does not have the drawbacks of the previous method. In particular, it is possible to extend schemata from the "outside" simply by creating new type declaration files and using them in document instances. However, this method has a few disadvantages of its own:

- Documents are required to use multiple namespaces, basically one namespace for each variation point. When single-namespace documents or no-namespace documents are required, this technique cannot be used.
- It is not possible to validate the master schema in isolation because the referenced types are not declared. But even if we provide type declaration files, schema validators may not find them as long as we don't supply schemaLocation attributes. With some parsers, we even witnessed problems with document instance validation. (Remember, the instance specifies the locations of the various schemata.)

So, the best advice is to treat this method cautiously but to keep it in mind as XML Schema–aware XML processors get more mature.

Relax NG

It didn't take long after the XML Schema Recommendation was released on May 2, 2001, until a specification for an alternate schema definition language was launched. It was August 11, and this was Relax NG. The proposal was backed by OASIS, one of the organizations behind the definition of the ebXML standard. OASIS *(www.oasis-open.org)* hosts some web pages that provide further information and tools regarding Relax NG [Clark2001] [Murata2001].

Relax NG has its roots in James Clark's TREX and in Murata Makoto's RELAX. For Relax NG, they got together to define a schema language that is of similar power to XML Schema, but more elegant and simpler to use. Make no mistake, I am not advocating that you now discard XML Schema and switch to Relax NG. The industry standard is XML Schema, and most XML tools and XML middleware support XML Schema and not Relax NG.

Relax NG is discussed here to give you a deeper understanding of the subject by comparing the two standards. The discussion will be somewhat shorter than for XML Schema. Relax NG does not currently define its own type system, but relies on the XML Schema type system, discussed in Section 5.2.

215

7.1 STRUCTURE

In this section, we discuss elementary Relax NG constructs for defining the structure of XML documents such as elements, attributes, groups, and particles.

7.1.1 The Relax NG Data Model

The data model of Relax NG is based on the XML Information Set (see Section 4.2). In Relax NG each XML document is represented by an element (the root element). Each element consists of

- A name consisting of namespace URI and the local name. An empty namespace URI represents the absence of any namespace.
- A context, consisting of a base URI and namespace map (in-scope namespaces), that maps prefixes to namespace URIs and may also declare a default namespace.
- A set of attributes. Each attribute consists of a name and a string value.
- An ordered sequence of zero or more children. Each child is either an element or a non-empty string. Consecutive children are allowed, but consecutive strings are not allowed. (Two consecutive strings collapse to a single string.)

7.1.2 Elements and Attributes

The definition of elements and attributes in Relax NG is straightforward. In fact, the definitions of elements and attributes are so similar that they can be discussed side by side.

```
<?xml version="1.0" encoding="UTF-8"?>

<grammar
  xmlns="http://relaxng.org/ns/structure/1.0"
  datatypeLibrary="http://www.w3.org/2001/XMLSchema-datatypes">

  <start>

    <element name="track">

      <data type="normalizedString"/>

      <attribute name="duration">

        <data type="duration"/>

      </attribute>

    </element>

  </start>

</grammar>
```

The attribute xmlns="http://relaxng.org/ns/structure/1.0" establishes a name-space for the Relax NG vocabulary.

Here is the equivalent DTD (ignoring type declarations):

```
<!ELEMENT track (#PCDATA)>
<!ATTLIST track
          duration CDATA #REQUIRED >
```

The children of an element are simply enclosed between the element tags. The sequence of definitions is binding for elements, but not for attributes. (Remember that attributes form an unordered set.)

Both element content and attribute values are declared with <data>, which can include a type definition. We already mentioned that Relax NG uses the XML Schema type system for simple types. This is specified in the <grammar> clause in the datatypeLibrary attribute, so Relax NG is open to other type systems, too. We will have a closer look at data types in Relax NG in Section 7.2.1.

A type system content specification is <text/>, which denotes text content. This is equivalent to #PCDATA in DTDs and to <data type="string"/>. There is also an abbreviation for

```
<attribute name="ID">
  <text/>
</attribute>
```

that can be written as

```
<attribute name="ID"/>
```

A similar abbreviation for elements is not possible.

7.1.3 Model Groups and Particles

Alternatives are enclosed in a <choice> clause; sequences are enclosed in a <group> clause. As we have seen, for top-level sequences (within an element def-inition), an explicit <group> definition is not necessary (in contrast to XML Schema, which would require an <xs:sequence> definition in this position). Here is a larger example:

```
<?xml version="1.0" encoding="UTF-8"?>

<grammar
        xmlns="http://relaxng.org/ns/structure/1.0"
        datatypeLibrary="http://www.w3.org/2001/XMLSchema-datatypes">

  <start>

    <element name="collaborationContext">

      <choice>
```

```
              <group>
                <element name="from">
                  <data type="date"/>
                </element>
                <element name="to">
                  <data type="date"/>
                </element>
              </group>
              <group>
                <element name="location">
                  <data type="normalizedString"/>
                </element>
                <element name="time">
                  <data type="dateTime"/>
                </element>
              </group>
              <group>
                <element name="time">
                  <data type="dateTime"/>
                </element>
                <element name="location">
                  <data type="normalizedString"/>
                </element>
              </group>
            </choice>
          </element>
        </start>
      </grammar>
```

Here is the equivalent DTD (ignoring type declarations):

```
<!ELEMENT collaborationContext
          ((from, to) | (location, time) | (time, location))>
<!ELEMENT from (#PCDATA)>
<!ELEMENT to (#PCDATA)>
<!ELEMENT location (#PCDATA)>
```

```
<!ELEMENT time (#PCDATA)>
<!ELEMENT time (#PCDATA)>
<!ELEMENT location (#PCDATA)>
```

It is possible to define alternatives of attributes, too, but in a different way than in XML Schema (and DTDs):

```
<element name="person">
  <choice>
    <attribute name="age"/>
    <attribute name="birthDate"/>
  </choice>
<element/>
```

Here, both attributes are mutually exclusive, a construct not possible with DTDs and XML Schema.

Interleaving

Relax NG contains a clause that is similar to `<xs:all>` or to the & operator in SGML. `<interleave>` defines an interleaving of the *content* of its child patterns. In the following example, the sequence of the child elements `location` and `time` does not matter.

```
<?xml version="1.0" encoding="UTF-8"?>
<grammar
        xmlns="http://relaxng.org/ns/structure/1.0"
        datatypeLibrary="http://www.w3.org/2001/XMLSchema-datatypes">
  <start>
    <element name="performedAt">
      <interleave>
        <element name="location">
          <data type="normalizedString"/>
        </element>
        <element name="time">
          <data type="dateTime"/>
        </element>
      </interleave>
    </element>
  </start>
</grammar>
```

However, `<interleave>` differs somewhat from the corresponding connectors in SGML and XML Schema: Although (a,b)&c is equivalent to (a,b,c)|(c,b,a), using `<interleave>` instead of & would produce all possible permutations of a, b, and c—that is, `<interleave>` cuts through all substructures:

(a,b,c)|(a,c,b)|(b,a,c)|(b,c,a)|(c,b,a)|(c,a,b)

As long as `<interleave>` contains only leaf items, it is equivalent to the `<xs:all>` connector in XML Schema. Remember that `<xs:all>` must not contain other connectors, a restriction that does not exist for `<interleave>`.

A common application for `<interleave>` is to interleave text between child elements:

```
<?xml version="1.0" encoding="UTF-8"?>
<grammar
        xmlns="http://relaxng.org/ns/structure/1.0"
        datatypeLibrary="http://www.w3.org/2001/XMLSchema-datatypes">
  <start>
    <choice>
      <element name="description">
        <interleave>
          <text/>
          <element name="albumTitle">
            <text/>
          </element>
          <element name="performer">
            <text/>
          </element>
          <element name="noOfTracks">
            <data type="positiveInteger"/>
          </element>
          <oneOrMore>
            <element name="trackNo">
              <data type="positiveInteger"/>
            </element>
            <element name="trackTitle">
              <text/>
            </element>
```

```
                  </oneOrMore>
                </interleave>
              </element>
            </choice>
          </start>
      </grammar>
```

(Remember that `<text/>` is equivalent to `<text/><text/>...<text/>`. In connection with `<interleave>`, one occurrence of `<text/>` can intermingle with all child nodes.)

Fortunately, there is a handy abbreviation for the same task, the connector `<mixed>`. Our example now looks like this:

```
<?xml version="1.0" encoding="UTF-8"?>
<grammar
        xmlns="http://relaxng.org/ns/structure/1.0"
        datatypeLibrary="http://www.w3.org/2001/XMLSchema-datatypes">
  <start>
    <choice>
      <element name="description">
        <mixed>
          <element name="albumTitle">
            <text/>
          </element>
          <element name="performer">
            <text/>
          </element>
          <element name="noOfTracks">
            <data type="positiveInteger"/>
          </element>
          <oneOrMore>
            <element name="trackNo">
              <data type="positiveInteger"/>
            </element>
            <element name="trackTitle">
              <text/>
            </element>
```

```
            </oneOrMore>
          </mixed>
        </element>
      </choice>
    </start>
</grammar>
```

Here is the equivalent DTD (ignoring type declarations):

```
<!ELEMENT description (#PCDATA | albumTitle | performer | noOfTracks |
                      (trackNo, trackTitle)+)*>
<!ELEMENT albumTitle (#PCDATA)>
<!ELEMENT performer (#PCDATA)>
<!ELEMENT noOfTracks (#PCDATA)>
<!ELEMENT trackNo (#PCDATA)>
<!ELEMENT trackTitle (#PCDATA)>
```

For attributes, it does not matter if we combine them with `<interleave>` or `<group>`. Because attributes always form an unordered set, the sequence of their definition does not matter.

Cardinality Constraints

The cardinality of model groups or single elements can be declared by embedding them into the following clauses:

- `<zeroOrMore>` defines a cardinality of [0:*] and is equivalent to the modifier * in DTDs.
- `<oneOrMore>` defines a cardinality of [1:*] and is equivalent to the modifier + in DTDs.
- `<optional>` defines a cardinality of [0:1] and is equivalent to the modifier ? in DTDs. This clause can also be used to define optional attributes:

  ```
  <optional>
    <attribute name="middleName"/>
  </optional>
  ```

The following example defines an album with exactly one title and one or several tracks.

```
<?xml version="1.0" encoding="UTF-8"?>

<grammar
        xmlns="http://relaxng.org/ns/structure/1.0"
        datatypeLibrary="http://www.w3.org/2001/XMLSchema-datatypes">
```

```
<start>

  <element name="album">

    <element name="title">

      <text/>

    </element>

    <oneOrMore>

      <element name="track">

        <text/>

      </element>

    </oneOrMore>

  </element>

</start>
</grammar>
```

Here is the equivalent DTD:

```
<!ELEMENT album (title, track+)>
<!ELEMENT title (#PCDATA)>
<!ELEMENT track (#PCDATA)>
```

Relax NG does not support the more general cardinality constraints of XML Schema (see Section 5.3.4) but restricts its functionality in this area to that of DTDs.

7.1.4 Empty and notAllowed

Empty elements are denoted by <empty/>:

```
<element name = "isALivingLegend">
  <empty/>
</element>
```

Here is the equivalent DTD:

```
<!ELEMENT isALivingLegend EMPTY>
```

In terms of regular algebra (see Section 1.6.3), the `<empty/>` clause is equivalent to the empty string. Concatenating it with other clauses within a group makes no difference. The following clause,

```
<group>
  <element name = "first"/>
  <empty/>
  <element name = "last"/>
</group>
```

is equivalent to

```
<group>
  <element name = "first"/>
  <element name = "last"/>
</group>
```

The `notAllowed` clause behaves similarly toward choice groups. In terms of relational algebra, the `notAllowed` clause represents the empty set: It never matches with anything.

```
<choice>
  <element name = "age"/>
  <element name = "birthDate"/>
  <notAllowed/>
</choice>
```

What is it good for? Usually, the `notAllowed` clause is used as a placeholder when we want to define abstract patterns and later merge in another pattern. This is discussed in detail in Section 7.2.3.

7.1.5 Annotations

Relax NG treats anything within a schema that does not belong to the Relax NG core namespace as an annotation. For example, we could use the annotation logic of XML Schema within Relax NG:

```
<rng:element name="album"
  xmlns="http://relaxng.org/ns/structure/1.0"
  xmlns:xs="http://www.w3.org/2001/XMLSchema">
  <xs:annotation>
    <xs:documentation>
```

```
      A web page describing a jazz album

    </xs:documentation>

  </xs:annotation>

  ...

</rng:element>
```

7.1.6 Default and Fixed Values

Relax NG does not support default and fixed values. There are various reasons for this:

- Default and fixed values modify the information set of a document instance. The document can have a different meaning when processed by a schema-aware application instead of a non-schema-aware application.
- Default and fixed values do not fit well into the calculus of Hedge-Regular Grammars (HRGs) (see Section 1.6.4). Relax NG schemata, however, are 100% pure HRGs.
- Default and fixed values behave badly when merging schemata with union and intersection.

Because many existing applications rely on the schema-defining default values for instance attributes, an accompanying specification [Clark2001a] provides the necessary compatibility with DTDs. Default values are defined via an annotation (see previous section). A special annotation tag `defaultValue` has been reserved to declare default values. The following DTD,

```
<!ELEMENT saxophone(#PCDATA)>
<!ATTLIST saxophone
  material (brass|plastic) "brass"
>
```

could be expressed in Relax NG as

```
<element name="saxophone"
    xmlns="http://relaxng.org/ns/structure/1.0"
    xmlns:a="http://relaxng.org/ns/compatibility/annotations/1.0"
>
  <optional>
    <attribute name="material" a:defaultValue="brass">
      <choice>
        <value>brass</value>
        <value>plastic</value>
      </choice>
```

```
      </attribute>
    </optional>
    <text/>
  </element>
```

In contrast to XML Schema, Relax NG only provides backward compatibility to DTDs; it does not support default values for elements.

7.2 TYPES, GRAMMARS, PATTERNS

In this section, we discuss how types are defined in Relax NG, and which constructs are provided for reusing existing declarations.

7.2.1. Data Types in Relax NG

As already mentioned, Relax NG does not have a system of simple types of its own. Instead, it allows us to adopt foreign type systems such as the built-in types from XML Schema (see Section 5.2). The <data> clause is used to specify the type system used for each document node individually:

```
<element name="from">_
  <data type="dateTime" datatypeLibrary=
            "http://www.w3.org/2001/XMLSchema-datatypes"/>
</element>
```

Each node inherits the datatypeLibrary attribute from its parent elements, so it is usually sufficient to specify this attribute for the root element only. An element containing a <data> clause must not contain child elements or <text/> children. However, it may contain attributes.

If the type system features parameterized types, the <data> clause may include parameters. For example, when using the XML Schema data types, parameter clauses can specify constraining facets that derive customized types by restriction (see Section 5.2.7):

```
<element name="duration">
  <data type="unsignedShort">
    <param name="maxInclusive">4620</param>
  </data>
</element>
```

Enumerations, of course, cannot be defined via parameters. Therefore, Relax NG allows the use of the <choice> clause for defining enumerations:

```
<element name="jazzMusician">
  <attribute name="kind">
    <choice>
      <value>instrumentalist</value>
      <value>jazzComposer</value>
      <value>jazzSinger</value>
    </choice>
  </attribute>
</element>
```

Here is the equivalent DTD:

```
<!ELEMENT jazzMusician EMPTY>
<!ATTLIST jazzMusician
  kind (instrumentalist | jazzComposer | jazzSinger) #REQUIRED>
```

It is also possible to define lists in Relax NG. Unlike XML Schema, where a list extends a given simple type (see Section 5.2.6), a list in Relax NG is a construct in its own right:

```
<element name="3dVector">
  <list>
    <data type="float"/>
    <data type="float"/>
    <data type="float"/>
  </list>
</element>
```

Obviously, this is a more powerful construct than in XML Schema because it allows combining items of different types in a list, such as

```
<element name="currencyAmount">
  <list>
    <data type="string"/>
    <data type="decimal"/>
  </list>
</element>
```

This allows us to specify the inner structure of elements, such as

```
<currencyAmount>USD 49.00</currencyAmount>
```

A list of unlimited length of such currency amounts could be defined by enclosing a cardinality constraint specification.

```
<element name="currencyAmount">
  <list>
    <oneOrMore>
      <data type="string"/>
      <data type="decimal"/>
    </oneOrMore>
  </list>
</element>
```

A union type (see Section 5.2.10) can be defined with the help of the <choice> clause:

```
<element name="unitedColor">
  <choice>
    <list>
      <data type="unsignedByte"/>
      <data type="unsignedByte"/>
      <data type="unsignedByte"/>
    </list>
    <choice>
      <value>red<value>
      <value>green<value>
      <value>blue<value>
    </choice>
  </choice>
</element>
```

Here we have combined a list of three unsignedByte items (R-G-B) with an enumeration of color names. Actually, we could drop the second pair of <choice> brackets because the choice operation is associative.

7.2.2 Grammars and Named Patterns

As we have seen, Relax NG relies on existing type systems in the case of simple types, with the XML Schema type system being the prime candidate. Relax NG also allows us to derive new simple types from these imported types, either by restriction (parameters, enumeration) or by extension (list, choice). As for complex types, we will seek in vain for such a thing in Relax NG. What we find instead is the construct of *named patterns*.

A pattern is anything discussed so far, such as element and attribute definitions, model groups, and particles. Naming these patterns allows us to reuse previous patterns, and also to introduce recursions. The concept of named patterns works like this:

```xml
<?xml version="1.0" encoding="UTF-8"?>
<grammar>
  <start>
    <element name="customer">
      <element name="CustomerID">
        <text/>
      </element>
      <ref name="pName"/>
      <element name="mailingAddress">
        <ref name="pAddressContent"/>
      </element>
      <element name="shippingAddress">
        <ref name="pAddressContent"/>
      </element>
    </element>
  </start>
  <define name="pAddressContent">
    <element name="street">
      <text/>
    </element>
    <element name="town">
      <text/>
    </element>
    <element name="state">
      <text/>
    </element>
    <element name="zip">
      <text/>
    </element>
```

```
      </define>
    <define name="pName">
      <element name="name">
        <element name="first">
          <text/>
        </element>
        <optional>
          <element name="middle">
            <text/>
          </element>
        </optional>
        <element name="last">
          <text/>
        </element>
      </element>
    </define>
  </grammar>
```

Here is the equivalent DTD:

```
<!ELEMENT customer (customerID, name, mailingAddress, shippingAddress) >
<! ELEMENT customerID #PCDATA >
<! ELEMENT name (first, middle?, last) >
<! ELEMENT first #PCDATA >
<! ELEMENT middle #PCDATA >
<! ELEMENT last #PCDATA >
<! ELEMENT mailingAddress (street, town, state, zip) >
<! ELEMENT shippingAddress (street, town, state, zip) >
<! ELEMENT street #PCDATA >
<! ELEMENT town #PCDATA >
<! ELEMENT state #PCDATA >
<! ELEMENT zip #PCDATA >
```

The <grammar> clause encloses one or multiple <define> clauses and a single <start> clause. These clauses behave just like production rules in a grammar for a formal language (see Section 1.6) and are called *patterns*. The <start> clause is where the production of the whole grammar begins. In fact, the <start> clause is a pattern itself. The <define> clauses contain the subpatterns. These subpatterns are applied via <ref> clauses, here contained in the start subpattern. Such a ref clause can refer to any named pattern within the same <grammar> clause.

As we can see in the example above, a pattern does not necessarily consist of a single element or attribute definition, but can contain multiples of these. It may even contain only the content of such a definition. A named pattern can therefore fulfill the role of global types, global elements, groups, and attribute groups known from XML Schema.

As mentioned earlier, named patterns can also be used to define recursive structures. The following defines a treelike structure of parts and subparts:

```
<?xml version="1.0" encoding="UTF-8"?>
<grammar>
  <start>
    <ref name="pPart"/>
  </start>
  <define name="pPart">
    <element name="part">
      <attribute name="partID">
      <zeroOrMore>
        <ref name="pPart">
      <zeroOrMore>
    </element>
  </define>
</grammar>
```

Here is the equivalent DTD:

```
<!ELEMENT part (part*) >
<!ATTLIST part
  partID CDATA #REQUIRED >
```

It is also possible to nest grammars. This is useful when we need to define patterns that are local to context. A typical application is the definition of locally different, but identically named structures. Take for example the definition of a schema for a musical instrument with all its parts. The part list is defined as a recursive structure. Additionally, we want to have a choice if all parts are declared with only a partID attribute or with a partID attribute and a price element. This requires that we define two independent recursive structures with the same name. In a DTD we have no way of expressing such a structure. In

XML Schema we have to resort to group definitions. In Relax NG we use nested grammars:

```xml
<?xml version="1.0" encoding="UTF-8"?>
<grammar>
  <start >
    <ref name="pInstrument"/>
  </start>

  <define name="pInstrument">
    <element name="instrument">
      <choice>
        <grammar>
          <start>
            <ref name="pPart"/>
          </start>
          <define name="pPart">
            <element name="part">
              <attribute name="partID">
              <zeroOrMore>
                <ref name="pPart">
              <zeroOrMore>
            </element>
          </define>
        </grammar>
        <grammar>
          <start>
            <ref name="pPart"/>
          </start>
          <define name="pPart">
            <element name="part">
              <attribute name="partID">
              <element name="price">
                <text/>
              </element>
```

```
        <zeroOrMore>
          <ref name="pPart">
        <zeroOrMore>
      </element>
    </define>
  </grammar>
</choice>
      </element>
    </define>
  </grammar>
```

7.2.3 External Patterns and Grammars

External patterns and grammars can be used in Relax NG for the construction of multi-component schemata. In the following sections, we discuss these composition techniques.

Referencing Patterns

We can, of course, also refer to patterns that are stored externally. If we had stored the grammar of the last example in file part.rng, then we could utilize it in the following definition:

```
<element name="instrument">
  <element name="color">
    <text/>
  </element>
  <oneOrMore>
    <externalRef href="part.rng"/>
  </oneOrMore>
</element>
```

Merging Grammars

Similarly, we can merge external grammars into the current grammar. This is done with the <include> clause, a direct child of the <grammar> clause:

```
<grammar>
  <include href="part.rng"/>
  ...
</grammar>
```

Redefinition

It is possible to override one or more named patterns when a grammar is included. This is done by embedding appropriate define clauses into the include clause. For example:

```
<grammar>
  <include href="customer.rng">
    <define name="pName">
      <element name="name">
        <text/>
      </element>
    </define>
  </include>
  ...
</grammar>
```

Here, we have replaced the name element of the pName pattern in the customer example from above with a pattern containing a simpler name element.

Customizing Patterns

When we merge grammars, it is not uncommon for two patterns with the same name to clash. For each pattern, we can control how the identically named patterns are merged with the combine attribute. This attribute may have the value choice or interleave. For example:

```
<define name="pName" combine="choice">
  <element name="name">
    <element name="first">
      <text/>
    </element>
    <element name="last">
      <text/>
    </element>
  </element>
</define>
<define name="pName" combine="choice">
  <element name="name">
    <element name="first">
      <text/>
```

```
      </element>
      <element name="middle">
        <text/>
      </element>
      <element name="last">
        <text/>
      </element>
    </element>
</define>
```

This results in a `<choice>` expression for both patterns. By factoring out `<first>` and `<last>`, we arrive finally at

```
<define name="pName">
  <element name="name">
    <element name="first">
      <text/>
    </element>
    <optional>
      <element name="middle">
        <text/>
      </element>
    </optional>
    <element name="last">
      <text/>
    </element>
  </element>
</define>
```

In the next example we use `interleave` to merge two attribute groups. Remember that attributes always form an unordered set; the sequence of their definition does not matter.

```
<define name="pInstrumentAttributes" combine="interleave">
  <attribute name="color">
  <attribute name="weight">
</define>
<define name="pInstrumentAttributes" combine="interleave">
```

```
    <attribute name="material">
  </define>
```

This results in

```
<define name="pInstrumentAttributes">
  <interleave>
    <attribute name="color">
    <attribute name="weight">
    <attribute name="material">
  </interleave>
</define>
```

Note that the `interleave` clause is actually redundant, as attributes always form an unordered set. It is actually sufficient that only one of the two patterns to be merged specifies a `combine` mode.

The big question, of course, is: What happens if one of two equally named patterns is defined with `combine="choice"` and the other with `combine="interleave"`? Not much—this is considered an error.

Abstract Patterns

In some cases, it is useful to be able to specify an empty pattern. This can be done with the `<notAllowed/>` clause introduced in Section 7.1.4:

```
<define name="pattern">
  <notAllowed/>
</define>
```

A grammar may specify such a pattern and reference to it. However, it becomes a valid pattern only if another grammar that contains equally named patterns is merged into the current grammar. This feature allows us to define generic (or incomplete) grammars that are concretized and completed by a later merge.

Let's assume we want to define a generic grammar that describes an abstract one-to-many relationship. We could use such a grammar to describe, for example, the relationship between musicians and collaborations, between musicians and instruments, between a collaboration and albums, and so on.

```
<?xml version="1.0" encoding="UTF-8"?>
<grammar>
  <start>
    <ref name="pOne"/>
```

```
  <zeroOrMore>
     <ref name="pMany"/>
  </zeroOrMore>
</start>
<define name="pOne">
  <notAllowed/>
</define>
<define name="pMany">
  <notAllowed/>
</define>
</grammar>
```

This grammar is perfectly valid, but it has no instance documents. If we include the two other grammars below, which provide definitions for pOne and pMany, we get a completed grammar, with the content of the pOne and the pMany roles depending on the definition of the included grammar(s):

```
<?xml version="1.0" encoding="UTF-8"?>
<grammar>
  <define name="pOne" combine="choice">
    <element name="multiInstrumentalist">

      ...

    <element/>
  </define>
</grammar>
<grammar>
  <define name="pMany" combine="choice">
    <element name="instrument">

      ...

    <element/>
  </define>
</grammar>
```

And the result is

```
<grammar>
  <start>
    <ref name="pOne"/>
```

```
        <zeroOrMore>
          <ref name="pMany"/>
        </zeroOrMore>
      </start>
      <define name="pOne">
        <element name="multiInstrumentalist">
          ...
        <element/>
      </define>
      <define name="pMany">
        <element name="instrument">
          ...
        <element/>
      </define>
    </grammar>
```

This ability to define abstract patterns should not be underrated. It allows us to formulate generic schema prototypes that solve common problems and to apply this solution later to concrete problem areas by instantiating the schema prototype with concrete patterns.

Section 6.4.2 discussed the design of schema families in the context of XML Schema. One example was the adaptation of generic business documents to specific country or region formats. In Relax NG, a generic invoice document schema would specify the pattern for the shipping and billing addresses as `<notAllowed/>`. Depending on where the schema is used, this abstract pattern could then be instantiated with a country-specific address pattern.

Here is the master invoice schema equivalent to the schema given in Section 6.4.2 but formulated in Relax NG:

```
<?xml version="1.0" encoding="UTF-8"?>
<grammar
        xmlns="http://relaxng.org/ns/structure/1.0"
        datatypeLibrary="http://www.w3.org/2001/XMLSchema-datatypes">
  <start>
    <ref name="abstractAddress"/>
    <element name="invoice">
      <ref name="abstractAddress"/>
      <oneOrMore>
        <element name="item">
```

```
                    <element name="amount">
                      <data type="positiveInteger"/>
                    </element>
                    <element name="productNo">
                      <data type="string"/>
                    </element>
                    <element name="price">
                      <data type="decimal"/>
                    </element>
                  </element>
                </oneOrMore>
                <element name="paymentTerms">
                  <ref name="element0"/>
                </element>
              </element>
            </element>
          </start>
          <define name="any">
            <element>
              <anyName/>
              <mixed>
                <zeroOrMore>
                  <choice>
                    <ref name="any"/>
                    <attribute>
                      <anyName/>
                    </attribute>
                  </choice>
                </zeroOrMore>
              </mixed>
            </element>
          </define>
          <define name="abstractAddress">
            <notAllowed/>
          </define>
        </grammar>
```

We see the definition of the abstract pattern `abstractAddress`. This is the anchor point for merging concrete address patterns, such as

```xml
<?xml version="1.0" encoding="UTF-8"?>
<grammar
        xmlns="http://relaxng.org/ns/structure/1.0"
        datatypeLibrary="http://www.w3.org/2001/XMLSchema-datatypes">
  <start>
    <element name="UKAddress">
      <element name="name">
        <text/>
      </element>
      <element name="street">
        <text/>
      </element>
      <element name="city">
        <text/>
      </element>
      <element name="country">
        <text/>
      </element>
      <element name="postcode">
        <text/>
      </element>
    </element>
  </start>
</grammar>
```

This schema illustrates another point: The pattern "any" shows how to translate an XML Schema element containing an `<xs:any>` definition. Relax NG does not provide a similar construct. Here, it is necessary to write a generic pattern that allows any content. This is done in pattern "any." This pattern defines a mixed element of any name (see Section 7.3.2) containing an unconstrained model group consisting recursively of either the pattern "any" or an attribute of any name.

7.2.4 Keys and Key References

Relax NG does not presently define its own concept for keys and key references. This is subject to a future specification. However, to provide compatibility with existing applications, it supports the key and key references concept of DTDs. Attributes defined with data type ID serve as keys, and attributes defined with data types IDREF and IDREFS serve as key references (see Section 4.4.4).

7.3 NAMESPACES AND NAME CLASSES

In this section, we discuss the use of namespaces and more classes in Relax NG. In contrast to XML Schema, Relax NG allows for multi-namespace schema definitions.

7.3.1 Namespaces

The treatment of namespaces in Relax NG is straightforward. They don't play a central role as in XML Schema, where they are used to identify the schema. Instead, multiple namespaces can be used within a single schema. Each element and attribute definition can be equipped with an individual namespace specification. This is done with the ns attribute:

```
<element name="style" ns="http://www.jazz.org">
   ...
</element>
```

It is not necessary to provide a namespace attribute for each element definition. If no namespace attribute is specified, the namespace of an element defaults to the namespace of the nearest ancestor element. If no such ancestor exists, the namespace defaults to the empty string. It is also possible to specify the empty string explicitly: ns="" overrides existing namespace definitions with the default namespace.

Attributes and Namespaces

For attributes, the behavior is different. If no namespace attribute is specified for an attribute, its namespace defaults to the empty string. This is because of the fact that the XML Namespaces Recommendation [Bray1999] does not apply the default namespace to attributes.

However, it is possible to force the defaulting behavior for attributes to be identical to that for elements. This can be achieved by specifying the name of the attribute as a *name class* (see Section 7.3.2):

```
<attribute>
   <name>duration</name>
</attribute>
```

Clauses such as <name>, <value>, and <nsName> also inherit namespace definitions from their nearest ancestor.

Namespace Prefixes

An alternative syntax for declaring namespaces for elements and attributes makes use of namespace prefixes:

```
<element name="j:jazzMusician" xmlns:j="http://www.jazz.org">
 <attribute name="j:ID"/>
  <element name="j:name">
    <element name="j:first">
      <text/>
    </element>
  </element>
  ...
</element>
```

This syntax can be more convenient in cases when we have to deal with multiple namespaces.

Chameleon Components

An earlier section discussed how external patterns can be included in the current grammar. When doing so, it is sometimes necessary to cast the included pattern into a new namespace. This can easily be achieved by adding an ns attribute to the externalRef clause. Given the example from Section 7.2.3 this would look like

```
<element name="instrument">
  <element name="color">
    <text/>
  </element>
  <oneOrMore>
    <externalRef href="part.rng" ns="http://www.jazz.org"/>
  </oneOrMore>
</element>
```

This would cause the included part definition to be converted to

```
<define name="pPart" ns="http://www.jazz.org">
    <element name="part">
      <attribute>
        <name>partID</name>
      </attribute>
```

```
      <zeroOrMore>
        <ref name="pPart">
      <zeroOrMore>
    </element>
</define>
```

The condition for the conversion is that the external pattern does not already have a namespace attribute. This is not the case here, so pattern pPart is assigned to the new namespace. This namespace definition would then be inherited by the element defined in this pattern, and also by the nested attribute definition because this was defined with an explicit <name> clause.

7.3.2 Name Classes and Wildcards

With the introduction of name classes and an algebra for name classes, Relax NG offers a powerful tool for the definition of generic elements and attributes, known as wildcards. In the examples above we have almost always defined elements and attributes with name constants, specified in the name attribute. For example, the element definition

```
<element name="track">
  <attribute name="duration">
    <data type="duration"/>
  </attribute>
  <text/>
</element>
```

would only match instances such as

```
<track duration="PT13M56S">What Love?</track>
```

where the element is called "track" and the attribute is called "duration."

In Relax NG, however, it is possible not only to define a name constant but also to define a name *class* for an element or an attribute. In this case, all those instances satisfy the schema where the respective attribute or element name belongs to the corresponding name class.

Generic Name Classes

The most generic name class in Relax NG is anyName (as we saw in Section 7.2.3 when simulating xs:any), which covers, as the name says, any attribute or element name regardless of its local name and its namespace URI. The definition

```
<attribute>
```

```
  <anyName/>
</attribute>
```

describes a generic attribute that can have any name.

Scoped Names

Then there is the name class nsName,

```
<element>
  <nsName ns="http://www.jazz.org"/>
  <text/>
</element>
```

which is satisfied by instance elements with any name belonging to namespace http://www.jazz.org.

Combining Name Classes

Name classes can be combined with <choice> and <except> clauses. For example,

```
<choice>
  <nsName ns="http://www.jazz.org"/>
  <nsName ns="http://www.review.org"/>
</choice>
```

contains all names that belong to the namespaces http://www.jazz.org or http://www.review.org. The next example,

```
<anyName>
  <except>
    <nsName ns="http://www.jazz.org"/>
  </except>
</anyName>
```

contains all names except those in the namespace http://www.jazz.org. It is possible to abbreviate this with

```
<except>
  <nsName ns="http://www.jazz.org"/>
</except>
```

Individual names can also be combined with name classes:

```
<choice>
  <nsName ns="http://www.jazz.org"/>
```

```
  <name>rev:source<name/>
</choice>
```

or

```
<except>
  <name>rev:source<name/>
</except>
```

This allows us, for example, to define a schema for an element review that may contain arbitrary child elements. But when a location child element is specified, it must have an href attribute:

```
<element name="review">
  <zeroOrMore>
    <element>
      <except>
        <name>location</name>
      </except>
      <mixed>
        <zeroOrMany>
          <attribute>
            <anyName/>
          </attribute>
        </zeroOrMany>
      </mixed>
    </text>
    </element>
  </zeroOrMore>
  <optional>
    <element name="location">
      <attribute name="href">
        <data type="anyURI"/>
      </attribute>
      <text/>
    </element>
  </optional>
</element>
```

First we have defined a sequence of arbitrary elements but have excluded elements with name `location` from this definition. Then we have added an extra optional definition for the element `location`.

7.3.3 Comparison with DTDs

Compared to the XML DTD, Relax NG has many advantages, but some of its concepts result in a few restrictions. One concept is that definitions that alter the information set of an XML document should not appear in a schema—a schema should only define the validation of documents. Consequently, Relax NG

- does not support the specification of default values
- does not support the specification of entities
- does not support the specification of notations
- does not specify whether whitespace is significant

All these definitions would influence the information set (the content) of document instances. The philosophy of Relax NG is that any content should be defined in the document itself. This improves the capability of processors to interpret a document instance correctly, even if the schema is not available.

While this is a very clean approach to schema definition, it has drawbacks in practical application. In many cases it is necessary to use Relax NG in combination with another schema language, such as DTDs or XML Schema. The accompanying specification RELAX NG DTD Compatibility [Clark2001a] therefore provides backward compatibility for default values.

In other areas Relax NG has significant advantages over DTDs:

- Relax NG uses XML syntax to represent schemata. XML processors such as parsers, XSLT stylesheets, and so on can be used on schemata as well.
- Relax NG supports data typing. Rather than reinvent the wheel, it supports foreign type systems—for example, the rich type system of XML Schema. Rumors have it that its own type system is under consideration.
- Relax NG supports XML namespaces.
- Relax NG does not require schemata to be deterministic. The grammar is defined in such a way that parsers don't get confused with nondeterministic constructs (see Section 5.3.18).

7.3.4 Comparison with XML Schema

Compared to XML Schema, Relax NG offers some advantages:

- Relax NG is a very lean language. The effort to learn the basic concepts of Relax NG is considerably lower than with XML Schema.

- Attributes and elements are defined in very much the same way. For instance, it is possible to define attributes that are mutually exclusive; this is not possible with XML Schema.
- By providing only two constructs for reuse—grammars and patterns—the concepts for schema modularization and module reuse are easier to grasp than in XML Schema, which, with its rich arsenal of reuse facilities, can be overwhelming to the beginner.
- In Relax NG, multi-namespace schemata can be defined without the need to split the schema into several files.
- Relax NG is directly based on the concept of Hedge-Regular Grammars (see Section 1.6.4), making it possible to exploit the properties of these grammars: It is easy to construct a grammar for the union, intersection, and difference between Relax NG–defined schemata. This makes the composition of grammars from building blocks easy and provides a good environment to facilitate schema evolution (see Chapter 12).
- Relax NG allows for nondeterministic structures. Schema authors do not have to deal with this technical issue.
- Parser construction for Relax NG–defined grammars is simpler and parsers can be faster.

Relax NG also has some disadvantages compared to XML Schema:

- As noted above, Relax NG intentionally does not provide support for default and fixed values, notations, and whitespace handling.
- For cross-references, Relax NG provides only backward compatibility with DTDs. In particular, multifield keys, typed keys, and scoped keys are not supported. Note, however, that multifield key/keyref constructs found in XML Schema can make a schema undecidable [Fan2001]. Keys and key references are subject to future Relax NG specifications.
- XML Schema has been designed with relational databases in mind. It was designed as a superset of the type and structural system of SQL-99, and consequently deriving XML schemata from relational schemata and vice versa should be simpler with XML Schema than with Relax NG. This is an important aspect in enterprise applications.
- XML Schema is an official W3C standard and already an established industry standard. RELAX, the predecessor of Relax NG, is an official standard in Japan.

7.3.5 Tool Support for Relax NG

Relax NG does not currently have the same strong industry support as XML Schema. For example, de facto industry standards such as the Xerces DOM can validate document instances against schemata written in XML Schema, but not against Relax NG schemata. The same is true for editors. Leading schema editors such as XML Spy offer support for editing and validating XML Schema visually, taking much pain out of the authoring process. This same level of support is currently not available for Relax NG.

However, the OASIS support page for Relax NG, at *http://www.oasis-open .org/committees/relax-ng/#resources,* lists quite a few Relax NG–enabled validators, generators, and converters that can help during the authoring and validation process of XML schemata. There are validators that can validate a schema definition, instance generators that can produce document instances from Relax NG schemata, and converters that can convert a DTD or XML Schema to Relax NG. In fact, a converter was used to produce some of the code in this chapter.

Interesting, too, is RelaxNGCC, a tool that can generate Java source code from a given Relax NG grammar. Basically, this is a compiler-compiler that translates a grammar into a parser.

From Conceptual Model to Schema

Our tour through DTDs, XML Schema, and Relax NG in the previous chapters ends here, where we are now going to apply our knowledge to the construction of schemata from a conceptual model.

First we take a look at the knowledge base for which we want to develop the schemata. We will then go through the various steps for implementation in XML Schema, beginning with design decisions and how to map business objects onto schemata. You will see how to create a type library and how to model inheritance relationships in the various schema languages. The application of substitution groups and the implementation of wildcards and cross-references are demonstrated. Then we repeat the whole process by implementing the model in Relax NG. The last section summarizes the implementation steps.

8.1 A KNOWLEDGE BASE

The following selection of XML documents forms the jazz knowledge base. These documents are of course neither complete nor representative. The same namespace is used for these documents as in the conceptual model: `http://www.jazz.org/encyclopedia`. In the schemata defined in Sections 8.2 and 8.3 we will specify that element names must be qualified within document instances, and that attribute names need not be qualified. The document instances below define each target namespace as the default namespace. This ensures that all element names are qualified.

8.1.1 Jazz Musicians

Keith Jarrett was born May 8, 1945, and has played piano since the age of 3. He has produced several solo albums, only one of which is listed here, and numerous albums in collaborations (see "Collaborations," below), especially within the Keith Jarrett Trio.

```xml
<?xml version="1.0" encoding="UTF-8"?>

<jazzMusician xmlns="http://www.jazz.org/encyclopedia"
              xmlns:xsi="http://www.w3.org/2001/XMLSchema-instance"
              xsi:schemaLocation="http://www.jazz.org/encyclopedia
                            ../schemata/jazzMusician.xsd" >

  <ID>JarrettKeith</ID>
  <name>
    <first>Keith</first>
    <last>Jarrett</last>
  </name>
  <birthDate>1945-05-08</birthDate>
  <kind>jazzComposer</kind>
  <instrument>piano</instrument>
  <produces>
    <album>
      <publisher>http://www.ecmrecords.com</publisher>
      <productNo>1064</productNo>
    </album>
  </produces>
</jazzMusician>
```

Gary Peacock is a bass player but plays piano and vibraphone, too. He has played with Paul Bley and Albert Ayler, and is a member of the Keith Jarrett Trio.

```xml
<?xml version="1.0" encoding="UTF-8"?>
<jazzMusician xmlns="http://www.jazz.org/encyclopedia"
              xmlns:xsi="http://www.w3.org/2001/XMLSchema-instance"
              xsi:schemaLocation="http://www.jazz.org/encyclopedia
                            ../schemata/jazzMusician.xsd">
    <ID>PeacockGary</ID>
    <name>
        <first>Gary</first>
        <last>Peacock</last>
    </name>
    <kind>instrumentalist</kind>
    <instrument>double bass</instrument>
    <instrument>piano</instrument>
    <instrument>vibraphone</instrument>
    <influence>
        <influencedBy>
            <jazzMusician><ID>BleyPaul</ID></jazzMusician>
        </influencedBy>
    </influence>
    <influence>
        <influencedBy>
            <jazzMusician><ID>AylerAlbert</ID></jazzMusician>
        </influencedBy>
    </influence>
</jazzMusician>
```

Born August 9, 1942, Jack DeJohnette is a jazz composer who also plays drums and piano. He is a member of the Keith Jarrett Trio but has also played with Miles Davis and others not listed here.

```xml
<?xml version="1.0" encoding="UTF-8"?>
<jazzMusician xmlns="http://www.jazz.org/encyclopedia"
              xmlns:xsi="http://www.w3.org/2001/XMLSchema-instance"
              xsi:schemaLocation="http://www.jazz.org/encyclopedia
                            ../schemata/jazzMusician.xsd" >
```

```
<ID>DeJohnetteJack</ID>
<name><first>Jack</first>
  <last>DeJohnette</last>
</name>
<birthDate>1942-08-09</birthDate>
<kind>jazzComposer</kind>
<instrument>drums</instrument>
<instrument>piano</instrument>
<influence>
  <influencedBy>
    <jazzMusician><ID>DavisMiles</ID></jazzMusician>
  </influencedBy>
</influence>
</jazzMusician>
```

Born July 13, 1936, saxophonist Albert Ayler was one of the most prominent proponents of Free Jazz.

```
<?xml version="1.0" encoding="UTF-8"?>
<jazzMusician xmlns="http://www.jazz.org/encyclopedia"
              xmlns:xsi="http://www.w3.org/2001/XMLSchema-instance"
              xsi:schemaLocation="http://www.jazz.org/encyclopedia
                               ../schemata/jazzMusician.xsd" >
  <ID>AylerAlbert</ID>
  <name>
    <first>Albert</first>
    <last>Ayler</last>
  </name>
  <birthDate>1936-07-13</birthDate>
  <kind>instrumentalist</kind>
  <instrument>saxophone</instrument>
  <belongsTo>
    <period>
      <from>1963</from>
      <to>1970</to>
    </period>
    <style>
```

```
          <name>freeJazz</name>
       </style>
    </belongsTo>
</jazzMusician>
```

8.1.2 Styles

As an example of style, we will use Free Jazz, which was dominant from the early 1960s to the mid-1970s. The `description` element contains text in XHTML format.

```
<?xml version="1.0" encoding="UTF-8"?>
<style xmlns="http://www.jazz.org/encyclopedia"
       xmlns:xsi="http://www.w3.org/2001/XMLSchema-instance"
       xsi:schemaLocation="http://www.jazz.org/encyclopedia
                           ../schemata/style.xsd">
  <name>freeJazz</name>
  <dominantDuring>
    <from>1960</from>
    <to>1975</to>
  </dominantDuring>
  <description>
    <p xmlns="http://www.w3.org/1999/xhtml">The term "free jazz" came into
usage through the title of the groundbreaking 1960 album <quote>Free Jazz -
A Collective Improvisation</quote> by the <em>Ornette Coleman Double
Quartet</em>.<br/>Free jazz continued to develop in the mid-1960s primarily
within the context of the Black Arts Movement that flourished from the mid-
1960s to the mid-1970s and had a renaissance in the mid- to late 1990s.</p>
  </description>
</style>
```

Note the namespace definition in element <p> under <description>. The element description contained a wildcard specifying the namespace http://www .w3.org/1999/xhtml and the processing as "lax." This requires an appropriate namespace definition for the content of the wildcard. Since many processors have the XHTML namespace built in, they will check this content for validity.

8.1.3 Collaborations

The Keith Jarrett Trio has existed in its present form since 1983, with bassist Gary Peacock, drummer Jack DeJohnette, and Keith Jarrett at the piano.

```
<?xml version="1.0" encoding="UTF-8"?>
<band xmlns="http://www.jazz.org/encyclopedia"
      xmlns:xsi="http://www.w3.org/2001/XMLSchema-instance"
      xsi:schemaLocation="http://www.jazz.org/encyclopedia
                          ../schemata/project.xsd" >
  <name>Keith Jarrett Trio</name>
  <period>
    <from>1983</from>
  </period>
  <result>
    <album>
      <publisher>http://www.ecmrecords.com</publisher>
      <productNo>1780</productNo>
    </album>
  </result>
  <jazzMusician>
    <ID>JarrettKeith</ID>
  </jazzMusician>
  <jazzMusician>
    <ID>PeacockGary</ID>
  </jazzMusician>
  <jazzMusician>
    <ID>DeJohnetteJack</ID>
  </jazzMusician>
</band>
```

8.1.4 Albums

Inside Out is a recent album of the Keith Jarrett Trio. We list the musicians with the instruments they play on this album. We list the five tracks, too, and finally, we have an MP3 sample for track 1.

```
<?xml version="1.0" encoding="UTF-8"?>
<album xmlns="http://www.jazz.org/encyclopedia"
       xmlns:xsi="http://www.w3.org/2001/XMLSchema-instance"
       xsi:schemaLocation="http://www.jazz.org/encyclopedia
                           ../schemata/album.xsd" >
  <publisher>http://www.ecmrecords.com</publisher>
```

```
<productNo>1780</productNo>
<title>Inside out</title>
<track trackNo="t1">
  <title>From The Body</title>
</track>
<track trackNo="t2">
  <title>Inside Out</title>
</track>
<track trackNo="t3">
  <title>341 Free Fade</title>
</track>
<track trackNo="t4">
  <title>Riot</title>
</track>
<track trackNo="t5">
  <title>When I Fall In Love</title>
</track>
<sample>
  <MP3>
     http://www.jazz.org/samples/JarrettKeith/InsideOut/FromTheBody
  </MP3>
  <track trackNo="t1"/>
</sample>
<plays>
  <instrument>piano</instrument>
  <jazzMusician>
    <ID>JarrettKeith</ID>
  </jazzMusician>
</plays>
<plays>
  <instrument>double bass</instrument>
  <jazzMusician>
    <ID>PeacockGary</ID>
  </jazzMusician>
</plays>
```

```
<plays>
  <instrument>drums</instrument>
  <jazzMusician>
    <ID>DeJohnetteJack</ID>
  </jazzMusician>
</plays>
</album>
```

The Köln Concert is one of Keith Jarrett's solo albums. There are four tracks.

```
<?xml version="1.0" encoding="UTF-8"?>
<album xmlns="http://www.jazz.org/encyclopedia"
       xmlns:xsi="http://www.w3.org/2001/XMLSchema-instance"
       xsi:schemaLocation="http://www.jazz.org/encyclopedia
                          ../schemata/album.xsd" >
  <publisher>http://www.ecmrecords.com</publisher>
  <productNo>1064</productNo>
  <title>The Koeln Concert</title>
  <track trackNo="t1">
    <title>Part I</title>
  </track>
  <track trackNo="t2">
    <title>Part IIa</title>
  </track>
  <track trackNo="t3">
    <title>Part IIb</title>
  </track>
  <track trackNo="t4">
    <title>Part IIc</title>
  </track>
  <plays>
    <instrument>piano</instrument>
    <jazzMusician>
      <ID>JarrettKeith</ID>
    </jazzMusician>
  </plays>
</album>
```

8.1.5 Reviews

A review of the album *Inside Out* appeared in the jazz e-zine *all about jazz,* written by Glenn Astarita.

```xml
<?xml version="1.0" encoding="UTF-8"?>
<review xmlns="http://www.jazz.org/encyclopedia"
        xmlns:xsi="http://www.w3.org/2001/XMLSchema-instance"
        xsi:schemaLocation="http://www.jazz.org/encyclopedia
                            ../schemata/review.xsd" >
  <ID>r1001_048</ID>
  <pubDate>2001-10</pubDate>
  <album>
    <publisher>http://www.ecmrecords.com</publisher>
    <productNo>1780</productNo>
  </album>
  <magazine>
    <name>all about JAZZ</name>
    <URI>http://www.allaboutjazz.com</URI>
  </magazine>
  <critic>
    <ID>AstaritaGlenn</ID>
  </critic>
</review>
```

8.1.6 Critics

Finally, here is the `critic` document for Glenn Astarita:

```xml
<?xml version="1.0" encoding="UTF-8"?>
<critic xmlns="http://www.jazz.org/encyclopedia"
        xmlns:xsi="http://www.w3.org/2001/XMLSchema-instance"
        xsi:schemaLocation="http://www.jazz.org/encyclopedia
                            ../schemata/review.xsd" >
  <ID>AstaritaGlenn</ID>
  <name>
    <first>Glenn</first>
    <last>Astarita</last>
  </name>
</critic>
```

8.2 IMPLEMENTATION IN XML SCHEMA

Let's return to the conceptual model of Section 3.7 (shown again here in Figure 8.1). This model has already been partitioned by introducing Level 2 Structures. Also, most of the inheritance relationships were resolved. Note that this was done in order to allow for easy manual implementation of the model. A computer-based modeling tool such as KLEEN [KLEEN2002] (*www.aomodeling.org*) would not require this step but would resolve inheritance relationships automatically.

8.2.1 Design Options

One extreme in the implementation of a model would be to create one schema for each asset. However, with this design decision, we would run into fragmentation problems similar to relational techniques. Because the existence of some asset instances can depend on the presence of other asset instances, we would have to implement extra constraints to keep the referential integrity of the model intact. If, for example, we deleted a certain instance of asset jazzMusician, we would also have to delete all instances of the assets belongsTo, influence, and produces that depend on that instance of jazzMusician.

The other extreme would be to create a single schema containing the whole model. Such an implementation, however, would not scale well. Since instances of assets may refer to each other, we would end up with a single huge document containing the whole knowledge base. Instances of such a schema can become very big, and consequently various operations (loading, saving, parsing, transformation, etc.) would become very slow. For example, deleting an instance of asset album would require reading the whole knowledge base, deleting one album node with its child nodes, and then writing back the whole model. This situation will improve when manufacturers of XML database systems implement partial update operations for documents, so that only a particular node is rewritten. But still it might be necessary to lock the whole document against concurrent updates while an update operation is in progress, because cross-references may point into the node being updated.

In addition, databases are not the only technology that is affected negatively by huge documents. The same applies for parsers, XSLT processors, browsers, and so on. So, the all-in-one document approach is not a good option, even in terms of schema maintenance. The resulting huge schemata are difficult to maintain, and the reuse of schemata is virtually impossible. The rule "divide and conquer," or modularization, has always been an important principle in software engineering.

8.2.2 Business Objects

There is a natural way to determine the boundaries of schemata. In enterprise software engineering, the term "business objects" denotes units that exist in

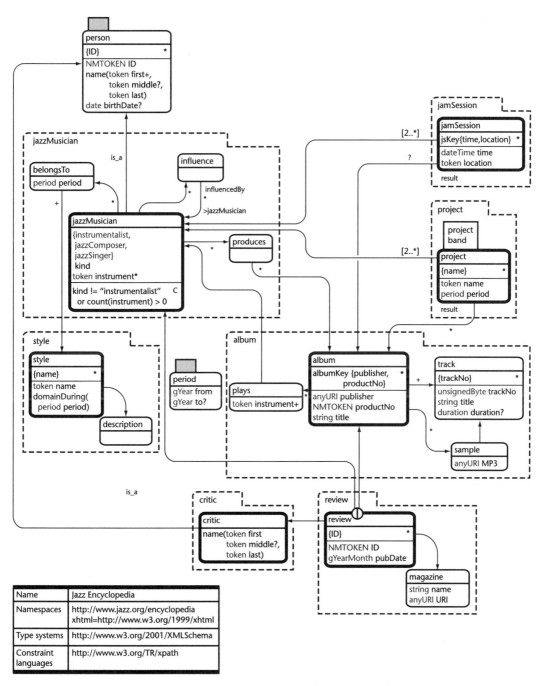

Figure 8.1 Conceptual model of jazz knowledge base revisited.

their own right (their existence does not depend on the presence of other units) and that play a role in the business process. When we determine our schema boundaries along such business objects, we get the following advantages:

■ As the existence of business objects does not depend on other objects, we do not have to watch integrity constraints when we insert, update, or delete schema instances in a database. Deleting a single business object, for example, does not require the deletion of other business objects, as each business object is a first-class citizen and has a life of its own.

■ Modifications done to a single business object do not lock the whole model. Concurrent update operations to other business objects remain possible.

■ The implementation fits well with current standards in application design. For example, the construction of a Java access layer for such a document would result in an implementation of the corresponding Java business object class.

■ The resulting set of schemata is very intuitive. Each schema instance (each XML document) represents a business object that is either a real-world object or a business document.

When we look at our AOM model in Figure 4.1, we see that the Level 2 Structures neatly correspond to business objects. Each of the units demarcated by a Level 2 Structure has instances that exist in their own right. Although these instances refer to instances of other units, they do not depend on them. In fact, the term "Level 2 Structure" is just a generic expression for the term "business object."

Our model has the following business objects: jazzMusician, style, jamSession, project, album, review, critic. This would result in a set of equally named schemata.

8.2.3 Creating a Type Library

In AOM every asset can be used as a type (see Section 2.5.5). In our model we have made explicit use of this feature by defining a *period* as asset period and using this type in various places. Of course, we would like to mirror this reuse strategy in our implementation. This is not difficult: We implement period as a separate complex type named period_type. In principle, we can implement each asset in this form, because formally each asset is a type, too. This technique makes the whole schema more flexible for later modifications to the schema. (See also Chapter 12 for schema evolution techniques.)

We can put all these type definitions into a separate file that acts as a type library. The definitions in this file can be reused between the various schema files (jazzMusician, style, jamSession, project, album, review, critic) if we include this file in each via an appropriate include statement. Let's call this type library JazzEncyclopedia_TypeLib.xsd.

Now, what does the code for period_type look like in XML Schema?

```
<xs:complexType name="period_type">
  <xs:sequence>
    <xs:element name="from" type="xs:gYear"/>
    <xs:element name="to" type="xs:gYear" minOccurs="0"/>
  </xs:sequence>
</xs:complexType>
```

This is a very simple schema part that defines a complex type consisting of a sequence of two elements (see Figure 8.2). Note that this is not the only way such a type could be implemented. Alternatively, we could have implemented the elements from and to as attributes, depending on our personal preferences. In the context of this example, however, we will stay with elements. The reason for doing so is simply that attributes would not show up in the XML Spy diagrams. A synopsis of the never-ending attribute vs. element debate is found in [Daum2002].

Of course, we could also implement period_type as a global group:

```
<xs:group name="period_type">
  <xs:sequence>
    <xs:element name="from" type="xs:gYear"/>
    <xs:element name="to" type="xs:gYear" minOccurs="0"/>
  </xs:sequence>
</xs:group>
```

However, we find that the tag name complexType quite satisfactorily describes what we want to define: the type of a node. Also, should we opt to implement some properties as attributes, complexType has the advantage of allowing the application of both elements and attributes within the same complexType definition. This is not possible with the group clause.

So, we use complexType for the definition of the other types, too. But before we can continue to create the code for the other assets in the model, we need to look at some finer points of inheritance.

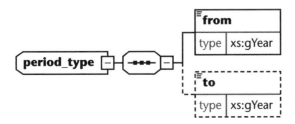

Figure 8.2 The structure of complex type period_type.

8.2.4 **Handling Inheritance**

Life would be too easy if we could continue in such a straightforward way as above. Implementing is_a relationships is a bit trickier. In our example we have two is_a relationships: one leading from jazzMusician to person, the other leading from critic to person.

Let's discuss XML Schema first. Implementing a person_type and inheriting from it into jazzMusician_type is straightforward. We simply use person_type as a base type of jazzMusician_type and extend it by appending the additional elements. This is depicted in Figures 8.3 and 8.4.

Here is the code for person_type:

```
<xs:complexType name="person_type">
  <xs:sequence>
    <xs:element name="ID" type="xs:NMTOKEN"/>
    <xs:element name="name">
      <xs:complexType>
        <xs:sequence>
          <xs:element name="first" type="xs:token"
                      maxOccurs="unbounded"/>
          <xs:element name="middle" type="xs:token" minOccurs="0"/>
          <xs:element name="last" type="xs:token"/>
        </xs:sequence>
      </xs:complexType>
    </xs:element>
    <xs:element name="birthDate" type="xs:date" minOccurs="0"/>
  </xs:sequence>
</xs:complexType>
```

Here is the code for jazzMusician_type derived from person_type:

```
<xs:complexType name="jazzMusician_type">
  <xs:complexContent>
    <xs:extension base="person_type">
      <xs:sequence>
        <xs:element name="kind">
          <xs:simpleType>
            <xs:restriction base="xs:string">
              <xs:enumeration value="instrumentalist"/>
```

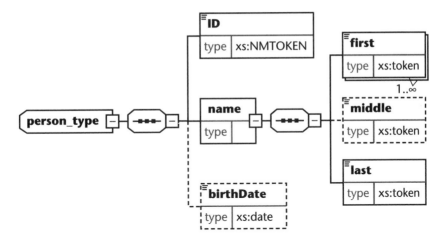

Figure 8.3 The complex type person_type.

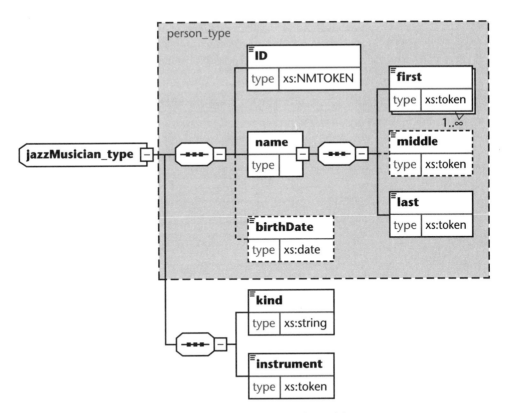

Figure 8.4 The complex type jazzMusician_type derived from person_type by extension.

```
            <xs:enumeration value="jazzComposer"/>
            <xs:enumeration value="jazzSinger"/>
          </xs:restriction>
        </xs:simpleType>
      </xs:element>
      <xs:element name="instrument" type="xs:token"
                  minOccurs="0" maxOccurs="unbounded"/>
    </xs:sequence>
  </xs:extension>
 </xs:complexContent>
</xs:complexType>
```

This has worked quite well, but this is only the simplest case of inheritance: No properties are overridden, and we don't have to deal with multiple inheritance. Things don't look so simple for the relationship between critic and person. Here, the subproperty first is overridden, because critic uses this subproperty with a different cardinality constraint. However, we are lucky. Since critic is a subtype of person (the narrower cardinality constraint for subproperty first diminishes the set of possible instances), we can derive this type by restriction (see Figure 8.5):

```
<xs:complexType name="critic_type">
  <xs:complexContent>
```

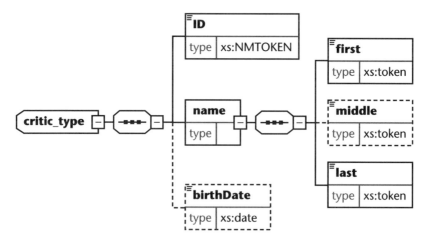

Figure 8.5 The complex type critic_type derived from person_type by restriction.

```
<xs:restriction base="person_type">
  <xs:sequence>
    <xs:element name="ID" type="xs:NMTOKEN"/>
    <xs:element name="name">
      <xs:complexType>
        <xs:sequence>
          <xs:element name="first" type="xs:token"/>
          <xs:element name="middle" type="xs:token"
                      minOccurs="0"/>
          <xs:element name="last" type="xs:token"/>
        </xs:sequence>
      </xs:complexType>
    </xs:element>
    <xs:element name="birthDate" type="xs:date" minOccurs="0"/>
  </xs:sequence>
</xs:restriction>
</xs:complexContent>
</xs:complexType>
```

Unfortunately, if properties are overridden in such a way that the new type is not a subtype of the inherited type (for example, if we want to allow multiple birth dates), we are out of luck. In these cases we can resolve the inheritance by the AOM inheritance rules (see Section 3.6), and then translate the resolved assets into a schema. But many inheritance relationships can be mapped to XML Schema, as we can always use combinations of type restriction and type extension.

8.2.5 The Complete Type Library

The creation of type definitions for the other assets is straightforward. Because we have already defined period_type, we can utilize this type in the definitions of belongsTo_type, project_type, and style_type. The implementation of these types is straightforward. We define each property and subproperty as a local element. This way, we do not run into name conflicts when the same property names should be used in different assets for different property types.

What is a bit out of the ordinary is the implementation of the property kind in asset jazzMusician. This property was defined as an enumeration with no specific type, so we will select the most general type for this element: xs:string. This built-in type will allow all enumeration values.

www_jazz_org_encyclopedia_TYPELIB.xsd

This file implements all asset types used in our model.

```xml
<?xml version="1.0" encoding="UTF-8"?>
<xs:schema targetNamespace="http://www.jazz.org/encyclopedia"
           xmlns="http://www.jazz.org/encyclopedia"
           xmlns:xhtml="http://www.w3.org/1999/xhtml"
           xmlns:xs="http://www.w3.org/2001/XMLSchema"
           elementFormDefault="qualified"
           attributeFormDefault="unqualified">
  <!--Asset type perso-->
  <xs:complexType name="person_type">
    <xs:sequence>
      <xs:element name="ID" type="xs:NMTOKEN"/>
      <xs:element name="name">
        <xs:complexType>
          <xs:sequence>
            <xs:element name="first" type="xs:token"
                        maxOccurs="unbounded"/>
            <xs:element name="middle" type="xs:token" minOccurs="0"/>
            <xs:element name="last" type="xs:token"/>
          </xs:sequence>
        </xs:complexType>
      </xs:element>
      <xs:element name="birthDate" type="xs:date" minOccurs="0"/>
    </xs:sequence>
  </xs:complexType>
  <!--Asset type period-->
  <xs:complexType name="period_type">
    <xs:sequence>
      <xs:element name="from" type="xs:gYear"/>
      <xs:element name="to" type="xs:gYear" minOccurs="0"/>
    </xs:sequence>
  </xs:complexType>
  <!--Asset type jazzMusician-->
  <xs:complexType name="jazzMusician_type">
```

```
    <xs:complexContent>
      <xs:extension base="person_type">
        <xs:sequence>
          <xs:element name="kind">
            <xs:simpleType>
              <xs:restriction base="xs:string">
                <xs:enumeration value="instrumentalist"/>
                <xs:enumeration value="jazzComposer"/>
                <xs:enumeration value="jazzSinger"/>
              </xs:restriction>
            </xs:simpleType>
          </xs:element>
          <xs:element name="instrument" type="xs:token"
                      minOccurs="0" maxOccurs="unbounded"/>
        </xs:sequence>
      </xs:extension>
    </xs:complexContent>
  </xs:complexType>
  <!--Asset type belongsTo-->
  <xs:complexType name="belongsTo_type">
    <xs:sequence>
      <xs:element name="period" type="period_type"/>
    </xs:sequence>
  </xs:complexType>
  <!--Asset type influence-->
  <xs:complexType name="influence_type"/>
  <!--Asset type produces-->
  <xs:complexType name="produces_type"/>
  <!--Asset type jamSession-->
  <xs:complexType name="jamSession_type">
    <xs:sequence>
      <xs:element name="time" type="xs:dateTime"/>
      <xs:element name="location" type="xs:token"/>
    </xs:sequence>
  </xs:complexType>
```

```xml
<!--Asset type project-->
<xs:complexType name="project_type">
  <xs:sequence>
    <xs:element name="name" type="xs:token"/>
    <xs:element name="period" type="period_type"/>
  </xs:sequence>
</xs:complexType>
<!--Asset type style-->
<xs:complexType name="style_type">
  <xs:sequence>
    <xs:element name="name" type="xs:token"/>
    <xs:element name="dominantDuring">
      <xs:complexType>
        <xs:sequence>
          <xs:element name="period" type="period_type"/>
        </xs:sequence>
      </xs:complexType>
    </xs:element>
  </xs:sequence>
</xs:complexType>
<!--Asset type description-->
<xs:complexType name="description_type">
 <xs:sequence>
  <xs:any namespace="http://www.w3.org/1999/xhtml"
          processContents="lax"/>
 </xs:sequence>
</xs:complexType>
<!--Asset type critic-->
<xs:complexType name="critic_type">
  <xs:complexContent>
    <xs:restriction base="person_type">
      <xs:sequence>
        <xs:element name="ID" type="xs:NMTOKEN"/>
        <xs:element name="name">
          <xs:complexType>
```

```
            <xs:sequence>
              <xs:element name="first" type="xs:token"/>
              <xs:element name="middle" type="xs:token"
                          minOccurs="0"/>
              <xs:element name="last" type="xs:token"/>
            </xs:sequence>
          </xs:complexType>
        </xs:element>
        <xs:element name="birthDate" type="xs:date" minOccurs="0"/>
      </xs:sequence>
    </xs:restriction>
  </xs:complexContent>
</xs:complexType>
<!--Asset type album-->
<xs:complexType name="album_type">
  <xs:sequence>
    <xs:element name="publisher" type="xs:anyURI"/>
    <xs:element name="productNo" type="xs:NMTOKEN"/>
    <xs:element name="title" type="xs:string"/>
  </xs:sequence>
</xs:complexType>
<!--Asset type track-->
<xs:complexType name="track_type">
  <xs:sequence>
    <xs:element name="title" type="xs:string"/>
    <xs:element name="duration" type="xs:duration" minOccurs="0"/>
  </xs:sequence>
  <xs:attribute name="trackNo" type="xs:ID"/>
</xs:complexType>
<!--Asset type sample-->
<xs:complexType name="sample_type">
  <xs:sequence>
    <xs:element name="MP3" type="xs:anyURI"/>
  </xs:sequence>
</xs:complexType>
```

```
<!--Asset type plays-->
<xs:complexType name="plays_type">
  <xs:sequence>
    <xs:element name="instrument" type="xs:token"
                maxOccurs="unbounded"/>
  </xs:sequence>
</xs:complexType>
<!--Asset type review-->
<xs:complexType name="review_type">
  <xs:sequence>
    <xs:element name="ID" type="xs:NMTOKEN"/>
    <xs:element name="pubDate" type="xs:gYearMonth"/>
  </xs:sequence>
</xs:complexType>
<!--Asset type magazine-->
<xs:complexType name="magazine_type">
  <xs:sequence>
    <xs:element name="name" type="xs:string"/>
    <xs:element name="URI" type="xs:anyURI"/>
  </xs:sequence>
</xs:complexType>
</xs:schema>
```

The highlighted piece of code in the definition of description_type shows
some detail that we have added to asset description. Remember that we left the
definition of asset description unfinished in Section 3.7 because we wanted to
add some detail later. We have now decided to leave that task (of adding detail)
to the W3C's XHTML Working Group, and to simply create a wildcard.

We have set processContents to "lax" (see Section 5.3.15) for this wildcard
and have declared the namespace as "http://www.w3.org/1999/xhtml". This will
cause processors to check the element for valid content if an XHTML schema
definition is available and accessible, but to accept the element as valid if such a
schema definition is not available or accessible. The namespace attribute reflects
the XHTML namespace URI.

In the definition of track_type, we have made an exception and implemented trackNo as an attribute of type ID. This is to provide backward compatibility with DTDs—trackNo is used as a key for cross-references. This backward
compatibility costs something: The preferred choice would be to implement
trackNo as an unsignedByte attribute or element to allow numeric key values.
Now, with type ID in place, all key values must start with a letter.

8.2.6 **Implementing a Business Object**

So far, we have only created complex types that perfectly describe the structure of each asset and have not bothered with the connecting arcs between the assets. This is what we want to do now. Each L2S contains a tree of assets, with the identifying asset in the top position. Remember that we chose the L2S in such a way that they represent business objects of our business scenario (see Section 3.7).

Let's begin with L2S jazzMusician. The identifying item here is asset jazzMusician. We implement this asset as the root element of the jazzMusician document. The type assigned to this element is derived from type jazzMusician_type by extension. The extension consists of the other assets in this L2S (belongsTo, influence, and produces) that are implemented as child elements of jazzMusician.

We use an include statement to access the type definitions in our previously defined type library. For a flexible schema layout, we implement each asset as a global element (which is always possible since asset names are unique within a model), and refer to these definitions as needed. Figure 8.6 (page 272) shows a diagram of the finished schema.

jazzMusician.xsd

This file implements the L2S jazzMusician with all outgoing arcs.

```
<?xml version="1.0" encoding="UTF-8"?>

<xs:schema targetNamespace="http://www.jazz.org/encyclopedia"
           xmlns:xs="http://www.w3.org/2001/XMLSchema"
           xmlns="http://www.jazz.org/encyclopedia"
           xmlns:xsg="http://www.aomodeling.org/KLEEN/XSDgenerator"
           elementFormDefault="qualified"
           attributeFormDefault="unqualified">

<xs:include schemaLocation="www_jazz_org_encyclopedia_TYPELIB.xsd"/>

<!--Asset jazzMusician-->

<xs:element name="jazzMusician">
  <xs:complexType>
   <xs:complexContent>
    <xs:extension base="jazzMusician_type">
     <xs:sequence>
        <xs:element ref="produces"
                    minOccurs="0" maxOccurs="unbounded"/>
        <xs:element ref="belongsTo"
                    minOccurs="0" maxOccurs="unbounded"/>
        <xs:element ref="influence"
                    minOccurs="0" maxOccurs="unbounded"/>
```

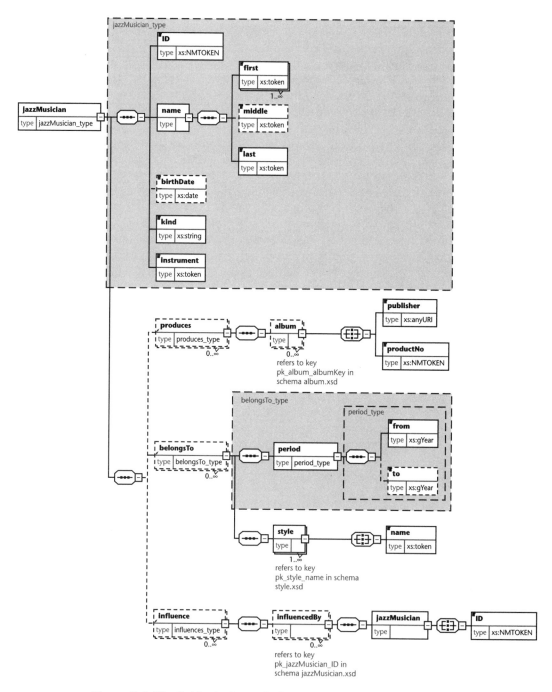

Figure 8.6 The finished schema for business object `jazzMusician`.

```
    </xs:sequence>
   </xs:extension>
  </xs:complexContent>
 </xs:complexType>
 <xs:key name="pk__jazzMusician_ID">
  <xs:selector xpath="."/>
  <xs:field xpath="ID"/>
 </xs:key>
</xs:element>
<!--Asset produces-->
<xs:element name="produces">
 <xs:complexType>
  <xs:complexContent>
   <xs:extension base="produces_type">
    <xs:sequence>
     <xs:element name="album" minOccurs="0" maxOccurs="unbounded">
      <xs:annotation>
       <xs:documentation>
          refers to key pk__album_albumKey in schema album.xsd
       </xs:documentation>
       <xs:appinfo>
         <xsg:refersToSchema
                xmlns:xlink="http://www.w3.org/1999/xlink"
                xlink:href="album.xsd"
                xlink:type="simple"
                keyName="pk__album_albumKey"/>
       </xs:appinfo>
      </xs:annotation>
      <xs:complexType>
       <xs:all>
        <xs:element name="publisher" type="xs:anyURI"/>
        <xs:element name="productNo" type="xs:NMTOKEN"/>
       </xs:all>
      </xs:complexType>
     </xs:element>
```

```
        </xs:sequence>
      </xs:extension>
    </xs:complexContent>
  </xs:complexType>
</xs:element>
<!--Asset belongsTo-->
<xs:element name="belongsTo">
  <xs:complexType>
    <xs:complexContent>
      <xs:extension base="belongsTo_type">
        <xs:sequence>
          <xs:element name="style" maxOccurs="unbounded">
            <xs:annotation>
              <xs:documentation>
                  refers to key pk__style_name in schema style.xsd
              </xs:documentation>
              <xs:appinfo>
               <xsg:refersToSchema
                    xlink:href="style.xsd"
                    xlink:type="simple"
                    xmlns:xlink="http://www.w3.org/1999/xlink"
                    keyName="pk__style_name"/>
              </xs:appinfo>
            </xs:annotation>
            <xs:complexType>
              <xs:all>
                <xs:element name="name" type="xs:token"/>
              </xs:all>
            </xs:complexType>
          </xs:element>
        </xs:sequence>
      </xs:extension>
    </xs:complexContent>
  </xs:complexType>
</xs:element>
<!--Asset influence-->
```

```
<xs:element name="influence">
 <xs:complexType>
  <xs:complexContent>
   <xs:extension base="influence_type">
    <xs:sequence>
     <xs:element maxOccurs="unbounded" minOccurs="0"
                 name="influencedBy">
      <xs:annotation>
       <xs:documentation>
          refers to key pk__jazzMusician_ID in schema jazzMusician.xsd
       </xs:documentation>
       <xs:appinfo>
        <xsg:refersToSchema xlink:href="jazzMusician.xsd"
                            xlink:type="simple"
                            xmlns:xlink="http://www.w3.org/1999/xlink"
                            keyName="pk__jazzMusician_ID"/>
       </xs:appinfo>
      </xs:annotation>
      <xs:complexType>
       <xs:sequence>
        <xs:element name="jazzMusician">
         <xs:complexType>
          <xs:all>
           <xs:element name="ID" type="xs:NMTOKEN"/>
          </xs:all>
         </xs:complexType>
        </xs:element>
       </xs:sequence>
      </xs:complexType>
     </xs:element>
    </xs:sequence>
   </xs:extension>
  </xs:complexContent>
 </xs:complexType>
</xs:element>
</xs:schema>
```

The first highlighted group represents the arcs to the assets belongsTo, influence, and produces. They are simply implemented as references to the global elements implementing these assets.

The next highlighted group sets up a key for the element jazzMusician. This is based on the key definition in the model. We select the only key field "ID" and compose a key name from the asset name and the key definition. The prefix pk_ identifies this key as a primary key (not that the key is really needed in this schema). Keys defined in XML Schema (or for that matter in a DTD or in Relax NG) are used to index elements with multiple occurrences within a document instance for cross-referencing. This is not the case for element jazzMusician. Within one document instance, we have exactly one root element jazzMusician, and it is not a target for cross-referencing. However, we keep this key definition as a schema representation of the original AOM key definition.

What follows is the code for the asset produces. This asset does not have properties, but it has an arc into another business object (to asset album). How do we implement such an arc? That depends primarily on how we want to process the documents later. In an instance document, we could, for example, represent such an arc with an XLink clause pointing to the referenced album document. Here, we have taken a relational approach and have created a foreign key represented by the element album. This element contains as its only elements the key fields of asset album. We used the connector xs:all to group the key fields together because the sequence of key fields does not matter. Document instances could contain values for publisher and productNo and thus refer to a concrete album instance.

Combining the corresponding instances of jazzMusicians and album would require a query language such as XQuery. Such a query language could evaluate the data in the foreign key fields in jazzMusician/belongsTo/album and in the primary key fields of an album instance, and could then join both documents. To make this connection visible to human and machine readers of the schema, it is documented in an annotation. The documentation clause is for human readers; the appinfo clause is for applications.

The same technique is used when implementing asset belongsTo. Here, we have created a foreign key element representing the asset style. This element contains as its only child element the key field name.

Again, the same logic is used to implement asset influence. Remember that the arrow with the role name influencedBy was declared with range constraint >jazzMusician. Thus, it can point to other instances of the jazzMusician schema. So, we don't implement this arc as an instance-internal cross-reference but in the same manner as the other arcs leading out of the Level 2 Structure jazzMusician. Note, too, that the element influence does not directly contain the element jazzMusician as a child. We have wrapped element influencedBy around jazzMusician to carry the role name of this arc into the schema.

We have added the attributes minOccurs="0" and maxOccurs="unbounded" to the definition of element influencedBy to reflect the unconstrained cardinality of this arc. Of course, we could have used a different method to implement this arc. We could have used data type NMTOKENS instead of NMTOKEN for the key field. This would allow us to get rid of the maxOccurs="unbounded" attribute. In case of multiple arc targets, the document instance would need only a single influencedBy element because multiple key values can be coded into the NMTOKENS key field. However, this technique is only possible with key data types that do not allow whitespace (such as NMTOKEN, ID, numbers, etc.) and when the key consists of a single field.

The next section discusses how to implement cross-reference arcs that are local to an instance.

8.2.7 Dealing with Cross-References

With the implementation of business object album, we arrive at a new problem: album does not have a hierarchical structure. True, both assets track and sample can be implemented as child elements of a root element album, but there is a cross-reference between track and sample. Please note that this arc does not have a range specification, so the arc is local to the instances of schema album—it always points from an album track to a sample of the *same* album.

This is a typical case for applying a cross-reference construct consisting of a key clause and a keyref clause. With the key clause, we define a primary key for each track—a primary key scoped to one instance document of schema album. The way to implement this in XML Schema is to introduce a key clause at the *origin* of the arc representing the cross-reference. This clause defines a local primary key for the tracks of an album document. It must be defined within the scope of the album element (the root element) because it must be accessible to other child elements (such as sample) of album.

Notice how the key "pk__track_trackNo" is defined in the schema below. The key selector is set to "./track" in order to select the track child elements for this key. The field clause specifies the single key field.

In the definition for element sample, the code that implements the arc leading from sample to track is highlighted. This is the same technique we used above for arcs that cross the boundaries of business objects. What is different is that we have also created a keyref definition named "fk__sample_track". This keyref definition establishes a foreign key, and it refers to our primary key "pk__track_trackNo". The selector clause specifies the element album/sample /track, which implements the arc. We were able to use the relative path notation ./track because this keyref definition is defined in the scope of element album/sample. Note that we have implemented the foreign key field trackNo as an attribute in order to provide backward compatibility with DTDs.

album.xsd

This file implements the L2S album with all outgoing arcs.

```xml
<?xml version="1.0" encoding="UTF-8"?>
<xs:schema attributeFormDefault="unqualified"
           elementFormDefault="qualified"
           targetNamespace="http://www.jazz.org/encyclopedia"
           xmlns="http://www.jazz.org/encyclopedia"
           xmlns:xs="http://www.w3.org/2001/XMLSchema"
           xmlns:xsg="http://www.aomodeling.org/KLEEN/XSDgenerator">
 <xs:include schemaLocation="www_jazz_org_encyclopedia_TYPELIB.xsd"/>
 <!--Asset album-->
 <xs:element name="album">
  <xs:complexType>
   <xs:complexContent>
    <xs:extension base="album_type">
     <xs:sequence>
      <xs:element maxOccurs="unbounded" ref="track"/>
      <xs:element maxOccurs="unbounded" minOccurs="0" ref="sample"/>
      <xs:element maxOccurs="unbounded" minOccurs="0" ref="plays"/>
     </xs:sequence>
    </xs:extension>
   </xs:complexContent>
  </xs:complexType>
  <xs:key name="pk__album_albumKey">
   <xs:selector xpath="."/>
   <xs:field xpath="publisher"/>
   <xs:field xpath="productNo"/>
  </xs:key>
  <xs:key name="pk__track_trackNo">
   <xs:selector xpath="./track"/>
   <xs:field xpath="@trackNo"/>
  </xs:key>
 </xs:element>
 <!--Asset track-->
 <xs:element name="track" type="track_type"/>
```

```
<!--Asset sample-->
 <xs:element name="sample">
  <xs:complexType>
   <xs:complexContent>
    <xs:extension base="sample_type">
     <xs:sequence>
      <xs:element name="track">
       <xs:complexType>
        <xs:attribute name="trackNo" type="xs:IDREF"/>
       </xs:complexType>
      </xs:element>
     </xs:sequence>
    </xs:extension>
   </xs:complexContent>
  </xs:complexType>
  <xs:keyref name="fk__sample_track" refer="pk__track_trackNo">
   <xs:selector xpath="./track"/>
   <xs:field xpath="@trackNo"/>
  </xs:keyref>
 </xs:element>
<!--Asset plays-->
 <xs:element name="plays">
  <xs:complexType>
   <xs:complexContent>
    <xs:extension base="plays_type">
     <xs:sequence>
      <xs:element name="jazzMusician">
       <xs:annotation>
        <xs:documentation>
          refers to key pk__jazzMusician_ID in schema jazzMusician.xsd
        </xs:documentation>
        <xs:appinfo>
         <xsg:refersToSchema xlink:href="jazzMusician.xsd"
            xlink:type="simple"
            xmlns:xlink="http://www.w3.org/1999/xlink"
            keyName="pk__jazzMusician_ID"/>
```

```
        </xs:appinfo>
       </xs:annotation>
       <xs:complexType>
        <xs:all>
         <xs:element name="ID" type="xs:NMTOKEN"/>
        </xs:all>
       </xs:complexType>
      </xs:element>
     </xs:sequence>
    </xs:extension>
   </xs:complexContent>
  </xs:complexType>
 </xs:element>
</xs:schema>
```

The element plays has an arc leading to business object jazzMusician. This is implemented in the usual way, as already explained in the previous section. Figure 8.7 illustrates the structure of business object album.

8.2.8 Using Substitution Groups

Now we define the two business objects that have been modeled as a single asset: project and band. This was expressed by decorating the asset project with two display labels: project and band. Consequently, we also create only one schema for them.

We implement this construct by first creating a complex type definition for asset project. We call this type project_asset. Next we define an element named project with the type project_asset. In this element we can include code for the key definitions made in asset project. Now we have two options to create an element band:

- We create it as a member of a substitution group. This is the preferred option because this way we do not have to replicate the key definition but can inherit it from the head element of the substitution group. This option was chosen in the code below: Element band refers to substitution group project.
- Another option would be to create the element band as a normal element of type project_asset. This would be necessary if we wanted to create this element as a local element because substitution groups can only be used on a global level.

Of course, we also could have created project_asset as an element and could have used it as the head of a substitution group. In this case we would need to

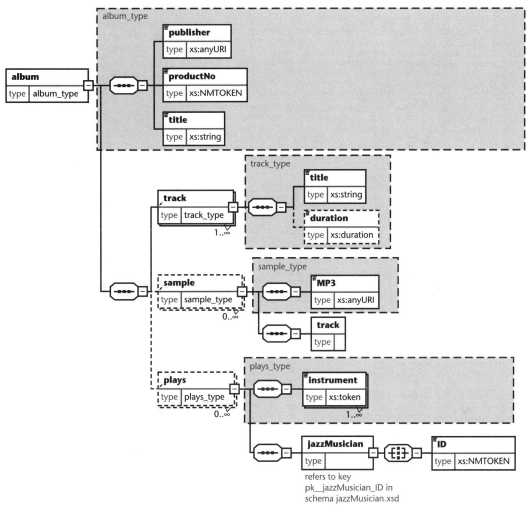

Figure 8.7 The structure of business object album. The identity constraints (key/keyref) are not visible in this diagram.

declare this element as abstract because the model does not allow instances of name project_asset. Because we experienced some problems with validators when the head element of a substitution group is declared as abstract, we have chosen this way of implementing project_asset as a complex type.

Finally, the last possibility is to choose a shortcut, and simply create an element for project and use it as the head element in the definition of element band. But this approach does not separate clearly between asset and display labels and could lead to problems later when the schema grows. It is better to use the kind of indirection shown in the code below.

project.xsd

This file implements the L2S project with all outgoing arcs. It also defines a substitution group for the display name band.

```
<?xml version="1.0" encoding="UTF-8"?>
<xs:schema targetNamespace="http://www.jazz.org/encyclopedia"
          xmlns:xs="http://www.w3.org/2001/XMLSchema"
          xmlns="http://www.jazz.org/encyclopedia"
          xmlns:xsg="http://www.aomodeling.org/KLEEN/XSDgenerator"
          elementFormDefault="qualified"
          attributeFormDefault="unqualified">
<xs:include schemaLocation="www_jazz_org_encyclopedia_TYPELIB.xsd"/>
<!--Asset project-->
 <xs:complexType name="project_asset">
  <xs:complexContent>
   <xs:extension base="project_type">
    <xs:sequence>
     <xs:element name="result" minOccurs="0" maxOccurs="unbounded">
      <xs:complexType>
       <xs:sequence>
        <xs:element name="album">
         <xs:annotation>
          <xs:documentation>
              refers to key pk__album_albumKey in schema album.xsd
          </xs:documentation>
          <xs:appinfo>
           <xsg:refersToSchema
                xlink:href="album.xsd" xlink:type="simple"
                xmlns:xlink="http://www.w3.org/1999/xlink"
                keyName="pk__album_albumKey"/>
          </xs:appinfo>
         </xs:annotation>
         <xs:complexType>
          <xs:all>
           <xs:element name="publisher" type="xs:anyURI"/>
           <xs:element name="productNo" type="xs:NMTOKEN"/>
```

```
            </xs:all>
          </xs:complexType>
        </xs:element>
      </xs:sequence>
    </xs:complexType>
  </xs:element>
  <xs:element name="jazzMusician"
              minOccurs="2" maxOccurs="unbounded">
   <xs:annotation>
    <xs:documentation>
       refers to key pk__jazzMusician_ID in schema jazzMusician.xsd
    </xs:documentation>
    <xs:appinfo>
     <xsg:refersToSchema xlink:href="jazzMusician.xsd"
                    xlink:type="simple"
                    xmlns:xlink="http://www.w3.org/1999/xlink"
                    keyName="pk__jazzMusician_ID"/>
    </xs:appinfo>
   </xs:annotation>
   <xs:complexType>
    <xs:all>
     <xs:element name="ID" type="xs:NMTOKEN"/>
    </xs:all>
   </xs:complexType>
  </xs:element>
 </xs:sequence>
 </xs:extension>
 </xs:complexContent>
</xs:complexType>
<xs:element name="project" type="project_asset">
 <xs:key name="pk__project_name">
  <xs:selector xpath="."/>
  <xs:field xpath="name"/>
 </xs:key>
</xs:element>
<xs:element name="band" substitutionGroup="project"/>
</xs:schema>
```

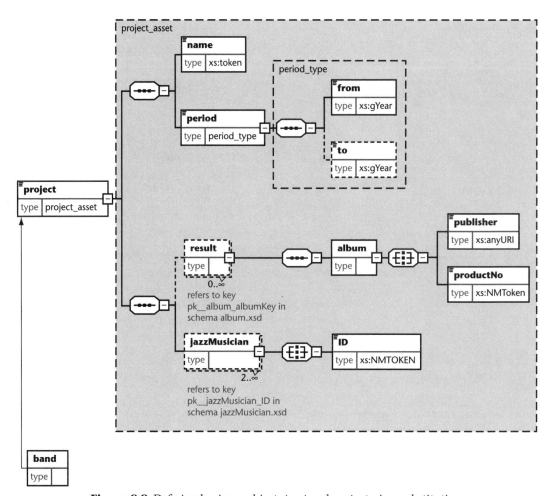

Figure 8.8 Defining business objects band and project via a substitution group.

Again, we have defined the arcs leading to jazzMusician and to album as elements whose child elements contain the foreign key values. Note that the element album is wrapped by element result because we wanted to carry the role name of the arc leading from project/band to album into the schema. Figure 8.8 illustrates the schema for project/band.

8.2.9 Implementing Clusters

Asset review contains a cluster with arcs leading to jazzMusician and album. This indicates that a review instance relates either to a jazzMusician instance or to an album instance—that is, a review either honors the life and work of a particular jazz musician, or praises the newest jazz album on the market.

The way to implement this in XML Schema is via a choice clause.

review.xsd

This file implements the L2S review with all outgoing arcs.

```
<?xml version="1.0" encoding="UTF-8"?>

<xs:schema targetNamespace="http://www.jazz.org/encyclopedia"
           xmlns:xs="http://www.w3.org/2001/XMLSchema"
           xmlns="http://www.jazz.org/encyclopedia"
           xmlns:xsg="http://www.aomodeling.org/KLEEN/XSDgenerator"
           elementFormDefault="qualified"
           attributeFormDefault="unqualified">

<xs:include schemaLocation="www_jazz_org_encyclopedia_TYPELIB.xsd"/>

<!--Asset review-->
 <xs:element name="review">
  <xs:complexType>
   <xs:complexContent>
    <xs:extension base="review_type">
     <xs:sequence>
      <xs:choice>
       <xs:element name="album">
        <xs:annotation>
         <xs:documentation>
            refers to key pk__album_albumKey in schema album.xsd
         </xs:documentation>
         <xs:appinfo>
          <xsg:refersToSchema xlink:href="album.xsd"
                      xlink:type="simple"
                      xmlns:xlink="http://www.w3.org/1999/xlink"
                      keyName="pk__album_albumKey"/>
         </xs:appinfo>
        </xs:annotation>
        <xs:complexType>
         <xs:all>
          <xs:element name="publisher" type="xs:anyURI"/>
          <xs:element name="productNo" type="xs:NMTOKEN"/>
```

```
      </xs:all>
    </xs:complexType>
  </xs:element>
  <xs:element name="jazzMusician">
   <xs:annotation>
    <xs:documentation>
      refers to key pk__jazzMusician_ID in schema jazzMusician.xsd
    </xs:documentation>
    <xs:appinfo>
     <xsg:refersToSchema xlink:href="jazzMusician.xsd"
                    xlink:type="simple"
                    xmlns:xlink="http://www.w3.org/1999/xlink"
                    keyName="pk__jazzMusician_ID"/>
    </xs:appinfo>
   </xs:annotation>
   <xs:complexType>
    <xs:all>
     <xs:element name="ID" type="xs:NMTOKEN"/>
    </xs:all>
   </xs:complexType>
  </xs:element>
  </xs:choice>
  <xs:element ref="magazine"/>
  <xs:element name="critic">
   <xs:annotation>
    <xs:documentation>
      refers to key pk__critic_ID in schema critic.xsd
    </xs:documentation>
    <xs:appinfo>
     <xsg:refersToSchema xlink:href="critic.xsd"
                    xlink:type="simple"
                    xmlns:xlink="http://www.w3.org/1999/xlink"
                    keyName="pk__critic_ID"/>
    </xs:appinfo>
   </xs:annotation>
   <xs:complexType>
    <xs:all>
```

```
            <xs:element name="ID" type="xs:NMTOKEN"/>
          </xs:all>
        </xs:complexType>
      </xs:element>
    </xs:sequence>
  </xs:extension>
 </xs:complexContent>
 </xs:complexType>
 <xs:key name="pk__review_ID">
  <xs:selector xpath="."/>
  <xs:field xpath="ID"/>
 </xs:key>
</xs:element>
<!--Asset magazine-->
<xs:element name="magazine" type="magazine_type"/>
</xs:schema>
```

The two arcs are implemented in the usual way, but they are simply connected via the choice clause. So an instance element review may only refer to one of either album or jazzMusician. The structure of business object review is shown in Figure 8.9 (page 288).

8.2.10 Business Objects critic and style

Finally, we show the schemata for the assets critic and style.

critic.xsd

This file implements the L2S critic (Figure 8.10, page 289).

```
<?xml version="1.0" encoding="UTF-8"?>
<xs:schema targetNamespace="http://www.jazz.org/encyclopedia"
           xmlns:xsg="http://www.aomodeling.org/KLEEN/XSDgenerator"
           xmlns:xs="http://www.w3.org/2001/XMLSchema"
           xmlns="http://www.jazz.org/encyclopedia"
           elementFormDefault="qualified"
           attributeFormDefault="unqualified">
  <xs:include schemaLocation="www_jazz_org_encyclopedia_TYPELIB.xsd"/>
  <!--Asset critic-->
```

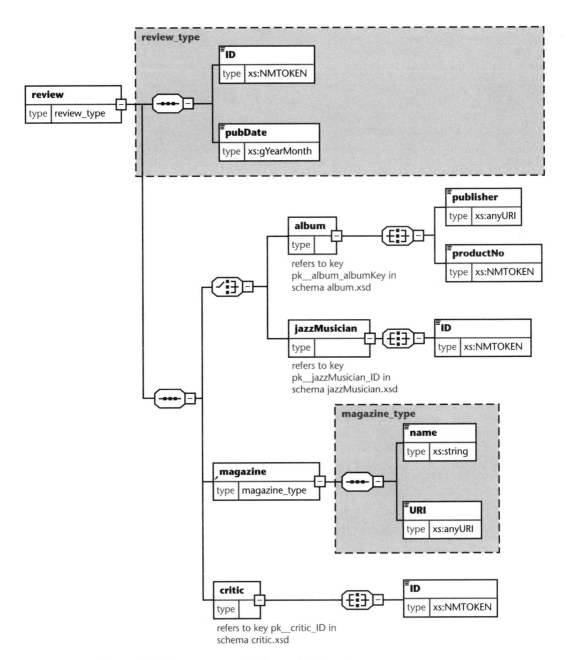

Figure 8.9 The structure of business object review.

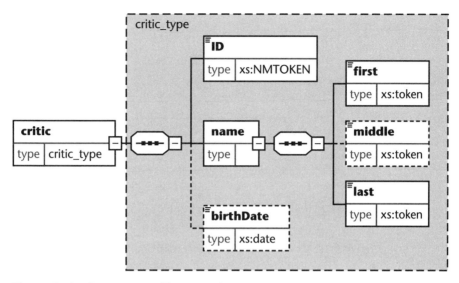

Figure 8.10 The structure of business object `critic`.

```
<xs:element name="critic" type="critic_type">
  <xs:key name="pk__critic_ID">
    <xs:selector xpath="."/>
    <xs:field xpath="ID"/>
  </xs:key>
</xs:element>
</xs:schema>
```

style.xsd

Finally, this file implements the L2S `style` according to the diagram in Figure 8.11 (page 290).

```
<?xml version="1.0" encoding="UTF-8"?>
<xs:schema targetNamespace="http://www.jazz.org/encyclopedia"
           xmlns:xsg="http://www.aomodeling.org/KLEEN/XSDgenerator"
           xmlns:xs="http://www.w3.org/2001/XMLSchema"
           xmlns="http://www.jazz.org/encyclopedia"
           elementFormDefault="qualified"
           attributeFormDefault="unqualified">
```

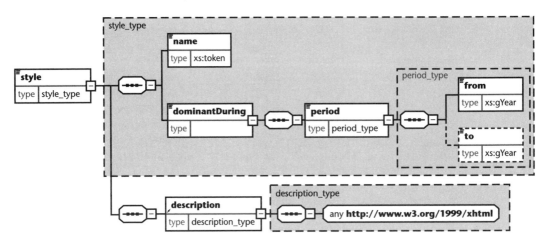

Figure 8.11 The structure of business object style.

```
<xs:include schemaLocation="www_jazz_org_encyclopedia_TYPELIB.xsd"/>
<!--Asset style-->
<xs:element name="style">
  <xs:complexType>
    <xs:complexContent>
      <xs:extension base="style_type">
        <xs:sequence>
          <xs:element ref="description"/>
        </xs:sequence>
      </xs:extension>
    </xs:complexContent>
  </xs:complexType>
  <xs:key name="pk__style_name">
    <xs:selector xpath="."/>
    <xs:field xpath="name"/>
  </xs:key>
</xs:element>
<!--Asset description-->
<xs:element name="description" type="description_type"/>
</xs:schema>
```

8.3 IMPLEMENTATION IN RELAX NG

For comparison, we implement the model shown in Figure 8.1 again, but this time in Relax NG.

8.3.1 Creating a Type Library

Again, our approach will be to first implement the asset types and then extend these definitions with the implementation of keys and arcs. Since Relax NG does not feature a type system similar to the complex types in XML Schema, we might consider using the more generic pattern feature instead for this task.

Let's start with the same asset as in Section 8.2. The asset period serves as a type that is used for property type declarations in various other assets. We implement this asset as a pattern named period_type.

period_type.rng

This file implements the asset type period.

```
<?xml version="1.0" encoding="UTF-8"?>
<rng:grammar xmlns:rng="http://relaxng.org/ns/structure/1.0"
             xmlns="http://www.jazz.org/encyclopedia"
             ns="http://www.jazz.org/encyclopedia"
  datatypeLibrary="http://www.w3.org/2001/XMLSchema-datatypes">


<rng:define name="period_type">
  <rng:element name="from">
    <rng:data type="gYear"/>
  </rng:element>
  <rng:optional>
    <rng:element name="to">
      <rng:data type="gYear"/>
    </rng:element>
  </rng:optional>

</rng:define>
</rng:grammar>
```

This pattern defines the content of any element of type period, its child elements, and their simple data types. As a target namespace, we have declared the namespace of our jazz encyclopedia model. This is done with attribute ns. We have also set the default namespace as identical to the target namespace; consequently, we have to prefix the Relax NG vocabulary.

As shown in Section 7.2.3, we can apply this pattern wherever an element of type period is used. For example:

```
<rng:element name="period">
  <rng:externalRef href="period_type.rng"/>
</rng:element>
```

The mechanism is very simple: It is a simple textual inclusion of the referenced file. As shown in Section 7.2.3, we can also pack together several such pattern declarations within a grammar. We can then include this external grammar in our current grammar and directly reference types with

```
<rng:ref name ="period_type"/>
```

instead of

```
<rng:externalRef href="period_type.rng"/>.
```

8.3.2 Handling Inheritance

Simple inheritance relationships could be resolved with the same technique. We could just include the pattern reference for the inherited type in the definition of the inheriting type. However, this technique does not work in more advanced cases of inheritance. Because we have no way to override definitions within a referenced pattern, we cannot use this technique to implement inheritance relationships where inherited properties are overridden by the inheriting asset. If we want to achieve that, we must break each structure into its smallest ingredients and define each as a pattern. This allows us later to override (or redefine) each property and subproperty of a type.

Let's see how the definition of the asset type person looks when we implement it this way.

person_type.rng

This file implements the asset type person.

```
<?xml version="1.0" encoding="UTF-8"?>
<rng:grammar xmlns:rng="http://relaxng.org/ns/structure/1.0"
            xmlns="http://www.jazz.org/encyclopedia"
            ns="http://www.jazz.org/encyclopedia"
        datatypeLibrary="http://www.w3.org/2001/XMLSchema-datatypes">
  <rng:define name="person_type">
```

```
    <rng:ref name="pID"/>
    <rng:ref name="pName"/>
    <rng:ref name="pBirthDate"/>
</rng:define>
<rng:define name="pID">
  <rng:element name="ID">
    <rng:data type="NMTOKEN"/>
  </rng:element>
</rng:define>
<rng:define name="pName">
  <rng:element name="name">
    <rng:ref name="pName.first"/>
    <rng:ref name="pName.middle"/>
    <rng:ref name="pName.last"/>
  </rng:element>
</rng:define>
<rng:define name="pName.first">
  <rng:oneOrMore>
    <rng:element name="first">
      <rng:data type="token"/>
    </rng:element>
  </rng:oneOrMore>
</rng:define>
<rng:define name="pName.middle">
  <rng:optional>
    <rng:element name="middle">
      <rng:data type="token"/>
    </rng:element>
  </rng:optional>
</rng:define>
<rng:define name="pName.last">
  <rng:element name="last">
    <rng:data type="token"/>
  </rng:element>
</rng:define>
```

```
<rng:define name="pBirthDate">
  <rng:optional>
    <rng:element name="birthDate">
      <rng:data type="date"/>
    </rng:element>
  </rng:optional>
</rng:define>
</rng:grammar>
```

We have defined a pattern around each individual element. This a bit lengthy, but the effort will pay off. Of course, we have to be careful about name clashes. We cannot just prefix each type with a *p* and use it as a pattern name. There may be several local type definitions with the same name. Since patterns are always defined on the global level, we must in such cases rename that pattern. A general approach is to use the full path of an element, as shown in the pName.first, pName.middle, pName.last patterns. Since pattern names don't appear in the document instance, we are completely free to choose any pattern name we like.

Let's assume that we stored this grammar in file person_type.rng. We can reuse this grammar for the definition of jazzMusician_type. We refer to the external grammar with an include clause. In the case of jazzMusician_type, the inheritance involves simple extension of the person type definition, so nothing needs to be overridden. We simply concatenate additional patterns containing definitions for the properties kind and instrument.

Again, we have implemented these properties as elements. Of course, we could have implemented some of these properties (for instance, the property kind) as attributes, but we stay with elements as in Section 8.2.

jazzMusician_type.rng

This file implements the asset type jazzMusician.

```
<?xml version="1.0" encoding="UTF-8"?>
<rng:grammar xmlns:rng="http://relaxng.org/ns/structure/1.0"
             xmlns="http://www.jazz.org/encyclopedia"
             ns="http://www.jazz.org/encyclopedia"
          datatypeLibrary="http://www.w3.org/2001/XMLSchema-datatypes">
  <rng:include href="person_type.rng"/>
  <rng:define name="jazzMusician_type">
    <rng:element name="jazzMusician">
      <rng:ref name="person_type"/>
```

```
      <rng:ref name="pKind"/>
      <rng:zeroOrMore>
        <rng:ref name="pInstrument"/>
      </rng:zeroOrMore>
    </rng:element>
  </rng:define>
  <rng:define name="pKind">
    <rng:element name="kind">
      <rng:choice>
        <rng:value>instrumentalist</rng:value>
        <rng:value>jazzComposer</rng:value>
        <rng:value>jazzSinger</rng:value>
      </rng:choice>
    </rng:element>
  </rng:define>
  <rng:define name="pInstrument">
    <rng:element name="instrument">
      <rng:data type="token"/>
    </rng:element>
  </rng:define>
</rng:grammar>
```

Note that Relax NG does not require us to define a data type for the enumeration values. They are just taken as text.

Next, we have the implementation of asset type critic, which is a subtype of person_type, too. However, critic overrides the cardinality constraints of name/first with a new value. So, we override the definition of the pFirst pattern when including the person_type grammar.

critic_type.rng

This file implements the asset type critic.

```
<?xml version="1.0" encoding="UTF-8"?>
<rng:grammar xmlns:rng="http://relaxng.org/ns/structure/1.0"
          xmlns="http://www.jazz.org/encyclopedia"
          ns="http://www.jazz.org/encyclopedia"
        datatypeLibrary="http://www.w3.org/2001/XMLSchema-datatypes">
```

```
<rng:include href="person_type.rng">
  <rng:define name="pName.first">
    <rng:element name="first">
      <rng:data type="token"/>
    </rng:element>
  </rng:define>
</rng:include>
<rng:define name="critic_type">
  <rng:ref name="person_type"/>
</rng:define>
</rng:grammar>
```

In contrast to XML Schema, where we derived the type critic_type from person_type by restriction and had to repeat all elements, including the ones that did not change, Relax NG only requires us to specify the changed pattern. Also, Relax NG can override patterns, even when the new type is not a restriction of the base type. Consequently, inheritance relationships can be mapped onto a Relax NG implementation in more cases than is possible with XML Schema.

Breaking complex structures into their smallest ingredients and defining each of those as its own pattern is only required for those types that are inherited by other types. However, I recommend this as a standard technique when defining reusable components and schemata with Relax NG. It allows the derivation of new schemata easily by including the old schema and overriding the patterns that have changed. Schemata implemented in such a way will lend themselves easily to later schema evolution (see Section 12.2.1).

8.3.3 The Complete Type Library

In the following type library, we will not follow this advice to break structures into their smallest parts. This will save a bit of space and improve the readability of the code.

When implementing schemata with Relax NG, it makes sense to implement each type in a separate file instead of storing all type definitions in one big type library. In particular, this is true when we want to inherit definitions between types across multiple inheritance levels, since we can override patterns only within the include clause.

The following code lists the remaining type definitions, each as a separate grammar stored in a separate file. period_type, person_type, jazzMusician_type, and critic_type are not listed again, as they have already appeared in the previous section. Comments are minimal, as the code is almost self-explanatory.

album_type.rng

This file implements the asset type album.

```
<?xml version="1.0" encoding="UTF-8"?>
<rng:grammar xmlns:rng="http://relaxng.org/ns/structure/1.0"
             xmlns="http://www.jazz.org/encyclopedia"
             ns="http://www.jazz.org/encyclopedia"
       datatypeLibrary="http://www.w3.org/2001/XMLSchema-datatypes">
<!--Asset type album-->
<rng:define name="album_type">
  <rng:element name="publisher">
    <rng:data type="anyURI"/>
  </rng:element>
  <rng:element name="productNo">
    <rng:data type="NMTOKEN"/>
  </rng:element>
  <rng:element name="title">
    <rng:text/>
  </rng:element>
</rng:define>
</rng:grammar>
```

belongsTo_type.rng

This file implements the asset type belongsTo.

```
<?xml version="1.0" encoding="UTF-8"?>
<rng:grammar xmlns:rng="http://relaxng.org/ns/structure/1.0"
             xmlns="http://www.jazz.org/encyclopedia"
             ns="http://www.jazz.org/encyclopedia"
       datatypeLibrary="http://www.w3.org/2001/XMLSchema-datatypes">

<!--Asset type belongsTo-->
<rng:include href="period_type.rng"/>
<rng:define name="belongsTo_type">
  <rng:element name="period">
    <rng:ref name="period_type"/>
```

```
    </rng:element>
  </rng:define>
</rng:grammar>
```

description_type.rng

This file implements the asset type `description`.

```
<?xml version="1.0" encoding="UTF-8"?>
<rng:grammar xmlns:rng="http://relaxng.org/ns/structure/1.0"
             xmlns="http://www.jazz.org/encyclopedia"
             ns="http://www.jazz.org/encyclopedia">

<!--Asset type description-->
<rng:define name="description_type">
  <rng:externalRef href="anyXhtml.rng"/>
</rng:define>
</rng:grammar>
```

Here we have to implement a wildcard. Relax NG does not have its own wildcard construct; instead we have to express the wildcard with a structure similar to that discussed in Section 7.2.3. We have put this definition into a separate file so that we can reuse it whenever we need it. The following pattern `anyXhtml` describes any content from the XHTML namespace. We have made use of a name class, to restrict the element names to this namespace (see Section 7.3.2).

anyXhtml.rng

This file implements a wildcard with the XHTML namespace.

```
<?xml version="1.0" encoding="UTF-8"?>
<rng:grammar xmlns:rng="http://relaxng.org/ns/structure/1.0"
             xmlns="http://www.w3.org/1999/xhtml">
<rng:start>
  <rng:ref name="anyXhtml"/>
</rng:start>

<rng:define name="anyXhtml">
  <rng:element>
    <rng:nsName ns="http://www.w3.org/1999/xhtml"/>
```

```
      <rng:mixed>
        <rng:zeroOrMore>
          <rng:choice>
            <rng:ref name="anyXhtml"/>
            <rng:attribute>
              <rng:anyName/>
            </rng:attribute>
          </rng:choice>
        </rng:zeroOrMore>
      </rng:mixed>
    </rng:element>
  </rng:define>
</rng:grammar>
```

influence_type.rng

This file implements the asset type influence.

```
<?xml version="1.0" encoding="UTF-8"?>
<rng:grammar xmlns:rng="http://relaxng.org/ns/structure/1.0"
             xmlns="http://www.jazz.org/encyclopedia"
             ns="http://www.jazz.org/encyclopedia"
        datatypeLibrary="http://www.w3.org/2001/XMLSchema-datatypes">
<!--Asset type influence-->
<rng:define name="influence_type">
  <rng:empty/>
</rng:define>
</rng:grammar>
```

jamSession_type.rng

This file implements the asset type jamSession.

```
<?xml version="1.0" encoding="UTF-8"?>
<rng:grammar xmlns:rng="http://relaxng.org/ns/structure/1.0"
             xmlns="http://www.jazz.org/encyclopedia"
             ns="http://www.jazz.org/encyclopedia"
        datatypeLibrary="http://www.w3.org/2001/XMLSchema-datatypes">
```

```
<!--Asset type jamSession-->
<rng:define name="jamSession_type">
  <rng:element name="time">
    <rng:data type="dateTime"/>
  </rng:element>
  <rng:element name="location">
    <rng:data type="token"/>
  </rng:element>
</rng:define>
</rng:grammar>
```

magazine_type.rng

This file implements the asset type magazine.

```
<?xml version="1.0" encoding="UTF-8"?>
<rng:grammar xmlns:rng="http://relaxng.org/ns/structure/1.0"
             xmlns="http://www.jazz.org/encyclopedia"
             ns="http://www.jazz.org/encyclopedia"
    datatypeLibrary="http://www.w3.org/2001/XMLSchema-datatypes">
<!--Asset type magazine-->
<rng:define name="magazine_type">
  <rng:element name="name">
    <rng:text/>
  </rng:element>
  <rng:element name="URI">
    <rng:data type="anyURI"/>
  </rng:element>
</rng:define>
</rng:grammar>
```

plays_type.rng

This file implements the asset type plays.

```
<?xml version="1.0" encoding="UTF-8"?>
<rng:grammar xmlns:rng="http://relaxng.org/ns/structure/1.0"
             xmlns="http://www.jazz.org/encyclopedia"
```

```
        ns="http://www.jazz.org/encyclopedia"
     datatypeLibrary="http://www.w3.org/2001/XMLSchema-datatypes">
<!--Asset type plays-->
<rng:define name="plays_type">
  <rng:oneOrMore>
    <rng:element name="instrument">
     <rng:data type="token"/>
    </rng:element>
  </rng:oneOrMore>
</rng:define>
</rng:grammar>
```

produces_type.rng

This file implements the asset type produces. Remember, the define clause must always contain a child element. Because asset produces does not have a property, we use the empty clause to specify the empty content model.

```
<?xml version="1.0" encoding="UTF-8"?>
<rng:grammar xmlns:rng="http://relaxng.org/ns/structure/1.0"
             xmlns="http://www.jazz.org/encyclopedia"
             ns="http://www.jazz.org/encyclopedia"
         datatypeLibrary="http://www.w3.org/2001/XMLSchema-datatypes">
<!--Asset type produces-->
<rng:define name="produces_type">
  <rng:empty/>
</rng:define>
</rng:grammar>
```

project_type.rng

This file implements the asset type project.

```
<?xml version="1.0" encoding="UTF-8"?>
<rng:grammar xmlns:rng="http://relaxng.org/ns/structure/1.0"
             xmlns="http://www.jazz.org/encyclopedia"
             ns="http://www.jazz.org/encyclopedia"
         datatypeLibrary="http://www.w3.org/2001/XMLSchema-datatypes">
```

```
<!--Asset type project-->
<rng:include href="period_type.rng"/>
<rng:define name="project_type">
  <rng:element name="name">
    <rng:data type="token"/>
  </rng:element>
  <rng:element name="period">
    <rng:ref name="period_type"/>
  </rng:element>
</rng:define>
</rng:grammar>
```

review_type.rng

This file implements the asset type review.

```
<?xml version="1.0" encoding="UTF-8"?>
<rng:grammar xmlns:rng="http://relaxng.org/ns/structure/1.0"
             xmlns="http://www.jazz.org/encyclopedia"
             ns="http://www.jazz.org/encyclopedia"
     datatypeLibrary="http://www.w3.org/2001/XMLSchema-datatypes">
<!--Asset type review-->
<rng:define name="review_type">
  <rng:element name="ID">
    <rng:data type="NMTOKEN"/>
  </rng:element>
  <rng:element name="pubDate">
    <rng:data type="gYearMonth"/>
  </rng:element>
</rng:define>
</rng:grammar>
```

sample_type.rng

This file implements the asset type sample.

```
<?xml version="1.0" encoding="UTF-8"?>
<rng:grammar xmlns:rng="http://relaxng.org/ns/structure/1.0"
```

```
                 xmlns="http://www.jazz.org/encyclopedia"
                 ns="http://www.jazz.org/encyclopedia"
        datatypeLibrary="http://www.w3.org/2001/XMLSchema-datatypes">
<!--Asset type sample-->
<rng:define name="sample_type">
  <rng:element name="MP3">
    <rng:data type="anyURI"/>
  </rng:element>
</rng:define>
</rng:grammar>
```

style_type.rng

This file implements the asset type style.

```
<?xml version="1.0" encoding="UTF-8"?>
<rng:grammar xmlns:rng="http://relaxng.org/ns/structure/1.0"
             xmlns="http://www.jazz.org/encyclopedia"
             ns="http://www.jazz.org/encyclopedia">
<!--Asset type style-->
<rng:include href="period_type.rng"/>
<rng:define name="style_type">
  <rng:element name="name">
    <rng:data type="token"/>
  </rng:element>
  <rng:element name="dominantDuring">
    <rng:ref name="period_type"/>
  </rng:element>
</rng:define>
</rng:grammar>
```

track_type.rng

Finally, this file implements the asset type track.

```
<?xml version="1.0" encoding="UTF-8"?>
<rng:grammar xmlns:rng="http://relaxng.org/ns/structure/1.0"
             xmlns="http://www.jazz.org/encyclopedia"
```

```
                    ns="http://www.jazz.org/encyclopedia"
             datatypeLibrary="http://www.w3.org/2001/XMLSchema-datatypes">
     <!--Asset type track-->
     <rng:define name="track_type">
       <rng:attribute name="trackNo">
         <rng:data type="ID"/>
       </rng:attribute>
       <rng:element name="title">
         <rng:text/>
       </rng:element>
       <rng:optional>
         <rng:element name="duration">
           <rng:data type="duration"/>
         </rng:element>
       </rng:optional>
     </rng:define>
     </rng:grammar>
```

The property trackNo is used as a key for cross-references. Because Relax NG relies on the DTD logic for keys and key references, we have to implement trackNo as an attribute of type ID.

8.3.4 Implementing a Business Object

As in Section 8.2.6, we start with the business object jazzMusician and the identifying item jazzMusician. We implement this asset as the root element of the schema jazzMusician.rng. The type assigned to this element is derived from type jazzMusician_type. The extension consists of the other assets in this Level 2 Structure (belongsTo, influence, and produces) that are implemented as child elements of jazzMusician.

At certain points, you will notice XML Schema language elements within this code, especially for key expressions and for annotations. All these elements are prefixed with xs:, so Relax NG will treat them as annotations. We have opted to implement only the primary and foreign keys of cross-references with the old DTD-style logic of ID and IDREF attributes, because only those are necessary for the validation of a single document. References across document and schema boundaries are not evaluated by the parser, but can serve as information for suitable XML middleware.

We implement each asset as its own pattern and refer to it with an rng:ref clause. As noted earlier, it is advisable to break down the structure even more and implement each property and subproperty as its own pattern. This provides a better basis for later schema evolution (see Chapter 12). We don't do this here, however, for reasons of space and readability.

The highlighted block in the implementation of asset jazzMusician declares an attribute that is not present in the conceptual model. This is attribute xsi:schemaLocation. The definition allows document instances to contain such an attribute. We thus achieve interoperability with XML Schema where document instances can declare a schema location via this attribute.

jazzMusician.rng

This file implements the L2S jazzMusician with all outgoing arcs.

```
<?xml version="1.0" encoding="UTF-8"?>
<rng:grammar xmlns:rng="http://relaxng.org/ns/structure/1.0"
             xmlns="http://www.jazz.org/encyclopedia"
             xmlns:xs="http://www.w3.org/2001/XMLSchema"
             xmlns:xsi="http://www.w3.org/2001/XMLSchema-instance"
             xmlns:xsg="http://www.aomodeling.org/KLEEN/XSDgenerator"
             ns="http://www.jazz.org/encyclopedia"
        datatypeLibrary="http://www.w3.org/2001/XMLSchema-datatypes">


<!--Asset jazzMusician-->
<rng:include href="jazzMusician_type.rng"/>
<rng:start>
  <rng:element name="jazzMusician">
    <rng:ref name="jazzMusician_type"/>
    <rng:attribute name="xsi:schemaLocation">
      <rng:data type="anyURI"/>
    </rng:attribute>
    <rng:zeroOrMore>
      <rng:ref name="produces"/>
    </rng:zeroOrMore>
    <rng:zeroOrMore>
      <rng:ref name="belongsTo"/>
    </rng:zeroOrMore>
    <rng:zeroOrMore>
      <rng:ref name="influence"/>
    </rng:zeroOrMore>
```

```
        <xs:key name="pk__jazzMusician_ID">
          <xs:selector xpath="."/>
          <xs:field xpath="ID"/>
        </xs:key>
      </rng:element>
  </rng:start>


  <!--Asset produces-->
  <rng:include href="produces_type.rng"/>
  <rng:define name="produces">
    <rng:element name="produces">
      <rng:ref name="produces_type"/>
      <rng:zeroOrMore>
        <rng:element name="album">
          <xs:annotation>
            <xs:documentation>
              refers to key pk__album_albumKey in schema album.xsd
            </xs:documentation>
            <xs:appinfo>
              <xsg:refersToSchema
                xmlns:xlink="http://www.w3.org/1999/xlink"
                xlink:href="album.xsd"
                xlink:type="simple"
                keyName="pk__album_albumKey"/>
            </xs:appinfo>
          </xs:annotation>
          <rng:interleave>
            <rng:element name="publisher">
              <rng:data type="anyURI"/>
            </rng:element>
            <rng:element name="productNo">
              <rng:data type="NMTOKEN"/>
            </rng:element>
          </rng:interleave>
        </rng:element>
      </rng:zeroOrMore>
```

```
      </rng:element>
  </rng:define>


<!--Asset belongsTo-->
<rng:include href="belongsTo_type.rng"/>
<rng:define name="belongsTo">
  <rng:element name="belongsTo">
    <rng:ref name="belongsTo_type"/>
    <rng:oneOrMore>
      <rng:element name="style" maxOccurs="unbounded">
        <xs:annotation>
          <xs:documentation>
            refers to key pk__style_name in schema style.xsd
          </xs:documentation>
          <xs:appinfo>
            <xsg:refersToSchema
              xlink:href="style.xsd"
              xlink:type="simple"
              xmlns:xlink="http://www.w3.org/1999/xlink"
              keyName="pk__style_name"/>
          </xs:appinfo>
        </xs:annotation>
        <rng:interleave>
          <rng:element name="name">
            <rng:data type="token"/>
          </rng:element>
        </rng:interleave>
      </rng:element>
    </rng:oneOrMore>
  </rng:element>
</rng:define>


<!--Asset influence-->
<rng:include href="influence_type.rng"/>
<rng:define name="influence">
  <rng:element name="influence">
```

```
      <rng:ref name="influence_type"/>
      <rng:zeroOrMore>
        <rng:element name="influencedBy">
          <xs:annotation>
            <xs:documentation>
              refers to key pk__jazzMusician_ID in schema jazzMusician.xsd
            </xs:documentation>
            <xs:appinfo>
              <xsg:refersToSchema xlink:href="jazzMusician.xsd"
                xlink:type="simple"
                xmlns:xlink="http://www.w3.org/1999/xlink"
                keyName="pk__jazzMusician_ID"/>
            </xs:appinfo>
          </xs:annotation>
          <rng:element name="jazzMusician">
            <rng:interleave>
              <rng:element name="ID">
                <rng:data type="NMTOKEN"/>
              </rng:element>
            </rng:interleave>
          </rng:element>
        </rng:element>
      </rng:zeroOrMore>
    </rng:element>
  </rng:define>
</rng:grammar>
```

8.3.5 Dealing with Cross-References

We now move to the implementation of business object album. (Compare this with Section 8.2.7.) album does not have a hierarchical structure—there is a cross-reference between track and sample.

Relax NG does not provide support for keys and key references, but for backward compatibility with DTDs, it allows the use of ID, IDREF, and IDREFS for attribute types. Attributes of this type act as keys and key references. A Relax NG–specific solution for keys and key references is expected for future releases.

Here, we have defined attribute sample/track/@trackNo as a key reference with type IDREF. The corresponding key track/@trackNo with type ID is defined in track_type.rng shown in Section 8.3.3.

album.rng

This file implements the L2S `album` with all outgoing arcs.

```xml
<?xml version="1.0" encoding="UTF-8"?>
<rng:grammar xmlns:rng="http://relaxng.org/ns/structure/1.0"
             xmlns="http://www.jazz.org/encyclopedia"
             xmlns:xs="http://www.w3.org/2001/XMLSchema"
             xmlns:xsi="http://www.w3.org/2001/XMLSchema-instance"
             xmlns:xsg="http://www.aomodeling.org/KLEEN/XSDgenerator"
             ns="http://www.jazz.org/encyclopedia"
    datatypeLibrary="http://www.w3.org/2001/XMLSchema-datatypes">


<!--Asset album-->
<rng:include href="album_type.rng"/>
<rng:start>
  <rng:element name="album">
    <rng:ref name="album_type"/>
    <rng:attribute name="xsi:schemaLocation">
      <rng:data type="anyURI"/>
    </rng:attribute>
    <rng:oneOrMore>
      <rng:ref name="track"/>
    </rng:oneOrMore>
    <rng:zeroOrMore>
      <rng:ref name="sample"/>
    </rng:zeroOrMore>
    <rng:zeroOrMore>
      <rng:ref name="plays"/>
    </rng:zeroOrMore>
    <xs:key name="pk__album_albumKey">
      <xs:selector xpath="."/>
      <xs:field xpath="publisher"/>
      <xs:field xpath="productNo"/>
    </xs:key>
  </rng:element>
</rng:start>
```

```
<!--Asset track-->
<rng:include href="track_type.rng"/>
<rng:define name="track">
  <rng:element name="track">
    <rng:ref name="track_type"/>
  </rng:element>
</rng:define>

<!--Asset sample-->
<rng:include href="sample_type.rng"/>
<rng:define name="sample">
  <rng:element name="sample">
    <rng:ref name="sample_type"/>
    <rng:element name="track">
      <rng:attribute name="trackNo">
        <rng:data type="IDREF"/>
      </rng:attribute>
    </rng:element>
  </rng:element>
</rng:define>

<!--Asset plays-->
<rng:include href="plays_type.rng"/>
<rng:define name="plays">
  <rng:element name="plays">
    <rng:ref name="plays_type"/>
    <rng:element name="jazzMusician">
      <xs:annotation>
        <xs:documentation>
          refers to key pk__jazzMusician_ID in schema jazzMusician.xsd
        </xs:documentation>
        <xs:appinfo>
          <xsg:refersToSchema xlink:href="jazzMusician.xsd"
                              xlink:type="simple"
                              xmlns:xlink="http://www.w3.org/1999/xlink"
                              keyName="pk__jazzMusician_ID"/>
```

```
        </xs:appinfo>
      </xs:annotation>
      <rng:interleave>
        <rng:element name="ID">
          <rng:data type="NMTOKEN"/>
        </rng:element>
      </rng:interleave>
    </rng:element>
  </rng:element>
</rng:define>
</rng:grammar>
```

8.3.6 Resolving Multiple Display Labels

In Section 8.2.8 we implemented the business objects band and project (which
have a shared definition in asset project) with the help of substitution groups.
In Relax NG we implement this asset as a single pattern. But instead of using a
name attribute for the top element definition, we use a name class definition
(see Section 7.3.2). This name class consists of the two names band and project.

We had to deal with another problem, too. The arc leading from project to
jazzMusician was decorated with the constraint [2..*]. The definition of such
general constraints is not supported in the Relax NG schema language. We have
to simulate this by concatenating two references to jazzMusician: Instead of
jazzMusician[2..*], we use jazzMusician, jazzMusician+. To achieve this with
the least effort, we have factored out the implementation of this reference into
a separate pattern called jazzMusician_Ref.

project.rng

This file implements the L2S project with all outgoing arcs.

```
<?xml version="1.0" encoding="UTF-8"?>
<rng:grammar xmlns:rng="http://relaxng.org/ns/structure/1.0"
             xmlns="http://www.jazz.org/encyclopedia"
             xmlns:xs="http://www.w3.org/2001/XMLSchema"
             xmlns:xsi="http://www.w3.org/2001/XMLSchema-instance"
             xmlns:xsg="http://www.aomodeling.org/KLEEN/XSDgenerator"
             ns="http://www.jazz.org/encyclopedia"
        datatypeLibrary="http://www.w3.org/2001/XMLSchema-datatypes">


<!--Asset project-->
<!--Asset band-->
```

```
<rng:include href="project_type.rng"/>
<rng:start>
  <rng:element>
    <rng:choice>
      <rng:name>project</rng:name>
      <rng:name>band</rng:name>
    </rng:choice>
    <rng:ref name="project_type"/>
    <rng:attribute name="xsi:schemaLocation">
      <rng:data type="anyURI"/>
    </rng:attribute>
    <rng:zeroOrMore>
      <rng:element name="result">
        <rng:element name="album">
          <xs:annotation>
            <xs:documentation>
              refers to key pk__album_albumKey in schema album.xsd
            </xs:documentation>
            <xs:appinfo>
              <xsg:refersToSchema
                    xlink:href="album.xsd"
                    xlink:type="simple"
                    xmlns:xlink="http://www.w3.org/1999/xlink"
                    keyName="pk__album_albumKey"/>
            </xs:appinfo>
          </xs:annotation>
          <rng:interleave>
            <rng:element name="publisher">
              <rng:data type="anyURI"/>
            </rng:element>
            <rng:element name="productNo">
              <rng:data type="NMTOKEN"/>
            </rng:element>
          </rng:interleave>
        </rng:element>
      </rng:element>
    </rng:zeroOrMore>
```

```
        <rng:ref name="jazzMusician_Ref"/>
        <rng:oneOrMore>
          <rng:ref name="jazzMusician_Ref"/>
        </rng:oneOrMore>
        <xs:key name="pk__jazzMusician_ID">
          <xs:selector xpath="."/>
          <xs:field xpath="ID"/>
        </xs:key>
        <xs:key name="pk__album_albumKey">
          <xs:selector xpath="."/>
          <xs:field xpath="publisher"/>
          <xs:field xpath="productNo"/>
        </xs:key>
      </rng:element>
  </rng:start>

  <rng:define name="jazzMusician_Ref">
    <rng:element name="jazzMusician">
      <xs:annotation>
        <xs:documentation>
          refers to key pk__jazzMusician_ID in schema jazzMusician.xsd
        </xs:documentation>
        <xs:appinfo>
          <xsg:refersToSchema xlink:href="jazzMusician.xsd"
              xlink:type="simple"
              xmlns:xlink="http://www.w3.org/1999/xlink"
              keyName="pk__jazzMusician_ID"/>
        </xs:appinfo>
      </xs:annotation>
      <rng:interleave>
        <rng:element name="ID">
          <rng:data type="NMTOKEN"/>
        </rng:element>
      </rng:interleave>
    </rng:element>
  </rng:define>
</rng:grammar>
```

8.3.7 Implementing Clusters

Asset review contains a cluster with arcs leading to jazzMusician and album. As in Section 8.2.9, the implementation with a choice clause is straightforward.

review.rng

This file implements L2S review with all outgoing arcs.

```xml
<?xml version="1.0" encoding="UTF-8"?>
<rng:grammar xmlns:rng="http://relaxng.org/ns/structure/1.0"
             xmlns="http://www.jazz.org/encyclopedia"
             xmlns:xs="http://www.w3.org/2001/XMLSchema"
             xmlns:xsi="http://www.w3.org/2001/XMLSchema-instance"
             xmlns:xsg="http://www.aomodeling.org/KLEEN/XSDgenerator"
             ns="http://www.jazz.org/encyclopedia"
    datatypeLibrary="http://www.w3.org/2001/XMLSchema-datatypes">


<!--Asset review-->
<rng:include href="review_type.rng"/>
<rng:start>
  <rng:element name="review">
    <rng:ref name="review_type"/>
    <rng:attribute name="xsi:schemaLocation">
      <rng:data type="anyURI"/>
    </rng:attribute>
    <rng:choice>
      <rng:element name="album">
        <xs:annotation>
          <xs:documentation>
            refers to key pk__album_albumKey in schema album.xsd
          </xs:documentation>
          <xs:appinfo>
            <xsg:refersToSchema xlink:href="album.xsd"
            xlink:type="simple"
            xmlns:xlink="http://www.w3.org/1999/xlink"
            keyName="pk__album_albumKey"/>
          </xs:appinfo>
        </xs:annotation>
```

```
      <rng:interleave>
        <rng:element name="publisher">
          <rng:data type="anyURI"/>
        </rng:element>
        <rng:element name="productNo">
          <rng:data type="NMTOKEN"/>
        </rng:element>
      </rng:interleave>
    </rng:element>
    <rng:element name="jazzMusician">
      <xs:annotation>
        <xs:documentation>
         refers to key pk__jazzMusician_ID in schema jazzMusician.xsd
        </xs:documentation>
        <xs:appinfo>
          <xsg:refersToSchema xlink:href="jazzMusician.xsd"
          xlink:type="simple"
          xmlns:xlink="http://www.w3.org/1999/xlink"
          keyName="pk__jazzMusician_ID"/>
        </xs:appinfo>
      </xs:annotation>
      <rng:interleave>
        <rng:element name="ID">
          <rng:data type="NMTOKEN"/>
        </rng:element>
      </rng:interleave>
    </rng:element>
  </rng:choice>
  <rng:ref name="magazine"/>
  <rng:element name="critic">
    <xs:annotation>
      <xs:documentation>
        refers to key pk__critic_ID in schema critic.xsd
      </xs:documentation>
      <xs:appinfo>
```

```
                    <xsg:refersToSchema xlink:href="critic.xsd"
                    xlink:type="simple"
                    xmlns:xlink="http://www.w3.org/1999/xlink"
                    keyName="pk_critic_ID"/>
                  </xs:appinfo>
                </xs:annotation>
                <rng:interleave>
                  <rng:element name="ID">
                    <rng:data type="NMTOKEN"/>
                  </rng:element>
                </rng:interleave>
              </rng:element>
              <xs:key name="pk_review_ID">
                <xs:selector xpath="."/>
                <xs:field xpath="ID"/>
              </xs:key>
            </rng:element>
        </rng:start>


        <!--Asset magazine-->
        <rng:include href="magazine_type.rng"/>
        <rng:define name="magazine">
          <rng:element name="magazine">
            <rng:ref name="magazine_type"/>
          </rng:element>
        </rng:define>


        </rng:grammar>
```

8.3.8 Business Objects critic and style

As before, the schemata for the business objects critic and style are presented last.

critic.rng

This file implements the L2S critic.

```
<?xml version="1.0" encoding="UTF-8"?>

<rng:grammar xmlns:rng="http://relaxng.org/ns/structure/1.0"
             xmlns="http://www.jazz.org/encyclopedia"
             xmlns:xs="http://www.w3.org/2001/XMLSchema"
             xmlns:xsi="http://www.w3.org/2001/XMLSchema-instance"
             xmlns:xsg="http://www.aomodeling.org/KLEEN/XSDgenerator"
             ns="http://www.jazz.org/encyclopedia"
        datatypeLibrary="http://www.w3.org/2001/XMLSchema-datatypes">


<!--Asset jazzMusician-->
<rng:include href="critic_type.rng"/>
<rng:start>
  <rng:element name="critic">
    <rng:ref name="critic_type"/>
    <rng:attribute name="xsi:schemaLocation">
      <rng:data type="anyURI"/>
    </rng:attribute>
    <xs:key name="pk__critic_ID">
      <xs:selector xpath="."/>
      <xs:field xpath="ID"/>
    </xs:key>
  </rng:element>
</rng:start>
</rng:grammar>
```

style.rng

Finally, this file implements the L2S style.

```
<?xml version="1.0" encoding="UTF-8"?>

<rng:grammar xmlns:rng="http://relaxng.org/ns/structure/1.0"
             xmlns="http://www.jazz.org/encyclopedia"
             xmlns:xs="http://www.w3.org/2001/XMLSchema"
             xmlns:xsi="http://www.w3.org/2001/XMLSchema-instance"
             xmlns:xsg="http://www.aomodeling.org/KLEEN/XSDgenerator"
             ns="http://www.jazz.org/encyclopedia"
        datatypeLibrary="http://www.w3.org/2001/XMLSchema-datatypes">
<!--Asset style-->
```

```
<rng:include href="style_type.rng"/>
<rng:start>
  <rng:element name="style">
    <rng:ref name="style_type"/>
      <rng:attribute name="xsi:schemaLocation">
        <rng:data type="anyURI"/>
      </rng:attribute>
    <rng:ref name="description"/>
    <xs:key name="pk__style_name">
        <xs:selector xpath="."/>
        <xs:field xpath="name"/>
    </xs:key>
    </rng:element>
</rng:start>
<!--Asset description-->
<rng:include href="description_type.rng"/>
<rng:define name="description">
  <rng:element name="description">
    <rng:ref name="description_type"/>
  </rng:element>
</rng:define>
</rng:grammar>
```

8.4 SUMMARY

After these rather extensive code examples, we give a short overview of the implementation steps and problems associated with the implementation.

8.4.1 Synopsis of Implementation Steps

The implementation process involves seven steps.

Step 1
Prepare the conceptual model for implementation. Resolve complex inheritance relationships, including key definitions, property definitions, incoming and outgoing arcs.

Step 2

Implement each asset type. This includes the asset's own and inherited properties.

- Under XML Schema, use complex types (see Sections 8.2.3 and 8.2.4). All type definitions belonging to a given namespace can be stored within one type library document (see Section 8.2.5).
- Under Relax NG, use grammars (see Sections 8.3.1 and 8.3.2). Implement each property and subproperty as a separate pattern. Each grammar should be stored in a separate file to allow for overriding each pattern later (see Section 8.3.3).

Step 3

Create separate schema documents for each business object—usually the top Level 2 Structures (see Sections 8.2.6 and 8.3.4). If a business object should contain assets from different namespaces and you are implementing under XML Schema, you must split the schema document into several documents—one for each namespace.

Step 4

Implement each asset (see Sections 8.2.6 and 8.3.4). Use the previous asset type definitions from step 2 as base types.

- Under XML Schema, implement each asset as a global element.
- Under Relax NG, implement each asset as a separate pattern.

Within each business object schema, select the identifying asset as the root element.

Step 5

Implement primary keys (see Sections 8.2.6 and 8.3.4). Although not always needed for the validation of the single instance elements, explicit definition of primary (and foreign) keys can help suitable processors to check referential integrity between documents. Under XML Schema, the key clause can be used to declare keys. Since Relax NG does not provide a key concept of its own, the same (XML Schema) key clauses may be used under Relax NG, too, where they are treated as annotations.

Step 6

For arcs there are four possibilities:

1. The arc carries a range attribute. In this case, the arc is treated like an arc to another business object (see case 4).
2. The arc establishes the tree hierarchy within the business object. In this case, the target element is implemented as a child element of the arc origin. This is done by referring to the global definition of the asset element.

In case 1 and in the remaining cases, 3 and 4, a foreign key definition must be implemented as a child element of the arc origin (see Sections 8.2.6 and 8.3.4). This key definition should contain an element for the role name (if any), an element for the target asset, and an xs:all (or rng:interleave) group containing the key fields of the arc target. The types of the foreign key fields should mirror the types of the primary key fields (except for type ID, which must be matched by IDREF).

3. The arc runs against the tree hierarchy. In this case, the arc must be implemented as a cross-reference (see Sections 8.2.7 and 8.3.5). If possible, choose an implementation form that is compatible with DTD standards (ID/IDREF), as not all XML processors support the full key/keyref construct introduced by XML Schema. Only in this case, the key and key reference definitions will be utilized for document validation. When implementing under Relax NG, you might want to include the XML Schema key and keyref clauses for documentation, as Relax NG does not have a key concept of its own.

4. Arcs that point to another business object cannot have a keyref definition, as this definition would not be able to refer to a key definition within the same schema. However, it makes sense to document the arc by including a suitable annotation.

Arcs emanating from clusters are implemented in the same way, except that they form a choice group with the other cluster members (see Sections 8.2.9 and 8.3.7). is_a arcs are not implemented.

Step 7
In the final step, we take care of display labels. Under XML Schema, we use substitution groups (see Section 8.2.8); under Relax NG, we use name classes (see Section 8.3.6).

8.4.2 Remarks

The example schemata shown in this chapter are directly derived from a normalized conceptual model in which the amount of redundant information has been minimized. Consequently, the instances of these schemata are not *navigational*. For example, an album instance does not contain information about the band that produced this album because this information is already contained in a band instance. Providing users with meaningful information, however, often requires including redundant information in a document (such as the name of the band that produced the album). Redundancy, on the other hand, makes updates to the document base complicated and error prone.

The solution is not to present the documents in their raw form to the user, but to provide "cooked" views of the document set. Such views can combine information from several document types (in our example, from album and band) in a new document type. Such views can be produced with various means, such as a Java servlet, an XSLT stylesheet, or an XQuery [Boag2002] expression, and typically require that the document base is stored in a database. In our jazz knowledge base, for example, we would have to find the band instance that refers to a given album in its result element. A database system would allow us to index the result elements of band and thus to quickly retrieve matching band documents. The primary and foreign key definitions that we have created in the various schemata are good clues for a database system as to which document elements should be indexed.

We should also not mistake the elements derived from conceptual arcs for navigational links (for example, the result element in band, which identifies an album). Although the navigational structure of a document base can be derived from the conceptual structure, it usually differs from the latter. For example, the navigational structure of our Jazz model would also contain reversed arcs (such as from album to band) and shortcuts. We might like to have hyperlinks from a jazzMusician instance to all album instances to which the musician has contributed. In many cases we would not want to insert these navigational structures into the original documents but, rather, keep them in separate documents, such as an XLink linkbase or a topic map [Daum2002], for easy maintenance. The arcs of the conceptual model serve as a basis from which such documents can be derived.

Validation beyond XML Schema

In this chapter we look over the fence of pure structural document validation. Although XML Schema does allow us to define constraints that refer to the content of elements of attributes in the form of simple data types, there are many aspects of semantic integrity that cannot be covered in this way.

The chapter discusses various methods for modeling and implementing advanced semantic constraints, such as cross-field and cross-document constraints. The classical method is to hard-code constraints using imperative programming with programming languages such as Java, C++, or Perl. Alternatively, it is possible to soft-code constraints as rules in the form of XSLT stylesheets or as Schematron schemata.

In all these methods, XPath plays a pivotal role as a common language to formulate constraints, one reason to adopt XPath for the conceptual model as well. In particular, the emerging XPath 2.0 specification [Berglund2002], with its support for XML Schema data types, looks very promising.

With this abundance of schema languages and validation methods, we analyze the individual steps during the validation of a document and how the various schema languages cover them. The last section discusses a current standardization effort for the integration of these diverse approaches to schema validation.

9.1 ABOUT MEANING

When XML became popular, one naïve opinion was that—in contrast to HTML—XML documents would express meaning, which would allow semantic processing of documents. This opinion was based on the fact that tags in XML documents are like spoken language—that is, they transfer the meaning of an element to the human reader. However, nothing stops a schema author from naming a field for body height with a `<salary>` tag. No XML processor would complain, and human readers would be completely misled. This is in contrast to HTML or XML-based application languages, such as SVG, SMIL, and many others, where the meaning of tags is clearly described in the language definition, and processors implement the desired behavior. In HTML, for example, the tag `<B>` has a clear meaning: The content of the element is to be printed in bold typeface. Tags in XML do not have predefined semantics—actually, the XML specification does not define specific tags at all. The same applies for attribute names, with a few exceptions. There are a few predefined attribute names in XML, such as `xml:lang` and `xmlns`, that, indeed, have clearly defined semantics.

To attribute XML tags with meaning requires extra effort beyond the definition of XML schemata. The buzzword is *ontologies*. An ontology is composed of a vocabulary and additional formal means to describe the semantic relationships between the members of the vocabulary, such as thesauri, semantic networks, constraint systems, and axioms. Ontologies are one subject of the standardization efforts of the W3C activity "Semantic Web" but also of standardization efforts such as ebXML. Here, the discussion will be restricted to constraints. For a detailed discussion of ontologies, see [Daum2002].

The fact that an XML schema does not associate individual tags with a specific meaning should not lead us to the conclusion that the same is true for the whole document. The next section will show that an XML schema imposes a set of constraints on the set of instance documents, and thus indeed defines a limited amount of formal semantics for those documents. Additional semantics can be specified for documents by using methods for constraint definition beyond XML Schema, such as the Schematron (see Section 9.4.3). And, of course, general semantics can be specified via XML processing instructions (see Section 4.2.5) or `appinfo` elements (see Section 6.3.7), which bind a document to a given application.

9.2 CONSTRAINTS

Apart from the definition of vocabularies and thesauri that can provide a base for understanding the meaning of tags, *constraints* are an important concept in the definition of formal semantics. This can be explained with a concrete example. Assume that we have a document containing the attribute duration in an element track:

```
<track duration="PT5M33.3S"/>
```

A human reader (who is acquainted with the ISO notation of time periods) can indeed derive some meaning from this element instance. For a nonvalidating XML parser, however, this element instance does not transmit any meaning. All the parser can recognize is that "track" is the element name, "duration" is an attribute name, and "PT5M33.3S" is a string value associated with this attribute name.

The picture changes when we define a schema for this element and make this schema accessible to an XML processor:

```
<xs:element name="track">
  <xs:complexType>
    <xs:attribute name="duration" use="optional">
      <xs:simpleType>
        <xs:restriction base="xs:duration">
          <xs:maxInclusive value="PT25M"/>
          <xs:minInclusive value="PT10S"/>
        </xs:restriction>
      </xs:simpleType>
    </xs:attribute>
  </xs:complexType>
</xs:element>
```

A validating processor that has access to this schema might gain some intelligence from it:

- First, it learns that the attribute value is of type duration and can interpret it accordingly. Because duration values are ordered, it can compare the duration values of document instances with each other.
- Second, it learns the upper and lower bounds of the duration value and can come to the conclusion that the value in the instance is not exceedingly small or exceedingly large.

The concept of constraints is not restricted to single values. In fact, a schema is nothing but a huge constraint itself. It constrains the set of valid documents to a subset of the alphabet's powerset (see Section 1.5). Even if the schema only imposed structural constraints, we could still get certain useful semantic information from this. Take for example the following schema definition:

```
<xs:element name="doc">
  <xs:complexType>
    <xs:all>
      <xs:element name="a"/>
      <xs:element name="b"/>
      <xs:element name="c"/>
    </xs:all>
  </xs:complexType>
</xs:element>
```

This schema allows elements a, b, and c to appear in any order within doc. Now compare it with the following structure:

```
<xs:element name="doc">
  <xs:complexType>
    <xs:sequence>
      <xs:element name="d">
        <xs:complexType>
          <xs:sequence>
            <xs:element name="a"/>
            <xs:element name="b"/>
          </xs:sequence>
        </xs:complexType>
      </xs:element>
      <xs:element name="c"/>
    </xs:sequence>
  </xs:complexType>
</xs:element>
```

From this schema we can learn that the elements a and b obviously have a closer relationship with each other than a and c or b and c. We are also told that sequence matters: b must follow a, and c must follow d, which unites a and b into a substructure. This schema does not inform us about the concrete semantics of the document instances; however, given that schema, we learn some semantic aspects about the document instances, such as the relationships between document elements. It is exactly this semantic aspect that gets lost when we flatten a complex structure into the relational First Normal Form to store it in a relational database.

Section 9.2.2 gives a practical example of how such structural constraints can be used to express semantic relationships between two document nodes.

9.2.1 Constraints in XML Schema

Apart from document structure, XML Schema allows us to define additional constraints for document instances:

- *Data types.* In contrast to DTDs, which provide only a few basic data types for attributes, XML Schema allows us to constrain both leaf elements and attributes with a large variety of simple data types. A hierarchy of built-in data types and a rich set of facets to construct additional data types with the help of constraining facets, list extension, and type union allow us to constrain element and attribute content in nearly any imaginable way (see Section 5.2.5).
- *Uniqueness and cross-references.* XML Schema refines and extends the cross-referencing concept found in DTDs. The unique, key, and keyref constructs complement the ID and IDREF data types known from DTDs (see Section 4.4.4). The cross-reference constraints are cross-field constraints, because they relate the contents of one document node instance to the contents of another.

As an example, we look again at the schema album from Section 8.2.7, along with its diagram, in Figure 9.1 (page 328). This schema already defines some cross-references, but it has been extended with additional constraints.

```
<?xml version="1.0" encoding="UTF-8"?>
<xs:schema attributeFormDefault="unqualified"
           elementFormDefault="qualified"
           targetNamespace="http://www.jazz.org/encyclopedia"
           xmlns="http://www.jazz.org/encyclopedia"
           xmlns:xs="http://www.w3.org/2001/XMLSchema"
           xmlns:xsg="http://www.aomodeling.org/KLEEN/XSDgenerator">
 <xs:include schemaLocation="www_jazz_org_encyclopedia_TYPELIB.xsd"/>
 <!--Asset album-->
 <xs:element name="album">
  <xs:complexType>
   <xs:complexContent>
    <xs:extension base="album_type">
     <xs:sequence>
      <xs:element maxOccurs="unbounded" ref="track"/>
      <xs:element maxOccurs="unbounded" minOccurs="0" ref="sample"/>
```

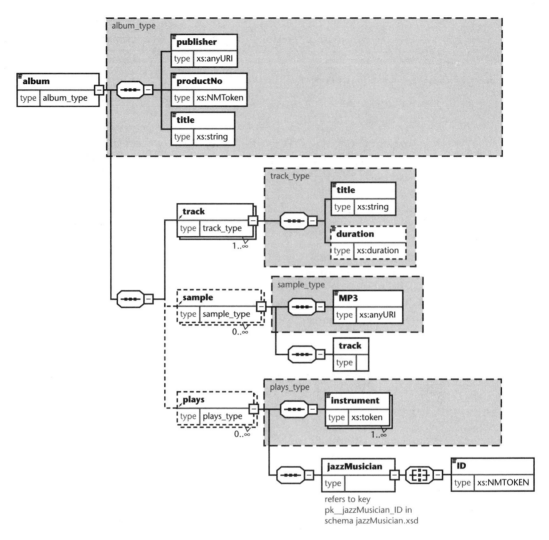

Figure 9.1 The structure of schema album.xsd.

```
        <xs:element maxOccurs="unbounded" minOccurs="0" ref="plays"/>
      </xs:sequence>
     </xs:extension>
    </xs:complexContent>
   </xs:complexType>
  <xs:unique name="unique__track_title">
   <xs:selector xpath="./track"/>
```

```
      <xs:field xpath="title"/>
    </xs:unique>
    ...
    <xs:key name="pk__track_trackNo">
      <xs:selector xpath="./track"/>
      <xs:field xpath="@trackNo"/>
    </xs:key>
  </xs:element>
  <!--Asset track-->
  <xs:element name="track" type="track_type"/>
  <!--Asset sample-->
  <xs:element name="sample">
    <xs:complexType>
      <xs:complexContent>
        <xs:extension base="sample_type">
          <xs:sequence>
            <xs:element name="track">
              <xs:complexType>
                <xs:attribute name="trackNo" type="xs:IDREF"/>
              </xs:complexType>
            </xs:element>
          </xs:sequence>
        </xs:extension>
      </xs:complexContent>
    </xs:complexType>
    <xs:keyref name="fk__sample_track" refer="pk__track_trackNo">
      <xs:selector xpath="./track"/>
      <xs:field xpath="@trackNo"/>
    </xs:keyref>
  </xs:element>
  <!--Asset plays-->
  ...
</xs:schema>
```

This schema defines a cross-field constraint by means of XML Schema. For each track referenced in a sample/track/@trackNo attribute, there must exist a track element with a corresponding album/track/@trackNo attribute. As shown above, this sort of constraint can be easily implemented with XML Schema. Note that we have applied this constraint to derived types. The definition of sample/track/@trackNo is contained in sample_type, while the definition of album/track/@trackNo is contained in track_type. The introduction of such a cross-field constraint to the album schema effectively sub-types the album element type.

We have added another constraint, too. We wanted to ensure that every track has a different title. We can define this constraint with the help of the unique clause as shown above. Note that this is a cross-field constraint, too, as it relates different album/track/title element instances to each other.

9.2.2 Constraints beyond XML Schema

The constraining power of XML Schema ends when it comes to general cross-field constraints or even cross-document constraints.

Cross-Field Constraints

Let's return to our jazz example. There are a few properties that are good candidates for cross-field constraints. Take for example the definition of type period-Type, which is used in several schemata:

```
<xs:complexType name="period_type">
  <xs:sequence>
    <xs:element name="from" type="xs:gYear"/>
    <xs:element name="to" type="xs:gYear" minOccurs="0"/>
  </xs:sequence>
</xs:complexType>
```

What immediately springs to mind is that the value of the from element must be smaller than or equal to the value of the to element if it exists. However, there is no way to define this in XML Schema.

For another example let's return for a moment to our album schema from the previous section. There is one more thing that we want to constrain: the total duration of an album. We want to restrict the sum of all track durations by an upper limit, let's say 240 minutes. Again, this constraint is impossible to express in XML Schema. (Section 9.4 discusses how we can validate such constraints.) But beware. Sometimes it is possible to express a constraint in XML Schema when it is not so obvious. Take for example the schema jazzMusician. During the modeling process we introduced a constraint: If a jazz musician is an instrumentalist, he or she must play at least one instrument (see Section 3.6). In Section 8.2.4 we arrived at the following type definition for jazzMusician:

```
<xs:complexType name="jazzMusician_type">
<xs:complexContent>
  <xs:extension base="person_type">
    <xs:sequence>
      <xs:element name="kind">
        <xs:simpleType>
          <xs:restriction base="xs:string">
            <xs:enumeration value="instrumentalist"/>
            <xs:enumeration value="jazzComposer"/>
            <xs:enumeration value="jazzSinger"/>
          </xs:restriction>
        </xs:simpleType>
      </xs:element>
      <xs:element name="instrument" type="xs:token"
                  minOccurs="0" maxOccurs="unbounded"/>
    </xs:sequence>
  </xs:extension>
</xs:complexContent>
</xs:complexType>
```

This schema, of course, does not implement the above constraint. But we can try to express this constraint by means of XML Schema.

We duplicate the sequence clause and place it into a choice clause. Within the first choice branch we restrict the possible values of kind to instrumentalist and set minOccurs="1" for element instrument (we could also just drop the minOccurs clause). In the second branch we restrict the values of kind to jazzComposer and jazzSinger.

```
<xs:complexType name="jazzMusician_type">
<xs:complexContent>
  <xs:extension base="person_type">
    <xs:choice>
      <xs:sequence>
        <xs:element name="kind">
          <xs:simpleType>
            <xs:restriction base="xs:string">
              <xs:enumeration value="instrumentalist"/>
            </xs:restriction>
```

```
          </xs:simpleType>
        </xs:element>
        <xs:element name="instrument" type="xs:token"
                    minOccurs="1" maxOccurs="unbounded"/>
      </xs:sequence>
      <xs:sequence>
        <!-- This violates the Unique Particle Attribution
             constraint! -->
        <xs:element name="kind">
          <xs:simpleType>
            <xs:restriction base="xs:string">
              <xs:enumeration value="jazzComposer"/>
              <xs:enumeration value="jazzSinger"/>
            </xs:restriction>
          </xs:simpleType>
        </xs:element>
        <xs:element name="instrument" type="xs:token"
                    minOccurs="0" maxOccurs="unbounded"/>
      </xs:sequence>
    </xs:choice>
  </xs:extension>
  </xs:complexContent>
</xs:complexType>
```

Well, this failed. Expressing the constraint

```
kind != "instrumentalist" or count(instrument) > 0
```

by means of type restriction and structure resulted in a nondeterministic schema—the schema does not satisfy XML Schema's Unique Particle Attribution constraint. Each branch of the choice clause begins with an element named kind. To decide which branch to take, the parser would have to look ahead into the content of each kind element and check the content against the respective type definition. So this schema is *wrong*!

The same schema translated to Relax NG, however, would be correct. Relax NG does not require nondeterministic content models:

```
<rng:grammar xmlns:rng="http://relaxng.org/ns/structure/1.0"
             xmlns="http://www.jazz.org/encyclopedia"
             ns="http://www.jazz.org/encyclopedia"
          datatypeLibrary="http://www.w3.org/2001/XMLSchema-datatypes">
```

```
        <rng:include href="person_type.rng"/>
        <rng:define name="jazzMusician_type">
          <rng:element name="jazzMusician">
            <rng:ref name="person_type"/>
            <rng:choice>
              <rng:group>
                <rng:element name="kind">
                  <rng:value>instrumentalist</rng:value>
                </rng:element>
                <rng:oneOrMore>
                  <rng:ref name="pInstrument"/>
                </rng:oneOrMore>
              </rng:group>
              <rng:group>
                <rng:element name="kind">
                  <rng:choice>
                    <rng:value>jazzComposer</rng:value>
                    <rng:value>jazzSinger</rng:value>
                  </rng:choice>
                </rng:element>
                <rng:zeroOrMore>
                  <rng:ref name="pInstrument"/>
                </rng:zeroOrMore>
              </rng:group>
            </rng:choice>
          </rng:element>
        </rng:define>
        <rng:define name="pInstrument">
          <rng:element name="instrument">
            <rng:data type="token"/>
          </rng:element>
        </rng:define>
    </rng:grammar>
```

In XML Schema a solution for this problem would be to define the type jazzMusician_type as abstract, to derive types intrumentalist_type, jazzComposer_type, and jazzSinger_type from this abstract type, and to use the xsi:type mechanism (see Section 6.2.4) to instantiate the abstract type in the document instance:

```xml
<xs:complexType name="jazzMusician_type" abstract="true">
  <xs:complexContent>
    <xs:extension base="person_type">
      <xs:sequence>
        <xs:element name="instrument"
                    type="xs:token"
                    minOccurs="0"
                    maxOccurs="unbounded"/>
      </xs:sequence>
    </xs:extension>
  </xs:complexContent>
</xs:complexType>
<xs:complexType name="instrumentalist_type">
  <xs:complexContent>
    <xs:restriction base="jazzMusician_type">
      <xs:sequence>
        <xs:element name="instrument"
                    type="xs:token"
                    minOccurs="1"
                    maxOccurs="unbounded"/>
      </xs:sequence>
    </xs:restriction>
  </xs:complexContent>
</xs:complexType>
<xs:complexType name="jazzSinger_type">
  <xs:complexContent>
    <xs:extension base="jazzMusician_type"/>
  </xs:complexContent>
</xs:complexType>
<xs:complexType name="jazzComposer_type">
  <xs:complexContent>
    <xs:extension base="jazzMusician_type"/>
  </xs:complexContent>
</xs:complexType>
```

Document instances of jazz musicians must now specify a concrete type using the xsi:type notation. This is also the reason why we were able to omit the element kind: The kind of jazz musician is sufficiently described via the xsi:type attribute.

```
<?xml version="1.0" encoding="UTF-8"?>
<jazzMusician xmlns="http://www.jazz.org/encyclopedia"
              xmlns:xsi="http://www.w3.org/2001/XMLSchema-instance"
              xsi:schemaLocation="http://www.jazz.org/encyclopedia
                                  ../schemata/jazzMusician.xsd"
              xsi:type="instrumentalist_type">
  <ID>JarrettKeith</ID>
  <name>
    <first>Keith</first>
    <last>Jarrett</last>
  </name>
  <birthDate>1945-05-08</birthDate>
  <instrument>piano</instrument>
  <produces>
    <album>
      <publisher>http://www.ecmrecords.com</publisher>
      <productNo>1064</productNo>
    </album>
  </produces>
</jazzMusician>
```

Cross-Document Constraints

Cross-document constraints are constraints that involve multiple documents, even documents from different document types. Typically we have four types:

- *Uniqueness constraints.* A document that has an identifying primary key may have the constraint that there is only one document with that key value. For example, if we have a jazzMusician document with an ID value of "Bley-Carla," we don't want to have other documents with the same ID value around.
- *Referential integrity constraints.* A document can rely on the fact that other documents to which it refers exist. For example, a band document "ArtEnsembleOfChicago" may rely on the presence of jazzMusician documents for the musicians collaborating in the band: "BowieLester," "Mitchell-Roscoe," "JarmanJoseph," "FavorsMalachi," and "MoyeDon."

■ *Cardinality constraints.* Given that a document relies on the existence of other documents, it may require that a certain number of those documents exist. Take for example the documents band, jamSession, project. All these collaborations refer to at *least* two jazzMusician documents. Otherwise we could hardly speak of collaboration

However, this constraint type can be expressed with a normal cardinality constraint for the document node that implements the foreign key. Thus, we can express the cardinality constraint by means of XML Schema, and referential integrity does the rest. In Section 8.2.8 the above relationship was expressed with

```
<xs:element name="jazzMusician"
 minOccurs="2" maxOccurs="unbounded">
 <xs:annotation>
  <xs:documentation>
     refers to key pk__jazzMusician_ID in schema jazzMusician.xsd
  </xs:documentation>
  <xs:appinfo>
   <xsg:refersToSchema xlink:href="jazzMusician.xsd"
              xlink:type="simple"
              xmlns:xlink="http://www.w3.org/1999/xlink"
              keyName="pk__jazzMusician_ID"/>
  </xs:appinfo>
 </xs:annotation>
 <xs:complexType>
  <xs:all>
   <xs:element name="ID" type="xs:NMTOKEN"/>
  </xs:all>
 </xs:complexType>
</xs:element>
```

What remains is to check the referential integrity for each jazzMusician element.

■ *General constraints.* There may be additional semantic relationships between different documents. For example, the period/from date in the band or project document or the time date in a jamSession document should not be smaller than the birth date of the jazz musicians collaborating in such a band, project, or jam session.

While cross-field constraints are relatively easy to validate (as we will see in Section 9.4), the same cannot be said for cross-document constraints. In relational databases, in contrast, constraints across multiple tables are not a big issue. SQL provides the necessary means to check these constraints, such as integrity rules and triggers (see Section 11.9).

That the situation with XML documents is different has nothing to do with the inherent properties of XML. What makes the validation of cross-document constraints difficult is not XML by itself but the fact that XML is used in a different scenario. In general, we cannot make a closed world assumption for a set of XML documents as we can for a relational database. Instead, we can expect that the documents will be distributed across several servers, even the whole Internet. Some of these servers may be mobile, and not all may be accessible at a given time. This makes it practically impossible to maintain referential integrity and other cross-document constraints at all times. The all too familiar 404-response code for dangling hyperlinks in HTML documents illustrates this situation. So, in many cases it will be necessary to replace the traditional cross-document constraint validation, which is executed before a document is stored or updated, with a process of synchronization and repair that is applied after a document has been stored.

9.3 CONSTRAINTS IN CONCEPTUAL MODELS

Defining constraints in a conceptual model requires a constraint definition language. Several formal constraint definition languages have been defined in the past. Most of these languages never left the academic sphere. Adoption in the industry has been poor because the formalism of these languages makes them difficult for industry programmers and designers to read. A specification language that is not understood by programmers is worse than an informal specification of constraints in natural language.

This is one reason for the definition of the *Object Constraint Language* (OCL), which has been part of the Unified Modeling Language (UML) since UML 1.1.

> There is a need to describe additional constraints about the objects in the model. Such constraints are often described in natural language. Practice has shown that this will always result in ambiguities. In order to write unambiguous constraints, so-called formal languages have been developed. The disadvantage of traditional formal languages is that they are useable to persons with a strong mathematical background, but difficult for the average business or system modeler to use. [OCL1997]

However, OCL is also not widely adopted. The tool support for OCL is patchy at best. One notable exception is a recent open source CASE tool, ArgoUML (*argouml.tigris.org*), and its commercial offspring, Poseidon (*www.gentleware .com*). Both include an OCL-to-Java compiler.

What makes the situation even more difficult for our purposes is that OCL is designed for object-oriented design methods and object-oriented implementations. OCL was not really designed with the document data model in mind.

That can make the definition of constraints for document-centric models difficult. Therefore, the following sections concentrate on the use of XPath [Clark1999] as a constraint language. This choice has several advantages:

- Document designers, stylesheet editors, and programmers familiar with XML know XPath well.
- XPath constraints can be easily translated into XSLT stylesheets or Schematron schemata (see Section 9.4.2), which can be used to validate documents.
- XPath is sufficiently powerful to express arbitrary constraints. Although XPath 1.0 does not support XML Schema data types (for example, comparison of date and time values), XPath 2.0 will offer full support.

The following example shows how to formulate constraints with XPath in an AOM conceptual model. AOM (see Chapter 2) is not limited to a single constraint language but allows the use of arbitrary constraint languages, even mixed within one model.

Now, let's see how we define a constraint for an asset property in AOM:

- Properties in an asset are addressed with an XPath expression consisting of the name of the property. Subproperties specify the path of the subproperty relative to the asset, for example, name/last.
- Properties in other assets are addressed by including the arc leading to this asset in the XPath expression. If the arc has a role name, we include the role name in the path, too. For example, if we want to address the property publisher in asset album from asset project, we write result/album/publisher.

Take for example the asset jamSession. We want to express the constraint that a jam session must not start before the birth date of a participating musician. We define the constraint within asset jamSession and do not specify an explicit context:

```
not(time <= jazzMusician/birthDate)
```

So, the context of this constraint defaults to jamSession, and time addresses property jamSession/time. The expression jazzMusician/birthDate addresses property birthDate in asset jazzMusician, which can be reached via an arc from asset jamSession. This arc has the cardinality constraint [2..*], and consequently this constraint must hold for at least two jazzMusician instances referred to by jamSession.

Let's briefly discuss the various constraints defined in the example, shown in Figure 9.2. First, the asset period contains the constraint

```
from <= to
```

which defines that the beginning of a period must be smaller than or equal to the end. This constraint applies to the assets belongsTo, style, project, and band because asset period is used in these assets as the type.

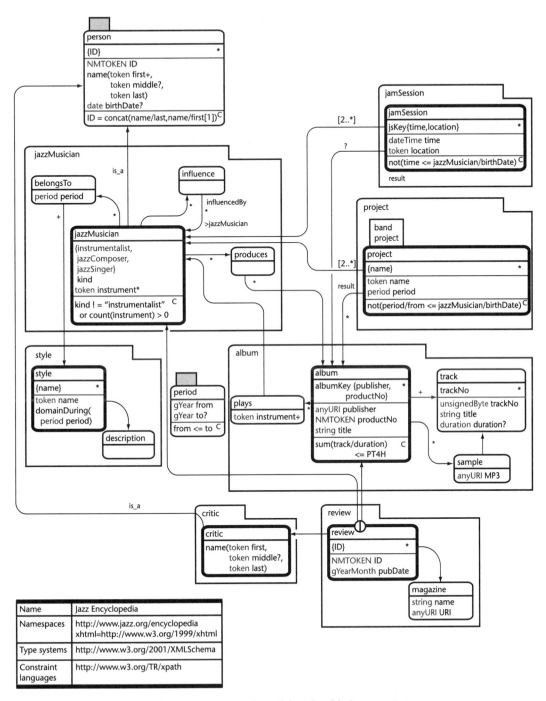

Figure 9.2 The Jazz conceptual model with added constraints.

Asset `person` contains the constraint

```
ID = concat(name/last,name/first[1])
```

This constraint postulates that the ID of a person must be obtained from the concatenation of its last name with the first occurrence of a first name. This constraint applies to both assets `critic` and `jazzMusician` because both inherit from `person` via the `is_a` relationship.

Next, the asset `jazzMusician` contains the constraint

```
kind != "instrumentalist" or count(instrument) > 0
```

This constraint specifies that an instrumentalist must play at least one instrument. As already pointed out in Section 9.2.2, it is possible to model this constraint completely by means of structure and type constraints. The conceptual model could reflect this by defining asset `jazzMusician` as

```
( {instrumentalist} kind
  token instrument+
| {jazzComposer,jazzSinger} kind
  token instrument*
}
```

However, the original definition with the added constraint has advantages in terms of readability.

The two assets `band` and `project` contain the constraint

```
not(period/from <= jazzMusician/birthDate)
```

This constraint makes sure that the beginning of the period during which a band or project exists is greater than the birth date of each participating musician. `period/from` refers to the subproperty `from` of property `period`. This subproperty is defined in the asset type `period`. Note that the simpler expression

```
period/from > jazzMusician/birthDate
```

is true when the birth date of at least one musician is greater than `period/from`. This is not what we want. In a similar way, the asset `jamSession` contains the constraint

```
not(time <= jazzMusician/birthDate)
```

which we have already discussed.

Finally, the asset `album` contains the constraint

```
sum(track/duration) <= PT4H
```

This constraint states that the sum of all track/duration properties must be less than or equal to four hours.

9.4 VALIDATION OF GENERAL CONSTRAINTS

This section covers how constraints, as discussed in Section 9.3, can be implemented. By formulating constraints in XPath, we have the advantage of choices among several implementation options.

9.4.1 Hard-Coded Constraint Checks

One of the most commonly used methods for validating general constraints (which often appear in the form of Business Rules) is hard-coding them into the application logic. For example, in a Java application, the application code would parse the document instances into DOM trees, and then would test the DOM nodes for compliance with the constraints.

An advantage to using XPath for constraint expressions is that these expressions can be used directly with newer DOM APIs, which can save a substantial amount of coding effort. The current working draft of the "Document Object Model (DOM) Level 3 XPath Specification" [Whitmer2002] defines an (optional) access layer to the document node via XPath expressions. This would allow us to address document elements directly with their path specification and formulate constraints as XPath filter expressions. For example, the constraint

```
ID = concat(name/last,name/first[1])
```

could be tested with the following Java DOM call,

```
if (!evaluate("ID = concat(name/last,name/first[1])",
        jazzMusician, null, XpathResult.BOOLEAN_TYPE, null).
                getBooleanValue() )
  throw new ConstraintException("ID does not match name");
```

where jazzMusician represents the root node of a jazzMusician document. Note that this code is hypothetical, as the specification mentioned above is still a working draft.

Current XPath processors usually come packaged within XSLT processors (because XPath was once a part of the XSL specification). However, there are also standalone XPath processors available, such as Jaxen (*www. jaxen.org*). An interesting development is also JXPath, which is part of Apache's Jakarta project. JXPath allows the use of XPath expressions to access Java data structures (*www.apache.org*).

Things get a bit more complicated when we want to check cross-document constraints. The following Java code illustrates how the constraint

```
not(time <= jazzMusician/birthDate)
```

which checks between jamSession and jazzMusician, can be validated by using standard DOM Level 2 API access methods:

```
public boolean checkEventDateVsBirthData(Document jamDoc) {
  // set result
  boolean result = true;
  // get a "time" element
  NodeList timeList = jamDoc.getElementsByTagName("time");
  Element startDateElement = (Element) timeList.item(0);
  // get start date value
  String startDateValue = getText(startDateElement);
  // convert to Date
  Date startDate = toDate(startDateValue);
  // Get jazzMusician elements
  NodeList musicians = jamDoc.getElementsByTagName("jazzMusician");
  // now loop over the "jazzMusician" children
  for (int i=0; i < musicians.getLength(); i++) {
    // get a single "jazzMusician" child
    Element oneMusician = (Element) musicians.item(i);
    // get the ID element
    NodeList ids = oneMusician.getElementsByTagName("ID");
    Element id = (Element) ids.item(0);
    // check if this item has content
    if (id.hasChildNodes()) {
      // get the string content
      String musicianID = getText(id);
      // Perform query for jazzMusicians identified by musicianID
      Document jazzMusicianDoc =
          performQuery("jazzMusician[ID"+"="+"'"+musicianID+"']"
      if (jazzMusicianDoc == null) {
        System.out.println("Error: Referenced jazzMusician"
                              +musicianID+" does not exist");
        result = false;
      } else {
        // get birthDate
        NodeList birthDateList =
            jazzMusicianDoc.getElementsByTagName("birthDate")
        Element birthDateElement = (Element) birthDateList.item(0);
        // get string value
```

```
          String birthDateValue = getText(birthDateElement);
          // convert to date
          Date birthDate = toDate(birthDateValue);
          // compare with startDate
          if (startDate.compareTo(birthDate) <= 0) {
            // Report violation of integrity constraint
            System.out.println
                ("Error: Start date before birth date of"
                                              + musicianID);
            result = false;
          }
        }
      }
    }
  }
  return result;
}
// Convert XML date formats into Java Date object
private Date toDate(String s) throws java.text.ParseException {
  // determine formatting string
  String f = (s.indexOf("T",0) >= 0 ?
                    "yyyy-MM-dd'T'HH:mm:ss" :     // dateTime
                    (s.indexOf(":", 1) >= 0 ?     // time
                    "HH:mm:ss" : "yyyy-MM-dd"));   // date
  // check for explicit time zone
  int p = Math.max (s.indexOf("+", 8),s.indexOf("-", 8));
  if (p >= 0) {
    f += "z"; // indicate time zone in formatting string
    s = s.substring(0,p-1)+"GMT"+s.substring(p);
                            // keep SimpleDateFormat happy
  }
  else if (s.charAt(s.length()-1) == 'Z') {
    // check for UTC time zone
    f += "z";
    s = s.substring(0,s.length()-1) + "UTC";
  }
  // create SimpleDateFormat object
  SimpleDateFormat df = new SimpleDateFormat ( f );
  // and use it as a parser
  return df.parse(s);
}
```

The method toDate() is required to convert the xs:date or xs:dateTime formats into java.util.Date objects.

What is not shown here is the implementation of the method `perform-Query()`. This method is used to fetch documents by key. The implementation of this method depends, as a matter of fact, on the storage medium: relational database, native XML database, file system, and so on.

9.4.2 XSLT

The advantage of such hard-coded constraints lies in performance benefits. The disadvantage, however, is that the change of a constraint requires rebuilding the application (at least to recompile all classes that implement this constraint). The alternative is to soft-code constraints. This can be done by writing an XSLT stylesheet [Clark1999a] that validates the document instances. Again, the use of XPath for constraint expressions has an advantage here: XSLT is based on XPath—both were once parts of the XSL specification. Running such an XSLT stylesheet against a document instance could result in another XML document containing an error report on which constraints have been violated.

The following stylesheet checks instances of the `album` schema (see Section 8.2.7) for the constraint

```
sum(track/duration) <= PT4H
```

I have deliberately chosen this constraint because it presents a problem. PT4H is an expression that is not understood by XPath 1.0 or XSLT 1.0, as neither specification supports XML Schema data types. We have the option of either using an XSLT extension—for example, one provided by EXSLT (*www.exslt.org*)—or waiting for the first XPath/XSLT processors supporting XML Schema data types. XPath 2.0 [Berglund2002] will support XML Schema data types, and so will XSLT 2.0 [Kay2002].

The other option would be to fall back to pre-XML Schema times and express the duration in seconds. Then the constraint would look like this:

```
sum(track/duration) <= 14400
```

But let's assume we already have an XSLT 2.0 processor. We create a little stylesheet to implement the above constraint. (For an introduction to XSLT, see [Kay2001].) First, we set up the namespaces for XSLT and for the Jazz model. For the Jazz model namespace we use `j:` as a prefix. We have also set up a namespace prefix `xf:` for *XPath and XQuery Functions,* which are needed to define a literal of type `xs:duration`.

```
<xsl:stylesheet xmlns:xsl="http://www.w3.org/1999/XSL/Transform"
                xmlns:j="http://www.jazz.org/encyclopedia"
                xmlns:xf="http://www.w3.org/2002/04/xquery-functions"
                version="2.0">
<!-- XSLT 2.0 required! -->
```

```
<xsl:template match="/">
  <xsl:apply-templates/>
</xsl:template>
<xsl:template match="j:album">
  <problems>
    <xsl:attribute name="album">
      <xsl:value-of select="j:title"/>
    </xsl:attribute>
    <xsl:if test="sum(j:track/j:duration) > xf:duration('PT4H')">
      <xsl:text>Total track duration exceeds 4 hours: </xsl:text>
      <xsl:value-of select="sum(j:track/j:duration)"/>
    </xsl:if>
  </problems>
</xsl:template>
</xsl:stylesheet>
```

The first template is the document node template and simply directs template processing to its child elements (which is the album element).

The second rule matches the context album—that is, the root element of album instances. It contains an <xsl:if> clause, which checks the constraint. Because we want to produce output when the constraint fails, the test clause contains the Boolean negation of the constraint:

```
sum(j:track/j:duration) > xf:duration('PT4H')
```

The expression xf:duration('PT4H') constructs a literal of type xs:duration with the specified value. The rest is just producing meaningful output.

Now we run the following document through this stylesheet:

```
<?xml version="1.0" encoding="UTF-8"?>
<album xmlns="http://www.jazz.org/encyclopedia"
       xmlns:xsi="http://www.w3.org/2001/XMLSchema-instance"
       xsi:schemaLocation="../schemata/album.xsd">
  <publisher>http://www.ecmrecords.com</publisher>
  <productNo>1780</productNo>
  <title>Inside out</title>
  <track trackNo="t1">
    <title>From The Body</title>
    <duration>PT1H</duration>
  </track>
```

```
    <track trackNo="t2">
      <title>Inside Out</title>
      <duration>PT1H</duration>
    </track>
    <track trackNo="t3">
      <title>341 Free Fade</title>
      <duration>PT1H</duration>
    </track>
    <track trackNo="t4">
      <title>Riot</title>
      <duration>PT1H</duration>
    </track>
    <track trackNo="t5">
      <title>When I Fall In Love</title>
      <duration>PT1H</duration>
    </track>
</album>
```

If our document instance contains tracks with a total duration longer than four hours, the following output document is produced:

```
<?xml version="1.0" encoding="utf-8"?>
  <problems xmlns:j="http://www.jazz.org/encyclopedia"
            album="Inside out">
    Total track duration exceeds 4 hours: xf:duration('PT5H')
  </problems>
```

The next example shows how to check constraints across documents. To do this, we make use of the XSLT document() function. We use XSLT 1.0 here despite the fact that XML Schema data types are involved. But first we have to explain how to address a document by key. When our documents are stored in a database system, retrieving a document by key is usually an efficient operation. Database systems can construct indexes and allow for searching data objects by key via an index.

The way such a query is passed to the database system—in particular within the parameter of the document() function—depends on the database system used. For example, a database system may require that the database is specified by URL and the document type and key are specified in the query part of the string. A query may consist of the following URL:

```
http://www.jazzserver.org/encyclopedia?jazzMusician[ID='PeacockGary']
```

However, the format of database access is currently not standardized in any way, and different database systems may use different formats. The format used here is that of the native XML database Tamino (*www.softwareag.com*). Here, we assume that all XML files are stored in a plain file system, and that the file name is constructed from the name of the document type and the key, such as

```
jazzMusician_PeacockGary.xml
```

and this is what we pass to the `document()` function.

The constraint, which we implement in the following stylesheet, is

```
not(period/from <= jazzMusician/birthDate)
```

Again, we first set up the namespaces and write the template for the document node:

```
<?xml version="1.0" encoding="utf-8"?>
<xsl:stylesheet xmlns:xsl="http://www.w3.org/1999/XSL/Transform"
                xmlns:j="http://www.jazz.org/encyclopedia"
                version="1.0">
<xsl:template match="/">
  <xsl:apply-templates/>
</xsl:template>
<xsl:template match="j:band">
  <problems>
    <xsl:attribute name="name">
      <xsl:value-of select="j:name"/>
    </xsl:attribute>
    <xsl:apply-templates/>
  </problems>
</xsl:template>


<xsl:template match="j:jazzMusician">
  <xsl:choose>
    <xsl:when test = "document(concat('jazzMusician_',j:ID,'.xml'))">
      <xsl:if test =
        "number(../j:period/j:from) &lt;=
        number(substring(document(concat('jazzMusician_',j:ID,'.xml'))
        /*/j:birthDate,1,4))">
        Unborn band member <xsl:value-of select="j:ID"/>
      </xsl:if>
```

```
      </xsl:when>
      <xsl:otherwise>
        Missing document
          <xsl:value-of select="concat('jazzMusician_',j:ID,'.xml')"/>
      </xsl:otherwise>
    </xsl:choose>
  </xsl:template>


  <xsl:template match="*">
  </xsl:template>
</xsl:stylesheet>
```

In the second template we prepare the output document and then apply templates to all child elements. This has the advantage of allowing us to process each jazzMusician element individually, thus producing a detailed error report. The third template contains the actual constraint check. First, in the <xsl:choose> clause, we make sure that the referenced jazzMusician file really exists (we do a check for referential integrity). If not, we give an error message.

Note that this does not work with all XSLT processors. Some processors may just throw an exception when the referenced document does not exist. When the document() function fails, an XSLT processor is free to throw an exception or to return an empty node list. The purpose of the <xsl:choose> clause is to catch the case of empty node lists.

In case of success, the <xsl:if> clause performs the actual constraint check. Because the period/from element only contains the year, we also extract the year from the birth date delivered by the document() function. Since XPath 1.0 is not type aware, we use the number() function to convert both strings into a number before we compare them. The final template is used to override the built-in default clause and does nothing.

9.4.3 Schematron

The technique discussed in the previous section has been sophisticated by Schematron (*http://www.ascc.net/xml/schematron*). Schematron can be used independently or in conjunction with DTDs, XML Schema, and Relax NG. With Schematron, schema authors do not need to dig deep into XSLT but can formulate constraints with XPath and a few additional statements. A Schematron schema can be formulated as a separate standalone document, or it can be embedded into XML Schema or Relax NG in the form of annotations. Validators that are not Schematron aware will ignore these statements, while Schematron processors can extract the embedded Schematron statements to process them. An interesting development is the Sun Multi-Schema XML Validator

Schematron Add-on, which can process Relax NG schemata with embedded Schematron statements in one step.

In the standalone form, the Schematron compiler translates the Schematron schema into an XSLT stylesheet and then utilizes the stylesheet to validate document instances. The Schematron compiler is actually implemented as an XSLT stylesheet, too. A Windows front end that streamlines this process is available at *www.topologi.com.*

Schematron introduces a few of its own declarations: schema, phase, pattern, rule, assert, report, key, and diagnostics. Figure 9.3 (page 350) shows the metamodel of Schematron with all language elements. The clauses assert and report define single tests (a single constraint). These can be grouped together with the pattern clause. The phase clause is used to organize the workflow within a validation suite. These declarations are covered briefly in the following pages.

Schema
The schema clause defines a Schematron schema.

Name	Attributes	Contains
schema	id?	title?
	fpi?	ns*
	ns?	p*
	defaultPhase?	phase*
	icon?	pattern+
	schema Version?	p*
		diagnostics?

Within the schema declaration, the definition of phase and pattern is essential. Patterns combine one or several assertion rules to a group. There must be at least one pattern group defined in a schema. Patterns are referenced by phases. Each phase element may refer to one or several patterns via child elements named active. Which phases are executed during a validation can be specified via parameters (such as command line parameters) when the validation sheet is executed against document instances. If no such phase is specified, the phase defined in attribute defaultPhase is executed. If no such attribute is specified, all phases in the schema are executed. If no phases are defined in a schema, all patterns are executed.

The functions of other child elements and attributes are as follows:

- The child elements title and p serve documentation purposes. title contains the schema title, while p elements may contain marked-up content for further description.
- The ns child elements can be used to declare namespaces used in the document instance. The syntax is <ns prefix="*prefix*" uri="*uri*"/> .

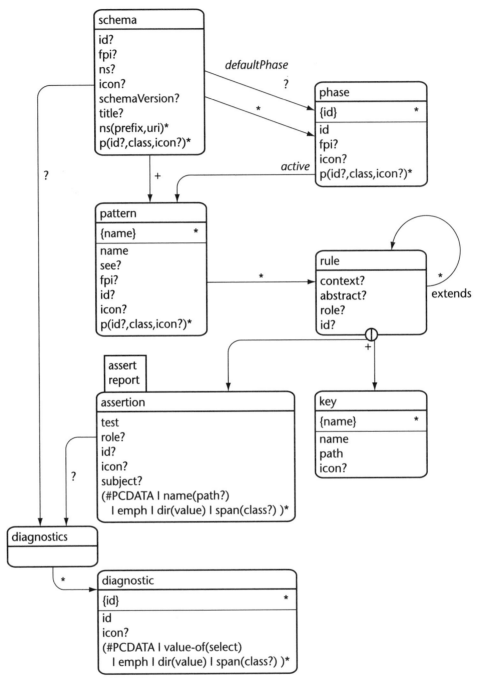

Figure 9.3 The metamodel of Schematron with all language elements.

- The ns attribute can define a namespace for the vocabulary defining role values (see "Rule" section).
- The icon attribute may specify a URI pointing to an icon such as a GIF file. This will appear in the output document.
- The fpi attribute allows specifying an SGML *Formal Public Identifier*.
- Finally, there is a group of diagnostics. This is a set of detailed descriptions that explain the reason why a rule has produced a message. These diagnostics are referred to by assert and report clauses (explained below). The output of diagnostics is optional and can be set with a parameter before execution.

Phase

The organization into phases allows various validation sequences that are executed on different occasions to be combined into a single schema. The patterns to be checked in a phase are specified via the active child elements.

Name	Attributes	Contains
phase	id	p*
	fpi?	active*
	icon?	

Phases are used to organize the workflow. For example, we could have a phase that is executed when a new document instance is created, and another phase that is executed when a document instance is deleted. Another application for phases is to combine validation sequences for different purposes. One phase could check document instances for structure violations, another phase could check for best practices or corporate standards, and another could check for accessibility. Or, we could have different phases for new documents, draft documents, and final documents.

Pattern

pattern clauses combine one or several rules into one group. Patterns are referred to by phases.

Name	Attributes	Contains
pattern	name	p*
	see?	rule*
	fpi?	
	id?	
	icon?	

Patterns are named; the name is displayed with the produced message in the output document. The id attributes may be used to identify a pattern. This value is specified by phase clauses via their active child elements to list a pattern as active. The see attribute may point to additional documentation via a URL.

Each pattern may list several rules to be executed. Which rule is executed depends on its context attribute (see "Rule"). The first rule with a matching context expression is executed; thereafter, the execution of the pattern stops. The context attribute consists of an XPath expression (XPath with the extensions defined in XSLT).

Rule

Rule clauses organize one or several constraints into one group. The context attribute controls the execution of the rule.

Name	Attributes	Contains
rule	context?	(assert | report | key | extends)+
	abstract?	
	role?	
	id?	

Rules can be declared as abstract. In this case they are not executed but are only referred to by other rules to inherit their properties. This is done via the extends clause: <extends rule="*rule-id*">. Abstract rules cannot define a context attribute; the context is defined by the inheriting rules.

The role attribute can be used by schema authors to classify or annotate the rule. The schema author may specify arbitrary values; a vocabulary can be defined with the ns attribute in the schema clause. The role attribute has no influence on the validation process.

Each rule contains one or several assert, report, key, or extends clauses.

Assert and Report

Both assert and report clauses are structurally identical:

Name	Attributes	Contains
assert	test	(#PCDATA | name | emph | dir | span)*
report	role?	
	id?	
	diagnostics?	
	icon?	
	subject?	

The test attribute contains the XPath expression to be checked by the rule within the specified context. An assert rule will fire when the test *fails*, while a report rule will fire when the test *succeeds*. The effect is that the message specified in the body of the clause is written to the output document. This message can be marked up with several tags (name, emph, dir, span):

- The name clause can be used to insert variable content into the text: <name path="*xpath-expression*">. If path is omitted, it defaults to ".", thus resulting in the current document node.
- emph, dir, and span have the same meaning as in HTML.

Key
The key clause exploits the key mechanism of XSLT within rules to check for cross-reference constraints.

Name	Attributes	Contains
key	name	
	path	
	icon?	

The attribute name specifies the name of the key. path specifies an XPath expression identifying the document node constituting the key. Defined keys can be referred to from XPath expressions within a rule via the XSLT function key(name,value). But beware: Only a few XSLT processors, such as Saxon and MSXML, support the key construct.

Diagnostics
The diagnostics attribute may specify one or several IDs of diagnostic messages (see "Assert and Report") that further explain the reason why the rule fired.

Name	Attributes	Contains
diagnostics		diagnostic*

Name	Attributes	Contains
diagnostic	id	(#PCDATA | value-of | emph | dir | span)*
	icon?	

The diagnostics section contains a set of diagnostic messages. These are identified by their id and referred to by assert or report clauses. The body of a diagnostic message contains text that can be marked up with value-of, emph, dir, or span. (value-of has the same meaning as in XSLT.)

Schematron Example 1

The following example implements the constraint

```
sum(track/duration) <= 14400
```

Again, we specify the duration in seconds (integers) because XSLT 1.0, on which Schematron relies, does not support XML Schema data types.

The schema contains only a single pattern and a set of diagnostics. There are no phases defined, so the only pattern is always executed when a document is validated by the schema. First, we declare the Schematron namespace as the default namespace, and a namespace prefix for our Jazz model. The latter is also defined in an ns child element. The xmlns:j attribute defines the namespace for the schema, while the ns child element defines the same namespace for the validation sheet generated from the schema.

```
<?xml version="1.0" encoding="utf-8"?>
<schema  xmlns="http://www.ascc.net/xml/schematron"
         xmlns:j="http://www.jazz.org/encyclopedia">
  <title>Schematron for jazz album</title>
  <ns prefix="j" uri="http://www.jazz.org/encyclopedia"/>
    <pattern name="album">
    <rule context="j:album">
      <assert test="sum(j:track/j:duration) &lt;= 14400"
              diagnostics="dur1 dur2"
              icon="bug10.gif">
          Total album duration too long.
      </assert>
    </rule>
</pattern>
<diagnostics>
  <diagnostic id="dur1">
    Sum over track durations should not exceed 14400!
  </diagnostic>
  <diagnostic id="dur2">
    The actual duration was
          <value-of select="sum(j:track/j:duration)"/>.
  </diagnostic>
</diagnostics>
</schema>
```

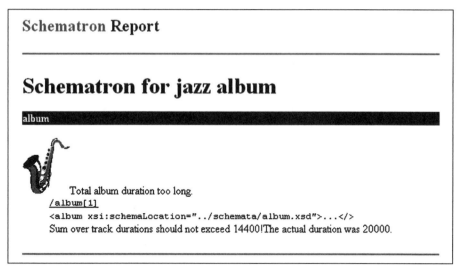

Figure 9.4 Schematron output for example 1.

The pattern contains a single rule with an `assert` clause. This clause sets up the context (root element `album`) and test for the constraint `sum(track/duration)` `<= 14400`. If this test fails, the message "Total album duration too long." is written to the output document. Since this `assert` clause refers to the diagnostic elements `dur1` and `dur2`, the messages defined in these elements will be written to the output document if the output of `diagnostics` was not suppressed. Also, an image pointer will be generated there because we have specified an icon.

The output is produced as an HTML file and should look like Figure 9.4.

Schematron Example 2
The next example is our cross-document constraint:

```
not(period/from <= jazzMusician/birthDate)
```

The implementation with Schematron makes use of the fact that Schematron accepts the XSLT extensions to XPath, in particular the `document()` function.

We have implemented two phases. The first phase checks only for referential integrity—that the `jazzMusician` document, to which `band/jazzMusician/ID` refers, exists. Note that, as above, depending on the XSLT processor used, an unresolved reference may abort the validation with an exception.

The second phase checks the actual constraint.

```
<?xml version="1.0" encoding="utf-8"?>

<schema xmlns="http://www.ascc.net/xml/schematron"
        xmlns:j="http://www.jazz.org/encyclopedia">
```

```
<title>Schematron for jazz band</title>
<ns prefix="j" uri="http://www.jazz.org/encyclopedia"/>
<phase id="Referential">
  <active pattern="integrity" />
</phase>
<phase id="Full">
  <active pattern="birthDate" />
</phase>
<pattern name="Referential Integrity" id="integrity">
  <rule context = "j:band/j:jazzMusician">
    <report test =
      "document(concat('jazzMusician_',j:ID,'.xml'))/jazzMusician"
          diagnostics="col1">
      Referenced document does not exist!
    </report>
  </rule>
</pattern>
<pattern name="Check birthDate" id="birthDate">
  <rule context = "j:band/j:jazzMusician">
    <report test = "number(../j:period/j:from) > number(substring
                   (document (concat('jazzMusician_',j:ID,'.xml'))
                   /*/j:birthDate,1,4))"
          diagnostics="col2">
      Unborn band member!
    </report>
  </rule>
</pattern>
<diagnostics>
  <diagnostic id="col1">
  No document for jazz musician <value-of select="j:ID"/> was found.
  </diagnostic>
  <diagnostic id="col2">
   The birth date of jazz musician <value-of select="j:ID"/> was after the
begin of the collaboration.
  </diagnostic>
</diagnostics>
</schema>
```

Also in this case, it would be possible to embed the Schematron instructions into the XML Schema file for band, as discussed in the next section.

Embedding Schematron into XML Schema

One of the nice things about Schematron is that we can include the above constraints as annotations in an XML Schema file. When this file is processed with the Schematron compiler, it will automatically harvest the Schematron statements from the annotation/appinfo elements. Here is the album schema from Section 8.2.7 with Schematron statements included:

```xml
<?xml version="1.0" encoding="UTF-8"?>
<xs:schema attributeFormDefault="unqualified"
           elementFormDefault="qualified"
           targetNamespace="http://www.jazz.org/encyclopedia"
           xmlns="http://www.jazz.org/encyclopedia"
           xmlns:xs="http://www.w3.org/2001/XMLSchema"
           xmlns:xsg="http://www.aomodeling.org/KLEEN/XSDgenerator"
           xmlns:sch="http://www.ascc.net/xml/schematron">
  <xs:annotation>
    <xs:appinfo>
      <sch:title>Schematron for jazz album</sch:title>
      <sch:ns prefix="j" uri="http://www.jazz.org/encyclopedia"/>
    </xs:appinfo>
  </xs:annotation>
  <xs:include schemaLocation="www.jazz.org_encyclopedia_TYPELIB.xsd"/>
  <!--Asset album-->
  <xs:element name="album">
   <xs:annotation>
     <xs:appinfo>
       <sch:pattern name="album">
         <sch:rule context="j:album">
           <sch:assert test="sum(j:track/j:duration) &lt;= 14400"
                       diagnostics="dur1 dur2"
                       icon="bug10.gif">
             Total album duration too long.
           </sch:assert>
         </sch:rule>
       </sch:pattern>
     </xs:appinfo>
   </xs:annotation>
   <xs:complexType>
```

```
      <xs:complexContent>
       <xs:extension base="album_type">
        <xs:sequence>
         <xs:element maxOccurs="unbounded" ref="track"/>
         <xs:element maxOccurs="unbounded" minOccurs="0" ref="sample"/>
         <xs:element maxOccurs="unbounded" minOccurs="0" ref="plays"/>
        </xs:sequence>
       </xs:extension>
      </xs:complexContent>
     </xs:complexType>
     ...
  </xs:element>
  <!--Asset track-->
  ...
  <!--Asset sample-->
  ...
  <!--Asset plays-->
  ...
  <xs:annotation>
    <xs:appinfo>
      <sch:diagnostics>
        <sch:diagnostic id="dur1">
           Sum over track durations should not exceed 14400!
        </sch:diagnostic>
        <sch:diagnostic id="dur2">
          The actual duration was
             <value-of select="sum(j:track/j:duration)"/>.
        </sch:diagnostic>
      </sch:diagnostics>
    </xs:appinfo>
  </xs:annotation>
</xs:schema>
```

To be consistent with the rest of the schema definition, we have here prefixed all Schematron element names with sch:. The default namespace is set to

our jazz target namespace. However, the prefix j: must still be specified with an ns element to identify the jazz namespace to the resulting validation sheet.

Embedding Schematron into Relax NG
Embedding Schematron declarations into Relax NG is even simpler, and using the multi-schema validator mentioned earlier allows us to validate the combined schema in one step. The validator currently only supports the Schematron declarations rule, assert, and report.

```
<rng:grammar xmlns:rng="http://relaxng.org/ns/structure/1.0"
             xmlns="http://www.jazz.org/encyclopedia"
             xmlns:xs="http://www.w3.org/2001/XMLSchema"
             xmlns:xsi="http://www.w3.org/2001/XMLSchema-instance"
             xmlns:xsg="http://www.aomodeling.org/KLEEN/XSDgenerator"
             xmlns:sch="http://www.ascc.net/xml/schematron"
             ns="http://www.jazz.org/encyclopedia"
        datatypeLibrary="http://www.w3.org/2001/XMLSchema-datatypes">
<!--Asset album-->
<rng:include href="album_type.rng"/>
<rng:start>
  <rng:element name="album">
    <rng:ref name="album_type"/>
    <rng:attribute name="xsi:schemaLocation">
      <rng:data type="anyURI"/>
    </rng:attribute>
    <rng:oneOrMore>
      <rng:ref name="track"/>
    </rng:oneOrMore>
    <rng:zeroOrMore>
      <rng:ref name="sample"/>
    </rng:zeroOrMore>
    <rng:zeroOrMore>
      <rng:ref name="plays"/>
    </rng:zeroOrMore>
    <sch:assert test="sum(track/duration) &lt;= 14400">
        Total album duration too long.
    </sch:assert>
  </rng:element>
```

```
</rng:start>

<!--Asset track-->
<rng:include href="track_type.rng"/>
<rng:define name="track">
  <rng:element name="track">
    <rng:ref name="track_type"/>
  </rng:element>
</rng:define>

...

</rng:grammar>
```

Here, it is not necessary to use a `rule` clause to specify the context of the assert clause. The context is simply defined by the location where the `assert` clause is specified (the `album` element).

9.5 AN XML PROCESSING MODEL

In this book we have looked at three different schema definition languages: DTDs (the legacy), the "object-oriented" XML Schema, and grammar-based Relax NG. Each has its merits and its weaknesses. The reader will have noticed that, for example, XML Schema and Relax NG do not cover external entities, so many applications will have to continue using DTDs. DTDs, on the other hand, cannot handle namespaces; and Relax NG has no concept of default and fixed values, and for cross-references, it relies on DTD logic.

We have also looked at several techniques to implement semantic constraints, which allow us to test not only if a document is valid but also if it is meaningful—an important topic as we move toward the Semantic Web. One of these techniques is Schematron, a schema language based on assertions.

For the implementer, this raises the question of how this all fits together. Which schema language is the correct one to use? Do we need to use a second schema language in addition to the first choice? What does the parser do, and what part of the implementation must be customized? In Figure 9.5, the document parsing process has been divided into sharply defined minitasks. This is in part based on Simon St. Laurent's analysis in "Toward a Layered Model for XML" [St.Laurent1999].

Most parsers handle several steps in this process. As mentioned in Section 9.4.3, there is actually a parser that does it all (Sun Microsystem's multi-schema validator with Schematron add-on). However, in other cases, it may be necessary to run a document through several parsers and passes, and combine the output from these passes.

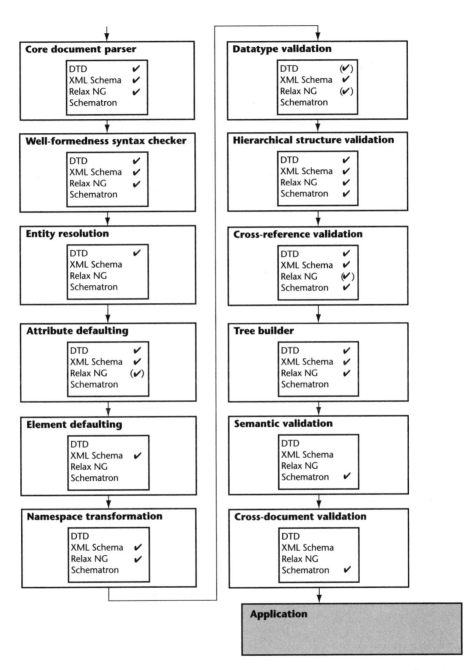

Figure 9.5 Tasks during the validation of an XML document. There is actually only one task (hierarchical structure validation) that is fully supported by all schema languages. (Checkmarks in parentheses denote partial support for a task.)

9.6 A FRAMEWORK FOR SCHEMA LANGUAGES

The multitude of schema languages indicates that there is not a single schema language fit for all purposes. XML Schema is best suited where XML is used in connection with databases and application-to-application messaging, such as electronic business and the integration of heterogeneous data formats. The traditional SGML community would probably like to stay with DTDs, enhanced by namespace support, or might migrate to Relax NG. In areas where documents need to be checked for complex structural constraints and for semantic constraints, Schematron shines.

A current standardization effort at ISO/IEC tries to combine the concepts of all of these schema languages into a modular framework. The *Document Schema Definition Language* (DSDL) [Holman2001] is "a multipart International Standard defining a modular set of specifications for describing the document structures, data types, and data relationships in structured information resources."

DSDL identifies six regions relevant to schema definitions:

- Grammar-oriented schema languages, naming Relax NG as an example.
- Primitive data type semantics, naming Part Two (data types) of the XML Schema Recommendation as an initial basis.
- Path-based integrity constraints, with Schematron as an initial basis.
- Object-oriented schema languages. This part is initially based on Part One (structure) of the XML Schema Recommendation and the sections of Part Two of W3C XML Schema describing the derivation of new simple types and the syntax for referring to primitive data types.
- Information item manipulation such as default values (as in DTDs), synonyms, and the eliding of information items.
- Namespace-aware processing with DTD syntax, basically covering the XML V1.0 specification plus XML namespaces.

Such a framework could help to gain a clearer understanding of the various schema languages and how they relate to each other. It could do the same for schema validation as the ISO layer model has done for communication.

THE ENVIRONMENT

Reality Check
The World Is Object-Oriented

Except in environments dominated by the documentation aspect, XML and XML schemata do not exist in isolation but have to integrate with other core technologies of enterprise IT, such as relational databases and object-oriented programming. This is probably the most important difference between SGML and XML. SGML flourished in documentation scenarios. XML, in contrast, intrudes into many traditional areas of enterprise technology: data storage, data integration, and message exchange. It is therefore essential that we get a clear understanding not only of the synergy effects between these existing technologies and XML but also of the "impedance mismatch" between these technologies and XML.

This chapter discusses XML Schema in context with object-oriented technologies; Chapter 11 deals with relational environments. The first part of this chapter explains some basic concepts of the object-oriented model and then compares it with the XML data model. We will see that both models follow concepts that are in parts alien, even opposed to each other. That will cause some problems when it comes time to implement integrated solutions in which object-oriented and document-related techniques are "married." What makes this

365

marriage so important is that object-oriented languages are the primary language used to combine processing logic with XML documents, despite the fact that functional languages such as Haskell are better suited to emulate the complex type system of XML. Java, especially, has strong XML support, followed by C++ and C#, but other OO languages such as SmallTalk or Eiffel provide XML access layers, too.

10.1 OBJECT-ORIENTED IMPLEMENTATIONS OF THE XML DATA MODEL

The most precise mapping of the XML Information Set onto object-oriented structures is the Document Object Model (DOM). The DOM defines a full application programming interface for XML documents on a generic level. It provides access to the various *nodes* of a document such as *document, element,* and *attribute,* and to *node lists.* By doing so, it allows clients not only to navigate within XML documents but also to retrieve, add, modify, or delete elements and content. To provide a language-independent specification, DOM uses the OMG IDL (Object Management Group Interface Description Language) as defined in the CORBA 2.2 specification. DOM bindings are defined for many languages, such as Java, C++, ECMAScript (JavaScript), and others.

There are currently three DOM API levels: Level 1, Level 2, Level 3 [LeHors 2002]. Apart from other improvements, DOM Level 2 adds an event model to the DOM specification, while DOM Level 3 adds an XML Content Model, load and save, document validation with DTD or XML Schema, better namespace handling, and optional support for XPath. I will not go into the details of DOM API programming, as these are usually well covered in the many excellent textbooks about XML with Java.

Section 9.4.1 gave an example for using the DOM API with Java. We saw how constraints can be checked using standard DOM Level 2 access methods or using the new XPath access methods defined as an add-on to DOM Level 3. What is discussed here is not a physical mapping of XML structures onto object-oriented structures as the DOM does, but a semantic mapping of conceptual structures onto both XML structures and object-oriented structures. In an OO application we want to be able to deal with `jazzMusician`, `band`, `album`, `customer`, and `purchaseOrder` objects instead of having to deal with `Document`, `Element`, `Node`, and `NodeList` objects. And, we want to be able to map existing OO class hierarchies onto XML structures.

So, what we need is a binding between XML structures and OO structures on the semantic level. Needless to say, there is no standard method to achieve that. In fact, it must be possible to customize such a binding according to the requirements of the application. And we want to keep the OO class hierarchy as similar as possible to the type inheritance hierarchy in the XML Schema.

Several products, such as Sun's JAXB (*java.sun.com/xml/jaxb*), Enhydra's Zeus (*zeus.enhydra.org*), and Breeze XML Studio (*www.breezefactor.com*), provide a framework to define such bindings. Other products are Castor (*www.castor.org*) and JaxMe (*jaxme.sourceforge.net*).

- JAXB is currently only available in an early access release supporting only DTDs. The final draft of JAXB v1.0, which supports XML Schema, should be available when this book publishes and will set the standard for Java-XML data binding. JAXB 1.0 will only support a subset of XML Schema, not covering wildcards, keys and key references, and NOTATION types.
- Zeus is an open source development currently in beta status. It supports XML Schema.
- Breeze Studio is a commercial product supporting XML Schema with the commitment to integrate JAXB when the standard becomes available.

Binding involves five phases—two phases when creating the application and three when running the application. The two phases during creation are

- Definition of the binding by the programmer. The programmer has to describe how elements and attributes defined in the schema are mapped to Java classes and fields.
- Generation of the classes. This step is performed by the binding framework.

The three phases when running the application are

- The *unmarshaling* process reads a document into fields of class instances. This involves the parsing of the document.
- In the *modification* process the client code modifies these fields via get... and set... methods.
- The *marshaling* process converts the instance fields back into an XML document.

Before describing these steps in detail, let's look at the similarities and differences between the object-oriented data model and the XML data model.

10.2 ENCAPSULATION AND BEHAVIOR

The term "object-oriented" gives a clear hint about the concept of OO languages. Similar to real-world objects, software objects expose only their exterior to the client. The internal structure is of no concern to the client. This is called *encapsulation.* The object encapsulates its internal mechanism. Its functionality is offered to the client via an *interface.* Take for example an electric lamp. The lamp has an internal structure: wiring, electric contacts, and so forth. What is exposed to the client is the switch with which to turn the lamp on or off. Taking a screwdriver and trying to switch on the lamp by connecting internal wires would be both inconvenient and dangerous. The same applies to software objects.

Objects also expose a *behavior.* Our lamp, for example, changes its state when I press the switch. Press the switch once, and the lamp is lit. Press the switch twice, and the lamp is switched off again. The lamp, it seems, has an internal state that influences the reaction that is caused by the press on the button. The behavior of each object can be described by stimulus-response patterns. Each stimulus (each client action at the object's interface) generates a certain response that can be observed by the client via the interface. This response depends on the stimulus and, of course, on the internal state. Or looked at another way, the internal state may be modified by a stimulus.

This sounds very much like an automaton, and, in fact, an object can be described as a finite state automaton. Its behavior can be completely described by a finite number of finite sequences of stimulus-response patterns. For software objects, the stimuli consist of *messages* that are sent to the object, and, similarly, the responses are messages that are sent back to the client. While some object-oriented languages (for example, SmallTalk) use this message metaphor, other object-oriented languages, such as Java and C++, have packaged the message concept into *method calls.* A method call consists of a method name, parameters, and a return value. Both name and parameters constitute the stimulus message that is sent to the object, while the return value contains the response message. In languages such as C++ and Java, methods are not classified by their name but by their signature. The method signature consists of the message name, the number of parameters, and the data types of all these parameters. For example, the method `switch(boolean)` is different from the method `switch(float)`.

Some OO languages support the concept of public object variables, allowing clients to access these variables. This may seem to violate the principle of encapsulation, but it does not. Object variables that are published at the object's interface are simply an abbreviation: The compiler translates *read* accesses to such a variable into a `get...()` method and *write* accesses into a `set...()` method. So, under the surface, the stimulus-response mechanism is still at work.

When we compare these object-oriented concepts of encapsulation and behavior with the document-centric model, we see that both models are in opposition. First, a document does not expose behavior. Second, a document is not encapsulated. Everything in a document is public. The contents may be encrypted, but they are still publicly visible.

10.3 CLASS, INSTANCE, TYPE

In this chapter we want to analyze how the type hierarchies in XML Schema relate to object-oriented type hierarchies. But before we do this, we must get a clear understanding of how type hierarchies in object-oriented languages are established, as we can identify three different concepts of hierarchy in these languages: class hierarchies, type hierarchies based on behavior, and type hierarchies based on syntax.

When taking a peek into the interior of an object, we can differentiate between the procedures that process incoming messages and the variables that hold state information. We say that objects belong to the same *class* if they have the same procedures. The individual objects of such a class, the class *instances*, differ only in the state they are currently in. If we regard objects as finite state automatons, we can say that two objects belong to the same class if they have the same state transition table. The actual state may differ for these two objects, but the state transition table is identical.

10.3.1 Class Hierarchies

Subclasses are classes that can be derived from a parent class by adding some functionality, such as new object variables or new methods. In terms of automaton theory, a subclass adds new states and new rows to the state transition table. However, most OO languages also allow us to derive subclasses from parent classes by overriding (modifying) existing functionality. By using inheritance mechanisms between parent class and subclass, it is only necessary to specify the new or modified functionality when implementing a class. The purpose of *class hierarchies* is to establish a mechanism for software reuse, not to establish an order relation between objects.

10.3.2 Type Hierarchies Based on Behavior

In contrast to class hierarchies, *type hierarchies* classify objects by behavior. *Behavior* in this sense means behavior at the interface: The same sequence of stimuli must generate the same sequence of responses. At this point we are not interested in side effects (writing to a file, drawing a window on the screen, playing a sound, etc.). Using stimulus response sequences, we can establish a subtype/supertype relation. A *subtype* must expose the same behavior as the parent type to all messages accepted by the object of the parent type but may expose additional behavior to other messages. The consequence is that we can substitute a parent type with a subtype without the client noticing (as long as the client is only looking at the interface). This is called *polymorphism*. Objects of the same type may belong to different classes as long as they expose the same behavior. These objects have a different implementation, but the functionality is identical.

Again, the object-oriented concept of types is opposed to the concept used in XML. In XML a type is defined by a set of structural constraints, while in object-oriented terms a type is a set of behavioral constraints.

10.3.3 Type Hierarchies Based on Syntax

Practical OO implementation, however, does not use this behavioral concept to establish a type hierarchy. This is because in order to support polymorphism, the compiler would have to know the exact behavior of a type. This is not always possible, as the implementation may not be available, and determining a behavioral type from an implementation is far from trivial. In terms of computational theory it is not decidable if two behavioral types are equal. Existing OO languages, therefore, use a different, syntactical notion of type. For example, a Java *interface* describes the methods that must be supported by a given type. It also can declare public variables, but we may ignore this here, as public variables are only an abbreviation for get... and set... methods. All methods are just described with their signature (name plus parameter types) and the return type.

Classes implement one or several interfaces. The type of a class instance, an object, is determined by the interfaces that the class implements. In fact, an object can belong to several types if the class implements several interfaces, and the object can be used in all places where such a type is expected. If, for example, the class MusicTeacher implements both interfaces Musician and Teacher, then an instance of MusicTeacher can be used in the role of type Musician and in the role of type Teacher.

Subtypes can be derived from parent types by adding method calls (or public variables) to the interface definition. This, of course, can also be achieved by combining several interface definitions. For example, we could define an interface MusicTeacher by combining Musician and Teacher. Consequently, Music-Teacher is a subtype of both Musician and Teacher. Subtypes can substitute a parent type in any occasion where the parent type is used, without violating type-safety. However, because this type concept is not based on behavior, this substitution can cause a complete change of the program's behavior.

10.3.4 Object-Oriented Types vs. XML Types

It is this notion of substitutability that establishes a type hierarchy in the OO world. In contrast, the notion of subtypes in XML is based on set theory. A document type A is a subtype of document type B if every instance of A is also an instance of B. The consequence is that the relationship between subtype and parent type is *not* maintained when we map XML structures on OO structures and vice versa.

Let's look at an example. The following XML type,

```
<xs:complexType name="CD_type">
  <xs:sequence>
    <xs:element name="title" type="xs:string"/>
    <xs:element name="productNo" type="xs:string"/>
  </xs:sequence>
</xs:complexType>
```

could be mapped on the following Java interface definition:

```
public interface CD_type {
    String getTitle();
    void setTitle(String);
    String getProductNo();
    void setProductNo(String);
}
```

We can now create a subtype of CD:

```
public interface CDforSale_type extends CD_type {
    java.math.BigDecimal getPrice();
    void getPrice(java.math.BigDecimal);
}
```

The corresponding XML Schema definition,

```
<xs:complexType name="CDforSale_type">
  <xs:complexContent>
    <xs:extension base="CD">
      <xs:sequence>
        <xs:element name="price" type="xs:decimal"/>
      </xs:sequence>
    </xs:extension>
  </xs:complexContent>
</xs:complexType>
```

is by no means a subtype of CD; the instances of CDforSale are not instances of the XML type CD because they contain an additional element.

Note that there is a slight inaccuracy in our mapping. Since all Java interface variables can contain the `null` value, too, our XML type definitions should have a `minOccurs="0"` with each child element:

```
<xs:complexType name="CD">
  <xs:sequence>
    <xs:element name="title" type="xs:string" minOccurs="0"/>
    <xs:element name="productNo" type="xs:string" minOccurs="0"/>
  </xs:sequence>
</xs:complexType>
```

and

```
<xs:complexType name="CDforSale">
  <xs:complexContent>
    <xs:extension base="CD">
      <xs:sequence>
        <xs:element name="price" type="xs:decimal" minOccurs="0"/>
      </xs:sequence>
    </xs:extension>
  </xs:complexContent>
</xs:complexType>
```

In this case, the XML type `CDforSale` is a supertype of XML type `CD` (while the Java type `CDforSale` is a subtype of Java type `CD`)!

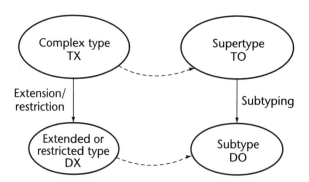

Figure 10.1 Hierarchical relationships between types can always be maintained when mapping XML Schema types onto object-oriented types.

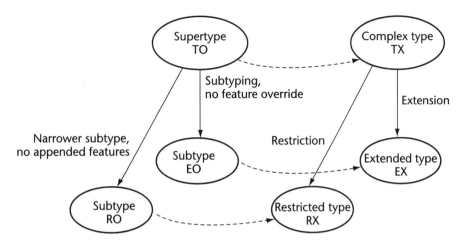

Figure 10.2 When mapping object-oriented types onto XML Schema types, the hierarchical relationships can only be maintained under certain conditions.

Conclusion: An XML Schema type DX constructed by extension from another XML Schema type TX can always be mapped onto a subtype SO of the corresponding OO supertype TO (see Figure 10.1). The same is true for derivation by restriction (because an OO subtype can override features of its supertype).

On the other hand, an OO subtype EO of an OO type TO can be mapped onto an extension EX of the corresponding XML Schema supertype TX only if the OO subtype SO does not override features of its supertype TO (see Figure 10.2). An OO subtype RO of OO type TO can be mapped onto a restriction RX of the corresponding XML Schema supertype TX only if the OO subtype TO overrides features of its supertype TO by narrowing them (making the set of instances smaller), and refrains from appending additional features.

10.4 SIMPLE TYPES

This section discusses how the simple types defined in XML Schema can be mapped onto types in OO languages. Some OO languages such as C++ and Java implement *primitive types* (types that are *not* objects). Java, for example, provides the following primitive types: byte, short, int, long, char, float, double, boolean.[1] Other languages such as SmallTalk do not have primitive types. In such languages every type consists of objects—in OO lingo, of *first-class citizens*.

---

1. The Sun XML Datatypes Library (xsdlib) is one example of a Java implementation of the XML Schema type system.

10.4.1 String Data Types

The primitive data type `string` as defined in XML Schema is based on the Unicode character set and is of unlimited length. In object-oriented languages the character set used depends on the particular language: While Java supports Unicode, most other OO languages support only ASCII. Most OO languages support strings of virtually unlimited length; some older languages such as Simula or object-oriented dialects of Pascal limit strings to a length of 255 characters. Java, for example, implements strings as first-class citizens in the form of the `java.lang.String` class, allowing a maximum number of characters of 2,147,483,647 (because the implementation stores the number of characters in an `int` variable).

XML Schema data types derived from `string`, such as `normalizedString` or `token`, are not supported as built-in data types in OO languages. However, it would be possible to implement such types in the form of user-defined classes. On the other hand, it is possible to define XML Schema data types derived from `string` that match the characteristics of a particular programming language, and to use these data types consistently when authoring XML schemata.

10.4.2 Binary Data Types

Since XML is text based, it does not support binary data in native format. Instead, XML Schema offers two encoded binary formats: `hexBinary` and `base64Binary`. Both formats support binary data of unlimited length.

Most OO languages do not provide an explicit concept for binary data. In Java, for example, binary data would be stored in arrays of data type `byte`.

10.4.3 The Boolean Data Type

XML Schema supports Boolean values with the data type `boolean`. Most OO languages implement a Boolean data type. Java, for example, has a built-in data type `boolean`.

10.4.4 Exact Numeric Types

The only primitive exact numeric data type in XML Schema is `decimal`. All other exact data types, such as `integer`, `long`, `int`, `short`, are derived from this data type by restriction. XML Schema does not restrict the upper and lower bounds of `decimal` but requires processors to support at least 18 decimal digits.

Most OO languages (except perhaps COBOL++) don't have built-in support for decimal data types but may provide appropriate support via class libraries. For example, Java 2 provides a decimal data type in the library `java.math`. The class `java.math.BigDecimal` supports decimal numbers with an unlimited number of decimal and fractional digits.

The `integer` data type is found as a built-in data type in most OO languages (except in those that don't have built-in data types at all, such as SmallTalk). In Java, for example, we find the following integer data types:

XML	Java	Range
integer	java.math.BigInteger	unlimited
long	long	–9,223,372,036,854,775,808 9,223,372,036,854,775,807
int	int	–2,147,483,648 2,147,483,647
short	short	–32,768 32,767
unsignedShort	char	0 65,535
byte	byte	–128 127

10.4.5 Approximate Numeric Types

XML Schema supports the approximate numeric types `float` and `double` for single and double precision floating-point numbers according to IEEE 754-1985. With these data types we find the highest compatibility with OO languages, as IEEE 754-1985 has been adopted by practically all OO languages.

10.4.6 Date and Time

XML Schema provides a rich set of date and time data types based on ISO 8601. `dateTime` specifies a precise instant in time (a combination of date and time), `date` specifies a Gregorian calendar date, and `time` specifies a time of day. All three types can be specified with or without a time zone. The data type `duration` specifies an interval in years, months, days, hours, minutes, and seconds, and allows negative intervals, too.

Not all OO languages provide built-in support for date and time. Java provides support for date and time in class library `java.util`: The classes `java.util.Date`, `java.util.Calendar`, and `java.util.GregorianCalendar` provide extensive support for date and time arithmetic. `java.util.Date` is almost equivalent to the XML Schema type `dateTime` with a resolution of milliseconds.[2]

---

2. However, these Java types always require the specification of a time zone, which is optional in XML Schema. Also, the date components (year, month, day, etc.) are restricted in size in Java, which is not the case in XML Schema.

Section 9.4.1 showed a conversion routine from the XML Schema xs:date and xs:dateTime formats into java.util.Date objects.

Most OO languages (including Java) do not provide built-in support for intervals. However, such a data type can easily be implemented as a specific class.

10.4.7 Other Data Types

XML Schema supports URIs with the data type anyURI. Java supports URLs (a subtype of URIs) with the class java.net.URL. Java 1.4 improves the support for URIs by adding class java.net.URI.

The QName data type in XML Schema specifies qualified names. It consists of a local part and a namespace part. It is relatively easy to represent such a qualified name in OO languages: It can be implemented as a tuple consisting of a namespace URI and the local name (string).

10.4.8 Type Restrictions

XML Schema provides a rich set of constraining facets to derive user-defined simple data types from built-in data types. Object-oriented languages allow us to implement user-defined data types that are directly or indirectly derived from built-in data types. The additional constraints can be implemented within the access method belonging to objects of these types.

10.4.9 Type Extensions

Restriction is not the only way in XML Schema to derive user-defined types. Type extensions such as type union and type extension by list are possible, too. In most OO languages there is no construct like a type union. (C++ recognizes the construct of a variant, which it inherited from C.) One solution is to use a type of the least common denominator, but some type-safety may be lost. In the worst case the most general type must be used, such as Object in Java.

Extension by list can easily be simulated in object-oriented languages through an appropriate collection type object such as java.util.List in Java. Some languages such as Eiffel support parameterized types, allowing the implementation of type-specific lists, such as a list of integers, a list of strings, and so on. Other languages such as Java must resort to a collection of general objects. (Java will support parameterized types with version 1.5.) This less type-safe solution requires casting a list element back into its specific data type when it is retrieved from the list.

10.4.10 Null Values

In OO languages, null values are possible when a data type is implemented as a class, and usually not possible when a data type is primitive. In Java, for example, the data types such as int, short, char, float, or double do not allow null values. For this purpose, Java provides wrapper classes: java.lang.Integer, java.lang.Float, or java.lang.Double.

Traditionally, OO null values are used to signal the absence of an XML element or attribute when an element or attribute is optional. This leaves us with the question of what to do when an element was defined as nillable (see Section 5.3.16). The answer is simple: It is in general not possible to represent a nilled element by a null value. The element may, for example, contain other attributes, so it must be represented by an object. Instead, the attribute xsi:nil="true" must be represented by a Boolean field within the object.

10.4.11 Implementing a Type Hierarchy

A consistent approach to mapping the XML Schema type system onto an OO language is not to map directly to built-in primitive types, but to implement a hierarchy of classes that closely matches the XML hierarchy of built-in types. A generic class XMLObject could be at the top of such a hierarchy. This class could provide some features that are common to all XML objects, such as marshaling and unmarshaling. Derived from this generic class, we would find classes such as XMLAnyType, XMLAnySimpleType, XMLString, XMLNormalizedString, XMLToken, XMLNM-TOKEN, and so on. These classes could implement the specific constraints for each built-in XML Schema data type. User-defined types could be derived from these classes, too.

10.5 COMPLEX TYPES

This section shows how the various constructs found in XML schemata, such as hierarchy, sequence, choice, and so on, can be mapped onto OO constructs. Java has been chosen as the implementation language.

10.5.1 Hierarchy

Leaf elements (elements that do not contain child elements) of a cardinality <= 1 and attributes can be implemented as simple fields of the data types shown in the previous section. Note that in Java it is not possible to express on a field level that an element is optional or not. However, it would be possible to add the necessary checks to the set...() access routines of a field. If an element is optional, it must be implemented as an object (reference) type and not as a primitive type (for example, as java.lang.Integer or our own XMLInteger instead of int) to allow for null values.

The following example shows how leaf elements can be translated into Java.

XML Schema

```
<xs:element name="name">
  <xs:complexType>
   <xs:sequence>
     <xs:element name="first" type="xs:string"/>
     <xs:element name="middle" minOccurs="0" type="xs:string"/>
     <xs:element name="last" type="xs:string"/>
   </xs:sequence>
  </xs:complexType>
</xs:element>
```

Java Interface

```
public interface Name {
  XMLString getFirst();
  void setFirst(XMLString first);
  XMLString getMiddle();
  void setMiddle(XMLString middle);
  XMLString getLast();
  void setLast(XMLString last);
  public static final String $Name = "name";
  public static final String $First = "first";
  public static final String $Middle = "middle";
  public static final String $Last = "last";
}
```

The last four instructions define the string constants that represent the tag names associated with this interface. These constants are used during the marshaling and unmarshaling process.

Java Implementation

```
public class NameImpl implements Name {
  private XMLString first;
  private XMLString middle;
  private XMLString last;
```

```
public XMLString getFirst() {
    return first;
}
public void setFirst(XMLString first) {
    if (first == null) throw new CardinalityException();
    this.first = first;
}
public XMLString getMiddle() {
    return middle;
}
public void setMiddle(XMLString middle) {
    this.middle = middle;
}
public XMLString getLast() {
    return last;
}
public void setLast(XMLString last) {
    if (last == null) throw new CardinalityException();
    this.last = last;
}
```

Complex elements with a cardinality of <= 1 are implemented in the same way, except that the child elements are represented by fields with the type of the child node.

XML Schema

```
<xs:element name="person">
 <xs:complexType>
  <xs:sequence>
   <xs:element name="name">
    <xs:complexType>
     <xs:sequence>
      <xs:element name="first" type="xs:string"/>
      <xs:element name="middle" minOccurs="0" type="xs:string"/>
      <xs:element name="last" type="xs:string"/>
     </xs:sequence>
    </xs:complexType>
   </xs:element>
   <xs:element name="birthDate" type="xs:date"/>
  </xs:sequence>
```

```
    </xs:complexType>
</xs:element>
```

Java Interface

```
public interface Name {
  XMLString getFirst();
  void setFirst(XMLString first);
  XMLString getMiddle();
  void setMiddle(XMLString middle);
  XMLString getLast();
  void setLast(XMLString last);
  public static final String $Name = "name";
  public static final String $First = "first";
  public static final String $Middle = "middle";
  public static final String $Last = "last";
}
public interface Person {
    Name getName();
    void setName(Name name);
    XMLDate getBirthDate();
    void setBirthDate(XMLDate date);
  public static final String $Name = "person";
  public static final String $BirthDate = "birthDate";
}
```

The representation of repeating elements requires some more effort. Such an element must be represented as a collection data type (List, ArrayList, LinkedList, Vector). These data types have their own interface, which makes it possible to iterate through the list, access list elements, and modify the list. Elements contained in a list always have the data type Object (the most general data type in Java). When retrieving an element from the list it is necessary to *cast* it into the appropriate type.

XML Schema

```
<xs:element name="album">
 <xs:complexType>
  <xs:sequence>

    ...
```

```
  <xs:element name="track" maxOccurs="unbounded">

    ...

  </xs:element>
  </xs:sequence>
 </xs:complexType>
</xs:element>
```

Java Interface

```
public interface Track {

  ...

}
public interface Album {

  ...

  java.util.List getTrackList();
  void setTrackList(java.util.List tracks);

  ...

}
```

Client Code

```
java.util.List tracks = myAlbum.getTrackList();
Track myTrack = (Track) tracks.get(0);
```

Alternatively, we could implement a type-safe access layer around such a collection type, replicating all its access methods. Languages such as Eiffel or Pizza allow us to use *generics* (parameterized types) to specify collection types such as a list of track elements. Again, control for cardinality constraints could be built into the implementation of setTrackList().

10.5.2 Sequence

Maintaining sequence information is normally not a big problem when translating XML schemata into OO interfaces, as access is always performed field by field and by name. Also, the sequence in repeating elements is maintained: List items are ordered and can be accessed by an index.

However, there is one case that causes a problem. Let's assume that a schema constructs a complex element by using an all connector. The consequence is that a sequence of elements in the document instance may arrive in a different order than the one defined in the schema. That does not really matter, as we normally access elements by name. But if we want to access an element by position, we are in trouble (XPath, for example, allows such things). We cannot determine the name of the element in question from the schema, because the instance may have a different element order. The relationship between tag and position is determined by the document instance.

XML Schema

```
<xs:element name="performedAt">
  <xs:complexType>
    <xs:all>
      <xs:element name="location" type="xs:string"/>
      <xs:element name="time" type="xs:time"/>
    </xs:all>
  </xs:complexType>
</xs:element>
```

XML Instance 1

```
<performedAt>
  <location>Cotton Club</location>
  <time>20:00</time>
</performedAt>
```

location has position 1, time has position 2, time follows location.

XML Instance 2

```
<performedAt>
  <time>20:00</time>
  <location>Cotton Club</location>
</performedAt>
```

location has position 2, time has position 1, time precedes location.

Java Interface

```
public interface PerformedAt {
  XMLString getLocation();
  void setLocation(XMLString location);
  XMLTime getTime();
  void setTime(XMLTime time);
  public static final String $Name = "performedAt";
```

```
    public static final String $Location = "location";
    public static final String $Time = "time";
}
```

Once converted to Java, the relationship between tag and position is lost. We are not able to ask: Was `time` given before or after `location`?

The problem also affects marshaling. Unmarshaling instance 2 into our Java structure should not cause problems: The unmarshaling process receives a tag and maps the element in the correct field. But when this data structure is marshaled again into XML, the information of the original sequence is no longer present, and the resulting XML will look like instance 1. This is, of course, unacceptable. The `<xs:all>` connector does not mean that the sequence of elements in an instance does not matter, it only means that all sequences are valid. (The XML Information Set [Cowan2001] (see Section 4.2) defines the child elements of a document as an ordered set.)

To solve this problem, it would be necessary to resolve the `all` connector into a choice of all possible permutations of the `all` list. However, this can result in a rather large amount of interface definitions. Section 10.9 discusses an alternate approach to this problem.

10.5.3 Repetition

One more point about sequences requires consideration: repeating sequences. Repetitions are mapped onto collection types such as `List`, `ArrayList`, and so on. The elements of such a collection type now do not contain an XML element but an XML model group (a sequence of elements). We represent such a model group with its own object type (`LocationAndDate`).

XML Schema

```
<xs:element name="tourDates">
  <xs:complexType>
    <xs:sequence maxOccurs="unbounded">
      <xs:element name="location" type="xs:string"/>
      <xs:element name="date" type="xs:date"/>
    </xs:sequence>
  </xs:complexType>
</xs:element>
```

Java Interface

```
public interface LocationAndDate {
  XMLString getLocation();
```

```
      void setLocation(XMLString location);
      XMLDate getDate();
      void setDate(XMLDate date);
      public static final String $Location = "location";
      public static final String $Date = "date";
    }
    public interface TourDates {
      java.util.List getLocationAndDateList();
      void setLocationAndDateList(java.util.List tourDates);
      public static final String $Name = "tourDates";
    }
```

Client Code

```
java.util.List Events = myTour.getLocationAndDateList();
LocationAndDate oneEvent = (LocationAndDate) Events.get(0);
XMLString loc = oneEvent.getLocation();
XMLDate date = oneEvent.getDate();
```

10.5.4 Choice

There is not much choice when we want to map a choice group onto OO structures: We have to implement it as a sequence (except in C++, where we might exploit the antediluvian variant construct), but with the additional constraint that only one of these fields in this sequence is not null. If we want to enforce this constraint, we have to provide an access method that sets all branches of the choice model group in a single step.

XML Schema

```
<xs:element name="item">
  <xs:complexType>
    <xs:sequence>
      <xs:choice>
        <xs:element name="amount" type="xs:unsignedShort"/>
        <xs:sequence>
          <xs:element name="quantity" type="xs:decimal"/>
          <xs:element name="unit" type="xs:token"/>
        </xs:sequence>
      </choice>
```

```
            <xs:element name="productNo" type="xs:NMTOKEN"/>
        </xs:sequence>
    </xs:complexType>
</xs:element>
```

Java Interface

```
public interface QuantityAndUnit {
  XMLDecimal getQuantity();
  void setQuantity(XMLDecimal quantity);
  XMLString getUnit();
  void setUnit(XMLString unit);
  public static final String $Quantity = "quantity";
  public static final String $Unit = "unit";
}
public interface Item {
  XMLUnsignedShort getAmount();
  QuantityAndUnit getQuantityAndUnit();
  void set AmountOrQuantityAndUnit(XMLUnsignedShort amount,
                                   QuantityAndUnit quantityAndUnit);
  String getProductNo();
  void setProductNo(String productNo);
  public static final String $Name = "item";
  public static final String $Amount = "amount";
  public static final String $ProductNo = "productNo";
}
```

Sequences within a choice group must be implemented as their own object type, as shown with `QuantityAndUnit`. The method `setAmountOrQuantityAndUnit` is used to set both branches of the choice group in one step. Thus, the implementation of this method can check if only one parameter is not `null`.

The implementation of repeating choice groups is similar to the implementation of repeating sequences. If the choice group in the example above were to repeat, we would implement it as a list of `AmountOrQuantityAndUnit` objects.

10.5.5 Recursion

Recursion is relatively easy to model. The recursive element is implemented as its own object type. This type contains fields that hold objects that refer recursively (directly or indirectly) to it.

XML Schema

```
<xs:element name="part">
  <xs:complexType>
    <xs:sequence>
      <xs:element name="productNo" type="xs:NMTOKEN"/>
      <xs:element name="name" type="xs:string"/>
      <xs:element ref="part" minOccurs="0" maxOccurs="unbounded"/>
    </xs:sequence>
  </xs:complexType>
</xs:element>
```

Java Interface

```
public interface Part {
  XMLString getProductNo();
  void setProductNo(XMLString product);
  XMLString getName();
  void setName(XMLString name);
  List getPartList();
  void setPartList(List parts);
  public static final String $ProductNo = "productNo";
  public static final String $name = "Name";
}
```

The objects contained in the list have type Part. Client code would have to cast these list elements to type Part:

```
List subparts = myPart.getPartList();
Part subpart = (Part) subparts.get(0);
```

10.5.6 Global and Local Elements

The mapping shown above works well for elements defined globally. However, in the case of complex elements that are defined locally, we may run into name clashes. Remember that elements defined locally with the same tag names may have different types. So far, we have derived the interface names directly from the tag names by capitalizing the first letter.

As a matter of fact, this problem is easy to solve. We just name interfaces for locally defined elements differently, preferably by using the full path name. Using such a naming convention for a locally defined element performedAt (as child of jamSession), we would arrive at the following interface:

```
public interface JamSessionPerformedAt {
  XMLString getLocation();
  void setLocation(XMLString location);
  XMLTime getTime();
  void setTime(XMLTime time);
  public static final String $Name = "performedAt";
  public static final String $Location = "location";
  public static final String $Time = "time";
}
```

The constant $Name for the tag name, however, stays the same.

10.6 GLOBAL TYPES

Global XML Schema types can be mapped onto OO structures in much the same way as XML elements. The only difference is that no tag name is declared for the type structure.

XML Schema

```
<xs:complexType name="CDType">
  <xs:sequence>
    <xs:element name="title" type="xs:string"/>
    <xs:element name="productNo" type="xs:string"/>
  </xs:sequence>
</xs:complexType>
```

Java Interface

```
public interface CD_type {
  String getTitle();
  void setTitle(String title);
  String getProductNo();
  void setProductNo(String productNo);
  public static final String $Title = "title";
  public static final String $productNo = "productNo";
}
```

An element CD defined with type CD_type

```
<xs:element name="CD" type="CD_type"/>
```

can then be declared as

```
public interface CD extends CD_type{
  public static final String $CD = "CD";
}
```

10.7 INHERITANCE

Section 10.3 already covered type hierarchies in OO languages. We found that object-oriented languages such as Java allow us to derive a subtype from a parent type by *extending* the definition of the parent type, and that the subtype inherits features from the parent type. This is very much in sync with derivation by extension in XML Schema. This inheritance mechanism should therefore be relatively easy to map between both data models. For example, if we want to extend the above CD_type with a price element, we can use the existing CD_type interface and extend it, too.

XML Schema

```
<xs:complexType name="CDforSale_type">
  <xs:complexContent>
    <xs:extension base="CD_type">
      <xs:sequence>
        <xs:element name="price" type="xs:decimal"/>
      </xs:sequence>
    </xs:extension>
  </xs:complexContent>
</xs:complexType>
```

Java Interface

```
public interface CDforSale_type extends CD_type{
  XMLDecimal getPrice();
  void setPrice(XMLDecimal price);
  public static final String $Price = "price";
}
```

XML Schema can also derive types by restriction, for example, by excluding optional child elements or attributes from the definition of a complex type. Within an OO implementation, such restricting constraints can easily be added by sharpening the constraints defined in the access method implementations (or by adding new constraints). For example, if we want to exclude an optional (minOccurs="0") element from a restricted type, we simply override its access methods with methods that throw an exception when they are used.

10.8 POLYMORPHISM

In object-oriented languages, the term *polymorphism* denotes the ability to use instances of a given type in the role of another type, usually instances of a subtype in the role of the supertype (substitutability). For example, given the above parent type CD_type and the subtype CDforSale_type, we can use CDforSale_type anywhere CD_type is used.

XML Schema has a similar concept. We can use a type that has been derived from a parent type anywhere the parent type is used.

- This applies, for example, to *substitution groups*. Elements that belong to a substitution group can replace the head element anywhere the head element is specified. Remember that the type of a substitution group element must be a type that is derived from the type of the head element.
- Similarly, *document instances* may explicitly declare a type (via xsi:type) for an element or attribute used in the document instance. The condition is that this type is derived from the type under which the element or attribute was declared in the schema.

Since the subtyping characteristic in Java and XML Schema is equivalent, as pointed out in the previous section, we can implement a Java binding of a given schema and trust that this binding can handle all documents with types derived from the original schema.

10.9 DYNAMIC MARSHALING

This section presents a proposal for how to solve the sequence problem with the <xs:all> connector (see Section 10.5). Two new fields are included in the interface definition: an integer field first and an integer array next:

```
public interface PerformedAt {
  XMLString getLocation();
  void setLocation(XMLString location);
  XMLTime getTime();
  void setTime(XMLTime time);
  public static final String $Name = "performedAt";
  public static final String $Location = "location";
  public static final String $Time = "time";
```

```
public int first;
public int next[] = new int[2];
}
```

These two fields are filled by the unmarshaling process, which records the sequence of elements found in the document instance. For example, if the document is

```
<performedAt>
  <location>Cotton Club</location>
  <time>20:00</time>
</performedAt>
```

the content of first is 0, the content of next[0] is 1, and the content of next[1] is –1. If the instance is

```
<performedAt>
  <time>20:00</time>
  <location>Cotton Club</location>
</performedAt>
```

the content of first is 1, the content of next[0] is –1, and the content of next[1] is 0.

Now the marshaling process, instead of just writing out the elements in the sequence of their definition, can use the information in first and next and write the elements in this sequence. The elements in the output document will have the same order as in the original document. The content of first and next could also be used to address elements by position.

10.10 CONSTRAINTS

As mentioned earlier, the object-oriented data model is based on encapsulation. The data within an object can only be accessed via methods. This makes it possible to implement all kinds of constraints in these access methods, including the constraints defined in an XML Schema.

10.10.1 Simple Types

The simplest constraints are those implied by simple types. These constraints are defined in XML Schema in the form of constraining facets such as minInclusive, maxExclusive, fractionDigits, pattern, and so on. Facets such as minInclusive or fractionDigits are easy to implement in very few instructions; pattern, however, can require serious programming in some OO languages. Fortunately,

Java 1.4 comes with a regex class that provides exactly the functionality to implement the pattern facet.

10.10.2 Cross-References

Cross-references that are defined in XML Schema via ID, IDREF, key, and keyref can, of course, also be checked. For example, a set... method for a list could check the list for duplicates and thus establish that the list elements are unique. Or, it could check if the list elements can be found in another specified list, and are thus suitable as references.

10.10.3 When to Check

Should we check constraints within access methods? Or would it be better to postpone the constraint validation until the final XML document is created (marshaled)? The problem with the first method is that constraints can get in the way when we want to modify content, especially if a constraint affects several fields. Also, a constraint can be checked more than once, which degrades performance.

However, the second method also has drawbacks. First, it is more difficult to identify the client code that caused the constraint violation. Second, if the document modification happens in an interactive environment—for example, when filling out a form—it is not very friendly to end users to tell them about a wrong field located at the beginning of the form after they have completed the whole form.

A good compromise is to implement constraints that affect a single field only in their respective access methods, and to test cross-field constraints in a separate step that can be invoked before the XML document is marshaled.

10.10.4 Conceptual Constraints

Conceptual models define additional constraints, in particular constraints that span multiple fields and multiple documents. Section 9.2.2 discussed such constraints that cannot be modeled with XML Schema. Section 9.4 showed how to check such constraints with application code, XSLT, and Schematron.

Section 9.4.1 showed an implementation of the constraint

```
not(time <= jazzMusician/birthDate)
```

for document type jamSession. There, we relied on the DOM API to access document nodes. The listing below shows an implementation based on an XML binding as outlined in the previous sections. Note that we deal with two document types: jamSession and jazzMusician. The binding for document type jazzMusician has been put into a separate Java package named jazzMusician to avoid name clashes.

```
public boolean checkEventDateVsBirthDate(jamSession jam) {
  // set result
  boolean result = true;
  // get a "time" element
  XMLDateTime time = jam.getTime();
  Date startDate = time.getValue();
  // Get jazzMusician elements
  java.util.List jazzMusicianList = jam.getJazzMusicianList();
  // now loop over the "jazzMusician" children
  for (int i=0; i < jazzMusicianList.getLength(); i++) {
    // get a single "jazzMusician" child
    JazzMusician oneMusician = (JazzMusician) jazzMusicianList.item(i);
    // now get ID of musician
    XMLNMTOKEN id = oneMusician.getID();
    // Perform query with this ID
    jazzMusician.JazzMusician jmdoc =
        performQuery("jazzMusician[ID"+"="+id+"']"
    if (jmdoc == null) {
      System.out.println("Error: Referenced jazzMusician"
                                    +id+" does not exist");
      result = false;
    } else {
      // get birthDate
      XMLDate birthDate = jmdoc.getBirthDate();
      if (startDate.compareTo(birthDate.getValue()) <= 0) {
        // Report violation of integrity constraint
        System.out.println
            ("Error: Start date before birth date of "+id);
        result = false;
      }
    }
  }
  return result;
}
```

10.10.5 Automatic Code Generation

The code above is much shorter than the code in Section 7.1.1, which is based on the DOM API. It is also more intuitive. However, it is not as short and compact as the original constraint specification:

```
not(time <= jazzMusician/birthDate)
```

This raises the question: Is there a way that we can automatically generate code like the above from the constraint specification given in the conceptual

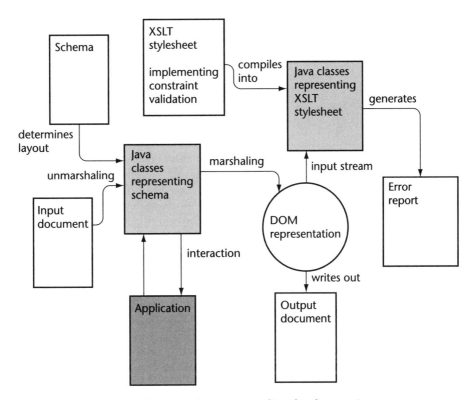

Figure 10.3 Applying XSLT stylesheets in XML/Java binding environment.

model? The answer is simple: not yet. The different implementations for binding XML Schema to object-oriented structures all generate different layouts, and many of these implementations have not yet reached a stable state. Once a standard binding method is established (this will probably be based on JAXB), the implementation of a constraint generator becomes an issue, too.

What is possible with current technology is shown in Figure 10.3. Instead of marshaling the Java data structures representing our input document to an output document file, we marshal it into a DOM representation. We can then use a suitable XPath processor (such as Jaxen) to apply the conceptual constraints formulated in XPath (see Section 9.3).

10.11 IDENTITY

The concept of keys (primary keys and foreign keys) is alien to the object-oriented concept. Instead, OO uses the concept of object identity. Objects are addressed by reference using an *object identifier* that is allocated whenever a new object is created. In contrast, relational databases (see Section 11.2) allow us to select table rows by content (XML databases also allow us to select XML documents by content, via XPath or XQuery).

This can create problems when we want to map several XML data types to OO structures and want to navigate within these structures. As discussed in Section 8.4.2, the XML documents may not contain the necessary navigation structures, and consequently the necessary object references in the OO implementation are missing. There are two ways to solve this:

- A map is created that describes the navigational model structure. Each map node points to the related map nodes and to the represented object.
- Content-based addressing is implemented. This can be done again, for example, with maps. Primary and foreign keys of an asset are mapped to their owning object. This allows all necessary navigation to be performed within a larger structure.

10.12 VISIBILITY

Most object-oriented languages implement a concept of visibility. An object class and its features can be defined with various degrees of visibility. Private features are only visible for the class itself; public features are visible for everyone.

In Java, the default setting for the visibility of a class or feature is visibility within the same package. A package combines classes that are in some sense interrelated. The concept of packages can be compared with XML namespaces, as packages are used to avoid name clashes as well. When mapping XML schemata onto Java classes, we usually want to map each namespace onto a separate package. Since packages can be nested, we can even mimic the hierarchical organization of XML namespaces. For example, given the namespaces

```
http://www.jazz.org/encyclopedia
```

and

```
http://www.jazz.org/shop
```

we can map those onto the packages

```
org.jazz.encyclopedia
```

and

```
org.jazz.shop
```

which are both contained in package jazz.

Reality Check

11
The World Is Relational

In today's enterprise environments, relational databases are the strategic method for data storage. For an enterprise-strength XML, it is crucial to integrate with this technology. This chapter explores paths of migration from and to relational databases as well as concepts of collaboration between the XML format and the relational format.

The chapter starts by giving an introduction into the relational data model and its implementation—SQL. We then compare the features found in SQL (data types and tables) with those offered by XML Schema. We will show how XML schemata can be translated into relational schemata, and vice versa. Finally, we will discuss two commercial implementations (Tamino X-Node and Experanto) that collaborate with relational databases via schema mapping.

11.1 MOTIVATION

Relational databases became a strategic data storage technology when client-server architectures in enterprises emerged. With different clients requiring different views on the same data, the ability to freely construct complex data structures from the simplest data atoms was crucial—a requirement that the classical hierarchical database systems could not fulfill. Relational technology made the enterprise data view possible, with one (big) schema describing the information model of the whole enterprise. Thus, each relational schema defines one ontology, one Universe of Discourse.

And this is the problem. Most enterprises cannot afford to be a data island anymore. Electronic business, company mergers, collaborations such as automated supply chains or virtual enterprises require that information can be exchanged between enterprises and that the cost of conversion is low. This is not the case if conversion happens only on a bilateral level, starting from scratch with every new partner.

XML represents a way to avoid this chaos. Because of its extensibility, XML allows the use of generic, *pivot* formats for various proprietary company formats. Usually business groups and associations define these formats. If such a format does not satisfy the needs of a specific partner completely, it is relatively easy to remedy by *dialecting*—extending the generic format with additional specific elements. This is why the integration of XML with relational technology is all important for enterprise scenarios. We will see that XML Schema has been designed very carefully with this goal in mind.

11.2 DATABASES

Logically, relational databases have a very simple structure. The fact that the implementation of a good relational database management system (RDBMS) is not simple at all, and that developers of RDBMSs have invested an incredible amount of work to get decent performance out of this clear and logical concept, is a different story.

When discussing relational databases in context with XML, there are two application areas to keep in mind:

- One application is to represent existing data in the RDBMS in XML format. This is important for organizations that store most of their enterprise data in relational form and want to leverage this data for electronic business.
- The second is to store existing XML data in relational databases. With mechanisms for referential integrity, transaction logic, backup, and recovery, a database always provides safer storage for data than a simple file system. Of

course, it is not always necessary to select an RDBMS for that purpose. Native XML databases can store XML data more efficiently and require less effort when creating an appropriate data model. However, a native XML database is not always at hand, and an RDBMS may provide easier access to the data from existing legacy applications.

The Standard Query Language (SQL) is the widely accepted standard for accessing an RDBMS (see Section 11.6). Originally developed to support database table creation, query, update, delete, and insert operations, SQL has been enhanced and expanded over the years and now includes additional means for constraint validation and support of object-oriented databases. SQL-99 goes far beyond the relational data model. However, most RDBMSs don't support SQL-99, and if they do, they only support a subset. I will therefore restrict the discussion to SQL-92 but give notice where new SQL-99 features solve problems that cannot be solved with SQL-92. Most RDBMSs implement a subset of SQL-92 but enhance it with proprietary extensions. In this discussion, I will stay close to the ANSI or ISO standard.

Representing the content of a relational database in XML is relatively easy. The SQL-99 table and type system (and hence the table and type systems of previous SQL editions) is a strict subset of the XML Schema type system. XML Schema looks the way it looks because it was designed to be compatible with SQL-99 (thanks to the intensive participation of DBMS manufacturers). Thus we can easily represent existing relational data with XML Schema without information loss. The opposite way—storing XML data in relational databases without information loss—is not so easy, however.

11.3 THE RELATIONAL DATA MODEL

A relational database basically consists of a set of two-dimensional *tables*. These tables are organized in unnamed *rows* and named *columns*. In relational algebra, tables are called *relationships*, columns are called *attributes*, and rows are called *tuples*. Each row contains a data record, and within such a record, each column represents a data field. Duplicate rows are not allowed. The sequence of rows and columns is *not* ordered. Two tables have the same *type* if they have the same set of columns.

Keys are used to identify rows in a table uniquely. Each key consists of one or several fields (columns) chosen in a way that the value or the combined values identify each row uniquely. A key that consists of a minimum number of fields and still satisfies this condition is called a *primary key*. *Foreign keys* are field combinations whose combined values can match with primary keys in other tables. This allows us to use tables as relationships: A table that has two foreign keys can relate two other tables to each other. That is the whole idea behind the relational data model: A table represents a relationship.

11.4 THE RELATIONAL ALGEBRA

Equally simple is the relational algebra. First, there are set operations:

- Union $A \cup B$
- Intersection $A \cap B$
- Difference $A - B$

The operations can be applied to two tables of the same type. The result (shown below) is a table with rows reflecting the union, intersection, and difference between the rows of the original tables.

Table A

productNo	title
53008	Round Midnight
3012	Take Five

Table B

productNo	title
9039	Sahara
53008	Round Midnight

$A \cup B$

productNo	title
53008	Round Midnight
3012	Take Five
9039	Sahara

$A \cap B$

productNo	title
53008	Round Midnight

$A - B$

productNo	title
3012	Take Five

Then there are three specific relational operations:

- Cartesian product
- Projection
- Selection

In a Cartesian product, given two tables A and B, the Cartesian product $A \times B$ consists of all rows $(a_1, a_2, \ldots, a_n, b_1, b_2, \ldots, b_n)$ where $(a_1, a_2, \ldots, a_n)$ is a row from A and $(b_1, b_2, \ldots, b_n)$ is a row from B. So, if A has 3 columns and 5 rows, and B has 2 columns and 3 rows, $A \times B$ has 5 columns and 15 rows. A smaller example is shown below:

Table A

productNo	title
53008	Round Midnight
3012	Take Five

Table B

productNo	price
3012	9.95
9039	17.95
53008	12.95

A × B

A.productNo	A.title	B.productNo	B.price
53008	Round Midnight	3012	9.95
3012	Take Five	9039	17.95
53008	Round Midnight	53008	12.95
3012	Take Five	3012	9.95
53008	Round Midnight	9039	17.95
3012	Take Five	53008	12.95

In projection, given a table A, $P(A,c_1,c_2, \ldots ,c_n)$ is called a projection of table A on $(c_1,c_2, \ldots ,c_n)$ if all columns a_i in A that are not specified in $(c_1,c_2, \ldots ,c_n)$ are removed from A. Duplicate rows that may have been created in the process are removed, too. For example:

Table A

productNo	title	artist
53008	Round Midnight	Thelonious Monk
3012	Take Five	Dave Brubeck

Table $P(A,artist,title)$

artist	title
Thelonious Monk	Round Midnight
Dave Brubeck	Take Five

In selection, given a table A and a Boolean function F with arguments from the set of columns $\{a_1, a_2, \ldots, a_n\}$ in A, the selection $A : F$ of table A with selector predicate F consists of all rows from A (and only such rows) satisfying predicate F. For example:

Table A

productNo	title
53008	Round Midnight
3012	Take Five
9039	Sahara

Table A : *productNo > 5000*

productNo	title
53008	Round Midnight
9039	Sahara

This is all we need. We can now derive two well-known relational operators from the basic operations defined above:

- The general *join* operation $A \times B : F$ is nothing but a Cartesian product of two tables A and B followed by a selection with some predicate F.
- In case of the familiar *natural join* operation $A \Leftrightarrow B$ the predicate F consists of a test of one or several column pairs from A and B for equality. Because this results in identical columns, a projection is also performed, to drop duplicate columns. The following example shows a natural join of tables A and B by column productNo:

Table A

productNo	title
53008	Round Midnight
3012	Take Five

Table B

productNo	price
3012	9.95
9039	17.95
53008	12.95

Table $A \Leftrightarrow B$

productNo	title	price
53008	Round Midnight	12.95
3012	Take Five	9.95

One problem with two-dimensional tables is that we must specify all fields in all records. For example, if we have a table person that contains columns for first name, middle name, and last name, then any person record stored in the table must have a first name, middle name, and last name. This is clearly not acceptable, and consequently, relational databases recognize the concept of null values. Any data field in a relational database can contain a "real" value or a null value that means a real value is not known. It is possible to deny the use of null values for certain columns. In particular, columns used for primary keys must not contain null values.

Null values allow the introduction of a new operation: the *outer join*. The outer join is constructed from the join operation by uniting the rows of the join with the rows of the original tables A and/or B. Because A and B have a different type than the result of the join $A \times B : F$, the rows of A and B are padded with null values before that operation: $(a_1, a_2, \ldots, a_n, null, null, \ldots, null)$ and $(null, null, \ldots, null, b_1, b_2, \ldots, b_n)$.

If only the padded rows of table A are added, we speak of a *left outer join*; if only the padded rows of table B are added, we speak of a *right outer join*. If both are added, we speak of the *full outer join*. The following example shows a right outer natural join by column productNo.

Table A

productNo	title
53008	Round Midnight
3012	Take Five

Table B

productNo	price
3012	9.95
9039	17.95
53008	12.95

Right Outer Natural Join

productNo	title	price
53008	Round Midnight	12.95
3012	Take Five	9.95
9039		12.95

11.5 NORMALIZATION

The design of relational models requires a sequence of normalization steps. Each step splits the complex data structures of the original model into simpler constructs and reduces redundancies and dependencies between data items.

This starts with First Normal Form (1NF), which requires that all column values are atomic. This is in stark contrast to the XML data model with its hierarchy of complex elements.

The relational normalization continues with Second Normal Form (2NF) up to 5NF. These Normal Forms deal more or less with the relationships between column values and keys. In the context of this book they are of no interest; it is the 1NF that causes us some problems.

When registering XML schemata with an XML-enabled relational database, it is the XML access layer of the database that will perform this normalization for us. It will resolve the hierarchical structure of the XML schema into a set of flat SQL tables. To understand this process, we will do this transformation manually.

11.5.1 Defining the Target Format

We will construct a small relational database and demonstrate normalization to First Normal Form. We sidestep a course in SQL for now by constructing our database in the form of an XML document! This has the additional benefit of showing us how relational structures can be implemented in XML.

The concept is simple: The root element of our document represents the whole database. The tables are represented as repeating child elements of this root element. The column values are child elements of these elements, that is, grandchildren of the root element. A person table, for example, would look like this:

```
<person>
  <firstname>Joe</firstname>
  <middlename xsi:nil="true"/>
  <lastname>Henderson</lastname>
</person>
<person>
  <firstname>Jelly</firstname>
  <middlename>Roll</middlename>
  <lastname>Morton</lastname>
</person>
...
<person>
  <firstname>Earl</firstname>
  <middlename xsi:nil="true"/>
  <lastname>Hines</lastname>
</person>
```

Note that we have used nil values here to represent relational null values. This is just to make the XML layout more similar to the relational layout. As nil values can only be used with elements and not with attributes, we always represent table columns with elements.

11.5.2 The Original Schema

What we are going to do is to normalize our `album` schema from Chapter 8. We have included all global definitions as local definitions and simplified this schema a bit—at this point we are not interested in data types and annotations. We have also enclosed this album in a root element `database`. Figure 11.1 shows a diagram of the database.

```
<xs:schema targetNamespace="http://www.jazz.org/encyclopedia"
           xmlns:xs="http://www.w3.org/2001/XMLSchema"
           xmlns="http://www.jazz.org/encyclopedia"
           elementFormDefault="qualified"
           attributeFormDefault="unqualified">

  <xs:element name="database">
   <xs:complexType>
    <xs:sequence>
     <xs:element name="album" minOccurs="0" maxOccurs="unbounded">
```

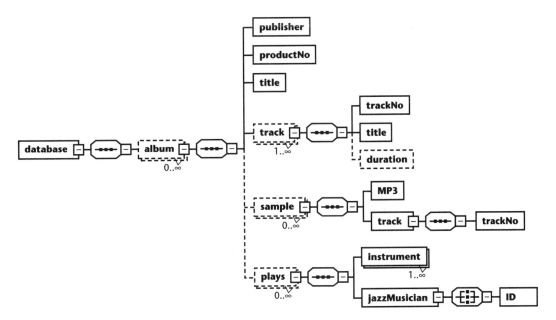

Figure 11.1 The `album` database, definitely not in Normal Form.

```
<xs:complexType>
 <xs:sequence>
  <xs:element name="publisher"/>
  <xs:element name="productNo"/>
  <xs:element name="title"/>
  <xs:element name="track" maxOccurs="unbounded">
   <xs:complexType>
    <xs:sequence>
     <xs:element name="trackNo"/>
     <xs:element name="title"/>
     <xs:element name="duration" minOccurs="0"/>
    </xs:sequence>
   </xs:complexType>
  </xs:element>
  <xs:element name="sample" minOccurs="0" maxOccurs="unbounded">
   <xs:complexType>
    <xs:sequence>
     <xs:element name="MP3"/>
     <xs:element name="track">
      <xs:complexType>
       <xs:sequence>
        <xs:element name="trackNo"/>
       </xs:sequence>
      </xs:complexType>
     </xs:element>
    </xs:sequence>
   </xs:complexType>
   <xs:keyref name="fk__sample_track" refer="pk__track_trackNo">
    <xs:selector xpath="./track"/>
    <xs:field xpath="trackNo"/>
   </xs:keyref>
  </xs:element>
  <xs:element name="plays" minOccurs="0" maxOccurs="unbounded">
   <xs:complexType>
    <xs:sequence>
```

```
              <xs:element name="instrument" maxOccurs="unbounded"/>
              <xs:element name="jazzMusician">
               <xs:complexType>
                <xs:all>
                 <xs:element name="ID"/>
                </xs:all>
               </xs:complexType>
              </xs:element>
            </xs:sequence>
           </xs:complexType>
          </xs:element>
        </xs:sequence>
       </xs:complexType>
       <xs:key name="pk__album_albumKey">
        <xs:selector xpath="."/>
        <xs:field xpath="publisher"/>
        <xs:field xpath="productNo"/>
       </xs:key>
       <xs:key name="pk__track_trackNo">
        <xs:selector xpath="./track"/>
        <xs:field xpath="trackNo"/>
       </xs:key>
      </xs:element>
     </xs:sequence>
    </xs:complexType>
   </xs:element>
</xs:schema>
```

11.5.3 Steamrolling the Schema

We are now going to convert this table into First Normal Form. Plainly speaking, 1NF means that each table field contains only a leaf element. This is clearly not the case with album. Three child elements (plays, track, sample) of album are repeating elements and, in addition, have a complex structure. They are tables themselves. We therefore remove these child elements from album and make them child elements of database; they become full database tables (see Figure 11.2, page 406).

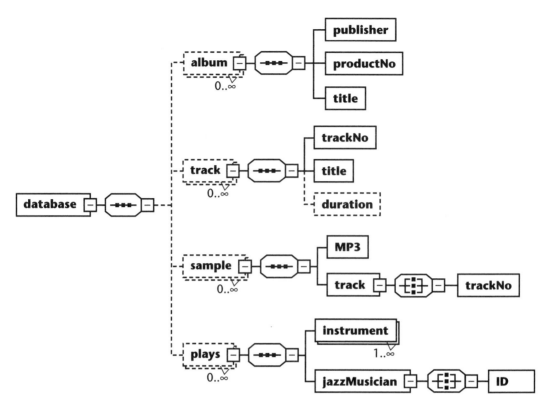

Figure 11.2 Much better, but still not perfect. Note that we made track optional because its former parent node album was optional.

There are still two columns that contain fields with complex structures: jazzMusician and track. This is easy to solve. We can simply collapse jazzMusician and ID into jazzMusicianID; track and trackNo into trackTrackNo.

11.5.4 Introducing Key Relationships

Unfortunately, our effort to flatten the album schema has resulted in a loss of structural information. The tables album, plays, track, and sample are completely uncorrelated. We solve this problem by declaring the combination of publisher and productNo as a primary key for album records, and by introducing elements albumPublisher and albumProductNo into the tables plays, track, and sample. These fields can then act as foreign keys relating to the album record to which a particular record from plays, track, or sample belongs (see Figure 11.3).

In the following listing, all the primary and secondary keys are defined. All keys are now defined on the database level. Because of this, trackNo as a key for track has become ambiguous—trackNo is only unique in the context of one

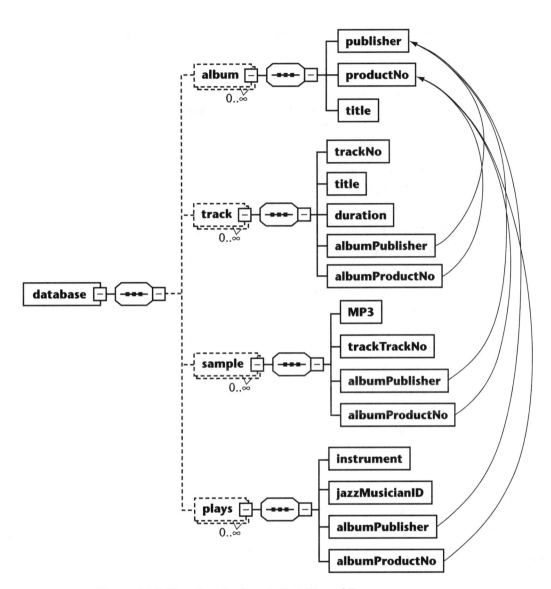

Figure 11.3 The album database in First Normal Form.

album element. We have fixed this by adding albumPublisher and albumProductNo to the keys pk_track_trackNo and fk_sample_track.

We have also removed the maxOccurs="unbounded" from plays/instrument. Instead of having one plays element with several instrument elements, we will have several plays elements with the same jazzMusician and album but with different instruments. (plays represents a ternary relationship between album, jazzMusician, and instrument.) Finally, we made element `duration` mandatory but nillable.

```
<xs:schema targetNamespace="http://www.jazz.org/encyclopedia"
           xmlns:xs="http://www.w3.org/2001/XMLSchema"
           xmlns="http://www.jazz.org/encyclopedia"
           elementFormDefault="qualified"
           attributeFormDefault="unqualified">

 <xs:element name="database">
  <xs:complexType>
   <xs:sequence>
    <xs:element name="album" minOccurs="0" maxOccurs="unbounded">
     <xs:complexType>
      <xs:sequence>
       <xs:element name="publisher"/>
       <xs:element name="productNo"/>
       <xs:element name="title"/>
      </xs:sequence>
     </xs:complexType>
    </xs:element>
    <xs:element name="track" minOccurs="0" maxOccurs="unbounded">
     <xs:complexType>
      <xs:sequence>
       <xs:element name="trackNo"/>
       <xs:element name="title"/>
       <xs:element name="duration" nillable="true"/>
       <xs:element name="albumPublisher"/>
       <xs:element name="albumProductNo"/>
      </xs:sequence>
     </xs:complexType>
    </xs:element>
    <xs:element name="sample" minOccurs="0" maxOccurs="unbounded">
     <xs:complexType>
      <xs:sequence>
       <xs:element name="MP3"/>
       <xs:element name="trackTrackNo"/>
       <xs:element name="albumPublisher"/>
```

```
        <xs:element name="albumProductNo"/>
      </xs:sequence>
    </xs:complexType>
  </xs:element>
  <xs:element name="plays" minOccurs="0" maxOccurs="unbounded">
    <xs:complexType>
      <xs:sequence>
        <xs:element name="instrument"/>
        <xs:element name="jazzMusicianID"/>
        <xs:element name="albumPublisher"/>
        <xs:element name="albumProductNo"/>
      </xs:sequence>
    </xs:complexType>
  </xs:element>
 </xs:sequence>
</xs:complexType>
<xs:key name="pk__album_albumKey">
 <xs:selector xpath="album"/>
 <xs:field xpath="publisher"/>
 <xs:field xpath="productNo"/>
</xs:key>
<xs:key name="pk__track_trackNo">
 <xs:selector xpath="track"/>
 <xs:field xpath="albumPublisher"/>
 <xs:field xpath="albumProductNo"/>
 <xs:field xpath="trackNo"/>
</xs:key>
<xs:keyref name="fk__plays_album" refer="pk__album_albumKey">
 <xs:selector xpath="plays"/>
 <xs:field xpath="albumPublisher"/>
 <xs:field xpath="albumProductNo"/>
</xs:keyref>
<xs:keyref name="fk__track__album" refer="pk__album_albumKey">
 <xs:selector xpath="track"/>
 <xs:field xpath="albumPublisher"/>
 <xs:field xpath="albumProductNo"/>
```

```
      </xs:keyref>
      <xs:keyref name="fk__sample_album" refer="pk__album_albumKey">
       <xs:selector xpath="sample"/>
       <xs:field xpath="albumPublisher"/>
       <xs:field xpath="albumProductNo"/>
      </xs:keyref>
      <xs:keyref name="fk__sample_track" refer="pk__track_trackNo">
       <xs:selector xpath="sample"/>
       <xs:field xpath="albumPublisher"/>
       <xs:field xpath="albumProductNo"/>
       <xs:field xpath="trackTrackNo"/>
      </xs:keyref>
     </xs:element>
    </xs:schema>
```

11.5.5 Preserving Sequential Order

Although we have now remodeled the parent-child relations of the original schema by introducing primary and foreign keys, we still face some information loss: The cardinality constraints are gone. The constraint that an album must contain at least one track is no longer there! We cannot express this constraint in terms of relational syntax. Relational database systems, however, allow expressing such constraints via *Integrity Rules* (see Section 11.9).

And there is still another information loss: Repeating elements in XML are ordered. In the original document we would have been able to address the second track element with the XPath expression album/track[2]. In a relational table, in contrast, the rows form an unordered set. There is no guarantee that a query returns the rows in the sequence in which they were inserted. Fortunately, our track table contains a column trackNo. We could use this field to sort returned records when we query the database. If the sequence of the plays and sample records were important, too, we would have to introduce similar numbering fields into these elements.

A document instance of our schema would now look like the following:

```
<?xml version="1.0" encoding="UTF-8"?>

<database xmlns="http://www.jazz.org/encyclopedia"
          xmlns:xsi="http://www.w3.org/2001/XMLSchema-instance"
          xsi:schemaLocation="http://www.jazz.org/encyclopedia
                              albumRDB.xsd">

    <album>
```

```
  <publisher>http://www.ecmrecords.com</publisher>
  <productNo>1780</productNo>
  <title>Inside out</title>
</album>
<album>
  <publisher>http://www.ecmrecords.com</publisher>
  <productNo>1064</productNo>
  <title>The Köln Concert</title>
</album>
<track>
  <trackNo>1</trackNo>
  <title>From The Body</title>
  <duration xsi:nil="true"></duration>
  <albumPublisher>http://www.ecmrecords.com</albumPublisher>
  <albumProductNo>1780</albumProductNo>
</track>
<track>
  <trackNo>2</trackNo>
  <title>Inside Out</title>
  <duration xsi:nil="true"></duration>
  <albumPublisher>http://www.ecmrecords.com</albumPublisher>
  <albumProductNo>1780</albumProductNo>
</track>
<track>
  <trackNo>3</trackNo>
  <title>341 Free Fade</title>
  <duration xsi:nil="true"></duration>
  <albumPublisher>http://www.ecmrecords.com</albumPublisher>
  <albumProductNo>1780</albumProductNo>
</track>
<track>
  <trackNo>4</trackNo>
  <title>Riot</title>
  <duration xsi:nil="true"></duration>
 <albumPublisher>http://www.ecmrecords.com</albumPublisher>
```

```
    <albumProductNo>1780</albumProductNo>
  </track>
  <track>
    <trackNo>5</trackNo>
    <title>When I Fall In Love</title>
    <duration xsi:nil="true"></duration>
    <albumPublisher>http://www.ecmrecords.com</albumPublisher>
    <albumProductNo>1780</albumProductNo>
  </track>
  <track>
    <trackNo>1</trackNo>
    <title>Part I</title>
    <duration xsi:nil="true"></duration>
    <albumPublisher>http://www.ecmrecords.com</albumPublisher>
    <albumProductNo>1064</albumProductNo>
  </track>
  <track>
    <trackNo>2</trackNo>
    <title>Part IIa</title>
    <duration xsi:nil="true"></duration>
    <albumPublisher>http://www.ecmrecords.com</albumPublisher>
    <albumProductNo>1064</albumProductNo>
  </track>
  <track>
    <trackNo>3</trackNo>
    <title>Part IIb</title>
    <duration xsi:nil="true"></duration>
    <albumPublisher>http://www.ecmrecords.com</albumPublisher>
    <albumProductNo>1064</albumProductNo>
  </track>
  <track>
    <trackNo>4</trackNo>
    <title>Part IIc</title>
    <duration xsi:nil="true"></duration>
    <albumPublisher>http://www.ecmrecords.com</albumPublisher>
```

```
        <albumProductNo>1064</albumProductNo>
     </track>
     <sample>
       <MP3>
          http://www.jazz.org/samples/JarrettKeith/InsideOut/FromTheBody
       </MP3>
       <trackTrackNo>1</trackTrackNo>
       <albumPublisher>http://www.ecmrecords.com</albumPublisher>
       <albumProductNo>1780</albumProductNo>
     </sample>
     <plays>
       <instrument>piano</instrument>
       <jazzMusicianID>JarrettKeith</jazzMusicianID>
       <albumPublisher>http://www.ecmrecords.com</albumPublisher>
       <albumProductNo>1780</albumProductNo>
     </plays>
     <plays>
       <instrument>double bass</instrument>
       <jazzMusicianID>PeacockGary</jazzMusicianID>
       <albumPublisher>http://www.ecmrecords.com</albumPublisher>
       <albumProductNo>1780</albumProductNo>
     </plays>
     <plays>
       <instrument>drums</instrument>
       <jazzMusicianID>DeJohnetteJack</jazzMusicianID>
       <albumPublisher>http://www.ecmrecords.com</albumPublisher>
       <albumProductNo>1780</albumProductNo>
     </plays>
     <plays>
       <instrument>piano</instrument>
       <jazzMusicianID>JarrettKeith</jazzMusicianID>
       <albumPublisher>http://www.ecmrecords.com</albumPublisher>
       <albumProductNo>1064</albumProductNo>
     </plays>
</database>
```

We now have a document with content in relational First Normal Form. The original element album that represented a business object is split into many separate records distributed over various tables.

11.5.6 Recomposing Original Document Nodes

We could apply relational operations on the content to create composite records that combine records from the various tables. To recombine all the tables album, plays, track, and sample we would need to perform the following steps:

1. Compute the natural left outer join between album and plays using the keys pk_album_albumKey and fk_plays_album as a selection constraint. We choose the outer join because albums without plays elements are allowed. In the process, the fields albumPublisher and albumProductNo from table plays are removed.

2. Sort the table track in ascending order using the field trackNo as sort criterion.

3. Compute the natural join between the result from step 1 and the sorted track table from step 2 using the keys pk_album_albumKey and fk_track_album as a selection constraint. We do not use an outer join here because albums require at least one track. In the process, the fields albumPublisher and albumProductNo from table track are removed.

4. Compute the natural left outer join between album and sample using the keys pk_album_albumKey and fk_sample_album as a selection constraint. We choose the outer join because albums without sample elements are allowed. In the process, the fields albumPublisher and albumProductNo from table sample are removed.

5. Finally, we have to consider the relationship between sample and track. We throw out all records for which the selection constraint given by the keys pk_track_trackNo and fk_sample_track does not hold. After this operation, the column sample/trackTrackNo has become redundant. We perform a projection to remove this column.

6. We have a name clash. Both album and track contain a column named title. We rename these elements albumTitle and trackTitle.

The above operations result in a set of records that looks like the following:

```
<album>
  <publisher>http://www.ecmrecords.com</publisher>
  <productNo>1780</productNo>
  <albumTitle>Inside out</albumTitle>
  <jazzMusicianID>JarrettKeith</jazzMusicianID>
  <instrument>piano</instrument>
  <trackNo>1</trackNo>
  <trackTitle>From The Body</trackTitle>
```

```
<MP3>
    http://www.jazz.org/samples/JarrettKeith/InsideOut/FromTheBody
</MP3>
</album>
<album>
  <publisher>http://www.ecmrecords.com</publisher>
  <productNo>1780</productNo>
  <albumTitle>Inside out</albumTitle>
  <jazzMusicianID>JarrettKeith</jazzMusicianID>
  <instrument>piano</instrument>
  <trackNo>2</trackNo>
  <trackTitle>Inside Out</trackTitle>
  <MP3>
      http://www.jazz.org/samples/JarrettKeith/InsideOut/FromTheBody
  </MP3>
</album>
...
```

For every valid combination of album, plays, track, and sample we get a new record. What we do not get with pure relational operations is the nice tree structure of the original document, although SQL provides some means for aggregation in queries (see next section). This is left to application logic, either expressed in some programming language or by means of SQL-99 [Krishnamurthy2000].

11.6 BRIEF INTRODUCTION TO SQL

This section gives a brief introduction to SQL-92 and then discusses how SQL-99 extends SQL-92. Note that this section is intended to give an overview about the features of SQL, not to provide an in-depth tutorial. Interested readers may refer to the many excellent textbooks about this topic, such as [Silberschatz 2001]. Although implementations of SQL-99 are scarce and incomplete, it is important because the type and structural system of XML Schema was designed as a superset of the type and structural system of SQL-99.

11.6.1 Queries

The query part of SQL is based on relational algebra with certain modifications and enhancements. A typical SQL query looks like

```
select C_1, C_2,...,C_n
  from t_1, t_2,...,t_m
 where P
```

with C_1, C_2, ..., C_n being column names, t_1, t_2, ..., t_m being table names, and P a predicate. If a column name does not uniquely identify a column, it must be prefixed with the table name, using the familiar dot notation. This query is equivalent to the following relational operations:

1. Constructing a *Cartesian product* from t_1, t_2, ..., t_m. This is specified in the from clause by listing the participating tables.

   The from clause may also specify a join. This is done by specifying the join type (inner join, left outer join, right outer join, full outer join), the join predicate (natural, on *predicate*), and which columns of the join are used (using C_1, C_2, ..., C_n); for example:

   ```
   from (t₁ natural full outer join t₂ using C₁, C₂,...,Cₙ)
   ```

2. Applying a *selection* with predicate P. This is done in the where clause. The where clause allows comparisons between columns and/or constants. Comparisons between arithmetic expressions and between string expressions are possible, too. These comparisons can be combined in a Boolean expression with the operators and, or, and not.

3. *Projecting* the result onto columns C_1, C_2, ..., C_n. This is specified in the select clause. Alternatively, the select clause may specify an asterisk (*) to denote all columns, meaning to skip this step.

   In contrast to pure relational theory, SQL allows duplicates in tables and query results. The keyword distinct can be specified after select to remove duplicates; the keyword all, to keep duplicates.

   The select clause can be used to apply arithmetic operations (+,-,*,/) on column names, provided these columns have a numeric type; for example:

   ```
   select prodNo, price*1.15
   ```

   Aggregating functions such as avg(), min(), max(), sum(), and count() are used to compute the average, minimum, maximum, sum, and number of rows over columns.

   A variety of string operations (concatenation, substring, conversion from upper- to lowercase and vice versa, etc.) are also available.

   The select clause can be used to rename the columns of the query result using the keyword as. For example,

   ```
   select C₁, C₂,...,Cₙ as R₁, R₂,...,Rₙ
   ```

   renames the columns C_1, C_2, ..., C_n to R_1, R_2, ..., R_n.

There are a few optional clauses that can be specified after the where clause:

- Sorting the result is possible by specifying the clause

  ```
  order by Cᵢ, Cⱼ,...
  ```

with C_i, C_j specifying the sort fields. The keywords asc or desc may be appended to specify ascending or descending order.

■ Aggregation of query results is possible with the clause

group by C_k, C_l,...

This will result in a single result record for each combination of C_k and C_l. The select clause must cumulate all columns that are not specified in the group by clause but are specified in the select clause with aggregating functions such as sum() or avg().

It is possible to apply additional predicates on the results of the group by clause to select only certain rows from the result set obtained by group by. This is done with the clause

having Q

where Q is a selection predicate.

Select statements can be nested—that is, the result of a query can be used as an input table for another query. The where clause provides several operators to relate to such result sets. For example,

```
select C₁, C₂,...,Cₙ
  from t₁, t₂,...,tₘ
  where P and (Cᵢ, Cⱼ) in
  (select D₁, D₂
    from u₁, u₂,...,uₘ
    where Q)
```

tests whether the value tuple (C_i, C_j) is found in the result set of the nested query. Similarly, it is possible to test whether a given value is greater or smaller than all or some of the values returned by the nested query.

Query results can be combined with set operations such as union, intersection, and difference. This is done with the operators union, intersect, and except. A condition is that both operands of such an operation have an identical column schema:

```
( select C₁, C₂,...,Cₙ from t₁, t₂,...,tₘ where P )
union
( select C₁, C₂,...,Cₙ from u₁, u₂,...,uₘ where Q )
```

Although there is more to know about SQL queries, this should be sufficient for a brief introduction. In addition to queries, SQL provides commands for table creation, for inserting, updating, and deleting table rows, and for administration.

11.6.2 Table Creation

Tables are created with the `create` command:

```
create table t (C₁ D₁ , C₂ D₂ ,..., Cₙ Dₙ ,
(integrity-constraint₁),
...,
(integrity-constraintₖ))
```

C_1, C_2,...,C_n define the column names, and D_1, D_2,...,D_n define the data types of each column (see Section 11.7). Each of the C_i D_i pairs can be postfixed with `not null` to indicate that no null values are allowed in this column.

Other integrity constraints are

```
primary key (Cᵢ, Cⱼ,...)
```

to define a primary key consisting of the columns C_i, C_j,... (similar to the key clause in XML Schema),

```
foreign key (Cᵢ, Cⱼ,...) references r
```

to define a foreign key consisting of the columns C_i, C_j,... (similar to the keyref clause in XML Schema) and referring to table t, and

```
check P
```

with P being a predicate over the columns C_1, C_2,...,C_n. This predicate is checked whenever a new row is inserted or a row is updated.

The command `alter table` is used to modify existing tables (adding or removing of columns), and the command `drop table` is used to remove tables from a schema.

11.6.3 Table Modification

Rows can be deleted from a table with the `delete` command:

```
delete from t where P
```

The `from` clause specifies the table, the `where` clause (see Section 11.6.1) specifies a predicate P, which selects the rows to be deleted.

New rows can be created with the `insert` command:

```
insert into t values (v₁, v₂,..., vₙ)
```

The `into` clause specifies the table; the `values` clause specifies a value for each column. As rows in a table form an unordered set, it is not necessary to specify where to insert the new row.

Existing rows can be modified with the update command:

```
update t set Cᵢ = Eᵢ, Cⱼ = Eⱼ,...where P
```

The set clause specifies which columns should be modified. The expressions E_i, E_j are the new values and can consist of constants, or arithmetic or string algebraic expressions computing a new value. These expressions can refer to existing column values. The where clause (see Section 11.6.1) specifies a predicate P, which selects the rows to be modified.

Multiple update, insert, and delete operations can be combined in transactions. The end of a transaction (and the beginning of the next) is defined with the commands commit work or rollback work.

11.6.4 Views

The ability to create views on a schema is an important facility of SQL. Views are typically used to give users restricted access to the tables of a schema. This allows decentralized maintenance of a data pool: In a large corporation, individual aspects of a table can be maintained by different departments without the need to perform each update through a central administration. For example, if we have a table customer, the sales department can be responsible for the sales contacts and sales history of a customer, the accounting department can be responsible for the customers' accounts, and so forth.

In SQL a view is created with the create view command:

```
create view v as Q
```

Q can be any legal query expression, including query expressions across multiple tables and on aggregations. The created view v can then be used in the from clause of a query instead of a table.

Updates on views are possible, too, but they are restricted on views that are defined by simple query expressions. Most implementations, for example, do not support updates on views that are defined with query expressions containing aggregates (group by).

Views can be defined across multiple tables by utilizing SQL's join facilities. Such a view can represent a set of multiple tables as a single virtual table to the user.

11.6.5 SQL-99

SQL-99 introduces object-orientation into relational databases. By doing so, it departs from pure relational theory; consequently, the approach of SQL-99 is called object-relational. Nevertheless, SQL-99 maintains backward compatibility with earlier versions of SQL. The most important change is that SQL-99 allows non-atomic, structured table columns (also called nested tables). In particular, SQL-99 introduces built-in constructors such as row and array. It is also possible to define your own structured data types:

```
create type T
    as (C₁ D₁, C₂ D₂,..., Cₙ Dₙ)
```

C_1, C_2,...,C_n define the column names, and D_1, D_2,...,D_n define the data types of each column, including other structured types and collections. These data types can be used everywhere types are specified, including the create table command.

We can access the components of such a structured type by using the familiar dot notation, for example, customer.name.first. User-defined types cannot be used directly in arithmetic expressions and comparisons; instead the user must provide appropriate access methods. Such methods are declared in the create type command:

```
create type T
    as (C₁ D₁, C₂ D₂,..., Cₙ Dₙ)
    method m (Cᵢ Dᵢ , Cⱼ Dⱼ,...)
```

But they must be implemented in a separate clause:

```
create method (Cᵢ Dᵢ, Cⱼ Dⱼ,...) for T
begin
    set self.Cₖ = Eₖ;
    ...
    set self.Cₙ = Eₙ;
end
```

E_k, ..., E_n are expressions derived from the parameters C_i, C_j,.... The table columns are addressed via $self.C_k$, ..., $self.C_n$.

SQL-99 allows the construction of type hierarchies. The expression

```
create type T1 under T2
```

establishes an inheritance relationship where T1 inherits columns and methods from T2.

Tables can be derived from a type,

```
create table t of T
```

with t specifying the table name and T the name of a defined type. The table t is created with a column for each property of type T. The table also inherits the methods of T. In terms of object-oriented programming, each row in table t is now an instance of type T. Because these rows are regarded as objects, an *object identifier* is generated for each row. These object identifiers can be used to refer to these rows. It is possible to store such identifiers in other tables: Their data type is ref(t), with t identifying the table that is referred to. This reference data type allows the new pointer notation in queries:

```
SELECT t₁.Cᵢ -> Cₖ
```

Given that C_i is a column of type ref(t_2), this expression results in column $t_2.C_k$ with the rows identified by the object identifiers stored in $t_1.C_i$.

Of course, there is much more to SQL-99. Its features would surely fill a book of its own.

11.7 SIMPLE DATA TYPES

For the description of SQL data types, I refer to the current working draft for SQL 200x (SQL-4) [Melton2001]. Earlier SQL standards (SQL-99, SQL-92, etc.) and existing implementations differ in some points from this description. However, this working draft is currently the best reference point for comparing XML Schema data types with SQL data types. The mapping between XML Schema data types and SQL data types is described in detail in [Melton2001a] and [Eisenberg2002].

11.7.1 String Data Types

The primitive data type string as defined in XML Schema is based on the Unicode character set (independent of the actual encoding!) and is of unlimited length. In SQL there are several corresponding *character string types*: CHARACTER, CHARACTER VARYING, CHARACTER LARGE OBJECT (CLOB). (There are also other spellings, such as CHAR and VARCHAR, which are used in earlier SQL editions.) CLOBs are restricted in certain aspects: They cannot be used in primary or foreign keys or unique column combinations.

All character string types are based on character sets supported by SQL. SQL supports various character sets, including ASCII and Unicode. This may require that XML strings be mapped to SQL strings and vice versa. This mapping is implementation defined. In addition, SQL string data types have a fixed or maximum length. The data type CHARACTER has a fixed, schema-defined length (the maximum length is implementation defined, varying between 255 and 4,000 in implementations), while the data type CHARACTER VARYING supports strings of variable length. Again, the maximum length is implementation defined. The CHARACTER LARGE OBJECT typically supports string lengths of up to 2GB. In XML, these data types can be modeled by restricting the string data type with the constraining facets length or maxLength.

In SQL, there are no equivalent standard data types for XML Schema data types derived from string, such as normalizedString or token.

11.7.2 Binary Data Types

Since XML is text based, it does not support binary data in native format. Instead, XML Schema offers two encoded binary formats: hexBinary and base64Binary. Both formats support binary data of unlimited length.

SQL supports the binary data type BINARY LARGE OBJECT that supports large strings of binary data. (Earlier SQL standards also recognize BIT and BIT VARYING.)

11.7.3 The Boolean Data Type

XML Schema supports Boolean values with the data type boolean. SQL supports Boolean values with data type BOOLEAN.

11.7.4 Exact Numeric Types

The only primitive exact numeric data type in XML Schema is decimal. All other exact data types such as integer, long, int, short, and so on, are derived from this data type by restriction. XML Schema does not restrict the upper and lower bound of decimal but requires processors to support at least 18 decimal digits. The SQL data type DECIMAL is almost equivalent to the decimal data type in XML Schema. The maximum number of decimal digits is implementation defined, ranging from 18 to 38 decimal digits.

There is no direct equivalent for the XML Schema integer data type in SQL. However, this data type can be represented in SQL by data type DECIMAL with no fractional digits. For the following integer data types there is a direct equivalence:

XML	SQL	Range
long	BIGINT–	9,223,372,036,854,775,808 9,223,372,036,854,775,807
int	INTEGER	–2,147,483,648 2,147,483,647
short	SMALLINT	–32,768 32,767

11.7.5 Approximate Numeric Types

XML Schema supports the approximate numeric types float and double for single and double precision floating-point numbers according to IEEE 754-1985. With these data types we find the highest compatibility between SQL and OO languages, as IEEE 754-1985 has been adopted by SQL-92 and practically all OO languages. However, the naming can be confusing:

XML	SQL	Precision
float	REAL	32 bit
double	FLOAT	64 bit

The SQL data type DOUBLE PRECISION (128 bit) does not have an equivalent in XML Schema.

11.7.6 Date and Time

XML Schema provides a rich set of date and time data types based on ISO 8601. dateTime specifies a precise instant in time (a combination of date and time), date specifies a Gregorian calendar date, and time specifies a time of day. All three types can be specified with or without a time zone. The data type duration specifies an interval in years, months, days, hours, minutes, and seconds, and allows negative intervals, too.

SQL supports date and time values with the data types TIME, DATE, and TIMESTAMP. While both TIME and TIMESTAMP can be specified with or without a time zone, DATE can only be specified without a time zone. (Note: The ODBC database interface does not support TIME and TIMESTAMP with time zone.) TIME and TIMESTAMP support fractions of seconds. The resolution is implementation dependent.

SQL provides a data type INTERVAL with features similar to the XML Schema data type duration. However, not many DBMSs implement this data type.

11.7.7 Other Data Types

XML Schema supports URIs with the data type anyURI. SQL does not have an equivalent to anyURI. However, URIs can easily be stored in CHARACTER VARYING fields.

The QName data type in XML Schema specifies qualified names. It consists of a local part and a namespace part. It is relatively easy to represent such a qualified name in SQL: It is simply mapped to a tuple consisting of a namespace URI and the local name (both stored in CHARACTER VARYING columns). Note that it would be wrong just to store a qualified name as a local name with a prefix! The mapping between prefix and namespace may change at any time.

11.7.8 Type Restrictions

XML Schema provides a rich set of constraining facets to derive user-defined simple data types from built-in data types. SQL allows parameterizing built-in types but in a limited way. For example, it is possible to control the length of a CHARACTER column, or to control the number of decimal and fractional digits in a DECIMAL column. Other parameters such as the constraining facets `minInclusive` or `maxExclusive` in XML Schema do not exist in the SQL type system. However, SQL offers other ways to constrain the value of a column (see Section 11.9).

11.7.9 Type Extensions

Restriction is not the only way in XML Schema to derive user-defined types. Type extensions such as type union and extension by list are possible, too. SQL-92 has no equivalent construct. If such types must be mapped onto relational types, the only choice is to store values of these types in their lexical representation, that is, to use the type `CHARACTER VARYING` or `CLOB` in SQL. In contrast, SQL-99 allows representing list extensions by defining an `ARRAY`. A `LIST` collection type is planned for future versions.

11.7.10 Null Values

All SQL data types support the notion of null values. XML Schema allows `nill` values for elements but not for attributes (see Section 5.3.16).

11.8 COMPLEX TYPES

Section 11.5 already showed a few examples of how complex types can be mapped onto relational structures. We have seen that relational fields that may either contain a value or null can represent optional elements. We have also seen that repeating elements almost always result in a separate table. Each record in this table contains a foreign key referring to the primary key of the former parent element.

This section discusses how to express hierarchy in relational terms, and how to implement the three basic regular expression operators (sequence, choice, recursion) with the relational methods of SQL-92.

SQL-99, in contrast, allows the definition of structured types. These types can then be used in a column definition to declare a column of complex content. Of course, this can make the SQL representation of XML content much simpler.

11.8.1 Hierarchy

Leaf elements (elements that do not contain child elements) of a cardinality <= 1 and attributes can be implemented as simple table columns (see Table 11.1). Complex elements and leaf elements with cardinality > 1, however, must be implemented as tables. Equipping the parent with a primary key and the child with a foreign key referring to this primary key can preserve parent-child relationships.

Table 11.1   Translating leaf elements into a relational schema. Note that we have to constrain the maximum length of string values, as SQL requires specifying a maximum length for VARCHAR.

XML Schema	SQL-92

``
<xs:element name="track">
  <xs:complexType>
   <xs:sequence>
    <xs:element name="trackNo"
      type="xs:unsignedByte"/>
    <xs:element name="title"
      type="xs:string"/>
    <xs:element name="duration"
      type="xs:unsignedShort"
      minOccurs="0"/>
   </xs:sequence>
  </xs:complexType>
</xs:element>
<xs:key name="pTrack">
  <xs:selector xpath="track"/>
  <xs:field xpath="trackNo"/>
</xs:key>
``
	``
	CREATE TABLE track
	(trackNo SMALLINT NOT NULL,
	   title VARCHAR(255) NOT NULL,
	   duration INTEGER,
	   PRIMARY KEY (trackNo)
	)
	``

Take for example the track element in the example in Section 11.5. Element track is a complex child element of album. Because it is complex, we have to implement it as a separate table. We introduce two fields albumPublisher and albumProductNo to form a foreign key. This key refers to the primary key defined for table album, which consists of the fields publisher and productNo (see Table 11.2).

Because track is defined as a repeating element in album, we also add the fields albumPublisher and albumProductNo to the primary key of track. Otherwise the key would not be unique, as trackNo is only unique within the context of one album instance.

In some cases, however, the creation of a separate table for a complex element can be overkill. Take for example a complex element such as name(first,middle?,last). In such cases we are better off resolving this element into three leaf elements, such as name_first, name_middle?, name_last.

As mentioned above, SQL-99 solves this problem by introducing user-defined structured types. It would be possible to define a structured type for name(first,middle?,last),

```
CREATE TYPE personName
AS ( first VARCHAR(20) NOT NULL,
     middle CHAR(2)
     last VARCHAR(30) NOT NULL
   )
```

Table 11.2 Translating complex element track into a relational schema.

XML Schema	SQL-92
| ```
<xs:element name="album">
 <xs:complexType>
  <xs:sequence>
   <xs:element name="publisher"/>
   <xs:element name="productNo"/>
   <xs:element name="title"/>
   <xs:element name="track"
       maxOccurs="unbounded">
    <xs:complexType>
     <xs:sequence>
      <xs:element name="trackNo"/>
      <xs:element name="title"/>
      <xs:element name="duration"
                minOccurs="0"/>
     </xs:sequence>
    </xs:complexType>
   </xs:element>
   ...
  </xs:sequence>
 </xs:complexType>
 <xs:key
     name="pk__album_albumKey">
  <xs:selector xpath="."/>
  <xs:field xpath="publisher"/>
  <xs:field xpath="productNo"/>
 </xs:key>
</xs:element>
``` | ```
CREATE TABLE album
  ( publisher
        VARCHAR(255) NOT NULL,
    productNo
        CHAR(32) NOT NULL,
    title
        VARCHAR(255) NOT NULL,
    PRIMARY KEY
        (publisher, productNo )
  )

CREATE TABLE track
  ( trackNo SMALLINT NOT NULL,
    title VARCHAR(255) NOT NULL,
    duration INTEGER,
    albumPublisher
        VARCHAR(255) NOT NULL,
    albumProductNo
        CHAR(32) NOT NULL,
    PRIMARY KEY (albumPublisher,
                 albumProductNo,
                 trackNo),
  FOREIGN KEY
    ( albumPublisher,
      albumProductNo )
    references album
  )
``` |

and then use it in a column definition:

```
CREATE TABLE person
  ( name personName NOT NULL,
    ID VARCHAR(32)
  )
```

The subfields of a type can be accessed via a dot notation, such as

```
person.name.last
```

11.8.2 Sequence

Again, as far as leaf elements are concerned, sequence is easy to establish. A sequence of leaf elements is simply translated into a sequence of table columns.

However, for complex elements we lose this sequence information when the complex element forms a table. If the sequence of complex child elements is essential, we must make sure in later queries that the various tables are joined in the right sequence. The SQL query

```
SELECT * FROM album NATURAL LEFT OUTER JOIN track WHERE ...
```

joins the two tables album and track in the correct order. The * notation after the SELECT stands for "all fields." In this case, where more than one table is specified after the FROM keyword, it delivers the Cartesian product.

In our case, however, it would be better to perform an explicit projection. There are three reasons for this: First, we were just lucky that the album schema specified all leaf elements in front of the complex element track. If, for example, the element title followed the element track, the query shown above would deliver the wrong result. Second, we need to rename a column because both album and track contain a title column. Third, we would like to remove the duplicate columns publisher/albumPublisher and productNo/albumProductNo.

```
SELECT publisher,
       productNo,
       album.title AS albumTitle,
       trackNo,
       track.title AS trackTitle,
       duration
  FROM album NATURAL LEFT OUTER JOIN track
  WHERE ...
```

The AS clause is used to rename a column.

For repeating elements (which form their own table), sequence information is lost, too. Rows in relational databases form an unordered set. To maintain the sequence information between the element occurrences, we must equip each of the table rows with a field that numbers the rows in the original sequence, such as trackNo in the table track. Later queries can then use the ORDER BY operation to reestablish the original sequence.

```
SELECT publisher,
       productNo,
       album.title AS albumTitle,
       trackNo,
       track.title AS trackTitle,
       duration
  FROM album NATURAL LEFT OUTER JOIN track
  WHERE ...
  ORDER BY publisher, productNo, trackNo
```

11.8.3 Choice

A construct such as the choice connector does not exist in relational schemata. If the choice connector combines two leaf elements, the implementation is relatively easy: Both elements become fields in the table. In each row, one of the fields must have a value and the other must be null (see Table 11.3).

For complex elements combined by a choice connector, the situation is tricky. Both elements are implemented as a table that points via a foreign key to the parent table. If we want to reconstruct the document instances in a query, we must compute the union of two subqueries: The first subquery joins the parent table with the left child table; the second subquery joins the parent table with the right child table. However, unions are only possible when both operands have the same structure. This can sometimes require some ingenuity. The general solution is to cast all noncompatible fields of each operand into a character string and then concatenate these fields into a single character string. This allows a successful union of both subqueries.

Let's assume the following table structure:

```
CREATE TABLE item
  ( amount INTEGER NOT NULL,
    productNo CHAR(32) NOT NULL,
    price DECIMAL(12,2) NOT NULL,
    PRIMARY KEY ( productNo )
  )
```

Table 11.3 Translating leaf element choices into a relational schema. Note that one of the columns amount or quantity must be null.

XML Schema	SQL-92

```<xs:element name="item">```
``` <xs:complexType>```
```   <xs:sequence>```
```   <xs:choice>```
```   <xs:element name="amount"```
```   type="xs:unsignedShort"/>```
```   <xs:element name="quantity"```
```   type="xs:decimal"/>```
```   </choice>```
```   <xs:element name="productNo"```
```   type="xs:NMTOKEN"/>```
```   </xs:sequence>```
``` </xs:complexType>```
```</xs:element>```
	```CREATE TABLE item```
	``` (amount INTEGER,```
	``` quantity DECIMAL,```
	``` productNo CHAR(32) NOT NULL,```
	```)```

```
CREATE TABLE product
 ( productNo CHAR(32) NOT NULL,
   name VARCHAR(40) NOT NULL,
   description(255)
   FOREIGN KEY
      ( albumProductNo )
        references album
 )
CREATE TABLE course
 ( productNo CHAR(32) NOT NULL,
   name VARCHAR(40) NOT NULL,
   duration INTEGER,
   trainer VARCHAR(20),
   FOREIGN KEY
      ( albumProductNo )
        references album
 )
```

Now let's assume that an item is the parent of either a product or a course. Product and course have a different layout, so a direct union is impossible. The following SQL query solves the problem:

```
( SELECT amount,
         productNo,
         price,
         name,
         description
   FROM item NATURAL INNER JOIN product )
UNION
( SELECT amount,
         productNo,
         price,
         name,
         '<duration>' || ( CAST duration AS VARCHAR(10) || '</duration>'
         || '<trainer>' || trainer || '</trainer>'
   FROM item NATURAL INNER JOIN course )
```

In the second SELECT clause we use string concatenation to combine duration and trainer into a single character string. This string is type compatible with description, so the UNION operator can succeed.

In SQL-99 the problem of alternative complex types is much simpler to solve. Both product and course can be defined as structured types. Table items would simply contain two additional columns product and course, where either one or the other is null. Querying this table would require neither a join nor a union.

Table 11.4 Translating recursive elements into relational structures.

XML Schema	SQL-92

``
<xs:element name="part">
  <xs:complexType>
    <xs:sequence>
      <xs:element name="productNo"
        type="xs:NMTOKEN"/>
      <xs:element name="name"
        type="xs:string"/>
      <xs:element ref="part"
        minOccurs="0"
        maxOccurs="unbounded"/>
    </xs:sequence>
  </xs:complexType>
</xs:element>
``
	``
	CREATE TABLE part
	(productNo CHAR(32) NOT NULL,
	  name VARCHAR(255) NOT NULL,
	  PRIMARY KEY (productNo),
	  FOREIGN KEY
	    (productNo)references part
	)
	``

```
CREATE TABLE item
  ( amount INTEGER NOT NULL,
    price DECIMAL(12,2) NOT NULL,
    product product,
    course course
  )
```

11.8.4 Recursion

Recursion is relatively easy to model. The recursive element is implemented as a table. This table has a primary key and a foreign key, with the foreign key referring to this primary key (see Table 11.4).

However, recursion is not easy to query:

Only SQL-99 introduces the ability to query recursive structures with an arbitrary depth. In earlier SQL standards it is possible to query such structures only to a limited depth.

11.9 CONSTRAINTS

SQL defines a rich arsenal for validating the integrity of relational data:

■ *Domain constraints* are the most elementary form of integrity constraints. Domain constraints are used to constrain the value of a single column. They are used to test values inserted into the database and to test queries to make sure that a comparison is valid. Domain constraints resemble the constraining facets for simple types in XML Schema but have more expressive power. For example, a domain constraint can contain a subquery, thus allowing the implementation of cross-field constraints.

SQL-99 introduces a SIMILAR predicate to test whether strings conform to regular expression syntax. This is comparable to the pattern facet in XML Schema, which constrains the lexical space of a data type to conform to the specified regular expression syntax. Consequently, the predicate SIMILAR can be used to mimic this constraining facet.

- *Referential integrity constraints* are used to declare columns or combinations of columns as unique, as a primary key, or as a foreign key. This functionality is practically equivalent to the unique, key, and keyref constructs in XML Schema. These constraints are applied when records are inserted, updated, or deleted. Operations that would violate these constraints are rejected.
- *Cascading actions* allow the DBMS to automatically maintain referential integrity by propagating operations such as DELETE or UPDATE along referential chains. For example, in our small database in Section 7.2.4, we established primary/foreign key relations from the tables plays, track, and sample to table album. If we deleted an album record, a cascading delete operation would also delete all records from plays, track, and sample that referred to this specific album record.
- *General assertions* are constraints that the database must always satisfy. An assertion defines a general query with a Boolean result. This query is executed with each operation that is performed on a table for which the assertion is defined. If the query fails, the operation is rejected. Since general assertions can contain complex queries, they can cause considerable overhead. There is no equivalent construct in XML Schema, but when storing XML documents in a relational database, general assertions can be used to maintain the structural integrity of the document instances.
- *Triggers* consist of SQL statements that are executed automatically by the DBMS as a side effect of database operations. Triggers contain a criterion that specifies under which conditions the specified statements are executed. Triggers are not defined in SQL-92, but many database implementations support them. SQL-99 defines a standardized model for triggers.

As you can see, the support for constraints in SQL far surpasses the possibilities provided by XML Schema. However, not every mechanism defined in the standard is implemented in existing DBMSs. For example, Oracle 9i does not support general assertions but supports triggers.

11.10 FROM RELATIONAL TABLES TO XML SCHEMA

Translating relational data into XML is a frequent operation. Especially when legacy enterprise data must be put on the Web, XML is the format of choice because XML is ideally suited to act as a pivot format from which many other web formats can be generated (Figure 11.4, page 432). The relational data is first translated into a presentation-neutral XML format, which can then be transformed into the target formats.

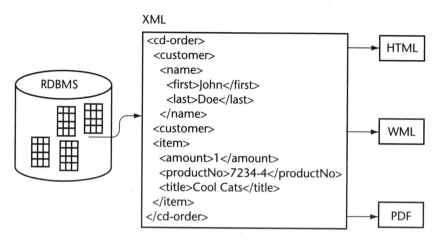

Figure 11.4 XML in the role of a pivot data format.

Constructing an XML schema from a relational table definition is simple and straightforward. The table is converted into an XML element; the sequence of table columns is converted into a sequence of child elements. Mapping SQL data types to simple XML Schema data types is also not a problem (see Section 11.6). Primary keys are converted into key clauses; foreign keys are converted into keyref clauses. Unique constraints are converted into unique clauses. Also, some suitable domain constraints may be represented by user-defined simple data types obtained by applying the appropriate constraining facets to built-in XML Schema data types.

However, with this technique, we only arrive at flat normalized XML schemata, similar to the one obtained in Section 11.5. To construct a deeply nested, treelike XML data structure from a relational schema requires a different approach:

- If we are still in possession of the conceptual model that served as a basis for the relational implementation, we can use this conceptual model to create the XML schemata. We can then map the elements of the relational schema onto the elements of the XML schema.
- If we are only in possession of the relational schema, a serious reengineering effort is required.

In the first step we re-create the conceptual model (see Chapters 2 and 3). Each table is remodeled as an asset; the table columns become properties. Foreign/primary key relations are translated into an arc originating from the asset to which the *primary* key belongs. The cardinality constraint of all arcs is "*" (no cardinality constraint).

However, this model is not really complete. We are unable to learn from the relational schema which columns and which key relationships represent alternatives. In many cases, it will be impossible to find out if two fields or two child tables are mutually exclusive. In some cases, however, this knowledge may be hidden in SQL constraints and SQL queries.

In the second step we determine Level 2 Structures, and in the third step we translate the conceptual model into XML Schema (see Chapter 8).

11.11 MEDIATION BETWEEN RDBMS AND XML DATABASES

In this section we introduce two commercial products, Tamino X-Node and Experanto, that can mediate between relational data structures and XML.

11.11.1 Tamino X-Node

Software AG's (*www.softwareag.com*) Tamino XML Server is one of the leading native XML databases. Tamino is able to handle generic (schema-less) XML documents, but for the most efficient operation it requires the definition of schemata where it uses a subset of XML Schema. Document instances can be validated against the schema.

In addition, a Tamino schema describes physical properties—for example, which document nodes should be used to index the document, and in which form. These additional definitions are included in `appinfo` sections in the schema file. These `appinfo` sections can also contain information about the storage location of each node—as native XML data within the Tamino data storage, or as relational data. Via its X-Node component, Tamino can access connected (and possibly remote) RDBMSs. Since the storage location can differ from document node to document node, Tamino can compose virtual XML documents from data stored in its own data storage, in relational databases, or other data sources. This not only works for retrieval but also for update, store, and delete operations. The following gives an overview of how the mapping between XML nodes and relational tables and columns is described within the schema's `appinfo` sections.

Let's assume that we store information about jazz albums in a relational database. The following tables are defined:

```
CREATE TABLE album

        ( publisher VARCHAR(255) NOT NULL,
          productNo CHAR(32) NOT NULL,
          title VARCHAR(255) NOT NULL,
          PRIMARY KEY (publisher, productNo )
        )
CREATE TABLE track
```

```
    ( trackNo SMALLINT NOT NULL,
      title VARCHAR(255) NOT NULL,
      duration INTEGER,
      albumPublisher VARCHAR(255) NOT NULL,
      albumProductNo CHAR(32) NOT NULL,
      PRIMARY KEY ( albumPublisher, albumProductNo , trackNo ),
      FOREIGN KEY ( albumPublisher, albumProductNo )
                    references album
    )
CREATE TABLE plays
    ( albumPublisher VARCHAR(255) NOT NULL,
      albumProductNo CHAR(32) NOT NULL,
      jazzMusicianID VARCHAR(64) NOT NULL,
      PRIMARY KEY ( albumPublisher, albumProductNo ,
                    jazzMusicianID, instrument ),
      FOREIGN KEY ( albumPublisher, albumProductNo )
                    references album
      FOREIGN KEY (jazzMusicianID )
                    references jazzMusician
    )
```

We want to map these SQL schemata to an XML schema similar to the `album` schema in Chapter 8. In the process, we want to extend the schema and add a `sample` node. The resulting XML Schema could look like the following:

```
<xs:schema xmlns:xs = "http://www.w3.org/2001/XMLSchema"
          targetNamespace = "http://www.jazz.org/encyclopedia"
          elementFormDefault = "qualified"
          xmlns = "http://www.jazz.org/encyclopedia">
  <xs:element name = "album">
    <xs:complexType>
      <xs:sequence>
        <xs:element name = "publisher" type = "xs:anyURI"/>
        <xs:element name = "productNo" type = "xs:NMTOKEN"/>
        <xs:element name = "title" type = "xs:string"/>
        <xs:element ref = "track" maxOccurs = "unbounded"/>
        <xs:element ref = "sample"
                    minOccurs = "0" maxOccurs = "unbounded"/>
        <xs:element ref = "plays"
                    minOccurs = "0" maxOccurs = "unbounded"/>
      </xs:sequence>
    </xs:complexType>
```

```
</xs:element>
<xs:element name = "track">
  <xs:complexType>
    <xs:sequence>
      <xs:element name = "title" type = "xs:string"/>
      <xs:element name = "duration" type = "xs:int"
                  minOccurs = "0"/>
    </xs:sequence>
    <xs:attribute name = "trackNo" type = "xs:ID" use = "required"/>
  </xs:complexType>
</xs:element>
<xs:element name = "sample">
  <xs:complexType>
    <xs:sequence>
      <xs:element name = "MP3" type = "xs:anyURI"/>
      <xs:element name = "track">
        <xs:complexType>
          <xs:attribute name = "trackNo"
                        type = "xs:IDREF" use = "required"/>
        </xs:complexType>
      </xs:element>
    </xs:sequence>
  </xs:complexType>
</xs:element>
<xs:element name = "plays">
  <xs:complexType>
    <xs:sequence>
      <xs:element name = "instrument" type = "xs:token"
                  maxOccurs = "unbounded"/>
      <xs:element name = "jazzMusician">
        <xs:complexType>
          <xs:all>
            <xs:element name = "ID" type = "xs:NMTOKEN"/>
          </xs:all>
        </xs:complexType>
      </xs:element>
    </xs:sequence>
```

```
        </xs:complexType>
      </xs:element>
  </xs:schema>
```

Note that the `duration` element has type `xs:int` instead of `xs:duration`. This was derived from the SQL tables where duration was defined as `INTEGER`. Most SQL databases do not support the SQL data type `INTERVAL`. We have also added the definition for element `sample` and have established a cross-reference between `sample` and `track`.

We can now use this schema as input for Tamino's Schema editor, as shown in Figure 11.5. This editor allows us to map the schema nodes to physical resources such as SQL tables and columns. Basically, each complex element such as `track` and `plays` is mapped to the corresponding SQL table. The leaf elements and attributes, in contrast, are mapped to columns of those tables. The exceptions are the element `sample` and its child elements. These elements are mapped to native fields within Tamino. The consequence is that album instance documents reside in part within Tamino and in part in the connected ODBC database. Nevertheless, it is possible to execute complex queries and to perform update operations (which are carried forward to the connected ODBC database).

Let's take a closer look at how the definition of the `album` node looks now:

```
<xs:schema
    xmlns:xs = "http://www.w3.org/2001/XMLSchema"
    xmlns:tsd =
      "http://namespaces.softwareag.com/tamino/TaminoSchemaDefinition"
    elementFormDefault = "qualified">
  <xs:annotation>
    <xs:appinfo>
      <tsd:schemaInfo name = "album">
        <tsd:collection name = "encyclopedia"/>
        <tsd:doctype name = "schema">
          <tsd:logical>
            <tsd:content>closed</tsd:content>
          </tsd:logical>
        </tsd:doctype>
      </tsd:schemaInfo>
    </xs:appinfo>
  </xs:annotation>
  <xs:element name = "album">
    <xs:annotation>
```

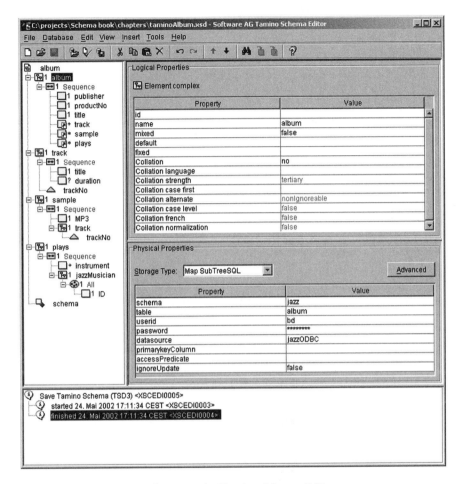

Figure 11.5 The album schema in the Tamino Schema Editor.

```
<xs:appinfo>
  <tsd:elementInfo>
    <tsd:physical>
      <tsd.map>
        <tsd:subTreeSQL schema = "jazz"
                        table = "album"
                        userid = "bd"
                        password = "password"
                        datasource = "jazzODBC"
                        sqlprimarykeys="&quot;publisher&quot;
                                &quot;productNo&quot;"/>
```

```
        </tsd.map>
      </tsd:physical>
    </tsd:elementInfo>
  </xs:appinfo>
</xs:annotation>
<xs:complexType>
  <xs:sequence>
    <xs:element name = "publisher" type = "xs:anyURI">
      <xs:annotation>
        <xs:appinfo>
          <tsd:elementInfo>
            <tsd:physical>
              <tsd.map>
                <tsd:nodeSQL column = "publisher"/>
              </tsd.map>
            </tsd:physical>
          </tsd:elementInfo>
        </xs:appinfo>
      </xs:annotation>
    </xs:element>
    <xs:element name = "productNo" type = "xs:NMTOKEN">
      <xs:annotation>
        <xs:appinfo>
          <tsd:elementInfo>
            <tsd:physical>
              <tsd.map>
                <tsd:nodeSQL column = "productNo"/>
              </tsd.map>
            </tsd:physical>
          </tsd:elementInfo>
        </xs:appinfo>
      </xs:annotation>
    </xs:element>
    <xs:element name = "title" type = "xs:string">
      <xs:annotation>
```

```
        <xs:appinfo>
          <tsd:elementInfo>
            <tsd:physical>
              <tsd.map>
                <tsd:nodeSQL column = "title"/>
              </tsd.map>
            </tsd:physical>
          </tsd:elementInfo>
        </xs:appinfo>
      </xs:annotation>
    </xs:element>
    <xs:element ref = "track" maxOccurs = "unbounded"/>
    <xs:element ref = "sample"
                minOccurs = "0" maxOccurs = "unbounded"/>
    <xs:element ref = "plays"
                minOccurs = "0" maxOccurs = "unbounded"/>
  </xs:sequence>
  </xs:complexType>
</xs:element>
<xs:element name = "track">
  <xs:annotation>
    <xs:appinfo>
      <tsd:elementInfo>
        <tsd:physical>
          <tsd.map>
            <tsd:subTreeSQL
                schema = "jazz"
                table = "track"
                userid = "bd"
                password = "password"
                datasource = "jazzODBC"
                sqlprimarykeys="&quot;albumPublisher&quot;
                           &quot;albumProductNo&quot;
                           &quot;trackNo&quot;">
            <tsd:accessPredicate>
              albumProductNo = album.productNo
                AND albumPublisher = album.publisher
            </tsd:accessPredicate>
```

```
                </tsd:subTreeSQL>
              </tsd.map>
            </tsd:physical>
          </tsd:elementInfo>
        </xs:appinfo>
      </xs:annotation>
      <xs:complexType>
        <xs:sequence>
          <xs:element name = "title" type = "xs:string">
            <xs:annotation>
              <xs:appinfo>
                <tsd:elementInfo>
                  <tsd:physical>
                    <tsd.map>
                      <tsd:nodeSQL column = "title"/>
                    </tsd.map>
                  </tsd:physical>
                </tsd:elementInfo>
              </xs:appinfo>
            </xs:annotation>
          </xs:element>
          <xs:element name = "duration" type = "xs:int" minOccurs = "0">
            <xs:annotation>
              <xs:appinfo>
                <tsd:elementInfo>
                  <tsd:physical>
                    <tsd.map>
                      <tsd:nodeSQL column = "duration"/>
                    </tsd.map>
                  </tsd:physical>
                </tsd:elementInfo>
              </xs:appinfo>
            </xs:annotation>
          </xs:element>
```

```
          </xs:sequence>
          <xs:attribute name = "trackNo" type = "xs:ID" use = "required">
            <xs:annotation>
              <xs:appinfo>
                <tsd:attributeInfo>
                  <tsd:physical>
                    <tsd.map>
                      <tsd:nodeSQL column = "trackNo"/>
                    </tsd.map>
                  </tsd:physical>
                </tsd:attributeInfo>
              </xs:appinfo>
            </xs:annotation>
          </xs:attribute>
        </xs:complexType>
    </xs:element>
    <xs:element name = "sample">
      <xs:complexType>
        <xs:sequence>
          <xs:element name = "MP3" type = "xs:anyURI"/>
          <xs:element name = "track">
            <xs:complexType>
              <xs:attribute name = "trackNo"
                            type = "xs:IDREF" use = "required"/>
            </xs:complexType>
          </xs:element>
        </xs:sequence>
      </xs:complexType>
    </xs:element>
    <xs:element name = "plays">
      <xs:annotation>
        <xs:appinfo>
          <tsd:elementInfo>
            <tsd:physical>
              <tsd.map>
```

```
                    <tsd:subTreeSQL
                        schema = "jazz"
                        table = "plays"
                        userid = "bd"
                        password = "password"
                        datasource = "jazzODBC"
                        sqlprimarykeys="&quot;albumPublisher&quot;
                                        &quot;albumProductNo&quot;
                                        &quot;jazzMusicianID&quot;
                                        &quot;instrument&quot;"/>
                </tsd.map>
            </tsd:physical>
        </tsd:elementInfo>
      </xs:appinfo>
    </xs:annotation>
    <xs:complexType>
      <xs:sequence>
        <xs:element name = "instrument"
                    type = "xs:token" maxOccurs = "unbounded">
          <xs:annotation>
            <xs:appinfo>
              <tsd:elementInfo>
                <tsd:physical>
                  <tsd.map>
                    <tsd:nodeSQL column = "instrument"/>
                  </tsd.map>
                </tsd:physical>
              </tsd:elementInfo>
            </xs:appinfo>
          </xs:annotation>
        </xs:element>
        <xs:element name = "jazzMusician">
          <xs:complexType>
            <xs:all>
              <xs:element name = "ID" type = "xs:NMTOKEN">
                <xs:annotation>
                  <xs:appinfo>
                    <tsd:elementInfo>
```

```
                         <tsd:physical>
                           <tsd.map>
                             <tsd:nodeSQL column = "jazzMusicianID"/>
                           </tsd.map>
                         </tsd:physical>
                       </tsd:elementInfo>
                     </xs:appinfo>
                   </xs:annotation>
                 </xs:element>
               </xs:all>
             </xs:complexType>
           </xs:element>
         </xs:sequence>
       </xs:complexType>
     </xs:element>
</xs:schema>
```

We can see that mappings to SQL tables used for complex elements are described with a `tsd:subTreeSQL` element. Specified in its attributes are the name of the SQL schema (the name of the database), the name of the table, user ID, and password to allow Tamino to access these tables, and the name of the ODBC data source through which this table is accessed. This setup would allow us to combine various tables from different data sources into one XML document.

The attribute `sqlprimarykeys` specifies the primary key fields of the specified table. For element `track`, the additional clause

```
<tsd:accessPredicate>
  albumProductNo = album.productNo
    AND albumPublisher = album.publisher
</tsd:accessPredicate>
```

specifies a join criterion to match records from table `track` to records of table `album`. The content of the `accessPredicate` clause will appear in the SQL WHERE clause generated by the Tamino X-Node.

For leaf elements and attributes, the mapping is simpler: We only have to specify the column of the SQL table that has been specified in the ancestor of the respective XML element or attribute. Take for example the element `plays/jazzMusician/ID`. We have specified column `jazzMusicianID`. Because the nearest ancestor with a table specification is the element `plays` and the table specified there is the SQL table `plays`, we refer to column `jazzMusicianID` in table `plays`.

11.11.2 Experanto

Another mediator software between relational databases and the XML world is IBM's Experanto (formerly XTABLES), which allows transparent access to RDBMSs and other data sources such as web services. Experanto features a completely different architecture from Tamino's. The core of the system is a powerful XQuery engine.

XQuery 1.0 is currently a W3C Working Draft [Boag2002]. XQuery builds heavily on XPath 2.0 and offers functionality similar to XSLT, but uses an SQL-like syntax to formulate queries. One of its strengths is that it is possible to define functions in XQuery, and XQuery functions may be used recursively as targets of new queries. An XQuery function thus defines a particular view of the information base.

Experanto exploits this feature of XQuery. For relational tables declared to the system, Experanto automatically generates a default view—an XQuery function that can retrieve a raw table record in XML format. Users can define custom views and queries on the basis of this default view. Because XQuery allows joining data sources, views across multiple tables can be defined.

Experanto is basically a schema-less system: The (virtual) document types are constructed by defining XQuery expressions, not by defining schemata using a common schema language. When a schema is needed for the virtual document type—for example, to serve as input to binding generators such as Sun's JAXB, Enhydra's Zeus, or Breeze XML Studio (see Section 10.1)—the author must create an additional explicit schema. In Section 13.1 we will discuss the problems of view definition in more detail.

Because XQuery—as the name says—is purely a solution for querying XML data sources, and not for their modification, Experanto can only query the connected data sources, but not update them.

Schema Evolution

Schemata usually do not stay the same over a long period of time. Instead they undergo an evolution to satisfy new requirements. This is a well-known phenomenon in the database community, and the daily bread of database administrators. XML schemata are no different. And since XML is used in an open and dynamic environment such as the Internet, changes to XML schemata are even more likely to happen. Basically, there are three types of changes that can be applied to an XML schema:

- New child nodes (elements or attributes) can be added to an element.
- Child nodes may be removed from an element.
- General structural changes are applied to the schema: Data types of elements or attributes may be changed; elements may be regrouped or groups may be resolved.

In real life, the second case (removal of child nodes) will rarely happen. Most of the time document schemata are extended to allow a wider variety of document instances. Therefore, only the first and third cases are discussed here.

12.1 DERIVED TYPES

Section 6.2.4 discussed how document instances can override the type definition of an element. In the case of complex types it is possible to append, for example, additional child elements to an existing sequence of child elements.

12.1.1 Schema-Conservative Evolution

Evolution techniques that do not require modifying the existing schemata are known as *schema-conservative evolution*. Usually, this requires that these schemata have been designed with flexibility and extensibility in mind. In particular, the new, extended types that we might want to use in our document instances must already be defined in the schema or in an associated type library.

Section 6.4 discussed several usage patterns for type libraries, such as chameleon components, type substitution, and dangling types. Let's see if and how these techniques can be used as a basis for evolvable schemata:

- *Chameleon components* (see Section 6.4.1) do not define their own namespace. Thus, they can blend into the namespace of the original schema. This technique requires that these components be *included* in the original schema. Because chameleon components can be derived from each other (provided their definitions were not declared as *final*), we can use them to implement evolvable schemata. The domain of a schema may be extended by adding new types to the included type library, without the need to modify the original schema. This allows for schema-conservative evolution. The next section gives an example using this technique.
- *Type substitution* (see Section 6.4.2) is based on abstract types and requires that a concrete type be explicitly specified in the document instance. This technique requires that the definition of concrete types used in the document instances be supplied by the original schema. The domain of the schema may only be extended by adding new concrete types to the original schema. Conservative schema evolution is not possible.
- *Dangling types* (see Section 6.4.2) is a technique whereby the master schema refers to undefined types belonging to different namespaces. The document instances define the location of the schemata for these namespaces and thus complete the type definition. However, it is hardly appropriate to classify dangling types as a schema evolution technique. Basically, each document instance constructs its own virtual schema, while the master schema defines a common pattern for all these virtual schemata. This means that new extended types can be added without touching the master schema. However, not every XML processor can deal with this sort of flexibility. An XML database, for example, may determine the document type and the physical storage requirements from a given schema and not from the virtual schema constructed by a document instance.

12.1.2 Using Chameleon Components

Let's look at an example of how to define and use chameleon components for schema evolution. Given the schema file `period type.xsd` defining type period_type that describes a period of time:

period_type.xsd

```
<?xml version="1.0" encoding="UTF-8"?>
<xs:schema xmlns:xs="http://www.w3.org/2001/XMLSchema"
           elementFormDefault="qualified"
           attributeFormDefault="unqualified">
  <xs:complexType name="period_type">
    <xs:sequence>
      <xs:element name="from" type="xs:gYear"/>
      <xs:element name="to" type="xs:gYear" minOccurs="0"/>
    </xs:sequence>
  </xs:complexType>
</xs:schema>
```

Note that we have defined this schema without a target namespace, so it can be included in any namespace. We can now define an extended type period-WithName_type for a period of time that is decorated with a name (like "Roaring Twenties," "Boring Eighties," etc.). This can be done within the same schema file or in a separate schema file. Here, we opt to define the new type in a separate schema file:

periodWithName_type.xsd

```
<?xml version="1.0" encoding="UTF-8"?>
<xs:schema xmlns:xs="http://www.w3.org/2001/XMLSchema"
           elementFormDefault="qualified"
           attributeFormDefault="unqualified">
  <xs:include schemaLocation="period_type.xsd"/>
  <xs:complexType name="periodWithName_type">
    <xs:complexContent>
      <xs:extension base="period_type">
        <xs:sequence>
          <xs:element name="name" type="xs:string" minOccurs="0"/>
        </xs:sequence>
      </xs:extension>
```

```
        </xs:complexContent>
    </xs:complexType>
</xs:schema>
```

The second schema definition includes the first schema definition and then refers to the type period_type defined there as a base type. Also, this schema is defined as a chameleon component, so it can blend into any namespaces when it is included in other schemata. The following schema, style_type.xsd, makes use of this by including both schemata defined above in its target namespace http://www.jazz.org/encyclopedia. It defines a complex type, style_type, that, in turn, refers to period_type. By including the schema periodWithName_type.xsd, too, we introduce a point of variability:

style_type.xsd

```
<?xml version="1.0" encoding="UTF-8"?>
<xs:schema targetNamespace="http://www.jazz.org/encyclopedia"
           xmlns:xs="http://www.w3.org/2001/XMLSchema"
           xmlns="http://www.jazz.org/encyclopedia"
           elementFormDefault="qualified"
           attributeFormDefault="unqualified"
           version="1.0">
  <xs:include schemaLocation="period_type.xsd"/>
  <xs:include schemaLocation="periodWithName_type.xsd"/>
  <xs:complexType name="style_type">
    <xs:sequence>
      <xs:element name="name" type="xs:token"/>
      <xs:element name="dominantDuring">
        <xs:complexType>
          <xs:sequence>
            <xs:element name="period" type="period_type"/>
          </xs:sequence>
        </xs:complexType>
      </xs:element>
    </xs:sequence>
  </xs:complexType>
</xs:schema>
```

We use this schema in the definition of the next schema, style.xsd, which also has target namespace http://www.jazz.org/encyclopedia:

style.xsd

```
<?xml version="1.0" encoding="UTF-8"?>
<xs:schema attributeFormDefault="unqualified"
           elementFormDefault="qualified"
           targetNamespace="http://www.jazz.org/encyclopedia"
           xmlns="http://www.jazz.org/encyclopedia"
           xmlns:xs="http://www.w3.org/2001/XMLSchema">
  <xs:include schemaLocation="style_type.xsd"/>
  <xs:include schemaLocation="description_type.xsd"/>
  <!--Asset style-->
  <xs:element name="style">
    <xs:complexType>
      <xs:complexContent>
        <xs:extension base="style_type">
          <xs:sequence>
            <xs:element ref="description"/>
          </xs:sequence>
        </xs:extension>
      </xs:complexContent>
    </xs:complexType>
    <xs:key name="pk__style_name">
      <xs:selector xpath="."/>
      <xs:field xpath="name"/>
    </xs:key>
  </xs:element>
</xs:schema>
```

This schema definition refers to the definition of period_type via style_type—that is, by default, period instances are of type period_type. However, instances can now override this default type with periodWithName_type because the schema contains a definition of periodWithName_type, and periodWithName_type is derived from period_type. This allows period instances to be extended with a name element:

```
<?xml version="1.0" encoding="UTF-8"?>
<style xmlns="http://www.jazz.org/encyclopedia"
       xmlns:xsi="http://www.w3.org/2001/XMLSchema-instance"
       xsi:schemaLocation="http://www.jazz.org/encyclopedia style.xsd">
```

```
<name>freeJazz</name>
<dominantDuring>
  <period xsi:type="periodWithName_type">
    <from>1960</from>
    <to>1975</to>
    <name>Sixties to mid-Seventies</name>
  </period>
</dominantDuring>
</style>
```

12.1.3 Creating Derived Schemata

Schema authors are normal human beings, too, who cannot foresee the future. It is unlikely that all future requirements are already covered in a schema or type library. When such requirements come up, we must create new schemata. We can derive new, extended schemata from a given schema with the help of the redefine clause (see Section 6.3.3). Redefinition allows us to modify the definition of complex and simple types and the definition of groups and attribute groups of the redefined schema.

Type definitions can be replaced with derived type definitions. Also, group and attribute group definitions can be replaced with subsets or supersets of themselves. Typical reasons for a schema redefinition are the following:

- We want to append a child element (or a group of child elements) to an existing complex type definition or to a group definition.
- We want to add an attribute to an existing complex type definition or to an attribute group definition.

However, there is one constraint. When we construct a new schema, we want to make sure that the instances that were valid under the old schema are also valid under the new schema. An existing document instance does not necessarily refer to a given schema file but may simply rely on the namespace association to identify the schema. When, for example, we registered the new schema with the XML client, the client would use the new schema definition for existing instances as well. So, the new schema definition must also cover the existing instances.

The new schema must therefore define a *supertype* of the original schema. This requires that when we extend a complex type definition, the extension must comply with the rules defined in Section 5.3.9, in particular:

- An extension of a complex type must not introduce cardinality constraints that are narrower than in the original definition.

- The types used for child elements and attributes must be supertypes of the types used in the original type definition (or equal).
- We must not introduce new default or fixed values for existing child elements and attributes. New fixed values could render existing instances invalid, while new default values could change the semantics of existing instances.
- If we introduce new child elements, we must make sure that these elements are optional (that minOccurs is set to "0"). New attributes must not be defined as *required*. The same logic applies when we extend existing groups or attribute groups.

12.1.4 Dialecting with Substitution Groups

Substitution groups (see Section 6.2.5) allow us to use differently named elements in lieu of the original head elements. The type of the substitution elements must be derived (restriction or extension) from the type of the head elements. This technique allows us to extend a schema by creating a *dialect* of the original schema. In contrast to redefinitions, where we *change* the definition of an element, we use substitution groups to *add a variant* of an existing element.

Section 6.4.2 discussed the use of substitution groups for the definition of schema families. There, we used abstract head elements within the definition of the master schema. Here, we do not deal with an abstract master schema, but with a concrete schema, possibly with existing document instances. The use of substitution groups will guarantee that the existing document instances are still accepted by the new schema because the original (nonabstract) head elements stay alive.

Let's look at an example of how to use substitution groups for schema evolution. Take for example the following little schema jazzMusicianList.xsd defining a list of jazz musicians:

jazzMusicianList.xsd

```xml
<?xml version="1.0" encoding="UTF-8"?>
<xs:schema targetNamespace="http://www.jazz.org/encyclopedia"
          xmlns="http://www.jazz.org/encyclopedia"
          xmlns:xs="http://www.w3.org/2001/XMLSchema"
          elementFormDefault="qualified"
          attributeFormDefault="unqualified">
  <xs:include schemaLocation="jazzMusician.xsd"/>
  <xs:element name="jazzMusicianList" type="jazzMusicianList_type"/>
  <xs:complexType name="jazzMusicianList_type">
```

```
        <xs:sequence maxOccurs="unbounded" >
          <xs:element ref="jazzMusician"/>
        </xs:sequence>
      </xs:complexType>
</xs:schema>
```

We now want to extend the definition of jazzMusician by inserting a contract number. We give the new element a new name: jazzMusicianWithContract. Since the type of element jazzMusician was already an extension of type jazzMusician_type, we simply repeat the definition of jazzMusician but insert the new element contractNo.

jazzMusicianWithContract.xsd

```
<?xml version="1.0" encoding="UTF-8"?>
<xs:schema targetNamespace="http://www.jazz.org/encyclopedia"
           xmlns:xs="http://www.w3.org/2001/XMLSchema"
           xmlns="http://www.jazz.org/encyclopedia"
           elementFormDefault="qualified"
           attributeFormDefault="unqualified">
  <xs:include schemaLocation="jazzMusicianList.xsd"/>
  <xs:include schemaLocation="www_jazz_org_encyclopedia_TYPELIB.xsd"/>
  <xs:element name="jazzMusicianWithContract"
              substitutionGroup="jazzMusician">
    <xs:complexType>
      <xs:complexContent>
        <xs:extension base="jazzMusician_type">
          <xs:sequence>
            <xs:element name="contractNo" type="xs:string"/>
            <xs:element ref="produces"
                        minOccurs="0" maxOccurs="unbounded"/>
            <xs:element ref="belongsTo"
                        minOccurs="0" maxOccurs="unbounded"/>
            <xs:element ref="influence"
                        minOccurs="0" maxOccurs="unbounded"/>
          </xs:sequence>
        </xs:extension>
      </xs:complexContent>
    </xs:complexType>
```

```
    </xs:element>
</xs:schema>
```

Under this schema we are now able to define `jazzMusicianList` elements containing both `jazzMusician` and `jazzMusicianWithContract` elements. The schema still accepts existing instance documents.

If we want to define a special list type containing only `jazzMusicianWithContract` elements, we can ripple the substitution through to the list definition. We add the following definition to schema `jazzMusicianWithContract.xsd`:

```
<xs:element name="jazzMusicianWithContractList"
            substitutionGroup="jazzMusicianList">
  <xs:complexType>
    <xs:complexContent>
      <xs:restriction base="jazzMusicianList_type">
        <xs:sequence maxOccurs="unbounded">
          <xs:element ref="jazzMusicianWithContract"/>
        </xs:sequence>
      </xs:restriction>
    </xs:complexContent>
  </xs:complexType>
</xs:element>
```

This restricts the content of the list type `jazzMusicianWithContractList` to `jazzMusicianWithContract` elements, as shown in Figure 12.1 (page 454).

12.1.5 Inhibiting Change

There may be cases where we want to protect schema definitions from change. XML Schema provides two mechanisms to do so:

■ The `final` attribute can be used to control the derivation of types and the definition of substitution groups in schemata (see Sections 5.2.5, 5.3.12, and 6.2.5).
■ The `block` attribute can be used to control the modification of types and the application of substitution groups in document instances (see Sections 6.2.4 and 6.2.5).

The values of these attributes are not inherited by derived types. However, it is possible to define default values for these attributes on the schema level, using the attributes `finalDefault` and `blockDefault`. Note that these attributes should be used cautiously in order not to prevent later schema extension.

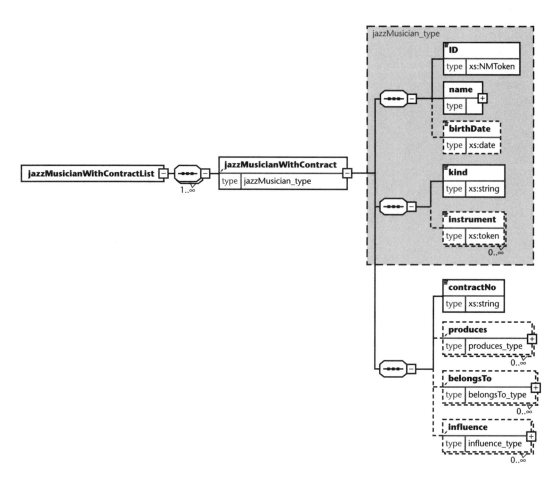

Figure 12.1 Creating a dialect with substitution groups: jazzMusicianWithContract is derived from jazzMusician by extending jazzMusician_type with contractNo, and jazzMusicianWithContractList is derived from jazzMusicianList by restricting its content to jazzMusicianWithContract child elements.

12.2 AUTHORING FOR REDEFINITION

In some cases, we will have requirements that cannot be met by extending an existing schema. Among those requirements are

- We want to extend an element that was declared with a simple type with an attribute.
- We want to append child elements to a nested structure of elements.
- We want to insert a new element at an arbitrary position in a sequence of elements.

■ We want to replace an element with a choice model group.

All these cases cannot be solved with the functionality of type derivation, in particular with the functionality of type extension. However, we can define a schema in such a way that it is open to the above extensions. In general, this is done with soft-coding techniques and indirections instead of hard-coding structures.

The following sections discuss what steps to take so that we can solve the above cases with normal type derivation, and thus by redefining the schema.

12.2.1 Adding an Attribute to a Simple Type Element

Restrictions and extensions can only refer to top-level type definitions. Such global type definitions are equipped with a name, and can consequently be referred to by that name. But what if we have an element declaration where the element is declared with a simple built-in type such as xs:string or xs:integer? Such an element does not have a global type definition, and thus could not be extended with an attribute definition.

Let's assume we have an original schema CD.xsd that contains an element price with a declared type of xs:decimal:

CD.xsd

```
<?xml version="1.0" encoding="UTF-8"?>
<xs:schema targetNamespace="http://www.nile.com"
           xmlns:xs="http://www.w3.org/2001/XMLSchema"
           xmlns="http://www.nile.com"
           elementFormDefault="qualified"
           attributeFormDefault="unqualified">
  <xs:element name="CD">
    <xs:complexType>
      <xs:sequence>
        <xs:element ref="title"/>
        <xs:element ref="publisher"/>
        <xs:element name="price" type="xs:decimal"/>
      </xs:sequence>
      <xs:attribute name="productNo" use="required"/>
      <xs:attribute name="year" use="optional"/>
    </xs:complexType>
  </xs:element>
</xs:schema>
```

Later we want to redefine this schema to add an attribute `currency` to the `price` element—no chance. The local type definition makes this impossible. If we really want this sort of flexibility, we have to author the original schema in a different way. For each element with a simple type we have to create a global complex type definition (see Section 5.3.12) with simple content (see Section 5.3.7). A similar technique was discussed in the context of creating type libraries with Relax NG (see Section 8.3.2).

Instead of declaring element `price` with

```
<xs:element name="price" type="xs:decimal"/>
```

we declare it with

```
<xs:element name="price" type="price_type"/>
```

and add the following type definition to the schema file:

```
<xs:complexType name="price_type">
  <xs:simpleContent>
    <xs:extension base="xs:decimal"/>
  </xs:simpleContent>
</xs:complexType>
```

This allows us later to redefine the original schema with

CD_priceWithCurrency.xsd

```
<xs:schema xmlns:xs="http://www.w3.org/2001/XMLSchema"
           elementFormDefault="qualified"
           attributeFormDefault="unqualified">
  <xs:redefine schemaLocation="CD.xsd">
    <xs:complexType name="price_type">
      <xs:simpleContent>
        <xs:extension base="price_type">
          <xs:attribute name="currency" type="xs:NMTOKEN"
                        use="optional"/>
        </xs:extension>
      </xs:simpleContent>
    </xs:complexType>
  </xs:redefine>
</xs:schema>
```

12.2.2 Appending Child Nodes to Nested Structures

Similarly, we run into trouble with redefinition when complex types are defined locally. In Section 8.2.4 we defined a schema for the type person_type. The element name within person_type was defined with a local complex type definition:

```
<xs:schema xmlns:xs="http://www.w3.org/2001/XMLSchema"
           elementFormDefault="qualified"
           attributeFormDefault="unqualified">

  <xs:complexType name="person_type">
    <xs:sequence>
      <xs:element name="ID" type="xs:NMTOKEN"/>
      <xs:element name="name">
        <xs:complexType>
          <xs:sequence>
            <xs:element name="first" type="xs:token"
                        maxOccurs="unbounded"/>
            <xs:element name="middle" type="xs:token" minOccurs="0"/>
            <xs:element name="last" type="xs:token"/>
          </xs:sequence>
        </xs:complexType>
      </xs:element>
      <xs:element name="birthDate" type="xs:date" minOccurs="0"/>
    </xs:sequence>
  </xs:complexType>
</xs:schema>
```

If we should want to extend this definition later by adding a nickname or a title to the name element, we are out of luck. But if the original schema definition looked like the following, we would have no problems:

```
<xs:schema xmlns:xs="http://www.w3.org/2001/XMLSchema"
           elementFormDefault="qualified"
           attributeFormDefault="unqualified">

  <xs:complexType name="person_type">
    <xs:sequence>
      <xs:element name="ID" type="xs:NMTOKEN"/>
      <xs:element name="name" type="name_type"/>
```

```
        <xs:element name="birthDate" type="xs:date" minOccurs="0"/>
      </xs:sequence>
    </xs:complexType>
    <xs:complexType name="name_type">
     <xs:sequence>
      <xs:element name="first" type="xs:token"
                  maxOccurs="unbounded"/>
      <xs:element name="middle" type="xs:token" minOccurs="0"/>
      <xs:element name="last" type="xs:token"/>
     </xs:sequence>
    </xs:complexType>
</xs:schema>
```

Note that we have already discussed a similar technique in the context of creating type libraries with Relax NG in Section 8.3.2.

We can now easily redefine this schema and extend the definition for name_type:

```
<?xml version="1.0" encoding="UTF-8"?>
<xs:schema xmlns:xs="http://www.w3.org/2001/XMLSchema"
           elementFormDefault="qualified"
           attributeFormDefault="unqualified">
  <xs:redefine schemaLocation="person_type.xsd">
    <xs:complexType name="name_type">
      <xs:complexContent>
        <xs:extension base="name_type">
          <xs:sequence>
            <xs:element name="title" type="xs:token" minOccurs="0"/>
            <xs:element name="nickname" type="xs:token"
                        minOccurs="0" maxOccurs="unbounded"/>
          </xs:sequence>
        </xs:extension>
      </xs:complexContent>
    </xs:complexType>
  </xs:redefine>
</xs:schema>
```

12.2.3 Inserting Elements at an Arbitrary Position

In the previous example we were able to add the child elements title and nick-name to the definition of element name. However, there was a hitch: We could only append these new elements to the end of the sequence of child elements. This is unfortunate because we would prefer the child element title at the top of the list and nickname between middle and last. Fortunately, there is a trick we can use to prepare the original schema for such extensions. Instead of (or in addition to) introducing the complex type name_type as in the example above, we add an *empty group* (see Section 6.2.2) at each position where we plan later extensions. Figure 12.2 (page 460) shows a diagram; here is the code:

```
<xs:complexType name="name_type">
 <xs:sequence>
  <xs:group ref="beforeFirst"/>
  <xs:element name="first" type="xs:token"
              maxOccurs="unbounded"/>
  <xs:group ref="beforeMiddle"/>
  <xs:element name="middle" type="xs:token" minOccurs="0"/>
  <xs:group ref="beforeLast"/>
  <xs:element name="last" type="xs:token"/>
 </xs:sequence>
</xs:complexType>

<xs:group name="beforeFirst">
  <xs:sequence>
  </xs:sequence>
</xs:group>

<xs:group name="beforeMiddle">
  <xs:sequence>
  </xs:sequence>
</xs:group>

<xs:group name="beforeLast">
  <xs:sequence>
  </xs:sequence>
</xs:group>
```

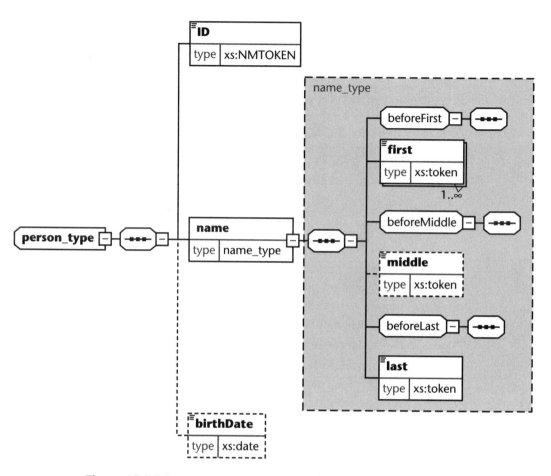

Figure 12.2 Schema person_type.xsd opened up for name extensions.

Now, we can easily insert new elements at any position within element name, just by redefining the appropriate groups:

```
<?xml version="1.0" encoding="UTF-8"?>
<xs:schema xmlns:xs="http://www.w3.org/2001/XMLSchema"
           elementFormDefault="qualified"
           attributeFormDefault="unqualified">
  <xs:redefine schemaLocation="person_type.xsd">
    <xs:group name="beforeFirst">
      <xs:sequence>
        <xs:group ref="beforeFirst"/>
        <xs:element name="title" type="xs:token" minOccurs="0"/>
```

```
        </xs:sequence>
      </xs:group>
      <xs:group name="beforeLast">
        <xs:sequence>
          <xs:group ref="beforeLast"/>
          <xs:element name="nickname" type="xs:token" minOccurs="0"/>
        </xs:sequence>
      </xs:group>
    </xs:redefine>
</xs:schema>
```

Similarly, we can allow the later extension of elements with attributes by declaring them with an empty *attribute group* (see Section 6.2.3). However, this is not really necessary. Attributes can always be appended via type extension, as their sequence does not matter.

12.2.4 Allowing Choices

Let's assume that at some point we are no longer satisfied with the mere option to specify a birth date for a person. Instead we would like to have a full curriculum vitae (CV) containing birth date, eventually a death date, and other events. However, because we still have to support existing documents, we have to create a supertype of personType. We can do this by replacing the element birthDate with a *choice* model group containing both birthDate and the new complex element CV.

The problem is that we cannot generalize a type in this way by type derivation. Type derivation would allow us only to append a choice group after birthDate, but this is not what we want. Again, we have to plan for this sort of extensibility in the definition of the original schema. We simply replace the element birthDate with a group reference. On the global level we define a group that contains a choice model group with element birthDate as the only alternative (see Figure 12.3, page 462).

person_type.xsd

```
<?xml version="1.0" encoding="UTF-8"?>
<xs:schema xmlns:xs="http://www.w3.org/2001/XMLSchema"
           elementFormDefault="qualified"
           attributeFormDefault="unqualified">
  <xs:complexType name="person_type">
    <xs:sequence>
      <xs:element name="ID" type="xs:NMTOKEN"/>
```

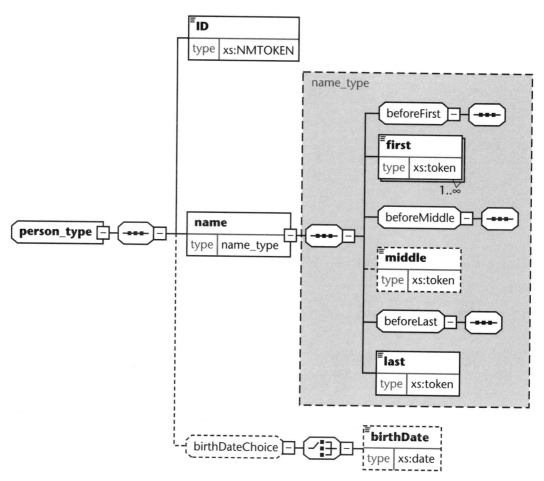

Figure 12.3 The person_type schema prepared for choice extensions.

```
        <xs:element name="name" type="name_type"/>
        <xs:group ref="birthDateChoice" minOccurs="0"/>
      </xs:sequence>
    </xs:complexType>
    <xs:group name="birthDateChoice">
      <xs:choice>
        <xs:element name="birthDate" type="xs:date" minOccurs="0"/>
      </xs:choice>
    </xs:group>
  </xs:schema>
```

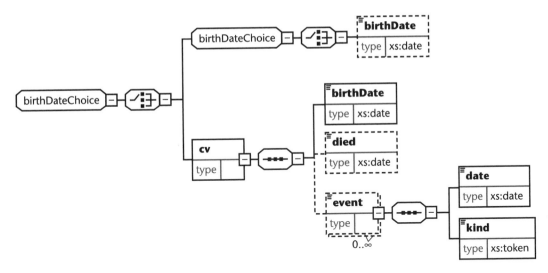

Figure 12.4 The redefinition of the choice group. Note the replication of `birthDateChoice` in the redefinition.

Now, we can easily redefine schema `person_type.xsd` and add alternatives to the choice group (see Figure 12.4).

personWithCV_type.xsd

```xml
<?xml version="1.0" encoding="UTF-8"?>
<xs:schema xmlns:xs="http://www.w3.org/2001/XMLSchema"
           elementFormDefault="qualified"
           attributeFormDefault="unqualified">
  <xs:redefine schemaLocation="person_type.xsd">
   <xs:group name="birthDateChoice">
    <xs:choice>
      <xs:group ref="birthDateChoice"/>
      <xs:element name="cv">
        <xs:complexType>
          <xs:sequence>
            <xs:element name="birthDate" type="xs:date"/>
            <xs:element name="died" type="xs:date" minOccurs="0"/>
            <xs:element name="event"
                        minOccurs="0" maxOccurs="unbounded">
              <xs:complexType>
```

```
        <xs:sequence>
          <xs:element name="date" type="xs:date"/>
          <xs:element name="kind" type="xs:token"/>
        </xs:sequence>
      </xs:complexType>
    </xs:element>
    </xs:sequence>
  </xs:complexType>
  </xs:element>
 </xs:choice>
 </xs:group>
 </xs:redefine>
</xs:schema>
```

12.2.5 Conservative Schema Modification

When redefining or modifying a schema to adapt to changing requirements, we want to make sure that the new schema also covers existing documents. This means that the new document type must be a supertype of the original document type. Keep these additional guidelines in mind when modifying schema:

■ A general rule is never to make cardinality constraints narrower. So, it is fine to make maxOccurs greater and minOccurs smaller. However, making maxOccurs smaller or minOccurs greater could exclude existing instances.

This logic also applies when adding new elements or attributes or when dropping elements or attributes. A nonexistent element can be seen as an element with minOccurs="0" and maxOccurs="0". If we want to add a new element, we just imagine that it already exists with minOccurs="0" and maxOccurs="0", and consequently we leave minOccurs at "0" and only increase maxOccurs to comply with the above rule. This means that all new elements must be optional. On the other hand, if we no longer need a given element, we simply set minOccurs="0". This makes the element optional, so both new and old instances are covered.

The same applies to attributes. New attributes should be added with use="optional", and for attributes that we no longer need, use should be set to optional, too.

■ Be cautious with the definition of fixed and default values. Never introduce new fixed or default values or modify existing fixed values, because this could render existing instances invalid. But, are we allowed to modify default values or to remove declarations for default or fixed values? Doing so would not make existing instances invalid, but it would change the content (and semantics) of these instances. Applications that rely on these values could fail.

So, the best thing is not to touch the definitions for default and fixed values during schema evolution.

- When changing the simple type of an element, only change it into a super-type. Otherwise it could exclude existing instances from the schema. This means that we can always extend a simple type with extension by list (see Section 5.2.6) or with a type union (see Section 5.2.10).

- When introducing a choice into a schema, the same rules apply as to all choices: The choice should not make the schema nondeterministic (see Section 5.3.18).

12.3 OPEN CONTENT MODEL

All the evolution techniques discussed so far require modifying existing schemata or creating new schemata. Document authors are usually not equipped to do this; they may not have the necessary knowledge, tools, or access rights to implement a new schema or modify an existing one. So, if a document author needs to embed new elements or attributes into a document, he or she may have to apply to the schema author. The modification may take time, especially if the schema author has a large backlog of work or has other priorities.

To solve this problem, XML Schema provides an extension mechanism that allows document authors to introduce elements that were not defined in the corresponding schemata. This mechanism is the wildcard extension mechanism (see Sections 5.3.15, 6.1.3, and [Costello2000]).

Other, earlier schema languages used a simple attribute on the schema level to indicate whether the content model of a schema was open or closed. An *open content model* means that the document author is free to introduce new elements and attributes whenever and wherever he or she desires. Early drafts of XML Schema also featured such an attribute, but it was dropped in favor of the more controlled approach with wildcards. The wildcard mechanism, though, requires a bit more work from the schema author.

Schema authors must specify an <any> or <anyAttribute> wildcard in any position where the document authors are later allowed to introduce their own elements or attributes. Take for example the following schema definition for person_type.

person_wildcard.xsd

```
<?xml version="1.0" encoding="UTF-8"?>
<xs:schema xmlns:xs="http://www.w3.org/2001/XMLSchema"
           xmlns="http://www.jazz.org/encyclopedia"
           targetNamespace="http://www.jazz.org/encyclopedia"
           elementFormDefault="qualified"
           attributeFormDefault="unqualified">

  <xs:complexType name="person_type">
```

```
        <xs:sequence>
          <xs:element name="name">
            <xs:complexType>
              <xs:sequence>
                <xs:any namespace="##other" processContents="lax"
                        minOccurs="0"/>
                <xs:element name="first" type="xs:token"
                            maxOccurs="unbounded"/>
                <xs:element name="middle" type="xs:token" minOccurs="0"/>
                <xs:element name="last" type="xs:token"/>
              </xs:sequence>
            </xs:complexType>
          </xs:element>
          <xs:element name="birthDate" type="xs:date" minOccurs="0"/>
          <xs:any processContents="lax"
                  maxOccurs="unbounded" minOccurs="0" />
        </xs:sequence>
        <xs:attribute name="ID" type="xs:NMTOKEN" use="required"/>
        <xs:anyAttribute processContents="lax"/>
      </xs:complexType>
      <xs:element name="person" type="person_type"/>
    </xs:schema>
```

This schema allows document authors to introduce new elements in the following positions:

- a single element as child element of element name before child element first
- an unlimited number of elements after element birthDate

Also, elements of type person_type may be equipped with an unlimited number of arbitrary attributes. Namespace control for all these elements and attributes is possible with the attributes processContents and namespace.

Note the use of the specification namespace="##other" for the first wildcard. This was done in order to avoid nondeterminism (see Section 5.3.18). Without this specification, the wildcard may contain elements from the same namespace. When encountering a first element in a document instance, a parser would not be able to decide if this element should be accepted by the wildcard or by the following element specification without looking ahead.

In the following example we have exploited this variability by creating a document instance with additional elements. We have inserted an e:title

element before person/name/first and appended an e:gender element after
person/birthDate.

```
<?xml version="1.0" encoding="UTF-8"?>
<person xmlns="http://www.jazz.org/encyclopedia"
        xmlns:e="http://www.jazz.org/encyclopedia/extensions"
        xmlns:xsi="http://www.w3.org/2001/XMLSchema-instance"
        xsi:schemaLocation="http://www.jazz.org/encyclopedia
                           person_type_wildcard.xsd"
        ID="NMTOKEN">
  <name>
    <e:title>Mrs.</e:title>
    <first>Billie</first>
    <last>Holiday</last>
  </name>
  <birthDate>1915-04-07</birthDate>
  <e:gender>female</e:gender>
</person>
```

Because we have not given a schema definition for namespace http://www
.jazz.org/encyclopedia/extensions and because processContents is set to "lax,"
XML processors will check the elements e:title and e:gender only for well-
formedness.

12.4 VERSIONING

When browsing the Web, we can find two best practices for reflecting version
changes in schemata:

1. Change the target namespace of the new schema version.
2. Do not change the target namespace of the new schema version.

In fact, both practices are applicable. Practice 1, however, only applies when
you want to inhibit existing instances from using the new schema version, and
when you want to inhibit other existing schemata from importing, including,
or redefining the new schema version, for example, in the following cases:

- A new schema version differs dramatically from former schemata, so that
  compatibility for existing instances and importing schemata cannot be
  maintained.
- The old schema contains a severe bug, so you want existing document instances to invalidate.

In such cases you can enforce invalidation of the new schema version for existing resources by introducing a new target namespace. In most cases, you may want to keep older schema versions around to allow existing applications to operate.

In all other cases we fall back to option 2. When you have designed the new schema in an upward-compatible way, so that existing resources can continue to use it, you have several options for indicating the version of a schema to applications. This will allow applications to evaluate the schema version and use the extended features of the new version.

1. Indicate the new schema version by storing it in a different location. The sooner you forget about this option, the better. The `xsi:schemaLocation` is only a hint to XML processors about where to locate a schema. The processor is free to decide otherwise.

2. Indicate the schema version via the standard `version` attribute in the `schema` clause.

```
<xs:schema version="1.0">
```

This attribute can indicate the schema version to the schema author and can be used to convey version information during the authoring process of schemata. For example, if we combine several schema components in one large schema, we want to make sure that the version attributes of each imported or included schema component fit with the version of the importing module.

However, XML parsers do not evaluate this attribute. Applications would be required to preparse the document and its schema to obtain the value of this attribute. In case of multipart schemata, this can become quite a task.

3. Indicate the schema version using a `version` attribute defined explicitly in the document root element (and possibly in child elements). This is probably the most versatile option for conveying version information to applications. An explicit attribute `version` with a fixed value is defined in the schema in the root element of the document. XML parsers will include this attribute in the document instance as seen by the parser's client; the application is automatically informed about the value of the version attribute.

```
<xs:schema xmlns:xs="http://www.w3.org/2001/XMLSchema"
           elementFormDefault="qualified"
           attributeFormDefault="unqualified"
           version="3.0">
  <xs:complexType name="period_type">
    <xs:sequence>
```

```
        <xs:element name="from" type="xs:gYear"/>
        <xs:element name="to" type="xs:gYear" minOccurs="0"/>
    </xs:sequence>
    <xs:attribute name="version" type="xs:NMTOKENS"
                  fixed="1.0 2.0 3.0"/>
  </xs:complexType>
</xs:schema>
```

This example uses the data type NMTOKENS for the version attribute. This allows us to specify a list of all valid application versions for that schema part. We can use version attributes to implement a finer-grained version control than on the global level. We can equip each document element with a version attribute to indicate the version of that particular element.

Such version attributes can either reflect the version of the schema (and should then be in sync with the version attribute in the schema clause), or they can reflect the version number(s) of compatible application versions. Of course, nothing stops us from introducing two different attributes: schemaVersion and applicationVersion.

Schemata in Large Environments

The large environments of certain corporations or government administration pose particular problems to schema developers. In some cases, existing schemata were developed in isolation by various business units; in other cases, schemata were inherited during the acquisition of whole companies. In most of these cases it is not possible to change these schemata to integrate them into one consistent set of schemata because these would render large information bases invalid. In such cases *mediation* techniques [Wiederhold1997] are necessary to make the various business units collaborate. These techniques are, of course, not restricted to large corporations; they can also be applied when small and medium companies cooperate in electronic business scenarios.

At the other end of the scale are enterprise data models: huge, consistent schemata that cover virtually every nook and cranny within an enterprise. These schemata are notoriously difficult to maintain. Both the relational discipline and the object-oriented discipline have developed techniques to manage the decentralized change of such schemata. We take a look at these techniques to see what we can learn from them for the decentralized change management of XML schemata.

13.1 COMBINING DIVERSE SCHEMATA

There are many situations in which we will not only have to extend an existing schema but will have to combine diverse schemata into a single, consolidated schema. Typical scenarios are company mergers or the establishment of a supply chain or virtual enterprise. The following sections will discuss the problems and possible solutions for the combination of diverse schemata. Please keep in mind that most of the topics discussed in these sections are subject to ongoing research and do not represent well-established industry standards.

13.1.1 The Problem

When we want to combine several schemata, we have a couple of options:

- Define a mapping between two schemata on a bilateral basis.
- Define a new schema covering the domain of the complete schema combination, and define a mapping between the new schema and the contributing original schemata.

In most cases we will select the second option, as this will reduce the number of mappings if we have more than two contributing schemata.

In some cases the original schemata will describe the same domain; for example, they may describe a certain product but will differ in the names used for elements and attributes. There may be structural differences, too: One schema might describe details that the other schema does not. Also, the content of instance elements may not be compatible. While one organization might specify the product dimensions in metric values, the other organization might use imperial measures.

In other cases, the domains of the original schemata might be fundamentally different but will overlap in certain areas. In such cases we might construct a fusion of both models in order to leverage synergy effects from the combination of both domains.

13.1.2 Model Fusion

Take for example the models given in Chapters 2 and 3. The model in Chapter 2 describes the information set of a bookshop (see Figure 13.1). In Chapter 3 we developed a model for a jazz knowledge base (see Figure 13.2). However, there is an area where both models overlap: The album asset type of the jazz knowledge base could be mapped to the CD asset type of the bookshop model. In this case a fusion of both models unleashes substantial synergies. Taken by itself our bookshop model would only allow queries such as:

Which CDs did customer A buy?

Which contributor was the most frequently named on CDs bought by customer A?

When was CD X bought by customer A?

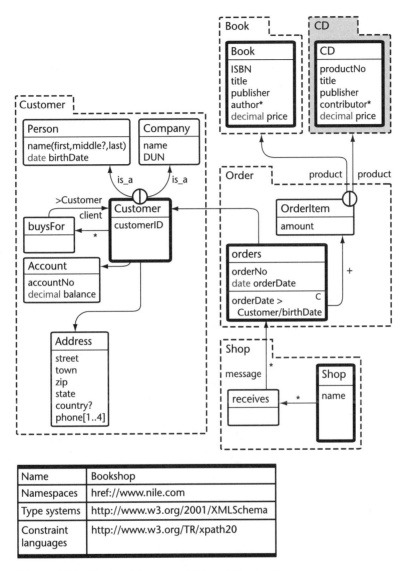

Name	Bookshop
Namespaces	href://www.nile.com
Type systems	http://www.w3.org/2001/XMLSchema
Constraint languages	http://www.w3.org/TR/xpath20

Figure 13.1 The bookshop model from Chapter 2.

But with a fusion of both models, we can exploit the knowledge contained in the jazz encyclopedia and give recommendations to a customer:

Which contributor was the most frequently named on CDs bought by customer A, and which other CDs produced by this contributor do we stock?

Which CDs belong to the same jazz style as CD X and were produced by musicians who have influenced the contributors of CD X or were influenced by them?

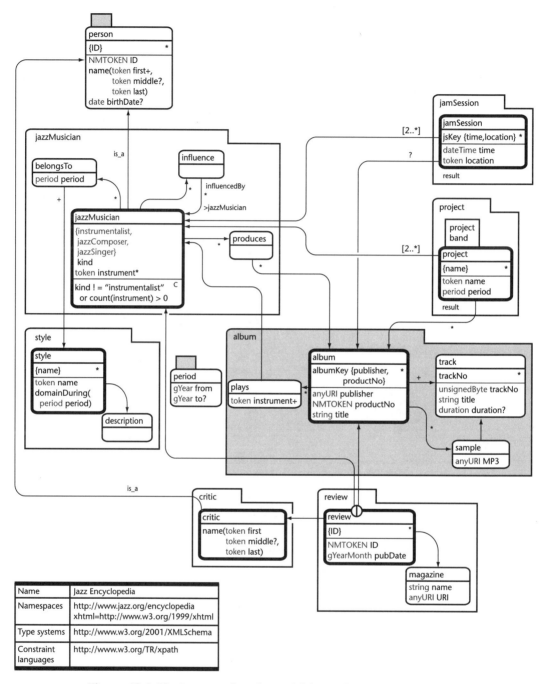

Figure 13.2 The jazz encyclopedia model from Chapter 3.

The following sections discuss how we can implement such a fusion between two overlapping information domains.

13.1.3 Combining Document Instance Sets

There are basically two options when we wish to combine two sets of document instances:

- Convert the instance documents of both information domains into a common, consolidated format.
- Leave the instance documents in their original format and use a *mediator* that facilitates the querying, navigation, and update across both instance sets.

The first option is only applicable when we deal with long-term integration between two different information bases and if the information bases are not accessed by third parties that might be affected by a format change. In all other cases, especially in cases of short-term and temporary collaboration, the original information bases are left untouched. Nevertheless, the use of mediators requires us to construct a new generic document format that can serve as a common document format for operations between the two disparate information bases.

In relational technology the combination of different data sources can be achieved by defining *views* across multiple tables (see Section 11.6.4). In XML scenarios we basically have the same option: to construct a view defining a virtual document type that is composed from various source document types. The technology to achieve this is currently only emerging. Section 11.11.2 mentioned XQuery. XQuery 1.0 is currently a W3C Working Draft [Boag2002], so you should regard the example given below with caution.

XQuery has strong relations to XPath 2.0 and to XSLT but has a more user-friendly syntax. One of the outstanding features of XQuery is its join facilities, which allow us to formulate queries across multiple document types. Since XQuery allows wrapping queries in explicit function definitions, it facilitates the formulation of views across multiple document types.

Let's look at an example. We have a collection of XML documents describing the CDs offered in our online bookshop. We assume that the instance documents are stored in a collection such as a file directory or a database with the name "bookshop."

```
<?xml version="1.0" encoding="UTF-8"?>

<CD xmlns="href://www.nile.com"
    xmlns:xsi="http://www.w3.org/2001/XMLSchema-instance"
    xsi:schemaLocation="href://www.nile.com CD.xsd">

  <productNo>cd1780</productNo>
```

```
<title>Inside out</title>
<publisher>http://www.ecmrecords.com</publisher>
<price>17.95</price>
</CD>
```

In addition, we have a collection, "encyclopedia," which contains a knowledge base about jazz musicians. In this collection there are documents of type album describing albums produced by jazz musicians:

```
<?xml version="1.0" encoding="UTF-8"?>
<album xmlns="http://www.jazz.org/encyclopedia"
       xmlns:xsi="http://www.w3.org/2001/XMLSchema-instance"
       xsi:schemaLocation="http://www.jazz.org/encyclopedia album.xsd">
  <publisher>http://www.ecmrecords.com</publisher>
  <productNo>1780</productNo>
  <title>Inside out</title>
  <plays>
    <jazzMusician><ID>JarrettKeith</ID></jazzMusician>
    <instrument>piano</instrument>
  </plays>
  <plays>
    <jazzMusician><ID>PeacockGary</ID></jazzMusician>
    <instrument>double bass</instrument>
  </plays>
  <plays>
    <jazzMusician><ID>DeJohnetteJack</ID></jazzMusician>
    <instrument>drums</instrument>
  </plays>
</album>
```

We want to combine these two document types into one virtual document type combinedCD. We want to match the CD documents to the album documents by publisher and productNo. Note that the product number of CD documents is prefixed with cd. This is not the case in the album documents.

The resulting documents should have a layout similar to the CD documents, but we want to add the information contained in the <plays> nodes of the album documents. We want to add this information in a modified layout, in the form of <musician> nodes, with the ID of each jazzMusician specified as an attribute.

The result of the query should look like this:

```
<combinedCD>
  <title>Inside out</title>
  <productNo>cd1780</productNo>
  <publisher>http://www.ecmrecords.com</publisher>
  <musician ID = "JarrettKeith">
    <instrument>piano</instrument>
  </musician>
  <musician ID = "PeacockGary">
    <instrument>double bass</instrument>
  </musician>
  <musician ID = "DeJohnetteJack">
    <instrument>drums</instrument>
  </musician>
  <price>17.95</price>
</combinedCD>
```

The following query does the trick:

```
namespace s="href://www.nile.com"
namespace j="http://www.jazz.org/encyclopedia"
  for $cd in collection("bookshop")/s:CD
    let $title := $cd/s:title,
        $productNo := $cd/s:productNo,
        $publisher := $cd/s:publisher,
        $price := $cd/s:price
    let $album :=
        collection("encyclopedia")/
            j:album[concat("cd",j:productNo/text()) =
                                        $productNo/text()]
    let $plays := $album/j:plays
    return
      <combinedCD>
      <title>{$title/text()}</title>
      <productNo>{$productNo/text()}</productNo>
      <publisher>{$publisher/text()}</publisher>
        {for $musician in $album/j:plays
            return
```

```
<musician ID={$musician/j:jazzMusician/j:ID/text()}>
        <instrument>{$musician/j:instrument/text()}</instrument>
    </musician>
  }
  <price>{$price/text()}</price>
</combinedCD>
```

The construction of this query is straightforward. The first section—after defining the two namespaces—contains the selection part of the query. Using for and let clauses, variables are instantiated with node lists extracted from the queried document base (collection). The for clause selects all CD documents from collection bookshop. The join to document type album is performed by the let $album clause. Note that we have used an XPath filter expression to select album documents with the matching productNo and publisher. The concat function is used to adapt the album product numbers to the CD product numbers.

The second part of the query (beginning with the first return clause) contains the construction part of the query where new document instances of the combined document type are produced. All construction elements are highlighted. Note that the construction part contains a subquery that transforms all plays elements into a different format (musician). This intermingling of selection and construction is typical for XQuery.

Let's now wrap this query in a function definition and use this function as a target for further queries:

```
namespace s="href://www.nile.com"
namespace j="http://www.jazz.org/encyclopedia"
define function combinedCDView() returns xs:AnyType {
  for $cd in collection("bookshop")/s:CD

  ...

}

for $x in combinedCDView()
  return
   <overview>
     <title>{$x/title}</title>
     <musicians>{count($x/musician)}</musicians>
   </overview>
```

We see that functions can be typed using the type system of XML Schema. The example above can only give a glimpse into the features of XQuery; a complete description would fill another book. XQuery is a powerful language and, despite its early stage (still a Working Draft), is already adopted by the industry:

IBM, Microsoft, Oracle, and Software AG have all produced working prototypes of XQuery processors.

Unfortunately, for our purpose of information integration, XQuery is of limited use. XQuery is a pure query language; update operations are not defined in XQuery. SQL, in contrast, provides update operations that can even be applied to views. The definition of a generic XML transformation and integration language is still very much a research topic. At present we know only one XML transformation language allowing the definition of updatable XML views: XPathLog [May2001] is a fusion of XPath with Prolog.

13.1.4 Schema-Driven View Definition

A view defined with a query or transformation language with a built-in set of construction operators, such as XQuery (or XSLT), effectively establishes a new document type. However, this document type is not explicitly represented by a schema written in standard schema language, such as XML Schema or Relax NG. When integrating information from diverse sources, we would want to use the new combined document type in lieu of the original schemata and would require a schema to support our XML development environment. For example, instead of using the original schemata for the document types CD and album, we would prefer to use a new schema, combinedCD. There are many reasons for creating a new, explicit schema definition for the combined document type, in particular:

- A schema can provide additional information that is not contained in document instances, such as defaults for elements and attributes.
- Visual schema editors can show the structure of the document type in the form of a diagram.
- Binding generators such as JAXB, Zeus, or Breeze XML Studio (see Section 10.1) need a schema to create a binding into an object-oriented language.
- Agents can exploit published schemata in order to navigate through complex information structures.

All this is not possible on the basis of only the XQuery view definition. Of course, most parts of a schema definition could be derived from the query definition, but not all: For example, the query does not contain information about default values or constraints such as keys and key references.

What we want to define is a schema like the one shown in Figure 13.3 (page 480). How can we now relate the query definition shown in the previous section to such a schema definition? Basically, we have two options:

- We embed query expressions into the schema definition and extract the complete query from the schema definition later. This technique will be demonstrated in the next section. This solution has two advantages: It is relatively easy to develop and maintain schema and query synchronously, and

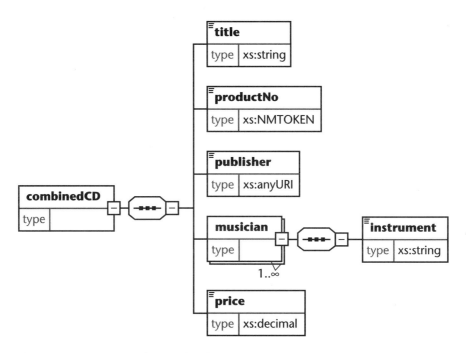

Figure 13.3 A schema diagram for the virtual document type `combinedCD`.

schema components with the embedded query parts can be reused. The disadvantage is that we have to touch the schema definition if we want to
change the mapping. For example, we might have to use different mappings
for the same schema in different scenarios.

■ The alternative is to rely on natural mapping between the elements and
attributes defined in the schema and the elements and attributes defined by
the construction part of the query based on the qualified names and paths of
these elements and attributes. The advantage is that we can easily exchange
the mapping while leaving the schemata untouched. The disadvantage is
that it is more difficult to keep the schema and the query in sync, especially
when schema components are reused.

13.1.5 Embedded Queries

As an example for the embedding of query expressions into a schema definition, we use the schema given in Figure 13.3. Into this schema definition we
embed XQuery fragments that describe the mapping between `combinedCD` and `CD`
with respect to `album`. We use the `annotation/appinfo` logic (see Section 6.3.6) of
XML Schema to specify the mapping. Similarly, we could embed the XQuery
fragments into Relax NG (see Section 7.1.5).

```
<?xml version="1.0" encoding="UTF-8"?>
<xs:schema xmlns:j="http://www.jazz.org/encyclopedia"
           xmlns:s="href://www.nile.com"
           xmlns:q="http://www.w3.org/TR/xquery"
           xmlns:xs="http://www.w3.org/2001/XMLSchema"
           elementFormDefault="qualified"
           attributeFormDefault="unqualified">
  <xs:annotation>
    <xs:appinfo>
      <q:query>

        namespace s="href://www.nile.com"
        namespace j="http://www.jazz.org/encyclopedia"
        define function combinedCDView() returns xs:AnyType

      </q:query>
    </xs:appinfo>
  </xs:annotation>
  <xs:element name="combinedCD">
    <xs:annotation>
      <xs:appinfo>
        <q:query>
      for $cd in collection("bookshop")/s:CD
        let $title := $cd/s:title,
          $productNo := $cd/s:productNo,
          $publisher := $cd/s:publisher,
          $price := $cd/s:price
        let $album := collection("encyclopedia")/
              j:album[concat("cd",j:productNo/text()) =
                                        $productNo/text()]

        </q:query>
      </xs:appinfo>
    </xs:annotation>
    <xs:complexType>
      <xs:sequence>
        <xs:element name="title" type="xs:string">
          <xs:annotation>
            <xs:appinfo>
              <q:query>$title/text()</q:query>
            </xs:appinfo>
          </xs:annotation>
```

```
    </xs:element>
    <xs:element name="productNo" type="xs:NMTOKEN">
      <xs:annotation>
        <xs:appinfo>
          <q:query>$productNo/text()</q:query>
        </xs:appinfo>
      </xs:annotation>
    </xs:element>
    <xs:element name="publisher" type="xs:anyURI">
      <xs:annotation>
        <xs:appinfo>
          <q:query>$publisher/text()</q:query>
        </xs:appinfo>
      </xs:annotation>
    </xs:element>
    <xs:element name="musician" maxOccurs="unbounded">
      <xs:annotation>
        <xs:appinfo>
          <q:query>for $musician in $album/j:plays</q:query>
        </xs:appinfo>
      </xs:annotation>
      <xs:complexType>
        <xs:sequence>
          <xs:element name="instrument" type="xs:string">
            <xs:annotation>
              <xs:appinfo>
                <q:query>$musician/j:instrument/text()</q:query>
              </xs:appinfo>
            </xs:annotation>
          </xs:element>
        </xs:sequence>
        <xs:attribute name="ID" type="xs:NMTOKEN" use="required">
          <xs:annotation>
            <xs:appinfo>
              <q:query>
                $musician/j:jazzMusician/j:ID/text()
              </q:query>
            </xs:appinfo>
```

```
              </xs:annotation>
            </xs:attribute>
          </xs:complexType>
        </xs:element>
        <xs:element name="price" type="xs:decimal">
          <xs:annotation>
            <xs:appinfo>
              <q:query>$cd/s:price/text()</q:query>
            </xs:appinfo>
          </xs:annotation>
        </xs:element>
      </xs:sequence>
    </xs:complexType>
  </xs:element>
</xs:schema>
```

The XQuery fragments (highlighted) are embedded into the schema by wrapping them in a <q:query> element. It is relatively easy to derive a complete XQuery query expression from this schema definition with the embedded fragments. The next listing shows an XSLT transformation that will do exactly this:

```
<?xml version="1.0" encoding="utf-8" standalone="yes"?>
<xsl:stylesheet xmlns:xsl="http://www.w3.org/1999/XSL/Transform"
                xmlns:q="http://www.w3.org/TR/xquery"
                xmlns:xs="http://www.w3.org/2001/XMLSchema"
                version="1.0" >
<!-- use text output mode because XQuery has a non-XML syntax -->
<xsl:output method="text" indent="no"/>
<!-- define key access structures for global elements  -->
<xsl:key name="global_element"
         match="//xs:schema/xs:element" use="@name"/>
<!-- process schema clause for namespace declarations  -->
<xsl:template match="xs:schema">
  <xsl:value-of select="xs:annotation/xs:appinfo/q:query"/>
  <xsl:apply-templates/>
</xsl:template>
<!-- process elements (in case of top-level only the first)  -->
<xsl:template
    match="xs:element[position() = 1 or name(..) != 'xs:schema']">
```

```
<!-- check if this refers to global element  -->
  <xsl:variable name="elem">
  <xsl:choose>
    <xsl:when test="./@ref">
<!-- yes - get global element via key  -->
      <xsl:copy-of select="key('global_element',../@ref)"/>
    </xsl:when>
    <xsl:otherwise>
<!-- no - just use current node  -->
      <xsl:copy-of select="."/>
    </xsl:otherwise>
  </xsl:choose>
  </xsl:variable>
<!-- get the element's name  -->
  <xsl:variable name="name" select="$elem/*/@name"/>
<!-- get the element's query expression  -->
 <xsl:variable name="query"
      select="$elem/*/xs:annotation/xs:appinfo/q:query/text()"/>
<!-- if this starts with 'for' or 'let' we have to generate before the
element and add a result clause  -->
  <xsl:variable name="isHead"
      select="starts-with(normalize-space($query),'for ')
        or starts-with(normalize-space($query/text()),'let ')"/>
<!-- Generate FLWR expression  -->
  <xsl:if test="$isHead">
    <xsl:text>{</xsl:text>
    <xsl:value-of select="$query"/>
    <xsl:text> return </xsl:text>
  </xsl:if>
<!-- Now generate the constructor  -->
<xsl:text>&lt;</xsl:text>
<xsl:value-of select="$name"/>
<!-- before closing the tag generate attributes  -->
  <xsl:for-each select="$elem/*/xs:complexType/xs:attribute">
    <xsl:call-template name="att-query">
      <xsl:with-param name="attribute" select="."/>
```

```
        </xsl:call-template>
      </xsl:for-each>
<xsl:text>&gt;</xsl:text>
<!-- was there a 'let' or 'for' expression  -->
   <xsl:choose>
     <xsl:when test="$isHead">
<!-- yes, just do child elements  -->
        <xsl:apply-templates/>
      </xsl:when>
      <xsl:otherwise>
<!-- no, insert query expression, but wrap in curly brackets  -->
        <xsl:value-of select='concat("{",$query,"}")'/>
      </xsl:otherwise>
   </xsl:choose>
<!-- closing tag  -->
        <xsl:text>&lt;/</xsl:text>
   <xsl:value-of select="$name"/>
   <xsl:text>&gt;</xsl:text>
<!-- closing bracket  -->
   <xsl:if test="$isHead">
        <xsl:text>}</xsl:text>
   </xsl:if>
</xsl:template>
<!-- template for attributes -->
<xsl:template name="att-query">
   <xsl:param name="attribute"/>
<!-- get attribute name  -->
   <xsl:variable name="name" select="$attribute/"@name"/>
<!-- get query expression  -->
   <xsl:variable name="query"
select="$attribute/xs:annotation/xs:appinfo/q:query/text()"/>
<!-- just insert a blank  -->
   <xsl:text> </xsl:text>
<!-- append the name followed by '='  -->
   <xsl:value-of select="$name"/>
```

```
<xsl:text></xsl:text>
<!-- and the query expression  -->
  <xsl:value-of select='concat("{",$query,"}")'/>
</xsl:template>
<!-- template to catch annotations  -->
<xsl:template match="xs:annotation">
</xsl:template>
</xsl:stylesheet>
```

To run this example, an XSLT processor that supports xsl:key clauses is required, such as SAXON. This example can handle global and local elements, and attributes, but is by no means complete. There is no support for multi-component schemata, nor for elements and attributes in global types or global groups, and so on. This is left to interested readers as an exercise.

Note that the original XQuery syntax is used for better readability. XQuery, however, features an alternative syntax that would be better suited for the embedded use of XQuery. XQueryX [Malhotra2001] provides the same semantics as XQuery, but uses XML syntax to allow processing of query expressions with XML processors. In particular, it would allow cross-checking the XML Schema definitions against the XQueryX definitions by means of XSLT.

This technique of embedding also works with addressing mechanisms and transformation languages other than XQuery. In simple cases we may succeed by embedding XPath expressions, but XSLT, XPathLog, and others are also candidates for schema-embedded view definition.

13.1.6 Model-Driven Schema Mediation

Another possibility for combining domains is to create a new conceptual model (see Chapter 2) of the combined domain. By using the modeling language's extension mechanism, we can describe the mapping between the domains within the conceptual model. An appropriate generator could produce both schemata and queries from these definitions.

In AOM we can use the annotation mechanism to include query expressions in the conceptual model. This allows us to define those query expressions wherever appropriate: in assets, in Level 2 Structures, and on the model level. To identify the query language, we use an appropriately defined namespace prefix. Figure 13.4 shows a possible mapping for the musician property of asset CD.

We assume that the prefixes j: and q: have been defined as

```
j=http://www.jazz.org/encyclopedia
q=http://www.w3.org/TR/xquery
```

```
┌─────────────────────────────────────────────────────────────┐
│ CD                                                          │
├─────────────────────────────────────────────────────────────┤
│ productNo                                                   │
│ title                                                       │
│ publisher                                                   │
│ musician(ID,instrument)+                                    │
│ decimal price                                               │
├─────────────────────────────────────────────────────────── A┤
│ musician::<q:map>                                           │
│   for$musician in j:album[concat("cd",j:productNo/text()) = │
│                                   productNo/text()]/j:plays  │
│   return                                                    │
│    <ID>{$musician/j:jazzMusician/j:ID/text()}</ID>          │
│    <instrument>{$musician/j:instrument/text()}<instrument>  │
│ </q:map>                                                    │
└─────────────────────────────────────────────────────────────┘
```

Figure 13.4 Asset CD with a mapping to j:album properties.

The context expression musician:: relates this annotation to the property musician; the query expression derives the instance values for the subproperties ID and instrument.

Since AOM supports the merging of models, we have the option of either specifying information structures and mappings within the same conceptual model, or separating them into two different models and later merging these models. This would allow reusing the same information structures with different mappings.

13.2 CENTRALIZED AND DECENTRALIZED CHANGE MANAGEMENT

The theme of centralized vs. decentralized change management of information resources is as old as the first time-sharing system. Centralized change management is quite easy to accomplish: All changes pass through a central instance—usually to the owner of the information object—to be approved or rejected. In large organizations, however, this can result in considerable bureaucratic overhead, slowing down operations.

Take for example a business object Customer. Such a business object may have a large number of features, such as billing address, shipping address, account, preferences, track record, and so on. In a large company, not every feature is important to every department: The shipping department is purely interested in the shipping address; the sales department is interested in the account, billing address, and the track record; the marketing department may want to know the preferences. It makes sense that the maintenance of these features is performed by the corresponding departments. A centralized change management, however, would slow down operation: To make a change to the account, the sales department would have to apply to the owner of the business object `Customer` (possibly the creator of that object) to perform this change.

This problem occurs on two levels: on the instance level and on the schema level. Let's first discuss decentralized change management for instances of business objects.

13.2.1 Decentralized Change Management of Document Instances

Relational technology has paved the way for decentralized change management. SQL allows for defining views (see Section 11.6.4) that restrict access to a set of relational tables constituting a business object. For example, the shipping department operates with a particular view that only gives them access rights to the shipping address of a customer. This technique allows each department to apply changes to those parts of a business object they are responsible for.

A similar technology for XML is currently not in sight. Section 12.4 described how views on XML documents could be defined with the help of XQuery, but XQuery is a pure query language that does not allow updates.

13.2.2 Decentralized Change Management of Document Schemata

The same problem occurs during the evolution of schemata. If, for example, the marketing department needs new elements and attributes in the schema parts describing the customer's preferences, it would not be appropriate to bother the core information object group with such a task. In SQL this problem is relatively easy to solve. The business object `Customer` exists in the form of multiple relational tables. So, it is possible to decentralize the maintenance of the schema by assigning the task of table maintenance to those departments that benefit the most from a table.

In object-oriented programming, a real problem exists. Business objects are usually implemented in OO as a large class hierarchy. Changes to members of the class hierarchy can easily break the delicate inheritance and containment relationships that exist in object-oriented structures. The problem of decentralized change management has therefore sparked the development of a new programming paradigm on top of the OO paradigm: subject-oriented programming [Ossher1994]. In subject-oriented programming, large business objects are segmented into so-called subjects, which can be maintained individually. Composition rules describe how the subjects are merged into a class hierarchy representing the business object.

The situation in XML is similar: Business objects tend to be large hierarchical structures (not an ensemble of flat atomic tables as in relational technology). In the past, when schemata were authored using DTDs, schema authors made extensive use of external entities. Typically, a complex DTD was segmented into a few dozen separate external entities. This allowed for the decentralized maintenance of the schema.

With XML Schema we have similar possibilities. We can use `include` and `import` to compose large schemata from smaller modules. Reusable structures such as named simple and complex type definitions, named group and attribute group definitions, and global elements allow for coarse- and fine-grained decomposition of schemata (see Chapter 6). The use of namespaces prevents name clashes between the different schema parts, as shown in Figure 13.5.

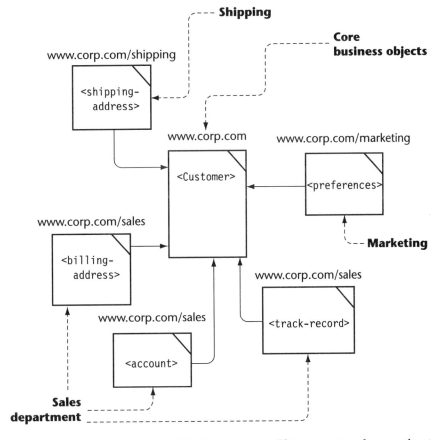

Figure 13.5 Managing change: The Core Business Objects group only cares about the core component of a business object and the integration. The individual aspects of a business object are implemented in the form of schema components that are imported into the core component. Using different namespaces for each aspect or each instance responsible for change helps to prevent name clashes.

Outlook

It is time to draw some conclusions. The definition of XML Schema marks a new step in the development of markup languages, but it doesn't stop there. For XML, XML Schema has opened the door to various information technologies such as databases and enterprise application programming, while for these technologies, it has provided a common exchange format that will lead to unprecedented levels of integration.

14.1 INTEGRATION OF CORE TECHNOLOGIES

XML Schema contributes to integration by combining existing concepts used in the enterprise world with markup technology. The core concepts are relational databases and object-oriented programming languages. Chapters 10 and 11 showed how XML Schema has integrated these concepts, for example, the SQL-99 type system. Future versions of SQL, such as SQL-200x, are being developed with the XML Schema type system in mind. It is likely that development of object-oriented languages will also reflect what XML Schema has achieved. Object-oriented languages will probably adopt a few things from functional languages (for example, Haskell), which are already well equipped to emulate the complex type systems found in markup languages like XML.

Object-oriented programming and relational databases evolved in the closed-world scenarios of client-server enterprise computing. For the new open world of electronic business and worldwide information exchange, their data models are far too rigid. The data models required for the new scenarios are best characterized by the document metaphor. Documents have accompanied business transactions as long as there has been written history, as seen in our discussion of ancient documents and grammars at the beginning of this book.

14.2. GRAMMAR-DRIVEN DATA MODELS

A core concept for describing documents, grammars are currently the most flexible method for describing complex data models. Formal grammars have been used for ages (well, at least since ALGOL 60) to describe the structure of computer programs. So it seems logical to use grammars to describe complex data structures, too. Grammar-driven data models can provide a strong basis for the global exchange of information. This, and because schema languages are based on grammars, is why a grammar-driven modeling method was adopted for this book. Chapters 2, 3, and 8 demonstrated how to describe conceptual data models with Asset Oriented Modeling (AOM) and how to derive XML schemata from such models.

The grammar metaphor will lead the way in the development of XML Schema. During the course of the book, especially in Chapters 7 and 8, we have compared XML Schema with an alternate schema language: Relax NG. Its foundation in regular grammars shows clearly on the surface, leading to a lean and elegant schema language. However, since Relax NG fails to integrate concepts from relational technology and object-oriented technology, it cannot make it into mainstream information technology. Nevertheless, XML Schema can learn from Relax NG, particularly in the area of nondeterministic schemata (*Unique Particle Attribution* and *Element Declarations Consistent*—see Section 5.3.18), where a more flexible approach is highly desired.

14.2.1 XML as a Mainstream Technology

Currently, the major base recommendations of the W3C are being redesigned to support XML Schema. In particular, XPath 2.0 (and with it XQuery) will support XML Schema data types, and so will XSLT 2.0. The IT industry has also taken XML Schema to its heart. Since May 2001, when the XML Schema Recommendation was published, XML Schema has gained considerable support from the industry, especially in the areas of tool support, APIs, databases, and middleware:

- A number of XML Schema–enabled productivity tools have been released. Among them are schema editors such as XML Spy and TurboXML. These tools already have a high degree of maturity and are invaluable aids when authoring XML Schema. As these tools become more and more sophisticated, they will ease the initially steep learning curve for XML Schema, bringing more schema authors to XML Schema and attracting people from outside the XML camp.

- XML Schema–compliant Application Programming Interfaces (APIs) exist in the form of XML Schema–compliant SAX and DOM implementations, in particular for the programming languages Java and C++. XML Schema–compliant binding technologies such as JAXB are in development.

- By the time this book goes to market, also the first native XML databases conforming to XML Schema or subsets will go to market. Relational databases that implement SQL-99 or SQL-200x or parts thereof should have no trouble supporting XML Schema.

- In the middleware area, basically all relevant standards have moved to XML Schema. The web services trinity (SOAP, WSDL, UDDI) is based on XML Schema, and so is ebXML. BizTalk moved to XML Schema at an early stage.

With XML Schema, enterprise IT has gained an industry-strength schema language that opens up the huge enterprise information resources to the open scenarios of the Internet and electronic business by providing a powerful tool for data integration and application-to-application communication. For the XML community, XML Schema has changed the scenario completely: It has transformed XML from a niche technology into a mainstream technology—a tremendous window of opportunity for those of us working in the field.

Regular Expressions for Patterns

The pattern facet uses the familiar regular expression syntax to restrict the lexical space of data types. This appendix gives an overview of the pattern syntax.

Complex regular expressions can be constructed from simpler ones with the help of operators. Let S and T be arbitrary regular expressions, c and d be normal characters, and C be a character class (listed below).

A normal character c is any character that is not a metacharacter. Metacharacters are ., \, ?, *, +, {, }, (,), [, and].

Expression	Meaning
c	The string consisting of character c.
C	The string consisting of a character belonging to character class C.
c-d	The string consisting of any single character whose code value is between c and d (inclusive).
ST	Concatenation. All strings st with s matching S and t matching T.
S|T	Choice. All strings s that match S or T.
^S	Negation. All strings s that do not match S.
S-T	Difference. All strings s that match S but not T.
S?	Option. All strings s that match S, or the empty string.
S*	Powerset. All strings s matching k repetitions of S (including $k = 0$).
S+	All strings s matching k repetitions of S (including $k > 0$).
S{n,m}	All strings s matching k repetitions of S ($n <= k <= m$).
S{n}	All strings s matching exactly n repetitions of S.
S{n,}	All strings s matching at least n repetitions of S.

Escape sequences can be used to represent characters that would otherwise be regarded as metacharacters.

Escape Sequence	Represented Character
\n	The newline character (#xA)
\r	The return character (#xD)
\t	The tab character (#x9)
\\	\
|		
\.	.
\-	-
\^	^
\?	?
*	*
\+	+
\{	{
\}	}
\(	(
\)	)
\[	[
\]	]

Character classes are represented by the following escape sequence:

\p{X}	A character belonging to the category denoted by X (see the following tables).

Letter categories:

Category	Represented Characters
L	All letters.
Lu	Only uppercase letters.
Ll	Only lowercase letters.
Lt	First character of a word may be uppercase depending on language (see Unicode technical report #21).
Lm	Modifier. Various characters such as accents modifying the pronunciation of a character.
Lo	Other.

Marks categories:

Category	Represented Characters
M	All marks.
Mn	All marks, except nonspacing marks.
Mc	Marks combined with whitespace.
Me	Enclosing marks.

Numbers categories:

Category	Represented Characters
N	All numbers. This includes numbers that do not rely on decimal digits such as roman numbers, encircled numbers, bracketed numbers, etc.
Nd	Only decimal digits.
Nl	Letter digits such as roman numbers.
No	All other digit symbols.

Punctuation categories:

Category	Represented Characters
P	All punctuation symbols.
Pc	Connector. All connecting symbols, for example, the underscore.
Pd	Dash. Various connecting dash symbols.
Ps	Open. All opening symbols such as opening parentheses or brackets.
Pe	Close. All closing symbols such as closing parentheses or brackets.
Pi	Initial quote (may behave like Ps or Pe depending on usage).
Pf	Final quote (may behave like Ps or Pe depending on usage).
Po	Other punctuation symbols.

Separator categories:

Category	Represented Characters
Z	All separators.
Zs	Separating space character.

Zl	Line separators.
Zp	Paragraph separators.

Symbol categories:

Category	Represented Characters
S	All symbols.
Sm	Mathematical symbols.
Sc	Currency symbols ($, €).
Sk	Modifier. Various characters such as accents modifying the pronunciation of a character, similar to Lm.
So	Other symbols.

Other categories:

Category	Represented Characters
C	All other characters.
Cc	Control. Nonprintable control characters.
Cf	Formatting characters.
Co	Private use for user-defined characters.
Cn	Not assigned (no specific meaning within Unicode).

Abbreviations:

Escape Sequence	Equivalent To	Legend
.	[^(\n|\r)]	Anything except newline or carriage return.
\s	[(#x20|\t|\n|\r)]	XML whitespace characters.
\S	[^\s]	XML non-whitespace characters.
\i	The set of initial XML name characters (Letter | '_' | ':').	
\I	[^\i]	Anything except initial XML name characters.
\c	The set of XML name characters (NameChar).	
\C	[^\c]	Anything except XML name characters.
\d	\p{Nd}	Decimal digits.
\D	[^\d]	Anything except decimal digits.

Glossary

Aggregation A complex entity composed of less complex entities.

AOM Asset Oriented Modeling (see Chapter 2). A modeling method based on regular grammars, and unifying the dual concepts of entities and relationships into the single concept of assets.

API Application Programming Interface. A description of the features of a program module for the client software wanting to use this module.

Asset In AOM an asset is an abstract notion for any object or relationship between objects that we want to include in a model.

Association A relationship that somehow correlates entities with others.

Browser A user agent that presents HTML or XML pages on a computer screen and supports navigation over the World Wide Web.

Business object A business object represents a real-world entity from the business problem domain that plays a role within the business scenario.

Business process A networklike construct of business objects to describe a complex value creating (or servicing) business activity.

Canonical form A preferred syntax and lexical representation for a given content. The canonical form allows comparison of objects by their string representation: When their string representations are equal, their content is equal, too.

CASE Computer-aided software engineering. CASE tools support the design of software systems and can automatically generate certain parts of the implementation. Roundtrip engineering allows changes in the implementation to be reflected back into the conceptual design.

Constraint A Boolean relation between the properties of one or more information items.

DOM Document Object Model. The DOM provides an API to describe, access, create, and modify SGML-based documents, such as XML or HTML documents.

DTD Document Type Definition. DTDs define the valid content of an XML document.

Encoding The code system used for a given text. Code systems define a supported character set and the mapping of the characters onto a range of integers (character codes).

Entity In XML, entities are used for text substitution, for single characters as well as for document parts. In conceptual modeling, an entity is an abstract notion of an object that we want to include in a model.

Facet In XML Schema, a specific constraint defining or restricting the domain of a data type.

Foreign key A key (a property or combination of properties) that can be used to refer to external information items. *See also Primary key.*

Information set The abstract description of XML document contents, independent of syntax.

Instance An individual of a certain class or type.

Internet The largest network in the world. The Internet features a three-level hierarchy consisting of backbone networks, midlevel networks, and stub networks. It spans many different physical networks around the world with various protocols, including the Internet Protocol TCP/IP.

Kleene star An operation that produces the set of all possible concatenations of symbols from a given set, including the empty string.

Lexical space In XML Schema, the lexical space of a data type is defined by the set of character strings required to represent all values of this data type. Each value may have several representations within the lexical space; one specific representation is designated as the canonical form.

Markup Syntactical means to make text more readable or to add meta-information to a text. In English prose, markup consists of punctuation, parentheses, dashes, footnotes, and so on. In XML, markup consists of tags.

Mediation A process that allows diverse software systems to interoperate. Mediation implies syntactical and semantic conversion. *See also Ontology.*

Namespace A concept to uniquely separate a set of identifiers from other identifiers. Namespaces are used to avoid name clashes. In XML, namespaces are identified by means of a unique URI.

Nil value In XML a nil value is an artificial value indicating that a given element does not have a value. However, a nilled element may own attributes.

Nondeterminism Feature of the p-calculus to describe the situation that the receiver of a communication when two or more processes "compete" for it cannot be predetermined. The process system evolves differently depending on who makes the race.

Normalized string A character string is normalized by reducing whitespace within the string to a single whitespace character and by removing any whitespace from the beginning and end of the string.

Null value In object-oriented programming and SQL, a null value is an artificial value indicating that a certain variable or column does not have a value.

Object Constraint Language (OCL) A language defining constraints, pre- and post-conditions, and navigation within UML diagrams.

Object-oriented programming A mainstream programming technique whereby data is encapsulated into object instances and can be accessed via the methods defined for a given object class.

Ontology An agreement about a shared conceptualization. Complete ontologies consist of vocabularies, thesauri, constraints, and axioms.

Parser A program that breaks a text string into a series of tokens, labeling each token with its grammatical role. XML parsers usually require that a document be well formed. Validating parsers can check a document instance against its schema definition.

Powerset *See Kleene star.*

Primary key A unique key (a property or combination of properties) that can be used to identify an information item. *See also Foreign key.*

Regular expression An expression describing a regular set.

Regular set A set of symbol strings is called regular if it can be obtained from a given alphabet of symbols with a finite number of concatenations, unions, and Kleene star operations.

Relational algebra Used to model the data stored in relational databases and queries defined on the data. The main relational functions are the set functions like union, intersection, and Cartesian product, plus selection (keeping only some rows) and projection (keeping only some columns). Relational algebra was developed by E. F. Codd.

Relational database management system (RDBMS) A database system based on the relational data model. Queries in relational databases are formulated with SQL.

Relax NG An alternate schema definition language, issued by the Organization for the Advancement of Structured Information Standards (OASIS).

SAX Simple API for XML. An API that provides methods for parsing XML documents (*see Parser*) and for retrieving elements.

Schema A definition that defines syntactic and semantic constraints of a certain class of information items.

SGML Standard Generalized Markup Language. A generic language for representing documents. SGML is defined in ISO 8879:1986.

SQL Structured Query Language. SQL is used as an interface to relational database management systems (RDBMSs). A series of standards by ISO and ANSI culminated in SQL-99 (SQL-3). While the original implementation of SQL in 1986 only supported flat tables, SQL-99 strives to provide relational support for complex objects. Currently, most RDBMSs support SQL-92.

Tag A syntactical means to mark up text. In XML, tags are enclosed in angled brackets and can own attributes.

Ternary association, ternary relationship A relationship between three information items.

Transformation The process of translating an XML document into a different—XML or non-XML—document, for example, for presentation purposes. Transformation may include changes in the structure, the vocabulary, the content, and the encoding of a document. Popular transformation engines are XSLT processors.

Unicode A 16-bit character set standard. Unicode covers all major modern written languages.

URI Universal Resource Identifier. A URI uniquely identifies a resource (typically a resource on the Internet) with a short string. URIs are defined in *http://www.w3.org/hypertext/WWW/Addressing/URL/URI_Overview.html*. The most common kind of URIs are URLs.

URL Uniform Resource Locator. A URL specifies the address of an Internet resource, such as a web page, an image, a sound file, or a script. URLs consist of a transfer protocol specification, such as *http:* or *ftp:*, a domain name, such as *www.w3.org*, and a path specification, such as *http://www.w3.org/hypertext/WWW/Addressing/URL/*.

View An interface to an information item or a set of information items, exposing only a limited property set.

W3C World Wide Web Consortium. A nonprofit organization responsible for the development of World Wide Web standards (recommendations).

Well formed An XML document is well formed if it complies with the syntax constraints defined in the XML 1.0 Recommendation.

Whitespace Any character that does not ink the paper when printed, for example: blank, newline, tab.

XML Extensible Markup Language. As a "slimmed-down" version of SGML, XML became a W3C recommendation in 1998. The XML V1.0 Recommendation specifies the syntax of well-formed documents and how document classes can be defined with a DTD.

XML Schema A W3C recommendation since May 2001, XML Schema introduces a hierarchy of built-in and user-defined data types, namespace support, and advanced facilities for structure definition and modularization of schemata, thus offering an alternative to schema definition with DTDs.

XPath The W3C recommendation for XPath defines the syntax and semantics of access operators to XML document nodes.

XQuery The W3C Working Draft for XQuery defines the syntax and semantics of an XML query language. XQuery is based on XPath V2.0.

XSLT The W3C recommendation for the Extensible Stylesheet Language (Transformations) defines the syntax and semantics of template-based document transformation. XSLT is based on XPath.

Bibliography

[Berglund2002] Anders Berglund, Scott Boag, Don Chamberlin, Mary F. Fernandez, Michael Kay, Jonathan Robie, Jérôme Siméon; XML Path Language (XPath) 2.0, W3C Working Draft; 15 November 2002

[Biron2001] Paul V. Biron, Ashok Malhotra (eds.); XML Schema Part 2: Datatypes, W3C Recommendation; 2 May 2001

[Boag2002] Scott Boag, Don Chamberlin, Mary F. Fernandez, Daniela Florescu, Jonathan Robie, Jérôme Siméon; XQuery 1.0: An XML Query Language, W3C Working Draft; 15 November 2002

[Booch1997] G. Booch, I. Jacobson, J. Rumbaugh; The Unified Modeling Language for Object Oriented Development, Documentation set, Version 1.0; Rational Software Corporation; 1997

[Boyer2001] John Boyer; Canonical XML, Version 1.0; W3C Recommendation; 15 March 2001

[Bray1999] Tim Bray, Dave Hollander, Andrew Layman; Namespaces in XML, World Wide Web Consortium; 14 January 1999

[Bray2000] Tim Bray, Jean Paoli, C. M. Sperberg-McQueen, Eve Maler; Extensible Markup Language (XML) 1.0 (Second Edition); W3C Recommendation; 6 October 2000

[Buck2000] Lee Buck, Jonathan Robie, Scott Vorthmann; The Schema Adjunct Framework, Draft; 30 November 2000; Extensibility specification

[Budd1997] Timothy Budd; An Introduction into Object-Oriented Programming, Second Edition; Addison-Wesley; Reading, MA; 1997

[Bush1945] Vannevar Bush; As We May Think; The Atlantic Monthly; July 1945

[Chen1976] P. P. Chen; The Entity-Relationship Model: Toward a Unified View of Data; ACM Transactions on Database Systems 1:1 pp. 9–36; 1976

[Chomsky1956] Noam Chomsky; Three Models for the Description of Language; IRE Transactions on Information Theory IT-2:113-124; 1956

[Christensen2001] Erik Christensen, Francisco Curbera, Greg Meredith, Sanjiva Weerawarana; Web Services Description Language (WSDL) 1.1; W3C Note; 15 March 2001

[Clark1999] James Clark, Steve DeRose; XML Path Language (XPath), Version 1.0, W3C Recommendation; 1999

[Clark1999a] James Clark (ed.); XSL Transformations (XSLT), Version 1.0, W3C Recommendation; 16 November 1999

[Clark2001] James Clark, Murata Makoto; RELAX NG Tutorial, Committee Specification; 3 December 2001; OASIS

[Clark2001a] James Clark, Murata Makoto; RELAX NG DTD Compatibility, Committee Specification; 3 December 2001; OASIS

[Codd1991] E. F. Codd; The Relational Model for Database Management (version 2); Addison-Wesley, Reading, MA; 1991.

[Costello2000] Roger L. Costello, John C. Schneider; Challenge of XML Schemas—Schema Evolution; The MITRE Corp.; 2000

[Cowan2001] John Cowan, Richard Tobin (eds.); XML Information Set, W3C Recommendation; 24 October 2001

[Cowan2002] John Cowan; XML 1.1, W3C Candidate Recommendation; 15 October 2002

[Daum2002] Berthold Daum, Udo Merten; System Architecture with XML; Morgan Kaufmann Publishers; 2002

[Eastlake2002] Donald Eastlake, Joseph Reagle, David Solo; XML-Signature Syntax and Processing, W3C Recommendation; 12 February 2002

[Eisenberg2002] Andrew Eisenberg, Jim Melton; SQL/XML is Making Good Progress; SIGMOD Volume 31, Number 2; June 2002

[Fallside2001] David C. Fallside (ed.); XML Schema Part 0: Primer, W3C Recommendation; 2 May 2001

[Fan2001] W. Fan, L. Libkin; On XML Integrity Constraints in the Presence of DTDs; In Proc. ACM PODS; 2001

[Finkelstein1998] Clive Finkelstein; "Information Engineering Methodology," Handbook on Architectures of Information Systems, eds. P. Bernus, K. Mertins, and G. Schmidt, Springer-Verlag, Berlin, pp. 405–427; 1998

[Goldfarb2000] Charles F. Goldfarb, Paul Prescod; The XML Handbook, Second Edition; Addison-Wesley; Harlow; 2000

[Grosso2001] Paul Grosso, Daniel Veillard; XML Fragment Interchange, W3C Candidate Recommendation; 12 February 2001

[Halpin1999] Terry Halpin; Entity Relationship Modeling from an ORM Perspective; The Journal of Conceptual Modeling; December1999–August2000

[Holman2001] G. Ken Holman; Information Technology—Document Description and Processing Languages, ISO/IEC JTC 1/SC34; 2001

[Hosoya2000] Haruo Hosoya, Jérôme Vouillon, Benjamin C. Pierce; Regular Expression Types for XML; Department of Computer and Information Science, University of Pennsylvania; 2000

[Hosoya2000a] Haruo Hosoya, Benjamin Pierce; XDuce: A Typed XML Processing Language (Preliminary Report), in Proceedings of Third International Workshop on the Web and Databases (WebDB2000)

[Kay2001] Michael Kay; XSLT Programmer's Reference 2nd Edition; wrox; 2001

[Kay2002] Michael Kay; XSL Transformations (XSLT). Version 2.0, W3C Working Draft; 15 November 2002

[Kleene1956] Stephen Cole Kleene; Representation of Events in Nerve Nets and Finite Automata; Automata Studies; Princeton; 1956

[KLEEN2002] KLEEN White Paper; *www.aomodeling.org;* 2002

[Krishnamurthy2000] Vishu Krishnamurthy, Muralidhar Krishnaprasad; Effectively Publishing XML Data Using Object-Relational Technology, H2-2000-457; Oracle Corporation; 2000

[Kroenke1995] David M. Kroenke; Database Processing: Fundamentals, Design, and Implementation; MacMillan; 1995

[LeHors2002] Arnaud Le Hors, Gavin Nicol, Lauren Wood, Mike Champion, Steve Byrne; Document Object Model (DOM) Level 3 Core Specification, Version 1.0, W3C Working Draft; 22 October 2002

[Malhotra2001] Ashok Malhotra, Jonathan Robie, Michael Rys; XML Syntax for XQuery 1.0 (XQueryX), W3C Working Draft; 7 June 2001

[Malhotra2002] Ashok Malhotra, Jim Melton, Jonathan Robie, Norman Walsh; XQuery 1.0 and XPath 2.0 Functions and Operators Version 1.0; W3C Working Draft; 15 November 2002

[Marjomaa2002] Esko Marjomaa; "Peircean" Reorganization in Conceptual Modeling Terminology; Journal of Conceptual Modeling, Issue 23; January 2002

[Marsh2001] Jonathan Marsh; XML Base, W3C Recommendation 27; June 2001

[Martin1993] James Martin; Principles of Object Oriented Analysis and Design; Prentice Hall, Englewood Cliffs, NJ; 1993

[May2001] Wolfgang May; Integration of XML Data in XPathLog; Institut für Informatik, Universität Freiburg, Germany; 2001

[Melton2001] Jim Melton (ed.); Foundation (SQL/Foundation), ISO-ANSI Working Draft; American National Standards Institute; 2001

[Melton2001a] Jim Melton (ed.); XML-Related Specifications (SQL/XML), ISO-ANSI Working Draft; American National Standards Institute; 2001

[Meyer1997] Bertrand Meyer; Object-Oriented Software Construction; Prentice Hall PTR; Upper Saddle River, NJ; 1997.

[Murata1995] Murata Makoto; Forest-Regular Languages and Tree-Regular Languages; 26 May 1995

[Murata2001] James Clark, Murata Makoto; RELAX NG Specification, Committee Specification; 3 December 2001; OASIS

[Naur1960] Peter Naur (ed.); Revised Report on the Algorithmic Language ALGOL 60; Communications of the ACM, Vol. 3 No.5, pp. 299-314; May 1960.

[Nelson1982] Ted. H. Nelson, Literary Machines; Mindful Press; 1982

[OCL1997] Object Constraint Language Specification, Version 1.1; joint document from Rational Software, Microsoft, Hewlett-Packard, Oracle, Sterling Software, MCI Systemhouse, Unisys, ICON Computing, IntelliCorp, i-Logix, IBM, ObjecTime, Platinum Technology, Ptech, Taskon, Reich Technologies, Softeam; 1997

[Ossher1994] Harold Ossher, William Harrison, Frank Budinsky, Ian Simmonds; Subject-Oriented Programming: Supporting Decentralized Development of Objects; IBM Thomas J. Watson Research Center; 1994

[Silberschatz2001] Abraham Silberschatz, Henry F. Korth, S. Sudarshan; Database System Concepts, Fourth Edition, McGraw-Hill; 2001

[St.Laurent1999] Simon St.Laurent; Toward a Layered Model for XML; simonstl .com; 1999

[Thalheim2000] Thalheim, Bernhard; Entity-Relationship Modeling; Springer-Verlag; Heidelberg; 2000

[Thompson2001] Henry S. Thompson, David Beech, Murray Maloney, Noah Mendelsohn (ed.); XML Schema Part 1: Structures, W3C Recommendation; 2 May 2001

[Whitmer2002] Ray Whitmer; Document Object Model (DOM) Level 3 XPath Specification, Version 1.0, W3C Working Draft; 28 March 2002

[Wiederhold1997] Gio Wiederhold, Michael Genesereth; "The Conceptual Basis for Mediation Services"; IEEE Expert, v. 12, n. 5, pp. 38–47; Sept.–Oct. 1997

[Williams2001] Stuart Williams, Mark Jones; XML Protocol Abstract Model; W3C Working Draft; 9 July 2001

Index

About the Author

Berthold Daum holds a Ph.D. in mathematics and was a codeveloper of NATURAL 4GL at Software AG. He has lectured in database design at the University of Karlsruhe (Germany) and has practical experience in the design and implementation of large distributed online systems. In the 1980s, he became involved in artificial intelligence and was a member of the ISO standardization committee for PROLOG. He has published various articles in trade magazines and scientific publications, and is coauthor with Udo Merten of *System Architecture with XML*. Currently he runs a consulting agency for industrial communication.